W9-CFJ-169

OF WINGS & THINGS

Volume I: 1972 - 1979

Reprints from *The Flyer*

The Nation's Aviation Newspaper

Copyright © 2000 by Flyer Media, Inc.

Library of Congress Cataloging-in-Publication Data pending.

Bowers, Peter M.
   Of Wings & Things, Volume I: 1972-1979
   1st Ed. September 2000
   ISBN 0-9703833-0-4

Cover photos from the Peter M. Bowers collection, Copyright 2000. All rights reserved.
Editing, layout and design by Kirk Gormley, Flyer Media, Inc.
Cover design by Roy McGhee, Flyer Media, Inc.

Printed in the United States by Consolidated Press, 600 S. Spokane St., Seattle WA 98134

Published by
Flyer Media, Inc.
P.O. Box 39099
Lakewood, WA 98439-0099
Tel: 253-471-9888, 800-426-8538
E-mail: comments@flyer-online.com
Web: www.flyer-online.com

Introduction

I first met Peter M. Bowers in 1970. Mary Lou and I had just purchased the aviation newspaper then known as The Northwest Flyer. We started attending aviation events in the Northwest and meeting people in the industry. Whenever we asked someone about an airplane with which we weren't familiar, they suggested we contact Pete Bowers.

After talking with Pete by phone and meeting him and his wife, Alice, at various events, we decided to ask him about writing for our publication.

Mary Lou, Pete, Alice and I met at a restaurant in what was then the Holiday Inn near the airport at Renton, Washington. Over a pleasant dinner and conversation, we broached the subject of a column and Pete readily agreed. That was the start of a wonderful relationship that we enjoy to this day.

Like many of Pete's fans, I have often said that I wish I had just a small fraction of his airplane knowledge. Pete was a Boeing engineer for more than 36 years and started writing articles in 1938. He is the author of more than 20 books, including a classic on Piper Cubs, and was a featured columnist in a national magazine for many years. He also started taking photos of airplanes and sharing the negatives with a number of other photographers around the United States. The net result was a library of photos and negatives of not only different planes, but also the different models of those aircraft.

In addition to his pursuits as an author, photographer and collector of aviation history, Pete is also a pilot and airplane designer.

He designed and built the Fly Baby, which won the 1962 Experimental Aircraft Association aircraft design contest. The plane, which can be built as a monoplane or biplane, became a popular project for homebuilders. He still sells plans for the aircraft, and many models are flying today. Following the Fly Baby, Pete designed and built a two-place aircraft called the Namu II.

Part of Pete's collection of aircraft photos and negatives was destroyed in a fire in the early 1990s, but he still has a collection that is the envy of many aviation museums.

A resident of Seattle, Washington, for over 50 years, Bowers is a founding member of the Museum of Flight on Boeing Field, and member of many aviation groups, including the OX5s in Seattle.

When a group of several hundred OX5 members was celebrating Pete's 60th birthday some years ago, we saw a great example of his sense of humor as well as his keen eye for aircraft. When the huge birthday cake was brought to the head table so he could blow out the candles, he proceeded to point out where the tiny airplane models that were situated on the cake needed alterations to their markings or colors or insignia.

The columns that have been published in the pages of The Flyer over the past 28 years are a treasure chest of knowledge, and evidence of a lifelong dedication to aviation. We are happy to present them to you in book form.

Dave Sclair
Co-Publisher
The Flyer

Foreword

The opening paragraphs of the Ercoupe/Aircoupe chapter on Page 2 of this book pretty well illustrate the thinking behind all of the columns that I have written for *The Flyer*. There has been no change in its concept over the past 28 years.

Not all of the columns, however, are reproduced here exactly as originally written. Misspellings and typographical errors have been corrected, and so have minor errors of fact that I call inexactitudes.

Other columns have undergone major changes for this book. In the early years the column had no fixed location in *The Flyer*. The text varied in length and the photo count ranged from one to eight. Sometimes the text had to be continued on a different page, or the text was on one page and the photos were on another. Due to space limitations, the columns were sometimes clipped by the editor, usually by deleting a photo or two rather than text. Whenever possible, deleted text and photos have been restored here.

Since the photos were not scanned electronically in the old days, I've had to retrieve the originals for this book. Most, fortunately, were still in my files, but some were not. They, as part of an active collection, were traded off or were loaned out and not returned. Whenever possible, in such cases, suitable substitute photos have been used.

In a very few cases, when photos were lost and could not be replaced, it has been necessary to go the undesirable route of using second-generation scans from the newspaper pages themselves.

In later years, some photos have been acquired that are more suitable to a particular column than were the originals. In such cases the later views have replaced the earlier ones.

Note that the date when each column appeared is printed on the page. Many of the

Peter M. Bowers

columns contained topical remarks as to the status or location of the subject that were correct at the time but are inaccurate today. In most cases, the material has been left as it originally appeared. So note and consider the date. In a few cases where new information was considered essential, a "2000 update" has been added to the column.

For those who check the dates, some columns may appear to be missing. Not so. Two things happened. First, I occasionally committed the author's No. 1 sin of missing a deadline. Second, because of limited space, the editor had to drop the then-floating column from a particular issue. Every column I've written through December 1979 is published in this book. Those apparently missing were merely shifted to subsequent issues.

There have been some interesting presentation problems over the years. At first, the photos were scattered throughout the column, each with its own caption. Some captions were short while others were necessarily long, and the photos were of various sizes. Such mismatches, however, didn't seem to create layout problems.

When a later editor began grouping the photos in a solid block, layout became complicated. Captions of different lengths were often not compatible with available space. Another editor neatly solved that problem by numbering the photos and the captions and then running the captions in a solid block of their own, as is done in this book.

Where do the ideas come from? Mainly, the photos in my extensive collection suggest themselves as subjects when I'm browsing the files. Others are the result of significant flight anniversaries, general conversations, current events, or my own broad interests in things aeronautical. Reader requests are also a significant source. I comply with them as I can, but problems arise when a relatively new reader suggests a subject that has been covered in recent years. I don't deliberately repeat subjects, but sometimes as a result of not carefully checking my old notes, I have repeated subjects quite a few years apart – sometimes, fortunately, with different approaches and different photos.

I try to spread the material broadly, mixing military and civil subjects, ancient and modern, as evenly as I can. In some cases a particular subject is broad enough to justify two or more columns.

Over the years I seem to have been doing things right. *The Flyer* and I get many supportive letters from our readers, and several nagging suggestions finally prompted this book, which covers the 181 columns I wrote from January 1972 through December 1979. If sales of this book merit it, we'll publish another collection of columns from the 1980s, and yet another from the 1990s.

When we finally decided to do this book, Editor Kirk Gormley and I had many discussions on its presentation. We thought of grouping the columns by subject matter, but dropped that in favor of running them in the random-subject sequence in which they ran in *The Flyer*. Each column, regardless of word and photo count as originally published, now appears on two facing pages, the text mostly on the left (even-numbered) pages and the photos on the right.

I hope that you enjoy reading this collection of my *Flyer* columns as much as I enjoyed writing them.

Peter M. Bowers
September 2000

Dedication

To the memory of James H. Dilonardo, 1927-2000,
a close friend for 50 years,
whose knowledgeable aeronautical discussions
have inspired many of these columns.

OF WINGS & THINGS

Volume I: 1972 - 1979

Reprints from *The Flyer*

The Nation's Aviation Newspaper

Ercoupes and Aircoupes

One was built by Erco, the other by Forney

1st January 1972

For some time now, Editor and Publisher Dave Sclair has been after me to do a column for the *Flyer* newspapers. As the idea was kicked around, it turned out that what he wanted was an illustrated first-person commentary on the wide-open field of all things aeronautical.

So that's what it will be – bits of history, oddities, and the "why and how" of things that fly. It won't all be mechanics and ancient history, however. If some current local or national aeronautical event is deserving of comment, that will be addressed too.

I had thought of a title like "Things with Wings," but that wouldn't be entirely correct because balloons and parachutes will sometimes be the subjects. So, we will talk "Of Wings & Things."

The problem of what subject to cover first was resolved when Dave asked about the differences between an "Ercoupe" and an "Aircoupe." The answer to that question was right at hand, and a dip into the files brought up some additional information about "Coupes," so here we go.

Back in the 1920s, most small two-seat airplanes had tandem-seat arrangements. Side-by-side seating was rare enough to rate a special designation. At first it was "sociable seater," but as enclosed models became popular, the term "coupe" came into use. As applied to the automobiles of the period, the French verb "to cut" meant cut off or cut down, as from a four-seat body style to two. As applied to airplanes, however, it meant only side-by-side seating for two.

Several designs of the late 1920s actually worked the word into the airplane names. There were, among others, the Ellias Aircoupe, the Swanson Kari-Keen Coupe and, of course, the immortal Monocoupe.

In 1937 the Engineering and Research Corporation (Erco) of Washington, DC, decided to develop and market a new light plane for what was then a growing market in two-seat sport and training types. The new Erco had many features that were new to private planes of the time, including a revival of the long-forgotten tricycle landing gear of pre-World War I days, twin vertical tail surfaces, and a two-control system with limited travel that not only made flying the plane as easy as driving a car, but made it spin-proof as well.

The side-by-side seating arrangement under a somewhat car-like top suggested a combination of the word "coupe" with the abbreviation of the company name, and the term "Ercoupe" was added to the vocabulary. There was a contemporary in the form of the Piper Cub Coupe, Piper's first side-by-side.

The Ercoupe, Erco's Model 415-C, was manufactured in a new plant at Riverdale, Maryland, from 1940 into 1942, when production ended after V-J Day. Deliveries resumed until the Korean War, when a combination of a weakening market for two-seaters and the demands of war work stopped the Ercoupe line once again.

Erco never built another Ercoupe. In 1955 the design was sold to a new firm, the aircraft division of the Forney Manufacturing Company in Fort Collins, Colorado. Forney put the airplane back on the market as the Forney F-1, but did not call it "Ercoupe." Instead, Forney revived the old 1927 Elias name of "Aircoupe." The model remained in production until 1959 in three versions – the Explorer, the Expeditor and the Exacta. They were still "Aircoupes," but were also coming to be called "Fornaires."

In 1959 Forney got out of the airframe business and sold the Aircoupe design to a rather surprising buyer – the city of Carlsbad, New Mexico. Carlsbad leased the manufacturing operation to the Air Products Company, but that

operation was short-lived.

In 1963 it was picked up by a new owner, Alon Incorporated of Wichita and nearby McPherson, Kansas. The model number was changed again to A-2 for Alon two-seater, but the "Aircoupe" name was retained. Noticeable changes were a sliding canopy instead of the old pushdown windows and somewhat later a spring-steel main landing gear. Alon merged with Mooney Aircraft in 1967 and the Aircoupe design was moved to Kerrville, Texas. There the Aircoupe identity vanished, as Mooney redesigned the plane as a single-tail type and renamed it the Mooney M-1 Cadet.

Again the production period was short, ending in 1970. A lot of corporate reshuffling was going on at the time, and Butler Aviation International, parent company of both Mooney and Aerostar, transferred the Cadet design to Aerostar. So far there has been no attempt to resume production. If Aerostar does build the old 1937 design again, would anyone like to bet that it will be called the "Aerocoupe"?

As a final sort-out of the names, Ercoupes were built only by Erco, the Engineering and Research Corporation.

Aircoupes were built by Forney, the city of Carlsbad, and Alon.

The photographs

1. The original Aircoupe, a pioneer light plane built by Elias Aircraft in 1927. With no small American engines available, this Aircoupe used an imported French Anzani six-cylinder twin-row radial.

2. Ercoupes were built by Engineering Research Corporation from 1940 to 1952. Only Erco built Ercoupes. A unique feature was the canopy. Its transparent portions on each side slid down into slots in the fuselage to permit full "open-cockpit" flying shown here.

3. An Alon A-2 Aircoupe with sliding canopy and a spring-steel landing gear to distinguish it from the Ercoupe and the predecessor Forney F-1 Aircoupe. Aircoupe production ended with Alon.

4. The final form of the old Ercoupe was the Mooney Cadet, which retained the Alon sliding canopy and spring-steel landing gear, but replaced the twin tail with a single.

How can a glider land on one wheel?

With long wings, and slow takeoff and landing speeds

2nd January 1972

When most of the general aviation planes of today take off or land, they have three wheels under them – two mains and either a tail wheel or a nosewheel. Since most of our gliders and sailplanes have only one wheel, how do they manage to operate without crashing?

Take a look at a sailplane at rest. For an otherwise conventional-looking aircraft, it just doesn't look right – more like a minor accident that just happened. One wingtip is on the ground. How can the pilot operate his bird with a landing gear that seems to have the stability of a pogo stick?

Well, it's really no problem. The answer is in those big, long wings and the relatively slow takeoff and landing speeds of the gliders. Actually, the whole takeoff-and-landing operation is an aeronautical balancing act that is a lot easier than merely standing on one foot for a minute.

It's a two-way balancing act, too – fore and aft to keep both the nose and tail skids off the ground during the takeoff and landing rolls, and laterally to keep the wingtips off the ground before and during those rolls. For fore-and-aft or longitudinal trim, the glider does not balance exactly on the wheel when static. The wheel is slightly ahead of or behind the loaded center of gravity of the glider. In addition to the single main wheel, either a nose skid, tail skid or wheel is in contact with the ground until takeoff roll is underway.

With a few miles per hour of forward speed, far less than that needed to become airborne, the elevator control becomes sufficiently effective to supply the trimming force that's needed to balance the glider longitudinally on the single wheel. If the pilot is flying a type that rests on the nose skid, he holds full back stick as the glider is towed forward to start the takeoff; as the air load on the elevator forces the tail down, he eases off on the back stick until it is practically in the neutral or level flight position as the glider rolls level or at near-flying speed. With full control established, the pilot then goes through with normal takeoff procedures. On "taildragger" gliders, the pilot applies full forward stick to raise the tail and then follows the same procedure.

Neither of these two systems, or skid arrangements, is better than the other; each has its advantages for a particular type of operation. The nose-skid system is particularly advantageous for training – it acts as a brake during jerky starts and, combined with hard forward stick and full brake application, can produce some amazingly short stops on landing. The forward position of the skid and the low center of gravity of the glider prevent nose-overs. For the high-performance contest types, the tail skid/tailwheel arrangement is preferred; it eliminates the weight and aerodynamic drag of the big nose skid.

It may surprise some power-plane pilots to learn that many gliders can be balanced laterally with no forward speed. Since the weight of the glider is equal on both sides of the center line and the wings are long, it takes very little trimming force to balance it. So little, in fact, that a slight breeze of 7 to 10 mph blowing over the wing from straight ahead will generate enough lift for the glider to be balanced by the pilot working the ailerons. A little more breeze, and he can raise a wingtip from the ground by aileron action. That trick was, and still is, used as a training exercise for new student glider pilots – sit them in a sailplane pointed into the wind and have them keep the wings level with the ailerons.

A normal glider takeoff involves a helper at the wingtip. In most operations he is an important middleman; not only does he raise the wingtip and hold it off the ground, he uses hand signals to relay the pilot's takeoff command to the pilot of the tow plane, the tow-car driver, or the winch operator, all of whom are a considerable distance ahead of the glider and unable to hear the pilot or even see him clearly. As a normal tow gets underway, the wingman runs forward with the glider, holding the wing level until it becomes self-supporting. Under no-wind conditions, ailerons and elevator become effective at about the same time, and the pilot can then balance the ship without outside help. During the landing, the glider tilts onto the nose or tail skid long before it stops rolling. With a breeze, the pilot can hold the wing level until a helper runs up to grab the tip or he can lower it to the ground gently by aileron action. Small skids, rollers or buffer pads are normal equipment for glider wingtip protection.

On all but the high-performance types, the wingtip man isn't absolutely essential to the takeoff even when there is no wind. On undermanned operations with no one available for the wingtip chore, the glider is parked on the runway at 45 degrees to the normal takeoff heading, with the trailing wingtip on the ground. The pilot conveys the takeoff signal by wagging the rudder. As the tow starts, the side load imparted by the tow rope, which is angled relative to the glider, slews the nose around. That gives extra velocity to the low, or "outside," wing and the aileron immediately becomes effective enough to raise the wing. After the pilot kicks in hard "outside" rudder to stop the turn on the runway heading, the rest of the takeoff is routine.

There are a number of advantages to the "monowheel"

1

2

landing gear, and various attempts have been made over the years to adapt the system to special-purpose airplanes.

So far, the closest successful approach has been the center line, or "bicycle" arrangement, of the Boeing B-47 jet bomber.

On smaller types, having one wingtip on or near the ground has complicated the taxi and steering problems, so the gliders, which are moved around by ground crews, still have a monopoly on the single-wheel landing gear.

The photographs

1. This old Schweizer 1-19 secondary glider with one-wheel landing gear and high-wing configuration emphasizes the tilt that results from having one wingtip on the ground. Note the husky steel-tube tip skids.

2. In an interesting training exercise, the wings of a motionless Frankfort Cinema sailplane are held level by aileron action alone. The author, left, is the instructor. The handkerchief he holds gives a good idea of the wind velocity.

The world's smallest airplanes

Do you measure by wingspan, weight or bulk?

1st February 1972

There are three contenders for the title of world's smallest airplane. But how do you define smallest? Is it by wingspan alone, by weight, or by the generality of "bulk"?

There have been many really small single-seat airplanes since shortly after the Wright brothers. Mostly, they have merely been sincere efforts to produce a practical flying machine for minimum cost of materials, man hours and powerplant. None were designed with the deliberate intention of becoming the world's smallest airplane.

Credit for the first design to actually seek this title was produced in 1948 by William Chana and Ken Coward of Bee Aviation Associates in San Diego, California. They called their product the Wee Bee. An all-metal monoplane, it was powered with a 20-horsepower Righter two-stroke-cycle engine taken from one of the large radio-controlled model airplanes that the Army used for antiaircraft gun targets.

Recognizing that one of the major handicaps to the performance of very small airplanes is the drag caused by the frontal area of an upright pilot, either enclosed completely in the fuselage or with his head and shoulders sticking out of an open cockpit, Bee Associates decided to reduce the drag by having the pilot lie prone on top of a fuselage so slim that he could not possibly get in it. That seemed to work, for the Wee Bee flew. Its performance wasn't such that it stood a chance of becoming everyone's handy-dandy low-cost airplane, but it was good enough to fly consistently and put in appearances at major air shows. It even went to England with a contingent of American performers.

The Wee Bee's major claim to the title of "smallest" was in its weight and very minimal cross section. Empty weight was only 210 pounds. Published wingspan was 18 feet, although it looked like less on inspection. Length was 15 feet, top speed was 80 mph, and the Wee Bee once achieved an altitude of 12,000 feet. Total cost reported by the builders was $275.

Other claims to the "smallest" title were made later by Ray Stits of Riverside, California. His SA-1 monoplane, named Junior, was built along much more conventional lines.

The pilot sat upright but was enclosed by a sliding hatch and raised turtledeck to reduce the drag associated with open cockpits and the pilot's head and shoulders.

Otherwise, the configuration was conventional but condensed. Length was 11 feet 4 inches, and the wingspan was only 9 feet 5 inches. With a Continental A-75 in the nose, empty weight was 398 pounds. With so much weight and so little wing area, the Junior had to fly at nearly 150 mph to stay in the air.

Not content to get by with only a 9-foot span, Stits soon had another "smallest" with a span of only 7 feet 2 inches. However, this time he had a little more wing area by virtue of two wings; his Sky Baby was a biplane. The full-cantilever wings were negatively staggered and had full-span flaps on the upper wing and ailerons on the lower. The aerodynamics must have been pretty weird, for there were slots on all four wingtips.

The Sky Baby had a bit more power, a C-85 Continental this time. Weight was 451 pounds, and top speed was approximately 200 mph.

So there they are: three claimants to the title of "world's small airplane" from three different viewpoints. My vote goes to the Wee Bee.

The photographs

1. The pilot of the Wee Bee didn't get into it; he laid down on top to reduce drag as much as possible.

2. The light weight of Bee Associates' Wee Bee, first claimant to the title of "world's smallest airplane," is demonstrated here by the pilot, who was able to lift the entire airplane off the ground.

3. Ray Stits' approach to small aircraft, a low-wing monoplane in which the pilot sat upright, was much more conventional. The enclosed cockpit eliminated the drag of his head and shoulders.

4. Ray Stits' claim to the "smallest" title for his Sky Baby was based on its wingspan of 7 feet 2 inches. The earlier Stits, Junior, was quite similar but was a low-wing monoplane.

1

2

3

4

On flying a pusher

Except for the propeller in back, they should be considered conventional aircraft

2nd February 1972

A lot of pilots these days fly "pushers" – airplanes with the propeller behind the engine instead of in front of it. Except for this particular detail of arrangement, the airplanes are pretty conventional in other respects and certainly do not have any significantly different handling characteristics. They are perfectly normal airplanes and take their place with others in the general aviation scene with no special distinction. They go by their own names and no one sees fit to distinguish them by adding the word "pusher."

Probably the best known, because it has been around for so long, is the Republic SeaBee amphibian. The mark of distinction with the SeaBee is that it is an amphibian, not a pusher. Then there is the later Lake, another amphibian that has also been known as the Colonial and the Skimmer. We also have the twin-engine Trecker Gull, developed by Piaggio in Italy and assembled in this country from Italian-built components. The most recent on the scene is that half-and-half ship, the Cessna Skymaster, which has one engine pulling and one pushing.

Among antiquers, homebuilders and history buffs, however, there is one model that is "The Pusher" before it is anything else. With variations in structure and powerplant, there are several in the country; all are based on the 1912 Curtiss Model E, and they are a class by themselves. They don't look like anything that's around today, and they certainly don't handle like anything with which we are familiar. Their appeal as a novelty and air-show item is great, but they are definitely not an average Sunday pilot's plaything. However, for those who want at least the essentials of the type of open-air flying that the 1912 model offers, plans are on the market for the "Breezy," a two- or three-seater that uses the wings, tail and most of the hardware of a more modern ship such as a Piper PA-12 Super Cruiser or a Cessna 140.

I own one of the 1912 replicas and have accumulated some 250 hours in it between 1957 and 1969. Since I am often asked how that thing flies, I'll tell about it here and describe the ship.

It was built in 1947 by Walter Bullock, a Northwest Airlines pilot who had owned an original after he learned to fly in 1916. He thought it would be fun to have one again. Unable to find an original to restore, he built a replica and made quite a few improvements. The basic frame is steel tubing instead of bamboo, and it uses a modern air-cooled 75-horsepower Continental instead of an old water-cooled Curtiss. It has brakes on the main wheels and 8.00 x 5 air wheels for shock absorption. The controls have also been modernized. In 1912, the wheel worked the rudder, the push-pull on the column worked the elevators, and a shoulder harness worked the ailerons on a "body English" principle. Old Glenn Curtiss had been a motorcycle racer and banked his airplanes like he banked the bikes, by leaning into the turn. That was carrying authenticity a bit far for a modern pilot, so Bullock put conventional controls on his latter-day replica. It also has conventional instruments where the original had none

at all.

The wings are very authentic, even to the original airfoil. Bullock couldn't find one in the available reference books, so he copied a side-view photo of his old ship, enlarged the end view of the wing, and set ordinates to the airfoil.

The first thing to be said about flying such a ship, despite all the improvements, is that it gives one a tremendous respect for the old-time pilots who taught themselves to fly without benefit of skilled instructors or the "feel" that is so essential today. Learning in those days was really trial and error. Let's go through a typical pusher flight and compare the "then" and "now" way of doing things.

First, when you sit in the seat, don't fasten your seat belt. Since the nosewheel is fixed and won't steer, you have to get off now and then to lift the nose around when you want to turn on the taxiway. Actually, they didn't taxi around much in the old days. The plane was pushed out of the hangar and headed into the wind, and the pilot took off from the point where the engine was started. He then set up the landing to roll to a stop in front of the hangar, switched off, and let the ground crew take over.

Starting is a hero's job. It's hard enough these days to find anyone who will prop a no-starter plane, much less climb in between those tail booms to do it. I generally have to show the local helper how to work the switches and throttle, and then prop it myself.

Visibility from that front seat is terrific, and you can see all over the field as you taxi out. If you hit a puddle, you really know it. When you are finally in takeoff position and all lined up on the runway, you finally fasten the safety belt. On the takeoff run, the control column has to be pulled back extra far to raise the nose because the main wheels are so far behind the center of gravity; they were located where they are as a structural convenience, not for the optimum balance point. Such refinements had not been developed in 1912. However, once in the air, you have too much back stick and have to go forward on the column fast. Since the major weight of the pusher is concentrated amidships, it is pretty sensitive in pitch. Most pilots who are new to the model tend to overcontrol considerably. They generally mange to get the see-sawing damped out about halfway down the runway. Once airborne, that way-out-front pilot position begins to present interesting problems. There you are, with no structural reference between you and the horizon. You are used to lining up some point of the nose with the horizon – but here, what nose? In the absence of one, you have to readopt one of the first bad habits they teach you in school – using your wings as the attitude reference. So, look out at the wings. If the outer struts are perpendicular to the horizon, you're level fore and aft. If the struts tilt back, you're nose-up; if they tilt forward, you're nose-down. If the tape where the flying and landing wires cross is below the horizon, that wing is low.

Another disadvantage of the no-nose feature is "point fixation." You navigate by some distant reference point ahead.

As the point gets closer, it gets lower in your line of sight. When it's real close, it doesn't disappear under the cowling. Rather, the pilot has a tendency to want to keep it in sight and starts to nose down to it.

There's an interesting vertigo problem at times, too, as when flying over a fog bank. You have to orient to the horizon in a hurry. One very interesting example occurred just after takeoff on a day with lots of little white clouds in a bright blue sky on a windless day. I swung out over a large glassy-smooth lake and had blue sky and white clouds below me as well as above for a few disconcerting moments.

Control procedures are by the modern movements, but the forces are vastly different. The ailerons are rather badly overbalanced on my particular model. You initiate a turn in the normal way by feeding in a little aileron, but then the over-balance takes over with a phenomenon known as "aileron snatch," and the things want to go full-stop on their own. This leaves you letting more aileron in by holding opposite force on the wheel.

Rudder is something else. With no vertical fin, there is no rudder "feel" whatever, and it won't center itself. You can be flying in a 10-degree crab and never know it. To tell if the rudder is straight, you either have to look over your shoulder at the rudder itself or look at your feet on the pedals to see if they are even.

Cruise speed is 45 mph, which makes wind blast tolerable. The fun here is when some other plane pulls alongside for a look-see. The pilot is watching the pusher, not his instruments, and doesn't realize how slow the thing is going. All of a sudden he's not there – he's stalled his plane. Then he remembers something he hasn't done since his private flight check – slow flight – and comes by again hanging on the prop.

Other performance numbers aren't always amusing. My pusher is probably the only plane around with a service ceiling below sea level. Service ceiling is the altitude where the rate of climb is 100 feet per minute and the pusher sometimes doesn't quite do that, particularly on a hot day. This sometimes has the pilot sweating the 100-foot trees a mile beyond the runway on takeoff. Rate of climb is a function of excess power, and the pusher uses so many of its 75 horses overcoming all the drag that there isn't much left for climb.

Landings can be made power-off if you don't mind coming down in a howling 30-degree dive. This is necessary to keep the speed up, again because of all the drag; the glide ratio is about 4:1 or 5:1 compared to about 10:1 for a Cessna 140. Preferred procedure is to come down at something over half throttle and control the altitude and sink with the stick.

Actual landing is made at 35 mph by rotating to put it down on the main wheels first. Then, stop on the runway, undo the safety belt, and get off and turn the nose. This ground procedure is almost an air show in itself.

Actually, I think that the main qualification for flying such a machine is the right attitude. Don't judge it by modern aircraft standards; think of it as what it is – something out of the stone age of aviation, and respect it as such.

One day I was working on it with the hangar door open when one of those guys who wouldn't fly anything with less than two engines and four radios came by.

"What are *you* doing?" he asked.

"Getting the pusher ready for re-license," I replied.

"Humpf!" he snorted. "Any inspector who would license a thing like that ought to be run out of town!"

Dale Mumford, the FAA inspector out of the Seattle office, re-licensed the pusher the next day, a Monday. The next Friday, he was transferred to Spokane, clear across the state. I've always wondered if there was a connection.

The photographs
1. The author in his Bullock-built replica of a 1912 Curtiss Pusher at its normal cruise altitude of 1,500 feet. It has gone as high as 6,000, but there is little point in flying high other than to get into smoother air on a bumpy day. A real speed demon at 45 mph, it once made the 90 miles from Portland International Airport to Olympia, Washington, in 2 hours 13 minutes.

2. With no nosewheel steering, the pusher pilot has to stand and lift the nose around to the desired heading. Here the author and his pusher are at the Whidbey Island Naval Air Station Air Fair in September 1966.

3. Propping the pusher is no job for the prop-shy. Here the author does his own propping with a friend on the controls. He can't back off any further because of the cross wires behind him.

Wingwalking then and now

Performers did more freelancing when the Jennys and Standards ruled

1st March 1972

One feature that has vanished completely from the modern air-show scene is the old-fashioned wingwalking act. True, a few daredevil performers still do what is called "wingwalking," but even with a relatively antique plane like the Stearman Kaydet, the act isn't the same. Nowadays, the performers don't get away from the center section of the upper wing; in most cases they start the flight perched on the center section and stay there through the landing.

It was considerably different in the unregulated heyday of the 1920s air shows. The performers really swarmed all over the airplane then. Usually they rode in the front cockpit during takeoff and climbed out when it was time to do the act. About the only point on the airplane that they didn't get to was in front of the propeller. I have a photo of one daredevil hanging from the tail skid!

The airplanes that were used for this work had a lot to do with making the act possible in the first place. Two models were used almost exclusively. One was the Curtiss JN-4D, a World War I surplus trainer that is best known by its nickname, Jenny. (It had a sister in the Canadian-built JN-4 model that was known as the Canuck, but we'll go into those differences at another time.) The other air show standby was the Standard J-1, another surplus trainer.

Powerplant for the Jenny and Canuck was the 90-horsepower Curtiss OX-5, which gave those ships a top speed of approximately 70 mph. The Standard originally had a 100-horsepower Hall-Scott, but about the first thing that a new postwar owner of a Standard did was get rid of the cantankerous Hall-Scott and put in an OX-5 or a 150-horsepower Hispano-Suiza. With Standards, the engine became part of the nomenclature, as "OX-5 Standard" or "Hisso Standard."

Several features of each airplane combined to make both an almost ideal vehicle for the wingwalking act. First, of course, was the maze of struts and wires that gave a wingwalker a lot of convenient hand-holds. The wires were round, and at an airspeed of 60 mph or less didn't cut into the daredevil's hands the way the sharp streamlined wires of a faster biplane like the Stearman would.

Both models had upper wings that were considerably longer than the lowers, and the overhang was braced on both sides with wires. A king-post arrangement was used on the top side of the upper wing as shown in the photos and gave the daredevil a very convenient working area. With one leg hooked over a king-post wire, a wingwalker could stand erect on the wing; with a good grip on the king post he could do a handstand as shown.

Another standard feature of both models was a semicircular skid under each lower wingtip. The skid was necessary to protect the tips during the fast blast-around turns that the top-heavy and brakeless planes had to make on the ground. They really leaned to the outside of the turn on those soft shock-cord landing gears. The tip skids, too, made a contribution to the act. They enabled the daredevil to work under the wings as well as on top of them.

Old-time wingwalking wasn't for just anyone who was after a fast buck or was merely looking for a thrill. It took a special breed to make a go of it. Absolute fearlessness was an important ingredient, of course, since all of this was done without benefit of parachute or safety line, but an athlete's physique and stamina had to go with it.

Take a look at the photo of Danny Grecco hanging from the wing skid of the Standard. Try that yourself in the ideal conditions of a gymnasium or your rec room. Hang from a bar at one arm's length and then try to raise yourself to that height by muscle power alone without the complication of a 60-mile wind, a lot of empty space below you, or the realization that you *have* to get yourself back up there . . . or else.

This type of wingwalking died out fast when the new airworthiness requirements of 1927 grounded the Jennies and the Standards. The few that flew for pay after that were in the Hollywood stunt squadron, doing their stuff for the movies. Unfortunately, most of the action for Jennies was in crash scenes.

The modern act is quite different. The daredevil usually stands on the center section of the upper wing of the Stearman for the entire act. Actually, he is not just standing there. He's propped against a short support, something like a shooting stick. He is held in tightly with four wires that run from a harness that he wears to four tiedown points on the wing. While he doesn't awe the crowd by climbing around the plane, his act does differ significantly from the old ones. Thanks to an inverted fuel system in the Stearman and his wired-in position on the wing, he can go through inverted maneuvers. So, loops, rolls and inverted fly-bys are the high points of the modern "wingwalking" act. The name is the same, but the action is different.

Sammy Mason, one of the well-known air-show pilots of the early years after World War II, wanted to revive the old type of wingwalking act but realized he couldn't do it with a Stearman. To restore the old action, he also had to restore a Jenny. He had one; or rather, he had the most important part of one. One of the old movie ships, it had been dismantled and stored in two hangars during the war. The hangar containing the fuselage burned down, so Mason built up a steel-tube fuselage and tail, and then installed a modern 200-horsepower Ranger engine to increase reliability a bit. That combination made for a funny-looking Jenny from the historian's point of view, but it was all right with the air-show crowds. The Ranger was soon replaced by a 220-horsepower Continental radial that altered the looks still more. The original Jenny wings, however, were the things that made the old-time act possible.

Now, I don't want to knock the present-day performers for their immobile acts. It's still a job that calls for surplus guts. While the precarious hanging-on part is gone, there are still very real risks – the possibility of a forced landing off the field because of engine trouble, or a ground loop or fast flip onto the back if a tire should blow on landing.

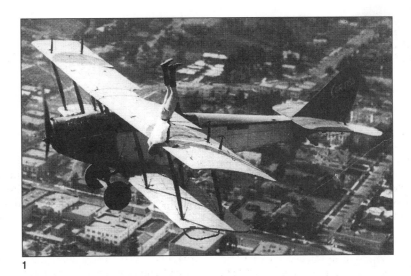

1

2

3

4

Today's wingwalkers still deserve all the applause you can give them. I just can't help thinking, though, how much better the act would be if only a Jenny or a Standard were available instead of a Stearman.

The photographs

1. Lieutenant Ormer Locklear makes full use of the king posts on the top wing of a Curtiss Jenny to do a hand-stand in 1920. Take a look at the altitude and location of this particular act and then imagine what the FAA would say to anyone who tried to duplicate it today.

2. Danny Grecco hanging at arm's length from the wing

skid of an OX-5 Standard in the early 1920s. Both Ormer Locklear and Grecco are wearing the uniform of the old air show business: riding boots and breeches.

3. Terry Holm is anchored to the top wing of Bud Fountain's special 450-horsepower air-show Stearman. It's an entirely different act these days, but it still thrills the crowds.

4. To revive the old-style wingwalking act in the post-World War II years, Sammy Mason rebuilt this Jenny to give his wingwalker a proper stage to perform. Wings like these were also good for pull-off parachute jumps, another extinct air show feature.

Communications without radios

Back in the 1920s and '30s, some planes served as flying billboards

1st April 1972

With airline, military and most general aviation airplanes equipped with radios these days, communications between airplanes and the ground or with other airplanes is no problem. The no-radio types (referred to as NORDOs by the FAA) generally operate in areas and in ways that do not require direct communications.

NORDO landings at uncontrolled airports are made by an established procedure. Those on the ground and others in the air know what a pilot's intentions are by the position of his airplane relative to the airport and what it is doing. If a NORDO wants to go into a controlled field, the normal procedure is to land at the nearest uncontrolled field and phone the tower for permission to come in on light-gun signals. Some specialized operations that call for precise positioning of the airplane, like dusting, are controlled from the ground by flaggers.

Back in the late 1920s and early 1930s, very few airplanes had radios of any kind. Special situations where communications were necessary were sometimes handled in interesting ways. One of the earliest was an airplane used by the San Diego Board of Air Control. It seems that there was quite a bit of questionable air traffic into Mexico back in those prohibition days, and the authorities had legitimate reasons for wanting to examine some of the transient airplanes and their cargo.

The way they prevailed upon a pilot to land for inspection was to fly up alongside him, where he could read the message painted on the billboard-size side of the official plane: "LAND AT ONCE."

I don't know how the pilots reacted, particularly if they had a faster plane and their numbers were a little hard to read. The picture is presented here to show one way of approaching the NORDO communications problem.

A similar practice was adopted shortly after World War II, when a high percentage of civil aircraft were still without radios or were not equipped to receive military frequencies. When the Air Force wanted to run some high-speed flight tests over Wright Field near Dayton, Ohio, it was necessary to clear all other aircraft, including the NORDOs, from the area. The method was to send up another "billboard" airplane, a Republic P-47D fighter, with the words "CLEAR WRIGHT FIELD AREA" clearly printed on the side.

Another example of communications-by-permanent-paint was used at a number of Navy primary training fields during World War II. The trainers, of course, were all NORDOs, and there were always a lot of them out in the practice areas at the same time. Upon occasions, such as the sudden approach of a storm, it was desirable to call all the birds in or divert them to another base. To accomplish that, officials at some bases put a highly conspicuous color scheme such as barber-pole stripes on one plane and used it exclusively as a recall plane. When needed to pass the word, it was flown to the practice area, where its pilot did his best to attract the attention of the cadets. They had been instructed as to the procedure to follow if the recall plane were to appear in their area.

Other occasions where messages were painted on the airplane did not involve such permanent markings. One good example is the communications with the Army Fokker C-2A , the "Question Mark," during its famous 150-hour endurance flight in January 1929. Various short messages, ranging from announcements of fuel or oil coming up with the next refueling plane or the status of a crew member's ailing wife, were chalked or painted on the dark olive drab side of a Boeing PW-9 fighter that was then flown into tight formation with the Fokker.

Another occasion calling for fast communications involved an experimental NORDO fighter at Chanute Field, Illinois, in the mid-1930s. Only one leg of the newfangled retractable landing gear came down during a test flight. The pilot was aware of the situation and was cruising around to burn off gas prior to making a one-wheel landing. Authorities on the ground had other ideas, however, and wanted the pilot, who had a parachute, to bail out rather than ride the crippled bird in. The word "JUMP" was quickly chalked on the side of another fighter, which then flew up to give him the message.

The pilot felt he was in command of the situation and shook his head to indicate he wouldn't comply. The messenger returned to the field, but was back again in a few minutes, this time with some more authoritative words. Above the word "JUMP" were two others: "COLONEL SAYS."

The photographs

1. The message on the fuselage should be clear to any pilot. The airplane is a single-engine version of the rare Prudden all-metal trimotor of 1927.

2. Army pilots and the Boeing PW-9 fighter used to carry messages to the "Question Mark" during its famous 1929 endurance flight.

3. The message is clear, but how does the Republic P-47D slow down enough so that the pilots of an errant light plane can read it?

The first T-6 racers

The originals were not as renowned as the latter-day versions

1st May 1972

When closed-course racing for North American T-6s was introduced at the 1968 Reno National Air Races, many thought they were seeing a brand-new competition. Actually, the noisy T-birds had been used as racers before. Because the airplanes are older than many people today, not many remember them.

The original T-6 races did not make the splash in their day that the current ones do because those events were overshadowed by other events, and with relatively slow airplanes running on the long Unlimited course, they didn't put on much of a show.

It's different nowadays. T-6 racing goes over big with the public because it is now held on the same short course used by the midgets and the sport biplanes and is therefore always in front of the crowd. The airplanes are evenly matched, but best of all, they make a lot of gratifying noise. The pilots also like the "new" event because the airplanes are readily available, the performance is something that can be handled easily, and the new "no modifications" rule heads off the costly airframe and powerplant modifications that are such a painful feature of the Unlimited racers.

So now we have T-6 races again, but what, the newcomers may ask, is a T-6? Time out for some history.

What we now call a T-6 was originally the two-seat North American AT-6, an advanced trainer (hence the AT) built for the U.S. Army from 1939 through the end of World War II. A development of the BC-1 (basic combat) model of 1937 and using the same 600-horsepower Pratt & Whitney R-1340 Wasp engine, a few were delivered as BC-1As before they were redesignated AT-6s. They became T-6s in 1948 when the new U.S. Air Force dropped the old AT, BT and PT designations and called all trainers T while retaining their original model numbers.

Other designations pop up, however, to confuse things. There are the letters SNJ and the names "Harvard" and "Texan." The SNJs up to -6 were mostly Navy versions of the various wartime Army AT-6s throughout AT-6F. The SN stood for scout trainer in the unique U.S. Navy aircraft designating system, and the J identified North American as the manufacturer. The SNJ-7 of 1949-51 was equivalent to the Air Force T-6G, some 2,000 of which were such extensive rebuilds of wartime models that they were considered new airplanes and were given new serial numbers.

The name "Harvard" appeared when Britain, which used names instead of numbers to identify military aircraft, bought hundreds of BC-1s just before World War II as Harvard 1s. Later AT-6 variants were bought as Harvard IIs, and some 1,500 built by Noorduyn in Canada under license were Harvard IIAs. Harvard IVs were rebuilds similar to SNJ-7s and T-6Gs.

The name Texan was applied to the AT-6s and the SNJs by the U.S. government in 1941, when it encouraged the use of popular names for public identification of military airplanes in place of their actual designations. That did not go over well at the time, but it's a convenience today as a blanket reference to all the nearly identical but differently designated models now flying.

Although the U.S. military didn't retire its last Texans until the late 1950s and the Canadians kept some until 1965, many became surplus to the military right after WWII. That is when their first short-lived racing careers began.

Except for the midget class that was introduced in 1947, all of the racers from 1946-49, when "big" racing was shut down for 15 years, were strictly war surplus. Fighters were in the Unlimited events like the Thompson Trophy and the Sohio races, but the Texans had an event of their own. Women were allowed to compete in the cross-country Bendix event, but they were not allowed to compete against the men in the pylon events. However, a separate all-women's pylon event was set up in the form of the Halle Trophy Race (1946-47) and the Kendall Trophy Race (1948-49) for women flying the relatively docile Texans with roughly half the speed of the unlimiteds.

The rules were not as tight then as now, and some modifications were allowed. The planes were still limited to 1,340-cubic-inch engines, but you could hop them up or go to more powerful versions than the stock military R-1340-AN-1s.

Airframes could be altered only to the point of cutting down the canopy. To keep the airplanes tame, no clipping of the wings was permitted.

In the interest of better streamlining, some of the racing Texans used the smaller Ranger V-770 that North American had already tried in an experimental model called the XAT-6E. That ploy was almost but never quite a winner. With only 770 cubic inches to the Wasp's 1,340, the V-770 put out 575 horsepower at 3,400 rpm, but didn't have the Wasp's stamina. The XAT-6E, racing with a stock canopy, qualified at 223 mph, but it could not hold that performance for a full race.

Top time for a winning T-6 racer was 234 mph in the 1948 Kendall, using a geared Wasp. The rules were changed in 1949 to prohibit geared engines and to require two-blade propellers. That mechanical restriction cut the winning 1949 time to 216 mph. The fact that these times top the current T-6 racing times does not mean that the women are out-flying the men. The current races are held around a three-mile course; the women raced on 10- and 15-mile courses where the speed could build up on the straightaways.

So T-6 racing is back, and we'll see a lot more of them rounding the pylons now than we did from 1946-49. We won't see all those interesting modifications, though.

The photographs

1. A stock AT-6A, photographed in March 1942, shortly before the colorful and distinctive Army tail stripes were deleted.

2. This Ranger-powered racer qualified for the 1947 Halle Trophy Race at 202.399 mph, but it crash-landed on the last lap.

3. When it came to extreme mods, this T-6 had an open

1

2

3

4

5

cockpit and a turbosupercharger for its Wasp engine.

4. A 1947 racing T-6 with only the rear part of the canopy cut down, but with a 750-horsepower geared Wasp engine and three-blade propeller. Ruth Johnson won the 1947 Halle Trophy Race in this one at 223.602 mph.

5. In this extreme modification of an SNJ-2, note the earlier BC-1 type of rudder that was used on SNJ-1s and -2s. The canopy has been cut down completely and a new one built to match the fuselage contours. Note the bubble for the rear-seat pilot's head.

Howard Hughes' airplanes

His interests ran the gamut from speed to photo reconnaissance to flat-out bulk

2nd May 1972

With all the publicity focused on Howard Hughes these days because of the Irving book hoax and Hughes' own mysterious changes of abode, let's look at some famous Hughes-designed aircraft. We'll skip the current helicopter and guided-missile lines and concentrate on the three older airplanes in whose design and development he is known to have played a large and personal part.

The first is a speed plane built in 1934 that was logically called the H-1. Often called the Hughes Racer, it was never flown against other airplanes, only against the clock.

While much of the design detail was handled by a young engineer named Richard Palmer, it incorporated many of Hughes' own ideas for faster airplanes. Hughes was a skilled pilot who, at the ripe age of 23, bought a civil version of the Army's brand-new Boeing P-12 fighter as a sport plane and used it to win several races in the early 1930s.

Actually, there was nothing really new or radical about the H-1. It was a very good collection of state-of-the-art items, plus a 700-horsepower Pratt & Whitney Wasp Jr. engine and a controllable-pitch propeller. The fuselage was metal monocoque and the wing was wood. The latter was covered with extra-thick plywood that was wrinkle-free and finished like glass.

On Sept. 13, 1935, Hughes set a world speed record for land planes at 352.388 mph in the H-1. On Jan. 19, 1937, after refitting it with a larger wing and a new engine, Hughes flew the H-1 from Los Angles to Newark, New Jersey, setting a transcontinental speed record of 7 hours 28 minutes at an average speed of 332 mph. Who held the old record? Howard Hughes, in a Northrop Gamma, in 9:27:10 on Jan. 13, 1936.

The next famous Hughes design was the XF-11 photo-reconnaissance plane that was built for the U.S. Army late in World War II. Looking like an oversized P-38 because of its twin fuselages and central nacelle, the XF-11 made news on two counts. First, Hughes was severely injured on July 7, 1946, when the first of two XF-11s crashed on its first flight. Failure of one of the contra-rotating propellers was responsible. The second and bigger story was the postwar congressional investigation of the Hughes Aircraft Company and how it got an order for 100 F-11s in the first place. The 98 production versions were canceled at war's end, but the two prototypes and the static-test article were completed.

Despite all the scandal and investigation, the second XF-11, which used single-rotation propellers, proved to be an excellent airplane for its intended mission.

The third Hughes model, and one that still makes the papers from time to time, is the H-4, or Hercules. With eight reciprocating engines and a wingspan of 320 feet, it is dimensionally the world's largest airplane although its estimated gross weight of 400,000 pounds has since been exceeded by planes like the Boeing B-52, the Lockheed C-5A and the Boeing 747.

This one started early in 1942 as an ambitious idea by Henry Kaiser, who figured the easiest way to overcome the German submarine menace would be to fly cargo across the ocean in very large airplanes. He believed they could be mass produced the way his famous Liberty Ships were being built. He interested Hughes in the idea and a joint organization was formed. Hughes was to build three prototypes in his Culver City plant and Kaiser would build the production models in a new factory adjacent to one of his shipyards. The government issued a contract for the construction of the three prototypes at $6 million each on Sept. 17, 1942, but they had very low priority.

Other than their size, the main feature of the otherwise conventional flying-boat design was that it was built of non-strategic material: wood. Also, Hughes had to agree not to pirate engineering or production personnel from the established wartime aircraft industry. With things off to a slow start, Kaiser pulled out and what started as the HK-1 became Hughes' own H-4.

Costs got way out of hand. When the government's $18 million ran out, Hughes added over $700,000 of his own to get a single Hercules completed after the war. When it was finished, a special dry-dock was built for it in Long Beach. On Nov. 2, 1947, the day after it was launched and right at the height of more congressional investigations of his affairs, Hughes staged a public taxi test and invited the whole investigating committee. He then took some of the dignitaries and press people for a high-speed taxi run up and down the harbor.

After he returned them to the dock, he taxied out again for more runs with only some technicians, but no copilot, aboard. One run felt so good (he said) that he just opened the throttles a little further and got the H-4 into the air at an altitude of about 80 feet for a mile before setting it down again.

2000 update — The H-4 was then put back in the dock and spent 36 years in storage. It was eventually donated to the Aero Club of Southern California and was put on display in a huge aluminum-dome hangar next to the Queen Mary at Long Beach, California. Ordered out of that facility, it became the subject of fierce competitive bidding and was sold. In January 1993, it was dismantled and moved to McMinnville, Oregon, where it will become the main exhibit in the Captain Michael King Smith Evergreen Aviation

2

1

3

Institute's museum, which is scheduled to open early in 2001.

The photographs

1. The first Hughes-designed airplane, the H-1 of 1934, set world and transcontinental speed records in 1935 and 1937.

2. The first XF-11, an ill-fated, single-seat photo-graphic plane with two Pratt & Whitney R-4360 engines and coaxial propellers. Prop trouble caused it to crash on its first flight.

3. The first and only flight of the Hughes H-4 at Long Beach, California, on Nov. 2, 1947. It was equipped with eight R-4360 engines, had a 320-foot wingspan and weighed 400,000 pounds at gross.

Airplanes to gliders and back again

Engines and landing gear extended the careers of many TG-5s, -6s and -8s

1st June 1972

Early in World War II the Germans surprised the world with their use of troop-carrying gliders. The rest of the major powers were quick to take note and some began crash programs to develop military gliders of their own.

While troop-carrying cargo models were being developed in the United States, it was also necessary to start a glider-training program. To that end, the Army Air Corps looked to the small U.S. sailplane industry and ordered several hundred examples of certificated two-seaters that were then in production.

The order included 45 Frankfort Cinema IIs that were designated TG-1A (for training glider), 32 Schweizer SGS-2-8s that became TG-2As, and 150 Laister-Kauffman LK-10s that became TG-4As. The military also contracted with Schweizer for the development of 153 examples of a new two-seater specifically for military training, the TG-3A. Then, to get a fast start, it also bought up a lot of privately owned single- and two-seat sailplanes. Other manufacturers soon developed prototype trainers, but the TG-1 through -4 models were the only sailplane types ordered in quantity.

The TGs were good training sailplanes, which was fine when the goal was to develop skilled soaring pilots. The problem was that the cargo gliders the pilots were to fly were not sailplanes. They were little more than boxy aerial trailers and certainly didn't handle like dainty and sensitive sailplane trainers.

Feeling that the trainers should handle more like the cargo types, the Army tried a different approach. It had Taylorcraft, Aeronca and Piper remove the engines and conventional landing gear from their standard 65-horsepower two-seat tandem light planes and add a longer glider-type nose with an extra seat in it to maintain the balance. With no propeller requiring long landing gear legs for ground clearance, these converted light planes used two wheels right under the lower longerons to provide a ground-stable gear similar to that used by the cargo gliders instead of the single-wheel type used by the sailplanes. After testing three prototypes from each manufacturer, the Army ordered 250 production models from each: TG-5s from Aeronca, TG-6s from Taylorcraft and TG-8s from Piper. The sailplane types were soon declared surplus and stored until war's end.

The last act was a mixed blessing for America's postwar soaring movement. The surplus sailplanes put cheap and plentiful soaring equipment into the hands of the pilots, but it also stifled the development of new (and much more expensive) models for more than a decade.

The converted light planes didn't work out too well as training gliders either, so the program was reoriented to give most of the initial glider training in light planes, after which the pilots transitioned to the cargo gliders. The converted light planes also survived in quantity to the end of the war, but did not get the warm welcome the surplus sailplanes enjoyed. There was just no place in the soaring movement for the odd three-seaters.

That did not hold up their sale, however. Except for the nose and landing gear, they were still standard light-plane airframes and would be reconverted to such by addition of the necessary engines, landing gear and other parts. So, having been derived from airplanes in the first place, many of the TG-5s, -6s and -8s were reconverted to airplanes.

One special feature that had been added to the glider configuration was a wing spoiler system. Pilots who had used similar devices fitted to some of the Army liaison planes thought they were great for steep approaches, but the FAA insisted that they be deactivated when the gliders became civilian airplanes. The key word there was "deactivated," not "removed," and it is interesting to note how many of those allegedly deactivated spoilers later managed to pop open at very convenient times.

The photographs

1. On tow is a three-place Aeronca TG-5 training glider, converted from the standard 1941 Aeronca Defender light plane. The attachment point for the removable glider nose is clearly visible.

2. Taylorcraft's entry in the light-plane-into-glider game was the TG-6. This one is fitted with an experimental aerial pickup device.

3. Unlike the Aeronca, the Piper TG-8 did not have separate fabric covering for the added nose section. It retained the famous J-3 Cub hinge-down door for the two rear seats but added a separate hinge-up canopy for the front seat.

4. When converted to a power plane, the Taylorcraft TG-6 was on the civil register as a converted TG-6, and did not carry a Taylorcraft model number. Twenty-six shops made power planes out of TG-6s. Each shop got a separate Category 2 certificate number.

1

2

3

4

The first American jet transports

Others came before the famous Dash 80

2nd June 1972

When the Boeing Company turned its 18-year-old Model 367-80 over to the Smithsonian Institution on May 26, 1972, the museum got what it regards as one of the 12 most significant airplanes of all time. The Dash 80, as it is called, is the direct prototype of the Boeing 707 jet transport that went into service in 1958 and revolutionized air travel.

While the subsequent Boeing Model 727, 737 and 747 transports were considerably different in appearance, the trusty old Dash 80, which first flew on July 15, 1954, was the test bed for many of their special features. It even did some testing relative to the late-lamented SST.

Because of its fame as an individual aircraft and the effect of the production 707 on the world airline scene, the Dash 80 is generally regarded as the first American jet transport. Not so. There were a couple of others, but those one-onlies have not been swamped by the publicity generated by the Dash 80 and are almost completely forgotten today.

The world's first jet transport, of course, was the British de Havilland Comet, which first flew on July 27, 1949, and began airline service on May 2, 1952. The Comet boosted airline speeds considerably, but did not exactly start a revolution. The airlines continued to buy big piston-engine types for nearly a decade after the Comet appeared. The world was much more ready for jet transports when the Dash 80 came along.

The first "American" jet transport, and the world's second, was a Canadian project, the Avro C-102. It was built at Malton, near Toronto, and first flew on Aug. 10, 1949. The C-102 used four 3,500-pound-thrust Rolls Royce Derwent engines paired in two nacelles attached to the wings in an installation that was almost a direct substitution of jets for piston engines in an otherwise conventional straight-wing airframe.

With a wingspan of 98 feet 1 inch and a length of 82 feet 9 inches, the C-102 had a gross weight of 60,000 pounds, about the same as a World War II B-17, and could cruise 430 mph at 30,000 feet. The C-102 made a very favorable impression on several American airlines, but the Korean War stopped further development and only the prototype was built.

The first U.S.-built jet transport was the Chase XC-123A, developed for the U.S. Air Force in 1951. The -123A, even more obscure today than the C-102, has very implausible origins. Considering that gliders are generally regarded as slow and jets are noted for their speed, one would hardly expect a glider to be converted to a jet transport, but that is what happened.

Chase Aircraft Company of West Trenton, New Jer-sey, had turned out several assault glider designs for the Air Force after World War II. The last was a pair of really clean all-metal models designated XG-20 (they were to have been XCG-20 for cargo glider, but the Air Force had just lumped all the glider types together under the single G-for-glider designation). By this time, the Air Force had decided that gliders had no further military use, but figured that some of the existing glider airframes might become good short-take-off transports if fitted with engines, which was done with the two XG-20s.

One, redesignated XC-123, was fitted with two 2,300-horsepower Pratt & Whitney R-2800 radial engines in conventional nacelles. The other, designated XC-123A, was fitted with modified inboard jet pods of the Boeing B-47 bomber, each containing two 5,200-pound-thrust General Electric J-47s. First flight of this new transport came on April 21, 1951, just a year before Boeing's board of directors authorized construction of the Dash 80.

The XC-123A was not a very successful conversion, and little information is available on it other than it had a wingspan of 110 feet and length of 77 feet 1 inch.

The XC-123, on the other hand, was very successful. Little Chase aircraft was not in a position to undertake large-scale production, so it teamed up with Kaiser-Frazer and built early production C-123Bs at Willow Run. Various difficulties resulted in cancellation of this contract, and the Air Force then awarded contracts to Fairchild for continued production. Although long since out of production, the C-123B (and modified versions with higher designations) is still a mainstay of operations in Vietnam while the unique XC-123A is just another forgotten airplane.

The photographs

1. Although Boeing's Dash 80 gets most credit for the development of passenger jets, Canada's Avro C-120 (pictured) was actually the first airliner in America to offer jet power.

2. The Chase XG-20, Air Force Tail No. 7787, was an all-metal cargo glider about the size of a Douglas DC-3. It even had retractable landing gear. Two were built. Cargo was loaded through a drop-down ramp at the rear of the cabin.

3. The G-20 7787 became the first U.S. jet transport when the two inboard jet pods of a Boeing B-47, each with two General Electric J-47 jet turbojet engines, were added.

4. The Boeing Company's prototype 707 now has a proud place in the Smithsonian Institution's Air & Space Museum. Officials consider the airliner one of the 12 most significant planes in history.

1

2

3

4

Finding antique airplanes

The days of discovering a jewel in the barn are pretty must in the past

1st July 1972

At one time or another, every antique airplane buff dreams of finding a really old airplane in a barn, acquiring it and restoring it. For a very few, that dream has become reality, but for most it remains unfulfilled.

Such discoveries are still possible but they are far less probable than 20 or even 10 years ago. Two conditions are essential to the continued existence of "undiscovered" antiques. One is that they have to be stored where they are not in anyone's way. The other is that the storage space doesn't cost the owner anything. That means they will most likely be found in out-of-the-way spots on private property, not at airports where storage space is at a premium.

Before the antique airplane boom started in the early 1950s, old airplanes did not have their present status, and a lot of long-stored oldies were burned as junk when the building in which they were stored was razed. Some were even burned by their owners just to get them out of the way. "No one wants that hunk of junk," one owner said as he burned a 1918 Spad in 1949.

Others, particularly unflyable military types from the 1920s and 1930s that were given to high schools and colleges, were scrapped when later equipment became available after World War II. Incidentally, the schools are not a good source for military antiques because of the restrictions under which the government donated them. It was stipulated that the plane could not be passed on as an identifiable airplane or for usable parts; it had to be returned to the government or scrapped. A 1926 Boeing FB-5 was scrapped at a well-known college in 1948 under this requirement.

A few of the military antiques that did survive the school route ended up in museums, not in the hands of individuals.

Every antiquer on the prowl hears all sorts of rumors — I'll call them put-ons — of old airplanes in barns "a few miles from here." Somehow, though, the guy who says he can take you there never has the time to do it. When the exasperated antiquer finally pins the guy down, or shows him the $20 bill that will be his when they get there, he gets an answer like, "Oh, that barn burned down a couple of months ago." Sound familiar?

Some real treasures do survive under odd circumstances. One antiquer knew of a pre-WWI Amercanized Bleriot in an old warehouse and wanted to borrow it to set up at an air show. When he asked the warehouse worker, the man said, "Yes, under one condition."

Figuring that the man wanted insurance coverage or a big deposit, the would-be borrower asked the condition.

"That you get the damn thing out of here and don't bring it back!"

The tragedy of that case is that the new owner was unable to restore it in the years that he had it. After he died, his family sold it to a museum.

Other true experiences can be frustrating. A young friend of mine was riding in a car with a fellow college student. They were on their way to some distant college function when the driver stopped to see a relative who was a farmer. Hanging in the barn was a wood-frame airplane that had been there when the family purchased the farm in 1930. By the time my friend mentioned this episode to me several years later, he couldn't remember the location of the farm or even the name of the student whose car he was in.

A few gems such as Jennies are found, but that's only part of the problem. Acquiring them is something else. I did get to a genuine Jenny in a barn, but the owner wouldn't sell. When he was away on a long trip, some other antiquers with a ready supply of the green stuff went to work on the man's wife and got the airplane.

In other cases the aging owner sets an impossibly high price – he seems to think that a basket case has the same value as a complete restoration. After years of this, the old codger dies off; the family moves in to clear up his affairs and casually burns the pile of old sticks that was out in the barn. Not all of these oldies are found as complete units. Some are acquired piece by piece over a period of many years.

The photographs

1. The U.S. Navy Vought UO-1 was built from 1923-25. In 1972 the author had some parts for one of these rare aircraft and was looking for others. He ultimately donated them to the Museum of Flight in Seattle, which also has the rudder to a Boeing 204 that Bowers turned over.

2. A dream realized — almost. The author inspects a Jenny that had been stored in an Oregon barn since 1928. Someone else, however, had gotten to it first. The aircraft was restored and put back in the air by its new owner.

3. This wooden Pietenpol Air Camper was hung in the rafters of an old foundry in the early 1930s. The author acquired it just before the building was torn down. With help from friends, it was back in the air in 1968.

4. Another find in a barn. Parts of a wooden 1928 Boeing Model 204 flying boat were found and examined by enthusiasts. After unsuccessfully trying to make a boat of the old hull, the owner had burned it.

1

2

3   4

The Sperry Messenger

The cutest little airplane the Army ever flew

2nd July 1972

Dick Betts sent in a photo of a small radio-controlled U.S. Army airplane. He shot the photo in 1924, and now he asks about the airplane. It just happens that I am very familiar with the history of this particular design and had planned to discuss it in a forthcoming column. Because of Mr. Betts' request, it got moved to the head of the line.

To use its correct designation, the airplane is a U.S. Army Engineering Division M-1, but it is better known as the Sperry Messenger. In any case, it qualifies in my book as the cutest airplane the Army ever had and is an excellent subject for a homebuilt replica project.

The design originated in 1920 in response to an Army requirement for what was essentially the aerial equivalent of a courier motorcycle – a small low-cost airplane that could land in small unimproved fields to carry messages between commanders in the field and their headquarters.

At this time the Engineering Division of the Air Service, located at McCook Field in Dayton, Ohio, did a lot of airplane design work and even built some prototypes.

Alfred Verville of the division designed the Messenger, which was designated M-1, but the Army shops did not build it. Instead, the manufacture of 42 airplanes was contracted to the Sperry Aircraft Company of Farmingdale, Long Island. President Lawrence Sperry was the son of Elmer Sperry of gyroscope fame. The first 22 built were M-1s, and the last 20 were M-1As.

Since they were messenger planes built by Sperry, it was entirely logical to call them "Sperry Messengers." The Army didn't like that, however, and eventually issued a directive to stop calling them Sperrys and use the proper alphanumeric military designation.

While the flying motorcycle concept did not work out, the Messenger proved to be a good little airplane – popular with pilots, aerobatic and fun to fly. Its low cost and structural simplicity subjected it to considerable experimentation at McCook Field. It underwent tests of different airfoils and wing shapes, variable-camber wings and hooking onto Army blimps in flight.

Sperry disappeared in 1923 while flying his Messenger from England to France. He was forced down in the channel and apparently tried to swim ashore. He should have stayed in the plane; it drifted ashore intact.

A number of Messengers were converted to radio-controlled flying bombs under the designation "MAT" (for messenger aerial torpedo). The local AT designation could not be used because the same letters already designated advanced trainers. One MAT was preserved in the original Air Force Museum but disappeared with a lot of other exhibits when McCook Field was closed in 1927.

The Messenger has a lot going for it as a present-day homebuilt. Its construction is all-wood, and its wings each have a 20-foot span, with an area of 160 square feet.

The original engine was the 60-horsepower Lawrence L-4, a three-cylinder air-cooled radial that weighed only 147 pounds. With a displacement of 223 cubic inches and turning a 78-inch-diameter prop at 1,800 rpm, it put out as much thrust as a Continental O-200 does today. Top speed was 96.7 mph, and gross weight was 862 pounds.

In 1962 I had an article about the Messenger in American Modeler magazine with fairly detailed drawings and all of the information that was available from the project documents in the Air Force Museum and other sources. That article, which was reprinted in Homebuilt Aircraft in 1967 and again in American Modeler in 1968, drew a lot of letters that indicated the Messenger's appeal as a homebuilt.

The would-be builders wanted more information, but none was available. I have since learned that the Air & Space Museum of the Smithsonian Institution has a set of original drawings, but I cannot say whether reprints are available or what they might cost.

The unavailability of little radials today is a severe setback to the authenticity of a Messenger replica, but sketches indicate that a modern flat-four engine using J-3 Cub air scoops doesn't hurt the looks at all (the purists will hate me).

A more important authenticity detail, at least to me, is the large-diameter wire wheels. Using fat modern 6.00 x 6s would compromise the looks of the Messenger to a far greater degree than would the change to a flat-four engine. Another adulteration I hope I can head off is the practice of some who build replicas of old-timers to put on a modern thick airfoil.

It is not a difficult job to fit brakes to wire wheels or make them work on a floating axle. To make the replica further compatible with present-day airport operations on pavement, it will be necessary to add a steerable tailwheel.

The Army retired its last Messenger in 1927, but with several individuals known to be building replicas from the magazine data, we can expect to see some Sperry Messengers – pardon me, Engineering Division M-1s – in the sky again.

The photographs

1. One of the experimental Sperry Messengers that were used to test variable-camber wings. A distinctive feature of the Messenger was the use of struts in place of conventional flying and landing wires. Interplane and landing-gear struts are laminated from wood as single units.

2. The little Messenger was light enough to hook on to an Army blimp without overloading it. The Army did not follow up on these 1924 tests; it remained for the Navy to carry on, building four-plane hangars into the rigid airships Akron and Macon.

3. Designer Lawrence Sperry takes off in his personal

1

2

3

4

5

Messenger from the Capitol Plaza in Washington, DC. Compare the size of the airplane with the people on the Capitol steps. Production of the M-1 totaled 42 for the U.S. Army.

4. Sperry also built an M-1 for himself. He lengthened the rear fuselage to make it a two-seater, and had to lengthen the nose to move the engine ahead for balance.

5. The little Messenger was small enough and had good enough control at low speed to participate in stunts like this.

The Moth variants

Original DH-60 was followed by the DH-60M, DH-82 and Stampe SV-4

1st August 1972

In response to a letter to the editor a few weeks ago, I promised to write a column on the de Havilland Moth biplanes and the Stampe SV-4. Here it is.

The original Moth was developed in 1925 at the de Havilland plant in Britain to fill a need for a simple, low-cost, easy-to-fly airplane for training and club use. Earlier government-sponsored attempts to develop ultra-light planes through a design contest had not been successful; engines in the motorcycle power range just didn't do the job.

De Havilland went ahead on its own and added power to a very traditional tandem-seat open-cockpit biplane design. The company drew heavily on its military designs, going back to 1915 models for aerodynamic features and structural details.

The Moth, as the DH-60 was named, was an all-wood design with a plywood-covered fuselage. Folding wings simplified storage. One relatively new innovation was the use of automatic slats on the leading edges of the upper wing to improve stall characteristics.

Since the rear-spar attachment fittings to the center section and the fuselage doubled as the wing hinges, they had to be in line with each other, so the Moth's wings were not significantly staggered. That put the front cockpit between the center-section struts. The access problem was somewhat alleviated by adding a small fold-down door on one side.

For all its excellent design features, the Moth had one serious problem even before it was built: There were no production engines that fit. That was solved by the quick redesign of a World War I surplus French Renault air-cooled V-8 into an inline four. In its early versions, the inline four delivered 60 horsepower and was just right for the Moth.

Thanks to large stocks of war-surplus material, the new Cirrus engine promised to be in production for several years (later versions, however, were built entirely new).

The Cirrus-powered Moth was an immediate success and became the dominant light plane throughout the British Empire and in many other countries. Early models retained the original wood fuselage, but later ones were switched to steel tubing and designated the DH-60M (for metal). The Cirrus engine was later replaced by the Gypsy, a similar 90-horsepower model that de Havilland designed on its own. This version was manufactured in the United States by Moth Aircraft as the DH-60GM. It received a U.S. approved type certificate (ATC) and was powered by an American version of the Cirrus. Built by Wright Aeronautical Corp., the engine was known as the Wright Gypsy.

The point of distinction was that the American engines turned right-hand props instead of the left-handers favored by the British. Moth Aircraft was taken over by Curtiss-Wright in 1930, but production was soon killed off by the Depression.

Meanwhile, back in merry England, de Havilland came up with an improved model, the 1931 DH-82 Tiger Moth. Intended as a military trainer, it had a 130-horsepower inverted de Havilland Gypsy engine.

The most noticeable change was in the wings. The center section was moved forward to put the center-section struts ahead of the front cockpit, which then made it necessary to sweep the outer wing panels back considerably for balance. With such a misalignment of the rear spar fittings, the wings of the Tiger Moth did not fold.

The Tiger Moth was second only to the Boeing/Stearman Kaydet in the number of biplane trainers built, with over 7,000 produced. It remained in British military service until the 1950s and is still going strong in many flying clubs.

Though it was an all-around good airplane, the Tiger Moth encountered licensing problems in the United States. It seems that none had been accepted in the U.S. under reciprocal agreements before 1937, when a lot of old-fashioned structural details became illegal for new designs.

Consequently, Tiger Moths did not qualify under a U.S. grandfather clause that allowed other aircraft with obsolete details to remained licensed.

Actor Cliff Robertson, however, fought the paperwork battle, and British- and Australian-built Tiger Moths can now be given standard licenses in the U.S.

However, the considerably refined Canadian-built DH-82C version, with steel-tube struts, brakes and steerable tail wheel – and some with cockpit canopies – are not eligible for licensing in the United States!

What about the Stampe? It fits in here because it is a very close copy of the Tiger Moth, using the wooden fuselage structure of the early DH-60. The SV-4B version of the Stampe even used the same inverted Gypsy engine as the Tiger Moth.

The original SV-4s were built in the late 1930s by the Belgian firm of Stampe-Et-Vertongen at Antwerp. After World War II, the SV-4C version, using a 140-horsepower French Renault engine that was based on the Gypsy, was built by the Societe Nationale des Constructions Aeronautique du Nord. That mouthful was one of several regional branches of the nationalized French aviation industry whose products are simply referred to as Nord.

SV-4Cs were used by the French air force as primary trainers and for many years thereafter in government-supported flying clubs.

1

2

3

4

Several Stampes have now been imported into the United States, but all so far seem to be operating on experimental licenses. It looks like we have the old Tiger Moth problem all over again. If satisfactory solutions are reached, I will be discuss them in a future column.

The photographs

1. This American-built DH-60GM Moth was photographed at Oakland Airport in 1940. NC-916M was later acquired by Ed Clark and became a fixture at air shows and fly-ins for many years. It was destroyed recently while performing in a movie. Note the leading-edge slats.

2. A British de Havilland DH-82A Tiger Moth of the Hampshire Aeroplane Club in post-World War II years. This

one has a folding instrument-training hood for the rear cockpit. British and Australian Tiger Moths operated without brakes and were fitted with tailskids. The Canadian DH-28C had brakes and a steerable tailwheel, and the mains were moved forward a bit. During a wartime engine shortage, some Canadian Tiger Moths were built with American Menasco engines.

3. It may look like a Moth, but this is actually a French-built Stampe SV-4C of Belgian design. The Stampe used the same Gypsy engine as the Tiger Moth.

4. The Belgian-designed, French-built Stampe SV-4A is almost a dead ringer for the Tiger Moth. The most notable difference is the lack of the classic de Havilland tail. The Stampe's wingtips are also more rounded.

What crowded skies?

Seven days in the air — and encounters with just six airplanes

2nd August 1972

There has been a lot of discussion in the aviation press lately about the problems of air traffic density — the crowded skies. There are those who advocate positive controls for all altitudes and putting everyone on IFR flight plans. I won't go into the pros and cons of that here, but will merely cover my own experience on a recent 3,900-mile cross-country.

I took the biplane version of my open-cockpit homebuilt Fly Baby from the Seattle area to Oshkosh, Wisconsin, for the annual fly-in of the Experimental Aircraft Association (EAA). The fly-in was held the first week in August. Admittedly, a trip in this kind of plane is not like one you would make in an up-to-date production airplane that's equipped with the typical electronic navaids, but it still gets where it is going.

My bird cruises at a slowpoke 85 mph and has a still-air range of 255 miles with a 20-minute fuel reserve. I don't use OMNI, and I seldom fly straight-line airways routes from Point A to Point B. I instead follow the highway through the mountains and the badlands. I fly low, generally 1,500 to 2,000 feet above the surface.

With the "crowded skies" problem well in mind before I started, I resolved to note every airplane I saw that wasn't in the immediate vicinity of an airport. For 3,900 miles of travel involving 44 hours and 10 minutes in the air, here is how the "other airplane" count went:

Eastbound

First day — No other planes seen in the air except one that I followed out of the pattern, so he doesn't count.

Second day — Only one airplane, a borate bomber working on a small forest fire about 30 miles west of Billings, Montana, and about a mile north of the highway I was following.

Third day — One airplane, an Air Force C-130, cut across my route at about 2,000 feet above the terrain some 20 miles east of Minneapolis, which I bypassed to the north. The low count this day was surprising; I had expected to find a lot of other no-radio airplanes that fly as I do converging on Oshkosh. I was told at gas stops that others had just been through, but I never saw any of them in the air.

Westbound

First day — Low ceilings and dirty weather moving in; weather forecasters told us that anyone still at Oshkosh Saturday night (the final day) would probably still be there on Tuesday. So along with many others, I left early. Didn't see any of them away from the field, however. Some 150 miles out, a Cessna 172 passed me. He was following a long straight road that intersected the power line I was following at a shallow angle. A little later I saw what could have been the same Air Force C-130 in the same place and at the same altitude as before.

Second day — No flying at all; stayed in a hotel in St. Cloud, Minnesota, all day. The wind and rain were so violent that even Molt Taylor driving his Coot amphibian home from Oshkosh on a trailer quit driving.

Third day — No other airplanes, even though I was traveling along many miles of highway where I had seen highway patrol planes on previous trips.

Fourth day — Another 172 passed me right at the summit of Pipestone Pass a few miles short of Butte, Montana. It's a short, steep descent to the airport from the pass. He put his flaps down and dived, and my bird, without flaps, was able to stay right with him. Because of repairs on an intersecting runway, I had intended to land long on 27, but the 172 landed short, so I had to circle once to let him clear.

Fifth day — Only one other airplane all day, a Piper Cherokee that passed me at my altitude and (properly) on the right as I approached Mullan Pass at 9,500 feet. It must have been at least the 235-horse model because of the speed he used to leave me behind. I found that it took me exactly an hour and a half to reach the pass from my takeoff at Missoula, 75 miles away. FSS had given me winds of 25-35 knots at 270 degrees, and the man was right.

So that's the "crowded skies" traffic count: six airplanes encountered in seven days of flying, and none of them what I would consider a hazard to me or me to them. Of course, I saw vapor trails from high-flying jets, but they don't count. At my altitude, I usually see quite a few working dusters, but it was too windy both going and coming for them to be out.

As you can see, it's still possible to get around most of the country in short-range no-radio planes and avoid controlled fields unless you want to get close to places like Long Beach, Chicago or New York City. For the really short-range ships like mine, there are occasional problem areas resulting from the prevailing wind conditions.

Eastbound, for example, I could make the 210 miles from Kellogg, Idaho, to Butte, Montana, nonstop and skip Missoula, the controlled-field midpoint. In fact, with the tail wind that came up, I could have just about made it another 70 miles to the next airport at Bozeman. I couldn't make Butte-Kellogg nonstop and had to put in at Missoula. That required a phone call to ask permission to come in on light signals. The 115 miles from Butte to Missoula took 90 min-

utes, and the 148 miles from Missoula to Coeur d'Alene took 2 hours 20 minutes.

Now before some of you question my sanity — and that of other pilots with similar equipment — for using such inadequate airplanes as transportation, I had better explain. Ships like these are not generally used expressly for transportation. They may take their owner-builders long distances to fly-ins, but the object is to get the airplane to the fly-in to participate in the activity.

A major disadvantage for long hauls in many of the smallest ships is the lack of baggage space. It was interesting at Oshkosh to see a lot of pilots down at the bus terminal, picking up or shipping their baggage home!

The photograph

The author and his 975-pound gross-weight homebuilt Fly Baby, ready to leave Boeing Field for Oshkosh on July 29, 1972. The 63 pounds of cargo, consisting of camera bag and four cameras, Air Force B-4 bag, camp stool, tiedown kit, tool kit, spare 8.00 x 4 inner tube, cockpit cover, maps, extra cushions and snacks are all carried internally. When a sleeping bag is carried, some of the items are carried in an external streamlined pod under the belly. Photo by Guenther Schmidt.

Fun with registration letters

A world of I-CANT, I-RENE, I-TALY, D-AMIT and G-WHIZ

1st September 1972

Back in 1919, most of the nations that were ambitious about civil aviation signed an international agreement that covered, among other things, the licensing and identifications of airplanes. Each country was assigned an identifying letter, such as F for France, G for Great Britain, D for Germany (Deutschland), etc.

The United States was assigned the letter N, even though it did not sign the treaty and did not start licensing its airplanes until 1927. The national letter was followed by a dash and four more letters, such as F-ABCD (except Germany, Austria and a few others; Germany used numbers until 1933).

For a while, some countries got extra mileage out of some of the letters. In Italy, the first two of the four indicated the district in which the airplane was licensed. In its 1933 system, Germany identified the airplane's weight category. In the British Empire, the first two letters of the four identified the dominion or commonwealth, such as G-CA (for Canada) and G-AU (Australia).

Canada also put civil registrations on its military airplanes for a while, but used a different series, G-CY. That particular system broke down by 1929, when those countries had more airplanes than they could cover with combinations of only the last two letters.

The problem was resolved by a simple change. Australia was given a new two-letter national and identification prefix (VH) and existing airplanes kept the last three letters of their original registration. G-AUSU became VH-USU.

Canada went at it differently. Its new identification letters were CF and the following combinations started at AAA. For a few years thereafter, planes licensed under the old system were allowed to operate under their old registrations.

Naturally, the use of five letters on an airplane resulted in occasional words, some deliberate and some accidental. That's where the fun comes in. The "Words on a Plane" game can be played by those who get to see non-U.S. airplanes or those who read foreign aviation magazines and books. Keep your eyes open and you may spot some good ones.

Sometimes the national letter becomes part of the word or a word pair. Sometimes not. Italy, with the national letter "I," has it good here, with such combinations as I-CANT, I-RENE, I-TALY, etc. Germany has come up with some lulus too, with D-AMIT and D-AMME. England offers the possibility of such things as G-WHIZ, G-RUNT, G-ROAN and G-RIPE (No photo confirmation on those). Czechoslovakia has a good one: OK-BAD.

Of course, quite a few can be overlooked because of not knowing the language. D-ESEL wouldn't mean anything to most people, but in German esel means donkey.

In general, except as noted, the governments issued the letters sequentially and did not permit jumping ahead for special combinations. Canada was pretty adamant about staying in sequence for a long time, but got more liberal a few years back and issued CF-RFC (for the World War I Royal Flying Corps) to a replica of a 1916 Sopwith Pup fighter that was built in Calgary.

Other special Canadian registrations have been even more specific. An excursion airline bought a single Boeing jet and had it registered CF-FUN. When it bought a second one, someone facetiously suggested that the airline get CF-SEX and thereby have the "Fun and Sex Airline," but it turned out that there was already a CF-SEX flying. We will assume that it was a sport plane.

While Canada's identification letters CF don't lead themselves readily to five-letter words, the last three turn up some good ones on their own. Seen at the recent Arlington fly-in were a Fairchild Cornell CF-FLY and a Luscombe CF-SHE.

Naturally, some corporations go for letter combinations that give their own airplanes corporate identity. Opel, in Germany, has or had D-OPEL on a plane. Fiat, in Italy, latched onto I-FIAT and had it on a long line of company-owned planes.

Some of the details and problems of the U.S. registration system will be covered in a future column.

The photographs

1. This Italian trimotor floatplane had an interesting tie-in of its registration letters and the company name. The plane was a CANT Z.1005; the letters were an abbreviation for Cantieri Navale Triestino.

2. Aircraft that use letters instead of numbers for their registration bore interesting words or word pairs. This German Dornier Superwal flying boat was built in Italy in 1929 and carried Italian registration letters spelling I-RIDE. A sister ship is I-RENE.

3 Germany switched from registration numbers to letters in 1933 and also came up with items in the word game. This Blohm and Voss Ha-140 of 1939 was registered D-AMME. Others were D-AMIT and D-AUTO.

4. An American Stinson SR-7 Reliant registered in Germany in the late 1930s. The letter D identified Germany (Deutschland) and the following letters identified the owner, the Opel Motor Co.

1

2

3

4

Stagger

Why have it, and what does it accomplish?

2nd September 1972

One of the nearly forgotten words in this age of monoplanes is "stagger." It has nothing to do with the erratic progress of a drunk down the street; it's a term that describes the longitudinal relationship of one wing of a biplane with the other. The word appears most frequently today in reference to the classic Beechcraft Model 17 biplane, which is widely referred to as the Beech Staggerwing.

As used here, it is somewhat of a misnomer. When that particular biplane appeared in 1932, its distinctive feature was the negative stagger arrangement of its wings. Most contemporary biplanes had positive stagger, which meant that the upper wing was located some distance ahead of the lower.

Walter Beech turned things around for a good reason. By having the lower wing forward, he was able to attach the landing gear directly to the lower wing in the manner of some low-wing monoplanes instead of to the fuselage, as was standard biplane practice. That made it possible to retract the landing gear into the wing, which gave the Beech 17 a big boost in performance.

Positive stagger was such a common feature of biplanes that no special mention was made of it. The use of negative stagger on the Beech was a rarity worthy of note. The airplane was initially described as the "negative-stagger Beech," but over the years the word "negative" was dropped and the term "Staggerwing" emerged to label the Beech 17.

All of which leads to the inevitable questions. Why have stagger in the first place? What does it accomplish?

According to the old aerodynamics textbooks, stagger contributes somewhat to longitudinal stability and also to maneuverability, which would seem to make it an asset on fighters and special aerobatic ships.

The fact that some famous fighters like the World War I Spad did not use it, plus the fact that the stagger was in use long before maneuverability become a competitive factor, would indicate that there are other reasons for its existence.

One reason is the simple matter of access, particularly in small airplanes. Take something like today's Smith Miniplane homebuilt as an extreme example. With the pilot seated almost on the center of gravity, he'd be under the upper wing if the plane had no stagger. With such a narrow wing gap, he wouldn't be able to get in or out without a big cutout in the side of the fuselage. Staggering the upper wing positively — that is, moving it ahead — plus a cutout in the rear of the center section allows the pilot to sit further aft relative to the upper wing and solves the access problem. In this matter, it should be noted that few big biplanes, from single-engine mail planes and bombers on up, had staggered wings. There was plenty of room between the top wing and the fuselage on these bigger ships for the crew to be able to climb into the cockpits. The passenger transports had doors in the side of the fuselage, so gap was no problem.

The military had considerations other than maneuverability. Early observation planes had the observer in the front seat, and his downward view was enhanced by the positive stagger that put the lower wing further back. Some fighters, such as the de Havilland 5 and the Sopwith Dolphin of World War I, had negatively staggered wings to improve the pilot's visibility in the critical upward-forward area, normally a blind spot on conventional single-seaters where the pilot sat behind the upper wing. However, despite that particular advantage, negative stagger remained rare on fighters.

What about biplanes with no stagger? There were plenty, particularly in the larger sizes as mentioned. The term "orthogonal biplane" was used to describe them. The word eventually took on a more specific meaning and was used to identify an unstaggered biplane with equal chord (and span) on both wings.

The photographs

1. A Waco cabin biplane, typical of all the 1931-41 Custom and Special lines. Like all Wacos and most other biplanes, this one has a positive stagger, with the upper wing located ahead of the lower. Note the pilot's position; his downward view is fine, but his upward view is nil without a skylight in the roof.

2. The famous Staggerwing, a Beech D-17S biplane on which the lower wing is located forward of the upper wing in an arrangement known as negative stagger. Downward view for the pilot is somewhat reduced compared to the Waco, but his upward vision is greatly improved.

3. Many biplanes were built with no stagger. When the wingspan and the chord were equal, and the gap between the wings equaled the chord, as on this Douglas M-1, the configuration was called an orthogonal biplane.

4. Most triplanes had their wings in alignment, but there were a few oddities, such as this experimental World War I Nieuport. At the height of the 1917 triplane craze, Nieuport tried three wings on the fuselage of its standard Model 17 biplane fighter and came up with this "double-stagger" gem.

1

2

3

4

Insignia proportions

Errors often pop up when restorers don't do their homework

1st October 1972

Getting the correct proportions on U.S. military aircraft insignia has always been a problem for illustrators, model builders and restorers of antique airplanes. It is really unfortunate that the final products of their many hours of effort often include serious errors in the area of markings.

This is not the result of carelessness or indifference on the part of the individuals involved. They simply don't have access to accurate reference materials. For current markings, which are primarily the concern of the military and the manufacturers of military aircraft, there is no problem; the necessary details are covered by military specifications and technical orders (TOs) that are readily available to those who have an official need for them.

Unfortunately for outsiders, this information is circulated only within official channels, even though it is not classified.

Specifications on the older markings are still around, but they are buried deep in the official archives. They are not readily available, even to the military when needed, as shown by the marking errors seen on some restored military airplanes in the Naval Aviation and Air Force museums.

The best sources for illustrators, modelers and airplane restorers who are unable to poke around in the archives themselves are the specialized books and magazines that have been written by and for aviation history and technical data buffs. Another source is the house organs of such organizations as the American Aviation Historical Society (AAHS), the Society of World War I Aero Historians (Cross & Cockade), Stearman Restorers Association, and the International Plastic Modelers Society (IPMS). The articles in the publications are usually the work of really dedicated buffs who are glad to spread the word. There is a communications problem, however, because too often an individual working alone who needs the information is not aware of its availability through these channels.

Now let's look at the basic U.S. military aircraft insignia and see what its proportions really are. In May 1917 the United States adopted a five-pointed white star (as on the U.S. flag) and backed it with a blue circle; a red circle was put in the center (Figure 1, facing page). The insignia was used until January 1918, when the United States adopted a three-color concentric circle for uniformity with the markings of its allies of the time; the star-in-circle was readopted in late 1919 and remained in use until May 15, 1942.

The most common error in latter-day applications of this marking is a red-center circle that is sometimes made so oversized that it touches the edge of the blue. The red circle is *tangent* to a line projected across the center of the star from the sides of the star points, as shown in Figure 1a.

The red center was dropped in May 1942 because of similarity to the Japanese "Rising Sun" insignia, which Allied pilots called the "meatball." U.S. aircraft then operated with just the plain white star on a blue circle until July 1943.

At that time, a decision was made to increase the visibility of the U.S. marking by adding a white rectangle to each side of the circle. As shown in Figure 2, it was equal in length to the radius of the blue circle and had a depth half the radius of the circle. The rectangles were positioned with their tops even with the top sides of the upper side points of the star, and the whole arrangement was surrounded with a *red* border whose width was one-eighth the radius of the blue circle.

The red border lasted only two months; in the heat of combat the red could still be mistaken for the Japanese marking, so the red was changed to blue. The decision to put a *blue* border next to the blue circle has created trouble for modelers, et al, ever since. The common error here is to ignore the fact that there is blue around blue. Many, including some manufacturers of civil aircraft who have sold off-the-shelf products to the military, think that the blue border surrounds only the rectangles; they bring the star points to the outer edge of the blue, as with the old markings. Take a look at model markings, and the painted illustrations in the magazines, and you'll see this error quite often when you're looking for it.

Actually, the blue-around-blue only made sense during the initial period of in-the-field conversions, when the original red border was painted over with blue. The blue-around-blue doesn't improve the visibility of the later applications a bit. In a few cases, it has actually been eliminated. On some black or dark blue planes of late World War II, the border was left off, as was the blue circle; such planes carried only the white star and the rectangles. The blue border has recently been depleted from a few of the planes that carry current camouflage schemes.

The final change to the national marking came in January 1947, when red was again put into the insignia in the form of a red stripe that had a width one-sixth the radius of the basic blue circle. It was painted along the long center line of each rectangle (Figure 2a).

The photographs

1. The most common error in applying the old star-in-circle marking to restored pre-1942 aircraft like this Fairchild PT-19 is to make the red center too large. Some people even enlarge it to where it touches the blue. Errors in applying the later white bars and blue borders are even more numerous.

2. In some applications the blue border around the insignia is conspicuous by its absence, as on this light gray McDonnell Douglas F-15A Eagle.

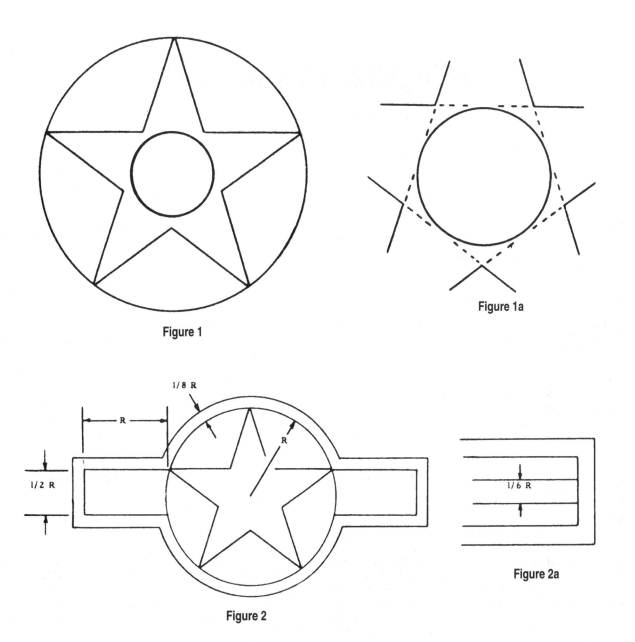

Figure 1

Figure 1a

Figure 2

Figure 2a

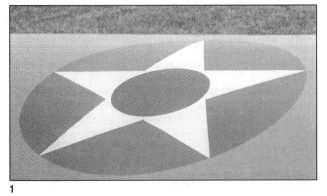

1

2

The B-40

A B-17 variant, it couldn't overcome the dead weight it was required to carry

2nd October 1972

Much has been written to describe the Boeing-designed B-17 as one of the great warplanes of all time. The aircraft certainly deserves the praise. A total of 6,980 were built by Boeing, 2,995 by Douglas and 2,750 by Lockheed. Though the B-24 was built in greater numbers (9,319 by Consolidated, 966 by North American, 964 by Douglas and 6,782 by Ford), the B-24s were taken out of service right after the war while the B-17s carried on in secondary Air Force roles until 1960. A few are still to be found, principally as borate bombers used in fighting forest fires.

A virtually unknown wartime variant of the B-17 is the B-40, which was the result of a not-very-successful experiment.

When long-distance U.S. bombing raids into Germany from bases in England were getting underway late in 1942, the fighter planes then in service did not have the range to accompany the B-17s all the way to the target and back. Existing planes that did have the range – the bombers themselves – were modified by deleting the bomb load and installing additional guns and armor, effectively converting them into escort fighters that could defend the bombers.

The job of developing the gunship variant of the B-17 was given to the Vega division of Lockheed, which was already involved in the B-17 program. Using a Boeing-built B-17F, Lockheed soon produced the XB-40. From one .30-caliber and nine .50-caliber machines guns that were used on the B-17E and early B-17Fs, the XB-40 had a total of 14 .50s.

The tail, top and belly twin-turret guns remained the same, but the single waist-gun installations, one to a side, were changed to pairs and a second top power turret replaced the single .50 in the radio compartment. The final touch was a new two-gun powered "chin" turret under the nose.

Normal ammunition load was 11,135 rounds to a maximum of 17,265 if the fuel weight was reduced accordingly. The result was an ammunition load of 1.8 to 2.8 tons, making the Flying Fortress really live up to its name (which had been bestowed in 1935 for the B-17's original mission of defending the U.S. coastline against surface fleets, not because of its firepower).

Without testing the XB-40 in combat, the Army ordered 24 service-test versions under the designation of YB-40. They were converted by Douglas from Lockheed-built B-17Fs and were rushed to England in April 1943 for combat trials. They proved to be a disappointment.

On the run to the target, the YB-40s could stay right with the B-17s because both models were flying at about the same gross weight. However, after each B-17 dropped several tons of bombs on the target, the YB-40s still had to carry their extra guns, armor and ammunition. This dead weight became a serious handicap to the YB-40s when they tried to keep up with the lighter B-17s on the return leg. As a result, and also because of recent increases in fighter range, the YB-40 gunships were withdrawn from service.

One YB-40 had a unique fling at glory, however. The Luftwaffe had a number of captured and flyable B-17s on hand. While most of them were flown in German markings for evaluation and to train Luftwaffe fighter pilots in the best ways to attack B-17s, a few were used for spy drops and other sneaky business. One trick was to shadow homeward-bound B-17 formations, acting like a crippled straggler and conning a B-17 into dropping back from the formation to fly cover for the supposed cripple. With the unsuspecting B-17 drawn away from the safety of the formation, the decoy either shot it down on its own or called in German fighters that had been alerted to the situation.

When the U.S. realized what was going on, it played some dirty pool of its own and planted one of the previously retired YB-40s in a B-17 formation. When the German "straggler" appeared, it was the YB-40 gunship, not a B-17, that dropped back to escort it. Once the YB-40's crew was positive that the straggler was under German control, it brought it down with a heavy broadside.

The photographs

1. Just another B-17? Look again; it's the XB-40. Lockheed added a second top turret, a chin turret and doubled the side guns of a Boeing B-17F to develop this gunship as a defensive escort for World War II bombers that operated beyond the range of standard fighter planes.

2. This close view of a YB-40 shows some of its extra firepower. Note the double waist guns and the additional top turret above the trailing edge of the wing. Also noticeable in this photo is the revised shape of the cockpit fairing. Although not successful in its intended mission, the B-40 left a legacy in the form of the "chin" turret, which was used on the later B-17G model.

3. Close-up of the chin turret installed in the XB-40. It was also used on the YB-40s that followed, and was standard equipment on some late B-17Fs and all the B-17Gs.

4. Interior of the XB-40 showing the double waist guns and the armor panels that protect the gunners from gunfire from the rear.

1

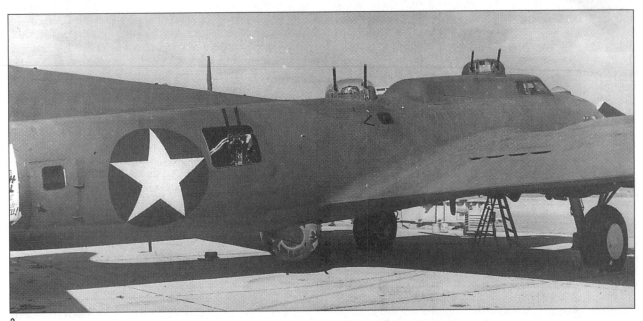

2

3

4

The wide-body Burnelli

The RB-1 of 1922 was a veritable ballroom when compared to other ships of the day

1st November 1972

"Wide body" is a term that has become common in commercial aviation since the advent of the Boeing 747, Douglas DC-10 and Lockheed L-1011. (Whatever happened to the term "jumbo jet"?) With "wide body" used as the current catchword, interior decorators are doing things to the insides of older transports like the Boeing 727 to give them the wide-body look.

Actually, wide-body transports – "wide" relative to the other dimensions of the airplane, not merely large – date back to 1921. Air travel was just getting underway in the United States, and while there were a few designed-for-the-purpose transports, they stuck pretty close to the traditional proportions that were developed during World War I. The fuselages were narrow and the cabins were cramped – uncomfortable for passengers and certainly unsuitable for bulk cargo.

A young aircraft designer named Vincent J. Burnelli decided that a change was in order. With the backing of T.T. Remington, he introduced his unique RB-1 (for Remington-Burnelli) transport in 1921. Perhaps the best way to describe this two-engine ship would be to call it a twin-fuselage design, something like the well-known P-38, only a biplane with the area between the two fuselages filled in to make a single large-volume unit. At 14 feet long, 14 feet wide and nearly seven feet high, this arrangement produced a veritable ballroom of a cabin.

Mere volume, however, was not Burnelli's only design goal. A much higher percentage of the total structure was used to enclose the passengers and cargo in the RB-1, a significant safety feature. Also, by utilizing an airfoil section for his extremely wide fuselage, he claimed that it added to the lift of the conventional wings and produced up to 40 percent of the total lift. That figure and the concept behind it have been a subject of controversy ever since.

Only one RB-1 was built. It was followed in 1924 by a near-duplicate RB-2 and in 1928 by a single CB-16 (for Chapman-Burnelli) 16-passenger monoplane.

Though the CB-16 featured the first retractable landing gear for a transport-type airplane, all-metal construction, wing flaps and the capability of climbing with one engine dead (and no assist from a feathering propeller), it did not win production orders. The UB-20 (for Uppercu-Burnelli) with fixed gear followed in 1929, and the UB-14, again with retractable gear, came along in 1934. Only one example of each model was built.

Progress toward a production version seemed to be made in 1937 when Cunliffe-Owen Aircraft, Ltd., was formed in England to produce a near-duplicate of the UB-14. One prototype designated OA-1 was built and licensed in November 1940, but World War II blocked further effort.

The final fling came in 1945 when the Cancargo subsidiary of Canadian Car and Foundry built the CBY-3, which was little more than an updated UB-14/OA-1. Under the name Loadmaster II, the CBY-3 had extensive service testing as a freighter and bush plane in Canada in the years immediately following World War II. Again, however, there were no production orders.

Granted, the wide-body Burnellis proved to be workable though not superior airplanes, it is questionable that their lifting fuselages worked quite the way Burnelli claimed.

Analyzed as a separate wing, the wide lifting fuselage appears logical at first; "X" number of additional square feet put to work generating lift. A second look raises some doubts. With a "wing" running the full length of the airplane, the center of pressure travel of the old-time airfoil would be considerable and should result in longitudinal trim problems. It is significant to note that the length of the fuselage lifting area was reduced on the CB-16 and subsequent models.

Still regarding the fuselage as a wing, there are the aerodynamic handicaps associated with a very negative (fractional?) aspect ratio, enormous tip losses, and a leading edge messed up with engines, propellers, air intakes and pilot cabins.

Obviously, the Burnelli's wide body does make some contribution to the overall lift of the airplane, but whether this is as much as Burnelli's claim of 40 percent or a considerably lower proportion can probably never be proven now that there are no more of these unique designs flying.

The photographs

1. The Remington-Burnelli RB-1 wide-body transport of 1921 with a single corrugated metal fuselage containing both engines. If the airfoil-sectioned fuselage can be regarded as extra wing area, the leading edge is pretty well messed up with the engines and open pilot cockpits.

2. The Chapman-Burnelli CB-16 of 1928 had a retractable landing gear, but the Uppercu-Burnelli UB-20 (shown) reverted to a fixed gear with the new low-pressure Goodyear Airwheels. Again, the leading edge of the lifting fuselage is distorted by the projecting Packard engines and their flat-faced radiators.

3. The Cunliffe-Owen OA-1 was a near-duplicate of the UB-14, with radial engines. Note the slightly projecting wheel of the retracted landing gear and the greatly shortened lifting portion of the fuselage, a detail shared with the CB-16, UB-20 and the subsequent CBY-3.

4. The most successful and longest-lasting of the Burnelli lifting-fuselage designs was the Cancargo CBY-3. After service in Canada and South America, it was registered as N17N in the United States and is now in the New England Air Museum at Windsor Locks, Connecticut.

1

2

3

4

O'han

The first seaplanes

They date to the work Glenn Curtiss conducted in 1908

2nd November 1972

Attempts to fly airplanes from the water began soon after the airplane became a workable reality. Glenn Curtiss, who got his start in aircraft design and construction with Alexander Graham Bell's Aerial Experiment Association in 1907 and '08, put twin floats under the association's highly successful June Bug in December 1908 and renamed it the Loon.

The Loon did a lot of taxiing, but it could not get off the water; the canoe-like floats had too much hydrodynamic drag, which prevented the aircraft from attaining a flying speed.

Curtiss then got busy with other projects and dropped the seaplane idea for a while. Late in 1910, a Frenchman named Henri Fabre managed to make a successful takeoff from water but did not land on it. His floats were little more than thick hydro skis with enough volume for buoyancy. His takeoff was a onetime event.

In November 1910, Curtiss set up a winter operation on North Island in San Diego Bay and set about in earnest to develop a successful seaplane. Starting with a large single float that was as wide as the original landing gear of the standard Curtiss pusher test vehicle, he tried dozens of sizes, shapes and auxiliary float arrangements before finding the combination that worked. What he ended up with was a single flat-bottom float 12 feet long, two feet wide and a foot deep. Lateral stability was provided by a single small float under each wingtip.

With Curtiss at the controls, this hydro-aeroplane, as it was called, made the first successful takeoff and landing on water on Jan. 26, 1911. It was no one-shot affair this time. Curtiss made several flights the same day and hydros immediately became a part of his San Diego operation.

Curtiss' next step was to increase the utility of the hydro by combining wheels and floats into an amphibious arrangement. He installed two retractable wheels in the normal land-plane position and added a small non-retractable wheel under the bow of the float. He then named the plane the Triad to indicate its ability to operate in three elements: land, sea and air. The Triad made its first flight on Feb. 26, 1911, just a month after the first successful full hydro had flown from the same spot.

The Triad made an immediate impression on the U.S. Navy, which had been cooperating with Curtiss in experiments involving airplanes that worked with the fleet. It ordered an improved Triad as its first airplane. The aircraft was delivered on July 1, 1911, at the Curtiss factory in Hammondsport, New York. The Navy bought other Curtiss pushers into 1914. Some were amphibians, some were land planes and others were straight hydros.

An interesting bit of aeronautical evolution paralleled the development of the hydros and the Triads. The standard Curtiss pusher of late 1910 had a fixed horizontal stabilizer and movable elevators behind the wing but also featured a biplane-type elevator ahead of the wing. This arrangement was used on the first hydro. By the time the Triad came along, the biplane forward surface had been cut down to a monoplane. The Navy's first Triad had a small monoplane elevator attached to the bow of the float instead of being carried on booms. When the 1912 production versions appeared, the forward elevator was done away with entirely.

One of the early Triads made another very important contribution to seaplane design: compartmentalization. The early floats had none. When compartmentalization was adopted for seaplanes, it was not for the standard nautical reason of isolating flooding to keep the ship from sinking. It resolved a balance problem.

On one flight in Hammondsport, Curtiss got into the air with a Triad after the float had picked up quite a bit of water. When he nosed down to land ashore, all the water ran to the bow of the float and made the plane so nose heavy that he could not get the nose up again with elevator.

Fortunately, the Triad crashed into the water, not on land. Curtiss, who had recognized the problem as soon as it appeared, survived and was able to make the necessary correction on subsequent hydros.

The photographs

1. Glenn Curtiss taxies the original Triad onto the beach from San Diego Bay in February 1911. Note the monoplane forward elevator carried on bamboo booms ahead of the wing.

2. This Curtiss Triad, the first Navy plane, was delivered in July 1911. The aircraft is resting with its wheels in shallow water. The forward elevator is mounted on the bow of the float. Curtiss kept the ailerons well between the wings until 1914.

3. This 1912 Curtiss did away with the forward elevator. The aircraft was a side-by-side two-seater with an early form of the throw-over control column developed by Curtiss. The filled-in areas between the inner struts are "skid plates." They were designed to prevent slips and skids in turns.

4. Glenn Curtiss holds the wheel of a 1911 Model D that was used for training. The control column can be swung over to the student in the right seat. Students today sit in the left seat, but on airliners the pilot sits on the left.

1

2

3

4

The first airplane

Those who claimed they flew before the Wright brothers were never able to prove it

1st December 1972

Dec. 17 is the anniversary of the first controlled powered flight by Wilbur and Orville Wright on the sands of Kitty Hawk, North Carolina, in 1903.

Throughout aviation history others have claimed to have flown before the Wright brothers, but they have been unable to prove it. The Wrights had five witnesses to their first powered flight, and they also had meticulous documentation of their earlier glider flights (also witnessed).

Best of all, they had the ultimate proof of repeatability; they not only continued to fly after their 1903 success, they taught others to fly, and they built and sold airplanes similar to the 1903 model.

Their first airplane was in most respects an oddity by today's standards. A development of their highly successful 1902 glider, it was fitted with a homemade 12-horsepower engine driving two eight-foot diameter propellers through chains. The pilot lay prone and controlled the elevators (located in front in what came to be called the canard configuration) with a rocking shaft. The wing-warping feature provided lateral control when the pilot swung his hips in a cradle-like device. The rudder was tied into the warping system for automatic yaw control.

The Wrights called their machine a flyer. The term aeroplane, which came into use soon after, actually referred to wings. The word later came to describe the machine as a whole. The Americanized version, airplane, did not come into general use until about 1916.

The Wright Flyer had no wheels, but rested on a dolly mounted on a wooden monorail that had been laid on the sand. The aircraft lifted off the dolly when it reached flying speed and landed on skids.

The first flight was to have been made on Dec. 14. Wilbur won the toss of a coin. The Flyer got into the air, apparently in a full stall or at least what today would be called the backside of the power curve, and flopped to the ground.

The damage was repaired by the 17th, at which time it became Orville's turn. The first flight lasted 12 seconds and covered 140 feet against a 20- to 27-mph wind. The second flight, by Wilbur, lasted 175 feet. Orville followed with a 200-foot flight. The big one was the fourth one, with Wilbur staying up for 59 seconds and covering 852 feet.

After the last flight, a gust of wind flipped the Flyer over and wrecked it. With a total air time of less than two minutes, it never flew again.

In 1916 Orville rebuilt the Flyer for display at the dedication of some new buildings at the Massachusetts Institute of Technology. It was necessary to recover the ship, but Orville saved some of the original fabric. After his death, the remnants were given to Lester Gardner, then editor and publisher of Aviation magazine. Gardner had the scraps cut into one-inch squares and mounted on printed cards outlining their history, along with the flight photo reproduced here, and distributed them to his many friends and associates. One of this author's most treasured possessions is one of these fragments of discarded Wright Flyer fabric.

At the time of the Flyer rebuild, the Smithsonian Institution asked Orville to donate it for permanent exhibit in the museum. Orville refused with some justification. He was highly displeased over the Smithsonian's claim that the 1903 Langley Aerodrome, built by its former secretary, Samuel Pierpont Langley, was, quote: "The first man-carrying aeroplane in the history of the world capable of sustained free flight."

Actually, it crashed during both of its catapult launches (a steam-powered scale model had flown successfully). The Smithsonian would not change the words, so in 1927 Orville sent the Flyer to the Science Museum in Kensington, England, on a long-term loan.

After World War II, interested parties prevailed upon a later generation of Smithsonian officials to reword the placard on the Langley in a manner acceptable to Orville, who then allowed the world's first successful airplane to return for permanent display in the most prestigious museum of its homeland.

The Flyer was hung in the Smithsonian on Dec. 17, 1948, the 45th anniversary of the flight. Orville, however, was not there. He had died the previous January.

The photographs

1. The famous photo of the first powered flight, taken Dec. 17, 1903. Despite the claims of a photographer who was given credit for this photo in later years, it was taken by a camera set up on a tripod by the Wrights. The Flyer tripped a wire when it reached the end of the rail and took its own picture.

2. A full-scale replica of the Wright Flyer. It was built for the Institute of Aeronautical Sciences by students of the Northrop Institute to celebrate the 50th anniversary of the first flight. The drooped wings do not indicate sloppy construction. The Wrights rigged their plane that way deliberately. Wingspan is 40 feet 4 inches, length is 19 feet 9 inches, and gross weight is 750 pounds for a wing loading of 1.47 pounds per square foot.

1

2

The flight of the Question Mark

Five-man crew set endurance mark of 150 hours in 1929

1st January 1973

A new aviation craze began the week of Jan. 1-7, 1929, when a five-man crew of the U.S. Army Air Corps kept a Fokker C-2 trimotor transport in the air for a record 150 hours. The aircraft, called the Question Mark, doubled the old record, thanks to a new method of keeping an airplane in the air.

Except for a short period in 1923, when the Army Air Service – it wasn't the Air Corps until 1926 – experimented with methods of refueling an airplane in flight, the time that a plane could stay up was limited by the amount of fuel it could carry on takeoff. Though the Army's 1923 tests proved that in-flight refueling would work, and set a record in the process, the method did not catch on at the time.

The subsequent endurance records were made entirely on single fuel loads until 1928. In that year, two European pilots raised the record to 60 hours 7 minutes by using in-flight refueling, but they did not achieve a significant breakthrough; the record was soon raised to 65 hours 25 minutes by the single-load method.

The Army got interested in in-flight refueling again in 1928 and tried an improved version of the 1923 system on a Keystone bomber. When the decision was made to go for the world's endurance record, it was obvious that a roomy cabin transport would be more suitable for the project than an open-cockpit bomber; hence the Fokker.

The target duration was 100 hours, plus whatever additional time could be attained before the engines or the crew gave out. Because of those unknowns, the plane was named the Question Mark. A question mark was even painted on each side of the fuselage. The locale for the attempt was the Los Angeles area, where continuous good weather could be expected in January.

Two tankers, a pair of Army Douglas C-1 cargo biplanes, were assigned to the project, each with its own crew. Other planes were on hand to observe, take photographs and transmit messages from the ground by chalking them on the side of the fuselage since the Question Mark did not carry a radio.

The Fokker's principle modification was a large hatch in the roof of the cabin for receipt of the hose nozzle and supplies, a receiver hopper and manifold system to transfer the fuel to the airplane's tanks, and revised lubricant-supply systems for the engines. Steel-tube walkways were added to each side of the nose so that the center engine could be serviced in-flight.

With Major Carl Spaatz in command; Captain Ira C. Eaker, Lieutenant Elwood R. Quesada and Lieutenant Harry A. Halverson serving as pilots; and Staff Sergeant Roy Hooe as mechanic, the Question Mark took off from Los Angeles Municipal Airport on New Year's Day.

The flight was routine, and 43 contacts were made with the tankers for fuel, oil and supplies. It ended after the left engine quit due to a clogged grease line. The Question Mark landed at Los Angeles with a record of 150 hours 14 minutes and 15 seconds. The entire crew was awarded the Distinguished Flying Cross.

With the wide publicity given the Question Mark's flight and its dramatic proof of the practicality of in-flight refueling, the boom was on. The endurance record was broken nine times in 1929 alone, and the craze continued into the 1930s.

In-flight refueling, however, did not become a regular part of military operations until 1948, when it was adopted to give global range to Air Force bombers and to extend the range of jet fighters.

The photographs

1. On the way to a world's endurance record, the U.S. Army Fokker C-2 transport Question Mark is refueled by a Douglas C-1. The Question Mark took off from Los Angeles on Jan. 1, 1929, and landed on Jan. 7 — 150 hours 14 minutes and 15 seconds later.

2. This looks like a different C-2A, but it's not. Photo No. 1 was taken on panchromatic film with a yellow filter, which makes yellow print quite light. This view was taken on orthochromatic film, which makes yellow print quite dark. Note the steel-tube work platform under the nose that permits work to be done on the center engine.

3. Since the "Question Mark" had no radio, messages were transmitted to it either with the supplies that were lowered from the tanker or they were painted on the side of another plane, like this Boeing PW-9D fighter.

4. Major Spaatz, commander of the flight, receives the refueling hose from the Douglas C-1 tanker and directs it to the receiving hopper.

5. The crew of the "Question Mark" at the end of their 150-hour flight. Left to right, Major Carl Spaatz, commander; Captain Ira Eaker, chief pilot; lieutenants Harry Halverson and Elwood Quesada, relief pilots; and Staff Sergeant Roy Hooe, mechanic.

1

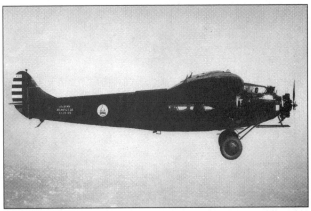

2

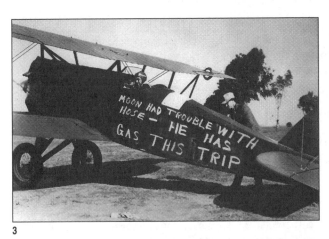

3

4

5

Airplane-size parachutes

Experiments with floating an airplane to earth began in the 1920s

2nd January 1973

Some aeronautical inventions work successfully but do not win acceptance and are so completely forgotten that other people reinvent them many years later.

That seems to be the case with a concept that is about as old as the personal parachute. The basic idea of the parachute was sketched by Leonardo Da Vinci in 1480, but the first recorded demonstration of one did not take place until 1783. From then until World War I, parachutes were primarily exhibition items, used by balloonist-acrobats at county fairs and the like for a grand finale descent from a hot-air balloon.

During the war, the parachute became a valuable life-saving device, mainly for the crews of observation balloons and in a few cases for airplane pilots. The major problem at the time was packing and stowage. The most significant years of practical personal-parachute development came in the early 1920s.

Enlargement of the canopy to handle a complete airplane was undertaken several times in the 1920s. The earliest experiment that I can confirm was the test of an expendable war-surplus Curtiss Jenny in 1927. In addition to testing the concept, the operation was also a publicity gimmick for the World War I air movie "Wings." The test was successful, and the Jenny suffered only a broken landing gear and some lower wing damage.

A short time later the same thing was tried again by the soon-to-be famous racing and stunt pilot Roscoe Turner, who used a later model Thunderbird biplane. The results were the same. The plane sustained some damage, but the Turner smile and waxed mustache came through intact.

Still another attempt was made, but it did not work as well. That one involved two parachutes. One was mounted on each panel of the upper wing of the biplane. Pilot Mickey McKeon slowed the plane down at an altitude of 5,200 feet at Tracy, California, and released the parachutes. Unfortunately, one did not open properly and got tangled in the wing structure. The plane began to spin instead of coming down in a level attitude. McKeon, who was wearing a personal parachute, went over the side. The faster descending plane almost did him in, however. It passed within 50 feet of him on the way down.

Aside from sky divers and other jumpers who have resort to a second parachute when No. 1 failed or who have done deliberate breakaways for show, McKeon is probably the world's first real two-stage parachutist, having made an emergency escape from a parachuting airplane by parachute.

2000 update — Bringing airplanes down by parachute under emergency conditions has been amply demonstrated. It began with ultralights in the 1980s and is now incorporated in Cirrus Design's four-seat SR-20 production aircraft.

The photographs

1. The solider hanging from the crown of this open parachute gives an idea of the size of canopy needed to bring a complete airplane down safely.

2. A 2,000-pound Curtiss Jenny descending in a successful test of an airplane-size parachute.

3. Here's a close-up of the modified Curtiss JN-4D Jenny that is seen descending under the parachute in Photo No. 2. This is obviously a "before" photo. Note the shortened wings, the ailerons that have been added to a lower wing, and the tail skid that has been moved far forward.

1

2

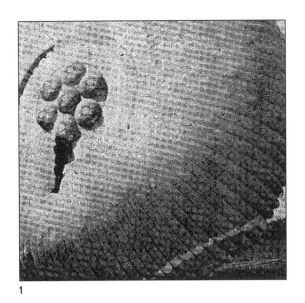

3

Fokker triplanes then and now

Fairly common during World War I, they've made a comeback in the replica movement

1st February 1973

While a triplane is regarded as a freak airplane today, it was not always so. The three-wingers were fairly common in the World War I years and for a while the existing designs outnumbered monoplanes.

The most famous of the triplanes by far was the single-seat Fokker Dr-1 of "Red Baron" fame. It appeared in mid-1917 after the German air force became impressed with the British Sopwith triplane and encouraged German designers to develop triplane fighters of their own. From more than 20 examples submitted for tests, only the Fokker and one other went into production. Fokker built 330 Dr-1s, and Pfalz built 10.

Even by the standards of the day, the prototype Fokker tripe could be considered a freak. The fuselage, landing gear, tail and engine installation were traditional except for the use of welded steel-tube construction instead of wood-and-wire. Fokker pioneered steel-tube construction and had the satisfaction of seeing it adopted as the world standard after the war.

Three wings, of course, were not unusual, but to see three wings without the traditional interplane struts and wires was a real shock. Fokker's designer, Rheinhold Platz, was pushing cantilever construction as a way to improve airplane performance by cleaning up the design. He almost went overboard with the V.4, the prototype triplane.

Each of the one-piece wings used two full-depth wooden box spars, which could carry their share of the load without the need for struts or wires. The upper wing was held in place by center-section struts, but the middle and lower wings attached directly to the upper and lower longerons.

The necessary torsional stiffness of the wing panels was obtained by bridging the two box spars, which were quite close together, with plywood to form a torsion box. The Fokker was a much cleaner airplane than the Sopwith.

The test pilots were pleased with the performance of the V.4 but were not comfortable with no wing struts in sight. They insisted on struts and got them on the V.5 second prototype and the production models.

The first three production models were designated F-1 in a continuation of the German air force's alphabetic designation system, but the rest became Dr-1, an abbreviation for dreidecker, which is German for triplane. Two of the F-1s were specials delivered to the two leading German aces of the time, Werner Voss and Manfred von Richthofen (the Red Baron).

Richthofen flew several Fokker tripes from mid-1917 until his death on April 21, 1918. Most of the Dr-1s were withdrawn from squadron service in June 1918, but a few stayed at the front until the Armistice.

A lot of nostalgia is involved in today's sport flying, as demonstrated by the popularity of antique airplanes and the high percentage of open-cockpit biplanes among the homebuilts. The Fokker triplane was reborn in 1957, several years before the Peanuts comic strip triggered Snoopy and the Red Baron.

Hobie Sorrell of Rochester, Washington, turned out a three-quarters replica that was powered with a 65-horsepower Continental. Almost simultaneously, Harry Provolt of Sunland, California, built a full-scale replica with a 125-horsepower Warner radial engine in place of the original 110-horsepower Oberursel rotary (a copy of the French LeRhone).

1

2

3

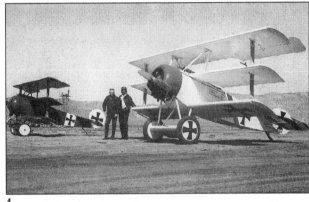

4

The Sorrell replica made a dandy little sport plane that was regarded more as a three-winged homebuilt that resembled a Fokker than as an accurately scaled replica. While the airplane could be scaled down, the pilot could not, so some distortion was necessary for getting him aboard, and also to fit in a flat-four engine.

Provolt had problems. His tripe was heavier than the original, and the so-called 125-horsepower from the modern Warner engine with 500 cubic inches was in no way comparable to the 110 old-fashioned horses delivered by the 922-cubic-inch Oberursel, which swung an 8-1/2-foot diameter prop at 1,225 rpm.

The building of replica Fokker tripes has caught on in a relatively big way. More Fokker replicas have been built than any other, and for good reason. The appeal is enormous. The airplane is famous to begin with and is very distinctive. It is relatively simple structurally and can handle a modern radial engine that does not compromise the authentic look.

Sorrell built another three-quarters replica that was powered with a 125-horsepower Lycoming. Other individuals have since completed a total of six full-scale models in the United States. One carries authenticity to the limit by using a genuine World War I rotary engine. Two others with radial engines were built in Europe for the "Blue Max" movie

and were seen in a later film called "Darling Lili."

Even the Sopwith has been revived in this latter-day triplane boom, with two full-scale examples flying.

The photographs

1. The first Fokker triplane, designated V.4, flew as shown in 1917 without interplane struts. Since only the designer had faith in this arrangement, it was soon modified to the standards of the production model.

2. Production Fokker triplanes reached the front in August 1917, but were temporarily withdrawn to repair their poorly built wings. Although the Fokker had short wings that spanned just 23 feet 7 inches, it was 9 feet 8 inches high.

3. Hobart Sorrell flying his three-quarters-scale Fokker triplane. Note the lengthened nose to accommodate the 65-horsepower Continental engine, which was longer than the original rotary. This plane started the reduced-scale replica movement.

4. The "Flying Circus" flies again. Fokker tripes are the most popular models in the modern replica airplane movement. The difference in size is not noticeable here, but the dark red tripe on the left is the second three-quarters-scale Sorrell-built replica. The white one on the right is a full-scale version built by Walt Redfern.

Old warplanes in the movies

Many World War I classics were destroyed in the name of entertainment

2nd February 1973

We seem to be in a period of high-budget aerial war movies, with the appearance of such epics as "The Blue Max" (World War I), "Tora, Tora Tora" and "The Battle of Britain (World War II). Others have covered both world wars and other actions, but I consider these the most notable.

There was another big boom in aerial war movies long ago. It started with "Wings" in 1927 and ended with the remake of the 1931 "Dawn Patrol" in 1937. True, the high-budget "Men With Wings," which had some WWI action, was made in 1938, but the flying represented only a brief period of a long story of aviation history. The warplanes in that picture received publicity that was out of proportion to their time on camera.

The tragedy of those early air classics was the large-scale destruction of genuine World War I airplanes. Many were crashed for the cameras and even more were blown up on the ground in airdrome strafing scenes.

As horrifying as the thought of destroying a genuine Nieuport or Fokker may be today, remember that there was no "antique" airplane movement in those days. The old wooden airplanes were considered junk, and the studios often had a tough time keeping enough of them in the air at the same time to get their full-squadron flight scenes. While some real WWI planes did fly in those old movies, the rough flying was done by more reliable modern types that were painted or slightly modified to look like the oldies

By contrast, one of the few surviving Thomas-Morse Scouts was "crashed" in the 1950s for the film "Lafayette Escadrille." The scene was realistic enough, but no harm came to the now-valuable plane even though it ended up on its back (it nosed over into a straw-filled pit at the end of the rollout). This same "Tommy" is now on display in the Air Force Museum near Dayton, Ohio.

While most of the warplane destruction was deliberate, others were damaged in frequent accidents. Some were used in the picture, but other necessitated retakes and sometimes a replacement airplane.

One of the best recent examples of capitalizing on an unplanned incident took place during the filming of "Tora, Tora Tora." One of the refurbished B-17s could not get a landing gear down. That meant a one-wheel landing that would put the ship out of commission for quite awhile. The fast-thinking director had the pilot land in front of the cameras, and the spectacular ground loop was used as part of the big Japanese attack scene. Additional scenes leading up to the one-wheel landing were then written and shot using the interior of another B-17.

One incident that was nearly fatal occurred during the big airdrome strafing scene in the 1931 "Dawn Patrol," in which an English pilot was to be shown shooting and bombing German planes on the ground. The bomb explosions were simulated by powder charges buried under the lined-up airplanes, and the charges were exploded electrically from a control point as the "Englishman" flew low along the line on his bombing run.

It didn't quite work out that way. Whoever was pushing the buttons got ahead of the attacking airplane and blew up one of the supposedly bombed Germans before the Englishman got past it. That goof put a column of dirt and airplane parts right in front of the startled pilot, who could only plow on through the debris and then nurse his damaged plane to a safe landing.

The pilot, Earl Robinson, was flying a 1929 Travel Air D-4000 that was painted to look like a French Nieuport 28. Four real Nieuports appeared in the film in British markings; the fact that the British did not use that model did not bother anyone at the time. The presence of real World War I planes was much more important than the accuracy of their markings.

The photographs

1. This famous German airdrome scene is from the 1931 "Dawn Patrol." Antique buffs will be interested in the World War I types shown here. In the background, from the left, are a Standard J-1, the fuselage of a Curtiss JN-4D and two rare Boeing Model C's. Along the flight line are three modified Curtiss JN-4Ds and one Standard J. All these aircraft were U.S. WWI trainers painted in the prevailing concept of what a German "Circus" looked like. The attacking "English" airplane is a 1929 Travel Air D-4000.

2. In this example of poor timing, the middle JN-4D was blown up just before the Travel Air passed over it during the filming. The pilot managed to get down safely.

3. Howard Hughes assembled these 37 airplanes at Oakland Airport for the big battle scene of his 1929 epic, "Hell's Angels." In the front row a 1924 Sikorsky is flanked by two WWI SE-5s. The second row has four authentic German Fokker D.VIIs and the de Havilland 4 camera plane. The third line has a D.VII at the left, while the rest are "German" Travel Airs of 1926-29 vintage. The rear rows are a mix of Travel Airs, Waco 10s, Eaglerocks and American Eagles.

4. Errol Flynn in the cockpit of a clipped-wing French Nieuport 28 in the 1938 remake of the 1931 "Dawn Patrol." David Niven is in the next Nieuport. The next two are clipped-wing Nieuports with I-struts, and the final three are U.S. Thomas-Morse S-4Cs. This was the last time that this many genuine 1918-vintage planes were brought together for a single movie scene.

1

2

3

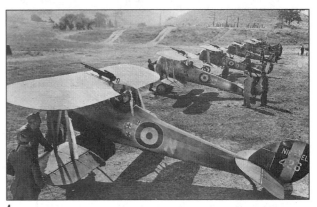

4

The Bücker Jungmann

It was designed in Germany as a low-powered primary and aerobatic trainer

1st March 1973

The campaign to help restore Professor Dave Rahm's Bücker Bu-131 Jungmann (German for "young man" or "freshman") raises the natural question, What is a Jungmann? The 15 examples in the United States are pretty well known as wonderful two-place aerobatic airplanes that are seen most often by the public while doing their special thing at air shows. But what of their background? What makes them so great?

The Bu-131 was designed late in 1933 by Carl Bücker as a low-powered primary and aerobatic trainer for the government-subsidized German flying clubs and the new German air force that was just coming into the open. With no significant private flying in Germany, the government was the principal customer. Bücker had built approximately 1,000 Bu-131s by time World War II got underway. In addition to export models, the Bestmann was built under license in Czechoslovakia, Japan, Switzerland, Spain and Hungary.

The original powerplant was an 80-horsepower inverted air-cooled Hirth HM-60R. The later Bu-131B used the 105-horsepower Hirth HM-504. The airframe was carefully designed to have the lightest possible structure compatible with the load requirements. The common economic convenience of using a lot of the same-sized tubing was discarded. That meant more work and higher prices, but resulted in a better airplane. The fuselage and tail were welded steel tubing; the wings were fabric-covered wood frame.

The attention to design detail carried over into the controls, and the Bu-131 has the best control harmonization of any plane in its class. The ailerons and elevator are aerodynamically and statically balanced, and there are ailerons on all four wing panels, which, incidentally, are interchangeable top to bottom. The 11-degree sweepback of the wings, resulting from the need to align the center of lift with the center of gravity after the center section was put ahead of the front cockpit to simplify the crew access problem, adds considerably to the Bu-131's snap-roll capability. The relatively short wingspan, 24 feet 3 inches compared to 32 feet 2 inches for the Stearman, helps the roll rate too.

Bücker also shortened the wings and fuselage of the Bu-131 to produce the even more aerobatic Bu-133 Jungmeister, but that is another story.

Though most of the Bu-131s in Germany were scrapped after the war, many in other countries survived and actually increased in numbers due to limited production into the 1960s.

Dave Rahm's hard-luck Jungmann was built in Czechoslovakia in 1963, according to its logbook. It was imported in 1964 by airplane pilot and former national speedboat champion Mira Slovak, who named it "The Poor Refugee" in recognition of his famous escape from the Soviet-bloc country. In 1965, Slovak replaced the Czech Walter Minor engine with a special 205-horsepower Lycoming because the original 105-horsepower model "did not have the muscles" for all-out air-show work at places like Reno.

In 1967, Slovak sold "Poor Refugee" to author-pilot Ernest K. Gann, who named it "Island in the Sky" after one of his books. In 1970 Gann sold it to Rahm, an up-and-coming acro-pilot whose title of "Flying Professor" is not just a piece of air-show ballyhoo. He is a professor of geology at Western Washington State College in Bellingham, Washington.

Rahm's problems with the white-and-black beauty were due to its years of the roughest kind of air-show work. While en route to the National Aerobatic Championships in 1971, a landing-gear fitting let go during a routine landing roll. The damage was not great, but a teardown inspection revealed other defects that resulted in a major rebuild and a new black-and-gold color scheme while retaining Slovak's gilded lion on the tail.

In 1972 the engine started throwing parts while returning from an air show; the absence of suitable landing area resulted in the need for major rebuild No. 2.

The photographs

1. The prototype Bücker Bu-131 Jungmann, photographed before its first flight on April 27, 1934. Note the high thrust line of the 80-horsepower Hirth engine.

2. Mira Slovak in his Czech-built Bu-131B in 1966, showing the revised nose contours that were a result of going with a 205-horsepower Lycoming engine.

3. After it was rebuilt in 1971 and '72, Dave Rahm's Bücker appeared in a black-and-gold color scheme but retained the heraldic rampant lion insignia that Mira Slovak had applied to the tail.

4. In 1935 Bücker introduced the Bu-133 Jungmeister, a single-seater with shortened Bu-131 wings and fuselage. The original had a 140- to 160-horsepower Hirth engine, but the production Bu-133B and C models (C shown) had a 160-horsepower seven-cylinder Siemens SH-14 radial engine under a "bump" cowling. Both Bücker models are still popular today as aerobats and antiques, though most use latter-day engines.

1

2

3

4

The Canuck

Canadian-built version of the JN-4 was created under odd circumstances

1st April 1973

We recently received a letter concerning the identity of an airplane in an old photo. The aircraft in question is a Canadian-built Curtiss JN-4. Powered with the famous 90-horsepower Curtiss OX-5 engine, it was widely used by the Canadian and U.S. Army air services as a primary trainer in World War I. It was called the Canuck to distinguish it from its American-built counterparts, the famous Jennies.

Many planes of both names were sold surplus after the war and, along with the similar Standard J, were the mainstays of the famous barnstorming fleet of the early 1920s. The Jenny was the most numerous and the best remembered; in fact, that period is often referred to as the Jenny Era. There is a tendency today to merge the identities of the Canucks and the Standards with the Jenny, though a lot of old-timers will maintain that both the Canuck and the Standard were better airplanes than the most common Jenny variant, the JN-4D.

The Canuck was created under rather odd circumstances. The famous Curtiss Aeroplane Company of Buffalo, New York, established a plant near Toronto in 1915 and built a small quantity of its established JN-3 models for the Royal Air Force. In 1916, with the plant nearly idle, the Canadian government took it over, along with some of the personnel, and renamed it Canadian Aeroplanes, Ltd. With an increased demand for trainers, an improved version of the JN-3 was designed and put into production. Since it was a direct development of the JN-3, it was logical to call the new model the JN-4. The Canadians, however, did not know that Curtiss was developing its own JN-4 at the same time.

The two JN-4 designs proved to be considerably different. With distinction between the two necessary, the Canuck label was bestowed by its users. It was never an official name, however. In U.S. Army paperwork, the Canadian-built model was the JN-4 (Can). It was sometimes shortened to JN-4C, but that was not an official designation. There was only two actual JN-4C airplanes, and those were American-built models using a different airfoil section for test purposes. Later, Canadian Aeroplanes built a number of American-designed JN-4As under license, but they were delivered as JN-4As; only the Canadian JN-4 models were called Canucks.

Distinguishing the Canuck from the American JN series is easy if you know what to look for. While it most resembled the basic American JN-4, with its low rounded rudder, the Canuck had a rudder that lined up with the bottom of the fuselage instead of projecting below it. Also, the stick-controlled Canuck had strut-connected ailerons on both wings while the American version had them only on the upper wings and used the wheel or "deperdussin" control system.

The differences became greater when Curtiss came out with the JN-4A. That airplane had wire-connected ailerons on both wings, but used entirely new tail surfaces and had six degrees of down-thrust for the engine. The JN-4B was similar but had upper-wing ailerons only and no down-thrust. The later JN-4D and its 150-horsepower Hisso-powered equivalent, the JN-4H (H for Hispano-Suiza), had upper wing ailerons only, switched to stick control, and added noticeable cutouts to the inboard ends of all wing panels. The D model re-adopted down-thrust and the final JN-6H had strut-connected ailerons on both wings.

The new licensing requirements of 1927 soon forced most of the Jennies and Canucks out of U.S. skies, and the Army scrapped its last Hisso Jennies in September of that year. A few struggled on for a few years in virtual bootleg operations. The few JNs that survive are either non-flying museum exhibits or are the treasured restorations of a few dedicated antiquers who fly them on experimental-exhibition licenses. Only one of the few that are flyable or nearing that condition is a Canuck.

The photographs

1. The first American JN-4, which the Canadians did not know about when they developed their own JN-4. Note the considerably different tail shape and the use of ailerons on the upper wing only.

2. The Canadian JN-4, or Canuck, developed from the Curtiss JN-3 of 1915. Note the rounded tail and the strut connecting the ailerons (a second aileron strut is hidden behind the right rear interplane strut). This particular Canuck is reported to be the first Canadian airplane to operate on skis.

3. This flight view of a U.S. Army Canuck emphasizes the pointed lower wingtips and differently shaped tail surfaces. Standard location of U.S. insignia on Army planes in 1918-19 was tangent to the forward inner corners of the ailerons.

4. This Curtiss JN-4D Jenny was beautifully restored by a Northwest Airlines pilot and, not counting replicas, was one of just four flyable JNs in the early '70s. The tail shape was standard for the JN-4A and subsequent models.

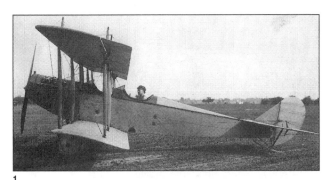

1

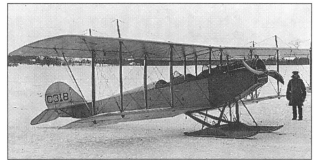

2

3

4

Two-letter registration prefixes

Sorting out the confusion with the old licensed and unlicensed planes

1st May 1973

A letter to the editor in the 1st April 1973 issue of the *Flyer* shows there is some concern about the use of the old prefix letters in connection with airplane registration numbers. Here's some history, plus a discussion of the situation today.

When the United States adopted licensing requirements in January 1927, the planes were identified by a sequential number. For planes that were licensed, the number was preceded by the letter N, which had been assigned to the United States by the International Convention in 1919 as its identifying letter (France was F, Great Britain was G, etc.).

A parallel list was set up for unlicensed planes that were merely identified by the number. That practice led to confusion, so the two lists were soon combined.

Meanwhile, the identification of the licensed types changed a bit depending on the status of the plane. Fully licensed commercial types that were eligible to fly outside of the country had NC ahead of their numbers, which were painted on the upper right wing, the lower left and on each side of the rudder. If the plane was to operate only inside the country, only the C was used. We then got the letters X and R to identify experimental and restricted licenses, again with the N prefix for international flights. Some state and federally owned civil models got NS licenses, meaning state-owned. By the early 1930s the N was applied to all the C licenses and only some of the X's and R's. The new G (for glider) and unidentified models operated without the N.

Late in 1928, when the registration numbers passed five digits, the actual numbers were shortened by adding a suffix letter to the end of the registration. They went to a maximum of three digits, but the suffixes were not adopted alphabetically. The first used was E, then H and M, plus others. After World War II, the number of digits to be used with suffix letters was expanded to four, and since the 1950s it has been possible to use two suffix letters.

The use of two prefix letters or the single-category letter without the N prevailed until World War II, when the identified G and NS categories vanished. There was an entirely different N situation in Oregon in the late 1930s, but that's a different story.

Everything was two-letter for a while after the war, with a new limited category, NL, added in 1946 to take care of certain war-surplus types that had useful capabilities but could not meet full licensing requirements.

A change came in 1948. The second prefix letter was dropped and only the N remained. It became mandatory for all aircraft. However, recognizing the possible hardship in the cost of repainting, the FAA allowed the second letter to be retained by all painted aircraft until the ship was repainted or recovered. Some owners stretched that to the absolute limit.

Other changes followed. With the adoption of the ADIZ zones during the Korean War, the use of foot-high numbers on the sides of the fuselage became optional in place of the old wing and tail numbers. That practice became mandatory in 1966.

The new marking requirements did not sit well with the very active antique group, whose members grumbled at the breach of authenticity involved in having to put 1966-style fuselage numbers on a restored 1926 antique or having foot-high numbers spoil the military colors of a restored warbird.

The FAA recognized the legitimacy of those gripes and allowed pre-1933 antiques to go back to the old-style wing and tail markings, NC letters and all. The agency subsequently allowed the same for later models of the same configuration and now seem to regard an age of 30 years as eligibility for old-style markings.

Unfortunately, the regulation as written is open to misunderstanding and the opinions of individual inspectors. Some allow any J-3, even post-WWII versions, to use the old NC on wings and tail while others insist on foot-high N's and numbers on the fuselages of the 1945 and later models.

A final break for the owners of the authentically marked military antiques was the authorization to apply the required civil registration numbers in figures only two inches high on both sides of the vertical tail or rear fuselage. Actually, this permission now extends to all recognized antiques; a few that could carry NC on wings and tail now use only the two-inch style. Maybe the owners are less concerned with authentic appearances than they are with the work involved.

In a few cases, you can fly legally with no numbers at all if the plane (usually an authentically marked military antique or replica) takes off, flies under continuous observation, and then lands back at the same field, as at an air show. One owner of a World War I Fokker replica did that as long as his ship was trailered to the shows. When he began flying it X-C, he had to add the numbers.

The photographs

1. This 1928 Kreider-Reisner Challenger C-1 (later Fairchild KR-31) has a full commercial license, but cannot fly outside the United States, as indicated by the absence of the letter N from its registration C7246.

2. A distinctly nonstandard application. This Travel Air Model 2000 left the factory with registration C6267. When it was upgraded to NC status, it was easier to paint the N above the existing numbers than to do them over in a smaller size that would get them on one line.

3. Larry Curry's replica Nieuport 17 has a neat way of combining the required N number with authentic World War I markings. He enlarged the N to the N-for-Nieuport as used by the French and made his registration number, 1920, look like the serial number as the French applied it.

4. An interesting marking error. The painter was told to add the letter C above the registration number on the rudder of this 1927 Boeing 40A and ahead of the number on the wings. He misunderstood and painted 3 instead of C. That snafu may have been the reason for those little blue VODG memo pads at Boeing: Verbal Orders Don't Go.

1

2

3   4

The rotary engine

The true ones, of course, actually rotate with the propeller

2nd May 1973

One of aviation's more interesting powerplants is the air-cooled rotary engine. The rotary was introduced in 1908 and saw wide use until the end of World War I. The principal models in the United States were the French Le Rhone and Gnome. The full details would fill these pages several times over, so the following is greatly simplified information.

As the name implies, the whole engine rotates. The crankshaft, which is anchored to the airframe, does not rotate and does not attach to the propeller; the prop hub attaches directly to the front of the crankcase of the radial-type engine. With the whole engine turning, the gas and oil cannot be supplied through conventional lines; the two come into the crankcase together through a common passage in the hollow crankshaft.

Castor oil is used because it is a vegetable oil that is not diluted by the gasoline. Considerably more of the stinky stuff than is actually needed is pumped through the engine, and the surplus is thrown out through the exhaust valve in each cylinder (not individual exhaust stacks or a collector manifold).

Most of the old rotary-powered airplanes used what look like modern NACA cowlings around the engines – which weren't for streamlining but to keep the castor from being sprayed all over the airplane. Unfortunately, even the best cowlings let a lot of oil escape, and the insoluble stuff was very hard to clean off.

Because of the popularity of the present-day Mazda automobile, which features the Wankel "rotary" engine, there is some confusion among many people as to just what a rotary, as applied to airplanes at least, really is. The root of the trouble lies in the misuse of the word "rotary" in connection with the Wankel. It is a rotary piston, not a true rotary, engine. Take a look at one in a car. You can hardly tell it from a regular reciprocating-piston engine.

A couple of generations of aviation-oriented people accustomed to seeing fixed air-cooled radial engines in airplanes since the middle 1920s sometimes have a hard time realizing that the very similar-looking rotary actually turned around with the propeller.

This lack of understanding has shown up several times in recent years in aviation art. The artists quite logically used photographs of rotary-engine airplanes for reference. However, flight photos were rare in the heyday of the rotary, so the references were photos taken on the ground with the engines shut off. Not knowing the essentials of rotaries, the artists who created action scenes showed the propellers spinning merrily away while the cylinders stool still, as they did on the familiar fixed radials.

Rotaries went out of production at the end of World War I when the more reliable air-cooled radial came in. However, hundreds served private owners of war-surplus planes into the early 1930s. No rotary-powered designs ever qualified for a U.S. approved type certificate, and except for short sightseeing hops, none were used in commercial operations.

During the 1930s, the use of rotaries was limited almost exclusively to the few antiques that flew for the movies. A surprising number of these unique engines survived even the World War II scrap-metal drives and have been put into some restored antiques and a few newly built replicas that are used primarily for exhibition.

The considerable operational limitations imposed by the rotary preclude it from being used for normal recreational or commercial flying. None throttle down well enough for normal taxiing or holding for clearance at the side of the runway; reduction of power for landing is achieved by switching the engine off and on intermittently on some models or by shorting out several spark plugs through a selector switch on others.

Today, the rotary-powered planes need the field to themselves when taking off or landing, so they operate from small private fields with light traffic and perform for the public only during the "closed field" periods at air shows. Few fly cross-country to these shows; most are brought in on trailers.

The photographs

1. When it isn't running, a rotary engine looks like the familiar static or fixed radial type. The finned cylinders of this 80-horsepower French Le Rhone of World War I vintage are machined from solid steel bars.

2. With the engine running, the cylinders of the rotary seem to disappear along with the propeller. The airplane is a replica of a 1915 German Fokker E-III built in 1961.

3. Starting a rotary engine is a three-man job. The pilot is in the cockpit, another person turns the propeller slowly, and a third presses open the exhaust valve of each cylinder with his thumb and applies raw gasoline from a squirt can. The engine is then ready for "Contact" and spinning the propeller.

1

2

3

The Army's first STOL

Patterned after the German Storch, the O-49/L-1 could take off in 225 feet and land in 75

1st June 1973

Back in 1937, the Germans demonstrated a remarkable new airplane at the U.S. National Air Races. It was a low-speed military observation plane that marked a complete break from the traditional big two-seaters that had been used for that role since World War I.

The airplane was the Fieseler Fi-156 Storch. It was relatively big for a two-seat monoplane, with a wingspan of 46 feet 9 inches. The span, however, paid off in light wing loading, and such auxiliary lift devices as full-span leading edge slots, big flaps and drooped ailerons gave it an amazingly short takeoff capability with only 240 horsepower. (Today we call such airplanes STOLs, for short takeoff and landing). The Storch could take off in 225 feet, and touch down and stop in 75.

The U.S. Army was duly impressed and set up specifications for a similar U.S. product. Three manufacturers submitted prototypes, but only one, the Stinson Model 74 (which the Army designated O-49) received production orders. One hundred were ordered in 1940, and another 182 O-49As were ordered in 1941.

The O-49 followed the general concept of the Storch, with a 50-foot-11-inch wing, slots, flaps and long-stroke landing gear, and a 295-horsepower Lycoming R-680-9 radial engine. Another feature adopted from the Storch was the outward slope of the cabin windows to improve the field of downward visibility. It had a top speed of 122 mph and could land at less than 30. Takeoff distance was about the same as the Storch. Not bad for a gross weight of 3,400 pounds.

With simple steel-tube fuselage and tail construction plus a wooden wing, the first O-49s went into Army service late in 1941. Four were quickly converted to O-49Bs by fitting them with litter accommodations for use as ambulance planes.

A designation change came along early in 1942. All the O-types then in production were redesignated as liaison planes, so the O-49s became L-1s with corresponding series letters, such as O-49A to L-1A.

A total of 104 L-1As were intended for lend-lease to the Royal Air Force under the designation of Vigilant I and were given RAF camouflage and markings at the factory. However, the Army took over most of them and flew them as L-1As with the British coloring.

The Army did not make much combat-theater use of the O-49s/L-1s. A few got overseas, but the L-mission there was pretty well monopolized by the Army version of the Piper J-3 Cub that was originally designated O-59 but became the L-4, and the Stinson L-5, which was just about halfway between an L-1 and L-4.

Conversion of the L-1As to the ambulance role resulted in redesignation to L-1C, and four L-1s converted to glider tugs became L-1Ds.

The addition of Edo amphibious floats to seven L-1s resulted in L-1Es while five L-1As similarly fitted became L-1Fs. Despite those new designations, a few L-1As operated as such on the amphibious floats.

Only a couple of these unique warbirds survive today. Last we heard, one was capitalizing on its unique low-speed performance by serving as a Hollywood camera plane. Its only competition in that work would be a helicopter.

The photographs

1. The German Fieseler Fi-156 Storch, introduced in 1937 and widely used throughout World War II, was the inspiration for the U.S. Army's Stinson O-49/L-1.

2. O-49Bs were stock O-49s converted to ambulance planes by installing litter facilities in the observer's station. This one was photographed on Dec. 6, 1941.

3. An L-1A in winter conditions in Alaska. Note the skis and the cold-weather shutter for the engine. Though the photo was taken in February 1943, the plane still has the old Army rudder stripes that were discontinued in May 1942.

4. Some O-49/L-1 models did get overseas. This L-1A on amphibious floats was photographed in Burma in 1943.

3

2

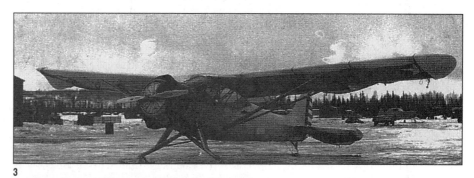

1

4

Loening's flying shoehorns

Inverted Liberty's high thrust line allowed float to be moved closer to the fuselage

2nd June 1973

Back in 1923, aeronautical engineer Grover C. Loening came up with a design idea for a new observation plane that he hoped to sell to the U.S. Army. It would take some doing, however, during a time of very limited procurement of new aircraft.

The Army had plenty of World War I surplus types on hand, particularly the de Havilland 4 observation plane, and there was no need to buy later versions of essentially the same airplane with the same 400-horsepower Liberty engine, which was the only suitable powerplant available.

Realizing that any Liberty-powered two-seater would show only a small performance gain over the DH-4, Loening went for a big improvement in utility. The Army engineering shops at McCook Field in Dayton, Ohio, had just come out with an inverted model of the famous Liberty. Loening capitalized on the new engine's high thrust line to design what was in effect a standard two-seat single-float seaplane with the float moved closer to the fuselage.

Instead of using the traditional struts between fuselage and float, he filled in the area with an extension of the fuselage structure to create a one-piece flying boat hull with the bow projecting ahead of the propeller. Then, by adding retractable wheels and a tail skid, he made the new boat amphibious.

At that point, Loening used some applied psychology. Knowing the distrust with which pilots and conservative military procurement officials regarded any departure from traditional forms (and the new amphibian hull was certainly unconventional), he decided to make the wings as conservative as possible. In fact, the wings were so similar to those of the DH-4 that they were interchangeable.

The trick worked. The pilots, seated in familiar open cockpits and looking out at familiar wings, felt right at home; the freakish bottom of the hull was out of sight, where it didn't bother them.

Since the Loening did show a performance gain over the DH-4 and had the advantage of being amphibious as well,

the Army gave Loening the first postwar order for new observation planes. The original Army designation was COA-1 (for Corps observation amphibian), later shortened to OA-1 and OA-2. Between 1924 and 1929, the Army bought 53, a sizable business for the time.

The Navy followed with orders of its own and actually took over some Army COA-1s before its own order could be completed. The aircraft were designated OLs in the Navy system (O for observation, L for Loening). Models with inverted Liberty and Packard engines were OL-1s through OL-7s; a switch to the air-cooled Pratt & Whitney Wasp radial engine in 1928 resulted in the OL-8 and OL-9 for a total of 108 Navy amphibs between 1925 and 1929.

Civil versions of the OL-8s became famous on short-haul airlines like the San Francisco-Oakland Air Ferries. Western Air Express used one between Wilmington and Catalina in the early 1930s.

When his firm was merged with Keystone to become Keystone-Loening in 1928, Loening left before the new organization was taken over by Curtiss-Wright in 1929. The basic "Shoehorn" amphibian, meanwhile, served the Navy through the end of World War II in the form of the Grumman JF and J2F Duck. The Duck was developed by LeRoy Grumman, who had been Loening's factory manager. Grumman left when Loening did and formed a new company of his own.

The photographs

1. An early Army Loening combination, the OA-1A of 1926. Note how the high thrust line of the inverted Liberty engine allows the "float" to be placed close to the "fuselage" to create the unique Loening hull design.

2. When a change to radial engines was made in 1928, the thrust line couldn't be lowered, so the forward visibility had to suffer. This is Admiral Moffett's OL-8 flying flagship. At the low airspeeds of the day, it was possible to fly real flags.

1

2

The origin of the word 'blimp'

The name is the result of a thump of the finger

1st July 1973

Blimp" is certainly one of the most appropriate names ever used for an object. In this case, the word and the object are very much alike without intending to be. The word sounds like the object looks: kind of silly, pompous and clumsy. Those who view anything that flies as beautiful may dispute that. For a comeback, one can ask if an airship really "flies."

"Blimp," which has been in the aeronautical vocabulary since the middle of World War I, was invented quite by accident. Only in recent years, however, have we accurately learned where it originated.

The previously accepted story was that the word developed out of the type and model designation of the airship. Back in the days of World War I there were two principal classes of airships: the big rigids, like the German Zeppelins; and the nonrigids, whose shape was maintained by the pressure of the gas inside their envelopes.

Somewhere along the line, a latter-day historian got the idea that the nonrigids were also called "limp" as the opposite of "rigid." Further, he or someone else got the idea that the British nonrigids of the era were designated by letters, as Model A, Model B, etc. It is from the double error of "Model B" and "limp" that the word "blimp" supposedly emerged.

Although that story was later proven to be incorrect by an article in the Bulletin of the Wingfoot Lighter Than Air Society and later in the Journal of the American Aviation Historical Society, the "B-limp" error still pops up.

For the benefit of those who have not seen the articles, here is where the word really came from:

On Dec. 15, 1915, Lieutenant A.D. Cunningham of the Royal Naval Air Service was inspecting the British nonrigid airship SS-12, No. 12 in the Sea Scout series. During the course of his inspection, Cunningham happened to snap his finger against the side of the taut envelope. The resulting sound, something like "blimp," was distinctive enough to draw his attention and repeated flicks of the finger. The sound was commented on to companions and repeated later in the mess hall. As spoken, the word "blimp" caught on and the station personnel soon found themselves referring to their nonrigid airships by that word, which to them seemed so well-suited.

The word spread and was solidly entrenched in the nomenclature of the service within a few months. Used only as a noun to identify nonrigid airships until World War II, it was then applied as a somewhat derisive term for a rather pompous, overblown and largely ineffectual military or public official, particularly in England, where the title Colonel Blimp was commonly used.

Although that use of the word has largely died out, "blimp" is still the generic term for nonrigid airships in practically all languages. It is even used by historians when referring to nonrigids that were in service years before the word was invented by chance in that English airship dock.

The photographs

1. An early British Sea Scout (SS) airship. This type helped coin the word "blimp" in December 1915. The airship car in this case is the fuselage of a B.E.2 airplane. Ram air from the propeller goes up the chute to an air ballonet that helps maintain gas pressure to keep the envelope taut.

2. The first SST was not a SuperSonic Transport. It was the British Sea Scout Twin of 1917. The T indicated that it was an SS type with twin engines. The cylinders suspended from the sides of the envelope are gasoline tanks. The U.S. Army got this one from the U.S. Navy, which got it from the British. Its original British markings were retained.

1

2

Corsair confusion

The name has been applied to a variety of warbirds

2nd July 1973

Many who are still active in aviation will remember the old Vought Corsair biplane. As the O2U, O3U and SU, the evolutionary model served the U.S. Navy from 1927 until the beginning of World War II. Many more people will remember the famous bent-wing bird, the Vought F4U fighter of WWII. It too was called the Corsair, but it did not conflict with the older biplane over use of the name since the biplane was effectively out of the military inventory by the time the F4U was operational.

Incidentally, the F4U was unique among propeller-driven WWII fighters in that it remained in production after the war. The last one was delivered in 1952 and the type remained in squadron service through 1955.

The name, already carried by two different designs by the same manufacturer, did not die out. In 1964 Vought submitted a new jet-powered attack model, the A-7, to the Navy. When ordered into production, it was given the name Corsair II, and the confusion began. The historians, remembering both the biplane and the bent-wing, maintained that the new A-7 should be called the Corsair III. The Navy stuck to II, and there's a reason for that.

Although the biplane version was widely known as the Corsair, the name was unofficially applied by the manufacturer and used in its advertising. The services did not use names for airplanes then. Names were not officially adopted for U.S. military aircraft until about the time the United States got involved in World War II. At that time, they were used as a convenient public reference to specific models without revealing their actual developmental status. The Corsair name covered all Vought F4Us, from the XF4U-1 prototype through

the final F4U-7 and the AU-1 attack variant. The duplicates built by Goodyear as the FG and by Brewster as the F3A were also called Corsairs. That practice worked fairly well with the public but not at all with the service personnel, to whom the difference between an F4U-1 and an F4U-4 were quite important.

Since the jet-powered Corsair was only the second Navy model to use the name officially, it had to be Corsair II instead of the III that many still feel it should be.

Then there was another confusing situation involving Corsairs from I through IV. The British had used names rather than numbers for their military airplanes since the end of World War I. When they acquired American aircraft for World War II, they applied names of their own, sometimes different than those officially applied by the U.S. services or manufacturers. For the bent-wing Corsair, however, they used the same name. Designations for the various American Corsairs that the British used were Corsair I (F4U-1), Corsair II (F4U-1A), Corsair III (F3A-1D) and Corsair IV (FG-1D).

The photographs

1. The Vought O2U biplane, widely known as the Corsair from 1927 until World War II, was never officially called that by the U.S. Navy.

2. The Navy's first official Corsair was the F4U fighter of WWII. The British used names instead of numbers for their service planes, and called their versions of the F4U Corsair I through IV.

3. The Navy gave the official name "Corsair II" to the Vought A-7 that was introduced in 1964. This is a two-seat UA-7H.

1

2

3

The adventures of 4N

1929 Waco has gone through a long series of owners, engines, wings and registrations

1st August 1973

Back in September 1929, the Waco Aircraft Company of Troy, Ohio, built a variation of its standard Taperwing model and powered it with the new 225-horsepower Packard Diesel radial engine. The plane got Registration No. X4N (X for experimental) and was designated the Waco Special.

It was sold almost immediately to the Packard Motor Car Company, builder of the engine. A Packard pilot cracked it up in 1930 while participating in the Ford Reliability Tour. Quickly repaired, the X4N was refitted with a set of "straight" Waco wings and qualified for a standard license as the Model HSO (H for the Packard engine, S for straight wings and O for the fuselage style in Waco's designating system). Packard operated the HSO, registered as NC4N, until 1934. A new owner then replaced the diesel engine with a 220-horsepower Wright J-5 Whirlwind, an old model that had been out of production since 1929. That change made NC4N identical to the Waco ASO (A for the J-5 engine), and it was redesignated as such.

NC4N had eight more owners and four more J-5 engines before it was sold to Central Aircraft in Yakima, Washington, in April 1945. Central converted it to a duster on a restricted license, and it became NR4N. The old J-5 was replaced with a 220-horsepower war-surplus Continental W-670 in January 1947, and the plane was redesignated as a Waco ASO Special. Since it had the same engine as the late-1930s Waco UPF-7, it would be logical to call it a Waco USO, but Waco had not used that engine in the old O-models, so the USO designation never existed.

In 1948 Central sold the Waco (now N4N because the second letter had been deleted from the U.S. registrations) to a crop duster in Chelan, Washington. The crop duster, who used the aircraft until 1963, was killed in a helicopter accident. Some time later his estate sold N4N to Richland Flying Service. In 1966 Richland reconverted N4N to a stock three-seater and got it back on standard license. Before selling the Waco in 1968, Richland switched its registration number with a Cessna 206 that it owned, so the old biplane went to its new owner as N4925F. It was then sold to two partners and was later resold to its current owner, a man in Vancouver, Washington.

The N4N number, meanwhile, was transferred to a homebuilt early in 1970. That aircraft was sold in 1972 but crashed on its transcontinental delivery flight, killing the new owner. The title to the wrecked airplane, and its older and shorter registration number, is apparently still held by the estate of its late owner. As of June 15, 1973, the number had not been canceled and returned to the FAA's list of available numbers.

The current owner has hopes, therefore, of being able to get the number and put it back on the old Waco that carried it for nearly 40 years.

The photographs

1. Built in 1929, this Waco Special had tapered wings and a Packard diesel engine. It carried the registration X4N to indicate its Experimental status.

2. A change to straight wings late in 1930 resulted in a designation change to Waco Model HSO and a standard license. A later change to the 220-horsepower Wright J-5 Whirlwind engine as shown in this late-1930s photo made NC4N a Waco ASO.

3. A change to 220-horsepower Continental engine in 1947 made N4N a Waco ASO Special. N4925F's change of registration in 1966, combined with all the other changes, makes it hard to believe that this is the same airplane as pictured in Photo 1.

4. To update the 1973 column in 2000, Willard Detour has been unable to get the old N4N number, but was able to come close with N4W, which he acquired from an airplane that was retired to a museum. It is shown in very small figures under the tail in this 1994 photo.

1

2

3

4

Airplanes that bite

'Shark mouth' has been around since World War I

2nd August 1973

From time to time throughout military aviation history, a number of entirely unofficial special markings have been applied. One of the most common, used by most of the world's major air forces at some time or another, is the "shark mouth" or some variation that put a face and very conspicuous teeth on the front of the airplane.

Isolated examples of this theme were seen on both sides early in World War I and then began to appear in almost full-squadron use on the German side late in 1916. Its use in the peacetime 1920s and 1930s was usually limited to special air-show appearances or private use.

Shortly before World War II, the Germans again began applying teeth as a squadron marking. British units that encountered such decorated Luftwaffe units in the Mediterranean Theatre soon adopted the pattern as their own and applied it to the Curtiss Tomahawk (the British name for the P-40) then operating in the African desert. The nose of the early P-40 was particularly well-suited to the application of a big painted mouth, and the RAF's African Tomahawks had the largest, most colorful and best standardized mouths to date.

It was publicly given to some of these 1941 British squadrons by The Illustrated London News, which brought the markings to the attention of the American Volunteer Group (AFG) then being formed to aid China. Although the AVG came to be known as the Flying Tigers, that was no deterrent to adding shark's teeth to their P-40s, which were actually British Tomahawk IIs released to China.

Thanks to good old American press agentry, the Flying Tigers became by far the best-known users of the shark-mouth motif – to the point, in fact, where many believed it originated with that outfit. It has become so thoroughly identified with the Tigers and their P-40s that it was adopted by many P-40 training units in the United States and has since became almost a mandatory feature for the handful of restored P-40s flying today as well as for countless scale models. When the Flying Tiger Line was formed after the war, its first airplanes carried the famous mouth. On a DC-3, however, the teeth merely looked silly instead of ferocious.

This group flew as the AVG for only the first half of 1942, but the famous fangs were carried over when it became part of the 14th U.S. Air Force and remained in use in China to the end of the war. On some AVG/ 14th AF planes the mouths were modified from shark to saber-tooth tiger by adding oversize incisors.

The British, Germans and Americans continued to use teeth on a variety of military aircraft throughout the war. Even the Russians and the Free French got into the act. There were some interesting variations, as applications of faces and teeth to drop tanks and even d/f antenna fairings. Some airplanes like the twin-fuselage Lockheed P-38 had a face on each fuselage and at least one British Avro Lancaster bomber had faces on all four engine nacelles.

Shark mouths have remained in almost constant military use since World War II and on through the Korean and Vietnam wars. In addition, they are on a number of private and commercial planes, including crop dusters and those restored P-40s. It is a safe bet that such a natural marking will be around for a long time to come.

The photographs

1. A lineup of German Roland C.IIs in 1916, with teeth on the near one. By coincidence, the model's name was Walfische (whale fish) because of its rounded, fish-shape fuselage.

2. Most famous users of the "shark mouth" motif were the P-40s of the Flying Tigers, the American Volunteer Group in China. Note the Chinese insignia under the wing. The sharp nose of the early P-40 actually helped the decoration to look sharklike.

3. Because of its odd-shaped nose, this German Henschel 129A looks more like a toad with teeth than a shark. Note that the forward gun ports have been painted to become eyes.

4. Even the big boys got into the act. This Boeing B-17G has a painted mouth gobbling the nose turret and an eye has been added above.

1

2

3

4

A double oddity

French Voisin's bicycle landing gear and twin-fuselage configuration didn't catch on

1st September 1973

Just about every conceivable arrangement of airplane components had been tried by the middle of World War I. There have been a lot of minor refinements since then, such as retracting the wheels or giving the wings variable sweep, but the basics have remained pretty much the same. When someone gets excited about a radically "new" airplane, it is often great fun to show him a photo of something very similar that was tried back around 1912 and then forgotten.

One design that qualified as "unusual" even in 1915 was the single-engine French Voisin pusher. In an attempt to clean up the conventional high-drag pusher of the time to get better performance, Voisin did away with the four-point landing gear of its standard model and tried the "bicycle" arrangement, with the wheels partly in the pod-like fuselage for still better streamlining. To achieve ground stability, it was then necessary to add outrigger skids under the lower wings.

Needless to say, this arrangement did not catch on. A few other designers tried center-line main landing gear through World War II, but never got anywhere with it. The only American production models to use it were the Boeing B-47, introduced in 1947, and the similar B-52 of 1951.

Voisin also tried other variations from the standard. Instead of the traditional four bamboo booms supporting the tail, the firm went to what were essentially two, and made them of steel tubing in an early application of that material. The bottom boom connected to the pod directly under the pusher Canton-Unne (later Salmson) water-cooled radial engine. The top boom divided into a Y at the forward end to permit attachment to the upper wing while avoiding the propeller.

As though the bicycle arrangement didn't make the airplane enough of an oddity, the Voisin firm made an even more notable oddity of it by putting two of the single-engine pushers together to create a new twin-engine, twin-fuselage, four-point design.

While that one did not sell either, the idea of joining two existing airplanes to make one new one did not die in 1915; one of the best-known latter-day examples is the German Heinkel He-111Z of World War II. This was a quickie effort to produce a high-powered tow plane for a 180-foot-span cargo glider by splicing two standard He-111 twin-engine bombers together and adding a fifth engine. Then there have been such interesting post-WWII onetime aircraft such as the twin-fuselage Ercoupe and Harold Wagner's twin-fuselage Piper Cub.

To paraphrase song that some may know well, "A really new airplane, nowadays, is hard to find."

The photographs

1. The odd Voisin "bicycle" pusher of 1915, with tandem wheels and outrigger skids. One wonders how it got around on the ground without nosewheel steering.

2. Two of the unique Voisin "bicycles" were put together to create a new twin-engine, twin-fuselage model with four-point landing gear.

3. From the front, the Voisin looked a lot cleaner than some of the contemporary twins. Would anybody care to try this with a Cherokee?

1

2

3

Suicide bomber

Used for Kamikaze missions, Ohkas were a prime example of specialized design

2nd September 1973

One of the most unusual weapons of World War II was the rocket-powered manned bomb that was developed by the Japanese in 1944. Mistakenly dubbed Baka (Japanese for fool) by the Allies, this unusual airplane cum missile was actually called Ohka (Cherry Blossom).

Its purpose was pinpoint bombing of Allied warships by having pilots dive right into the target. There was no pull-out from the dive, which started upon release from a high-flying bomber that carried it to the vicinity of its target. This practice came to be known in English as kamikaze, a word today that refers to a reckless pilot but has an entirely different meaning in Japanese — God's wind.

At other times in aerial warfare, pilots have deliberately rammed enemy aircraft or ground targets, but those were usually impulsive moves – the last act of a critically wounded pilot who knew he was a goner. The Japanese developed the Ohka as a deliberate suicide weapon to be flown by volunteer pilots who knew long in advance what they were supposed to do and were systematically trained to do it.

The Ohka itself was a prime example of specialized design. The conventional metal monocoque fuselage, which was 19 feet long, contained a 1,200-kilogram (2,646-pound) warhead in the nose, a conventional canopied cockpit with minimum instrumentation for the pilot, and three powder rockets in the tail.

The rockets had a combined thrust of 1,764 pounds for eight to 10 seconds and could boost the dive speed to 403 mph. The span of the wooden wing was 16 feet 5 inches, and the area was 65 square feet, the same as today's Formula 1 racers. The gross weight was 4,850 pounds instead of 800. Would you believe a wing loading of 75 pounds per square foot?

Altogether, 775 examples of the standard bomber version, designated Ohka 11, were built. The 10 prototypes built at the Japanese Naval Air Arsenal were designated MXY-7s. Some had extra instrumentation and landing skids because it was necessary to get the aircraft (and the pilots) back in order to evaluate the performance and iron out the bugs.

As an indication of the serious preparations that were made for the kamikaze missions, 45 Ohka K-1s were built as trainers. They had water ballast in the nose in place of the warhead. The water could be dumped to lighten the ship and lower the landing speed. There were no rockets on the trainer; the rear of the fuselage was fitted with a streamlined tail cone to create what was undoubtedly the world's faster glider. Landing was made with a spring skid as used by conventional gliders.

While the one-way weapon concept was simple and supposedly indefensible, it did not work as planned. The weak point was the airlift to the target. The slow and obsolescent bombers used for the job were highly vulnerable to fighter attack, and many were shot down short of the release area. Even in a dive the Ohka could be caught by fighters, and many others stopped by the almost solid wall of antiaircraft shells that were put up by the targeted ships. Few U.S. vessels were damaged or sunk by Ohkas or by the conventional planes that were also used for kamikaze purposes.

The first Ohka operation took place April 1, 1945, a date that may have suggested the Allied code name of Baka for the military airplane with the world's shortest range.

The photographs

1. The Ohka 11 was the standard version of the rocket-powered Japanese navy suicide attacker named Baka by the Allies. This unused model, brought to the United States after World War II, was exhibited at Wright Field. Several still exist in aviation museums throughout the world.

2. The Ohka K-1 was the trainer version of the kamikaze bomber. Note the longer and untapered nose, streamlined tail cone, glider landing skid and wing flaps. Unfortunately, this rare version has since been modified to look like the standard for museum exhibition.

3. An Ohka as it was found by U.S. troops after the capture of the Japanese-held island of Okinawa, a base for the Kamikaze attacks on Allied shipping.

4. To increase the diving speed of the Ohka, the designers installed a small turbojet engine in the tail in place of the original solid-fuel rockets. The Allies code-named this one "Baka 22."

1

2

3

4

The nosy B-18s

Obsolete as bombers for WWII, they carried radar and magnetic anomaly detectors

1st October 1973

Back in 1935 the Army Air Corps held a fly-off bomber design competition. The winner on points was the Douglas Model DB-1 (for Douglas bomber). The aircraft was an adaptation of the contemporary DC-2 transport with a few preview details of the imminent DC-3. As the winner, Douglas received a production order for 133 articles to carry the Air Corps designation B-18 (B for bomber, 18 for the 18th B model developed since the series began in 1924).

The B-18 had a more aerodynamically refined nose than most bombers of the time. It was neatly rounded, with a flat bomb-aiming window at the bottom. The top section was movable to form the front half of a manually swung machine-gun turret containing a single .30-caliber gun. When an additional 177 B-18As were ordered in 1937, the nose was considerably revised. The bomb sight was moved to the former gun position and put in a forward-projecting "snout" that imparted a very sharklike look. The gun was relocated to the former bombsight location and mounted in a smaller hemispherical turret.

The whole B-18 series was obsolete by the time the United States got into World War II, so the aircraft did not go to war as a bomber. A number of B-18As were converted to B-18Bs and -Cs and used for coastal and antisubmarine patrol. While they could carry bombs on those missions, their principal payload was radar and magnetic anomaly detectors. The presence of the radar resulted in the installation of a large plastic bubble on the nose in place of the former bombardier's "snout."

After the war, the surviving B-18s of all series went on the surplus market. Some were acquired by operators of the many nonscheduled freight lines that were then formed. The big radomes on the B-18Bs and -Cs did not stand up very well as they aged. Since there were no replacements, the operators had to patch them as best they could. In 1956, one operator had an entirely new and nicely streamlined nose section formed of fiberglass by Transocean Airlines, which operated a maintenance and modification shop in Seattle. Another modification made to this particular B-18 was to cut a large cargo door in the left side of the fuselage.

Later, the Air Force Museum acquired this same B-18 and faced the same problem of original parts. Rather than build a whole new but authentic nose from the factory drawings, the museum decided to display the B-18 in the same oddball configuration in which it was obtained. The only concession that was made to displaying the B-18 as a military airplane was to apply an essential coat of silver paint and apply standard U.S. military marking much later.

The photographs

1. A Douglas B-18 with the round nose that was used on the prototype and the first production model. The top portion is a gun turret.

2. When the nose-gun and bombsight positions were switched on the B-18A, the aircraft ended up looking like a shark trying to swallow a basketball.

3. B-18As converted to B-18Bs and -Cs were equipped with search radar in the former bombardier's station. The shark nose was replaced with a plastic radome.

4. The civilian owners of this surplus B-18A had a new fiberglass nose built. The Air Force Museum later acquired it and painted it as shown.

1

2

3

4

The Fairchild 71

Most of these big airplanes have to earn their keep

2nd October 1973

The Fairchild 71 is representative of a special category of antique airplane that still exists. That would be the "Big Airplane" – one that is too large and too costly for the average single hobbyist to own and maintain. Other than a handful that are owned by extremely wealthy folks, most of the biggies manage to survive only by earning their way in competition with much later designs.

The main job today seems to be barnstorming at air shows, where they cash in on nostalgia (who would pay $3 to $5 for a quick trip around the pattern in a modern twin?). Others, like the 1929 Fairchild 71, capitalize on their roomy cabins and large doors to haul bulky cargo in the bush country or lift skydivers in more populous areas.

The Model 71 was Fairchild's 1929 production model of a basic cabin monoplane design that Sherman Fairchild originated in 1925 when he needed a custom airplane for his aerial mapping work.

The FC-1 prototype originally had a World War I surplus 90-horsepower Curtiss OX-5 engine, but that was quickly changed to a 200-horsepower Wright J-4 radial. Production versions of the aircraft were the FC-2, which started with the 220-horsepower Wright J-5 and worked up to the FC-2W2 with a 450-horsepower Pratt & Whitney Wasp. The culmination was the 71, a big seven-seater that was powered by the Wasp. One feature common to all was folding wings, a gimmick that was intended to cut down on storage problems and costs, but one that never became popular.

The stability and high-altitude capability of the 71 impressed the U.S. Army to the point where it bought a single photo-and-transport variant as the XC-8. It did well enough to produce a follow-up order for eight F-1 photo planes (F for foto) and six F-1As. All were later redesignated C-8s and

C-8As in the light-transport category, but were used mainly for photography. When the last one was scrapped late in 1942, it was the oldest plane in the Army Air Forces.

The Navy liked the Fairchild too, and ordered one FC-2W2 under the utility designation of XJQ-1 and one 71 as XJ2Q-1. Those and the Army models are included in the totals of approximately 100 FC-2s. Of that total, only one FC-2 and four 71s are known to survive in the United States.

The 71 illustrated here is owned by Jack Ady, who has it based at Harvey Field in Snohomish, Washington, where it is a popular vehicle for skydivers. Among its many modifications are a much later 600-horsepower Wasp with constant-speed prop, doors on both sides of the cabin, special step-rails for the jumpers, and elimination of the wing-fold feature. Ady hopes to retire his 71 in a couple of years and restore it to plush originality – folding wings and all.

The photographs

1. The Fairchild 71, which could operate on wheels, skis or floats, was a highly successful bush plane in Canada and Alaska.

2. The pilot of the Fairchild 71 sat alone at a single set of controls in the narrow nose. The pilot's side windows slid back to open; other plate-glass windows cranked down like automobile windows.

3. The C-8A was the U.S. Army version of the 1929 Fairchild 71 seven-place light transport. Under the earlier F-1 designation, it was the first model in the Army's F-for-foto series.

4. Jack Ady's 1929 Fairchild 71 in September 1973. For most people, big birds like these are too costly to operate as a hobby; they have to earn their way. This one has just dropped a load of skydivers.

1

2

3

4

Strutless biplanes

The Germans took the lead with cantilever-wing fighters in World War I

1st November 1973

One of the complaints about biplanes concerns the complexity and drag of the struts and wires between their wings. An old joke often heard was that the final rigging check on such-and-such model was to put a chicken between the wings. If the fowl got out, a wire was missing.

Designers recognized the disadvantages of struts and wires for as long as there were biplanes, and they took steps to reduce their number within practical limits. One of the main arguments that was advanced by the monoplane advocates was that the one-winger did away with the need for most of the struts, while the cantilever monoplane needed none at all.

Biplanes pretty well dominated the scene back in World War I days, but by 1918 the monoplane finally managed to attract some serious attention, and a few orders were placed for production-model cantilever monoplanes. Biplane designers took note. They knew that bipes still had the edge in maneuverability, but they also knew that extensive cleanup was necessary to improve speed.

As a consequence, several manufacturers, mostly German, came out with "strutless" cantilever-wing biplane fighters late in the war. Struts were still used, but only to keep the upper wing above the fuselage. The best known model was the German Dornier D-I, which had significant advances in other areas, such as all-metal smooth-skin construction, single-strut landing gear, and a streamlined droppable fuel tank.

It had one serious deficiency, however. The elimination of wires was carried to such an extreme that there were no roll wires in the center section. Consequently, the center-section struts were subjected to bending loads that resulted in the loss of the upper wing of one of the prototypes. The correction was to beef up the struts, after which limited production was ordered. Dornier later abandoned the strutless bi-plane concept and adapted the basic D-I airplane to a parasol monoplane.

The only serious American effort along these lines produced the Arrow Sport biplane of late 1926. The airplane had cantilever wings with only center-section struts (and roll wires). Arrow soon found, as had others, that there was an aerodynamic interaction between the two unconnected wings that had detrimental torsional effects. The company responded by equipping the production Sports with steel-tube N struts in the classic location, but did not add flying wires.

Probably the best looking and most widely publicized strutless biplanes were the two little two-seat Darmstadt sport planes, the D-18 and D-22 that were built in Germany in the early 1930s. The last example was the Sorceress sport bi-plane racer. It handled the high loads of racing to everyone's satisfaction, but its manufacturer was forced to add struts in order to stay in the game simply because the rules specified that biplane racers had to have struts.

The photographs

1. The German Dornier D-I strutless fighter biplane of 1918 pioneered many features that later became standard, such as smooth-skin metal construction, single-strut landing gear, and streamlined droppable fuel tank.

2. When introduced in 1926, the American Arrow Sport did not have struts on its full-cantilever wings. Struts were required to add torsional stiffness to the two wings.

3. The super slick Darmstadt D-22 sport plane of 1932. Structural details closely followed the all-wood, high-performance gliders that were also built by the Akafleig Darmstadt.

4. Don Beck's Sorceress Sport Biplane-class racer of 1976 was designed as a full cantilever biplane without struts. Note that the lower wing supports the landing gear. Struts were added because the biplane race rules require them.

1

2

3

4

The first shipboard landings

The trick was getting the airplane launched and bringing it back aboard

2nd November 1973

After the world's navies began to acquire airplanes shortly before World War I, efforts were made to operate them from surface ships. The main problem, of course, was to launch the airplane and then get it back aboard.

In an experiment on Nov. 14, 1910, Curtiss test pilot Eugene Ely flew a standard Curtiss pusher land plane from a 26- by 83-foot platform that was built over the foredeck of the U.S. Navy cruiser Birmingham. The ship was at anchor in Hampton Roads, Virginia, and Ely took off over the bow.

On Jan. 18, 1911, Ely landed a similar plane on a similar 50- by 130-foot platform on the afterdeck of the cruiser Pennsylvania, which was anchored in San Francisco Bay. He landed forward, using an early form of the deck arrester gear that's still in use today and stopped in 60 feet. An hour later, he took off over the stern and returned to shore.

While those experiments worked, they weren't practical for combat ships. Seaplanes were launched by catapults, with subsequent landing on the water and retrieval by crane, but that too had its drawbacks.

By late 1915, the British navy had modified some fast passenger ships to launch seaplanes from a rail on the fore deck. Land planes, however, were needed to go after the German Zeppelins that were shadowing the fleet, so the fore deck of another passenger ship was converted to a fly-off deck for land-plane fighters. The adaptations paid off, and other ships were converted to "one-way" carriers. The system was fairly effective and Zeppelins were shot down, but the short-range planes either had to make it to a shore station to land or had to ditch at sea. No provision was made for landing back aboard.

One of the successful "one-way" carriers that was operating in 1917 was the HMS Furious, which had its takeoff deck on the roof of a 10-plane hangar. Like other ships, the takeoff area was forward, ahead of the standard ship's superstructure.

On Aug. 2, 1917, Squadron Commander E.H. Dunning decided to try a landing when wind conditions were right. He then took off in an 80-horsepower Sopwith Pup fighter and made an approach from the stern when the ship was steaming directly into the wind. He flew close alongside, then side-slipped in ahead of the superstructure and made a successful landing. No deck arrester gear was used, and of course the Pup had no brakes. Dunning had equipped his plane with several loops of rope that people on the deck were to grab and hold onto as he glided over them at nearly zero deck speed.

Two days later, he tried it again, but with disastrous results; he dropped onto the deck hard enough to blow a tire, after which the Pup swerved and dived over the side. Dunning was drowned, and orders were issued prohibiting any further landings on the foredeck.

In March 1918, the HMS Furious was fitted with arrester gear on a new afterdeck and some successful landings were made despite turbulence from the superstructure. The landing operation was still impractical. The true aircraft carrier arrived soon after in the form of the HMS Argus, which had a full-length obstacle-free deck for takeoffs and landings.

The photographs

1. Making the first carrier landing, Eugene Ely touches down on the 130-foot "flight deck" of the USS Pennsylvania on Jan. 18, 1911. A hook on the landing gear caught ropes stretched between the two rows of sandbags and held above the deck by the two longitudinal rows of 2 x 4s.

2. Squadron Commander E.H. Dunning makes the second carrier landing in his Sopwith Pup on the fore deck of the HMS Furious on Aug. 2, 1917.

3. A Sopwith Pup landing on HMS Furious. It was thought that skids would slow the plane more than wheels. Note the longitudinal deck-guide cables and the vertical cable barrier to keep the plane from ramming the ship's superstructure.

4. A Sopwith Pup makes a rough landing on HMS Furious. Turbulence behind the ship's superstructure while it was underway was a serious problem for pilots.

1

2

3

4

The flying bicycle

Frenchman's twin-propeller pusher had three sets of 'tail' surfaces

2nd December 1973

Back in 1909 the configuration and proportions of the airplane as we know it had not been standardized. Many designs of the time that would be regarded as outright oddities today did not come in for undue comment then. Any flying machine was something of an oddity, and one shape had no more reason for evoking any more comment than another.

One that does deserve mention, however, is the little 15-horsepower biplane built by M. Louis Lejeune of France. The airplane was relatively conservative in some respects, but pretty unusual in others.

First, it was a twin-propeller pusher in the tradition of the Wright brothers, with the props turning in opposite directions by the simple expedient of crossing the left-side chain loop. Where the Wrights had used metal sprockets that were inspired from their bicycle background, Lejeune used turned wooden pulleys, apparently without considering the drag that they would produce.

Like the Wrights, Lejeune had his engine, a little air-cooled "fan" Anzani that was offset to the right of the airplane's center line. It was balanced by offsetting the pilot's seat to the left.

Altogether, there were three sets of "tail" surfaces. Out in back, at the end of four bamboo booms, Lejeune had a rudder and a biplane structure that served only as a horizontal stabilizer. The actual elevators, again as with the Wrights, were up front. However, they were up there with a difference.

Instead of a single biplane unit held in front of the plane by a set of booms projecting forward from the center section, Lejeune used two sets of biplane forward elevators and mounted them on two sets of wire-braced double booms attached to the outer wing struts. The units could be operated in parallel as elevators or differentially as ailerons. With this dual arrangement, Lejeune introduced the "elevons" that were used on many subsequent tailless designs that used a single surface as both an aileron and an elevator.

Another Lejeune feature that was so advanced that it did not get into production until the Boeing B-47 came along after World War II was the bicycle landing gear with outboard wheels for ground stability. There was one notable difference, however. Since the rear wheel of the B-47 was too far behind the center of gravity for the plane to be able to "rotate" for takeoff and landing, the gear was built to hold the B-47 at proper takeoff and landing attitude. Lejeune's sat level, also with the rear wheel well behind the center of gravity.

However, with all that drag, the shaky forward booms and only 15 horsepower, I don't think that "rotation" ever got to be a problem with Lejeune No. 1.

The photographs

1. Monsieur Louis Lejeune in the offset pilot's seat of his Aeroplane No. 1. Notice the wooden pulleys for the chain-driven propellers and the "fan" arrangement of the three cylinders of the 15-horsepower Anzani engine.

2. The "bicycle" main landing gear, stabilizing wheels on the wingtips, and the unique elevator-aileron combinations ahead of the wing are all shown here. Note also the French mud that became so famous during World War I.

1

2

The Lockheed F-94 Starfire

Aircraft's lineage evolved from fighter to trainer to fighter

2nd January 1974

Would you believe that a first-line fighter could evolve from a two-seat trainer? Well, it happened, but the story isn't quite that simple.

Near the end of World War II, Lockheed came up with the P-80 Shooting Star, the first operational U.S. jet fighter. Two got to Europe before V-E Day, and production continued into 1950. Since there were no jet trainers in the U.S. inventory at the time, Lockheed took a standard P-80C – the designation was changed from P-for-pursuit to F-for-fighter in June 1948 – and lengthened the fuselage to accommodate a second seat for an instructor.

A new one-piece bubble canopy was then designed to go over both seats. Armament was deleted and the new model became the TF-80C, meaning a fighter modified for training. Lockheed built 128 before May 1949, when the designation was changed to T-33 in the T-for-trainer series.

Production of the T-33 continued until August 1959, by which time 5,691 had been built. They are still around in considerable numbers. An oddity here was that the trainer was slightly faster than the original fighter because the longer fuselage improved the streamlining.

The two-seat conversion of the single-seat P-80 worked out so well that the Air Force thought it could be used in combat. Two T-33s, including the TF-80/T-33 prototype that had been a P-80C, were converted to radar-equipped all-weather fighters. The rear seat was occupied by a radar operator and the radome was built into the nose just above the guns, which were essentially in their old P-80 positions. The combination worked, and beginning in 1949 110 production F-94As were built. The 357 F-94Bs were essentially the same except for revised hydraulics and instrumentation, and tip tanks that were centered on the wingtips instead of being slung underneath.

A major redesign of the F-94B was to have been designated the F-97A. It had so much parts commonality with the F-94s, however, that it was redesignated F-94C before it was built. Major changes were adding sweep-back to the horizontal tail, replacing the 6,000-pound-thrust Allison J-33 engine with an 8,300-pound Pratt & Whitney J-48, and adding a ring of 24 "Mighty Mouse" 2-3/4-inch air-to-air rockets around the nose radome. Two pods, each containing 12 additional "mice," could be fitted to the leading edges of each wing. An oddity of the nose rocket installation was that the crew was temporarily blinded from the smoke when the rockets were fired. Three hundred eighty-seven F-94Cs were built in addition to the two YF-94C prototypes that were converted from F-94Bs.

While the Starfires were in production before and during the Korean War, they were used primarily in the United States by the Air Defense Command. As such, they were the first jet-powered all-weather interceptors. Later, many were assigned to Air National Guard squadrons.

A few were used for experimental armament installations and the development of such new weapons as the Hughes GAR-1 Falcon missile. One of the most interesting F-94 guinea pigs was an F-94B, which was used to test the guidance system of the Boeing IM-99 Bomarc missile. The IM-99, a ram-jet-powered pilotless airplane in its own right, was originally designated F-99 in the fighter-plane series. It then became the IM-99 (for interceptor missile) after the Air Force decided that only piloted aircraft would use standard

1

2

3

4

aircraft designations. It is now CIM-10 in the renumbered missile series.

Anyhow, the gimmick with the F-94B was that its nose was cut off just ahead of the nose gear, and a whole Bomarc nose and guidance section was installed. Instead of launching vertically with the help of booster rockets like the Bomarc, the modified F-94B took off normally and was headed toward the incoming target by the pilot. The Bomarc guidance then took over and flew the plane; the pilot just rode along. He'd take over again after passing the theoretical intercept point and bring the long-nosed F-94B back to its base.

The photographs

1. The prototype F-94A Starfire was a radar-equipped two-seat fighter that had been converted from the prototype T-33 jet trainer. This same airframe had originally been a single-seat P-80C that was lengthened to accommodate an extra seat. The later F-94B was identical in appearance except for center-line wingtip tanks.

2. The F-94C had a bigger engine, swept-back horizontal tail, and 24 "Mickey Mouse" air-to-air rockets around the nose radome. The optional wing rocket pods are not installed here.

3. In an example of instant instrument flight, the crew of an F-94C loses all forward visibility at the moment they fire the nose rockets. Wing-mounted rocket pods are installed here.

4. One of the most unusual experimental variants of the F-94 was this F-94B, which was fitted with the complete nose and guidance equipment of a Boeing Bomarc missile.

The ageless DC-3

Its first flight was 32 years to the day of the Wright brothers'

1st February 1974

On Dec. 17, 1973, we celebrated "Kitty Hawk Day," the 70th anniversary of powered flight. That wasn't really so long ago, only the Biblical "three score and 10" of a normal lifetime.

Another Dec. 17 of significance came along in 1935, 32 years later, when the first Douglas DC-3 made its first flight. Since that was a little over 38 years ago, it chronologically establishes the DC-3 as a genuine antique by airplane standards.

Realize, now, that the DC-3 appeared more than halfway back to Kitty Hawk. It should also be pointed out that despite its age, no one seems to take the DC-3's status as an antique very seriously in the usual sense – that of an obsolete and uneconomical airframe maintained as a hobby or for exhibition by individuals or historical organizations.

The DC-3 is also too much airplane and too expensive to fly to be any individual's hobby horse; it has to pay its way in order to survive. Would you believe that there are 533 DC-3s still in scheduled airline service outside of the United States? Now add an intermediate number in nonscheduled U.S. operations and government service. The Air Force still operates the C-47 and C-117 military versions; the Navy retired its last C-47 in 1973 but still has some C-117s. Ironically, the FAA, which forced DC-3s off the U.S. trunk airlines many years ago as uneconomical, still operates a fleet of DC-3s. Due to be retired "next year" for several years, they are now scheduled for retirement in 1974. Someone should bake a very special cake when that occasional finally rolls around.

Altogether, 609 civil DC-3s are currently registered in the United States, compared to 922 in 1948 and 806 in 1952. The worldwide total is currently estimated at over 2,000.

The DC-3 was not really a new airplane in 1935. It was actually a slightly fattened version of the DC-2 airliner of 1934, itself the production version of the 1933 DC-1. The DC-1 (for Douglas commercial) was developed by Douglas at the specific request of TWA, which could not get the revolutionary Boeing 247 because of Boeing's commitment to United Air Lines.

The 14-passenger DC-2 was very successful. Although a better airplane than the 247, it still was not a money-maker. It remained for the 21-passenger DC-3 to become the first airliner that could pay its own way and operate without subsidy. The first DC-3s were actually 14-passenger sleepers designated DST for Douglas sleeper transport. They were developed from the DC-2 at the request of American Airlines. The original DC-3s and DSTs had Wright R-1820 Cyclone engines. The same models with Pratt & Whitney R-1830 Twin Wasps were DC-3As and DST-As. Convertible day-or-sleeper models with R-1830s were DC-3Bs.

Altogether, 961 civil DC-3s, as distinguished from the Army C-47 and the Navy R4D with cargo doors and reinforced floor, were built. Paratrooper versions without the big doors and reinforcements were C-53s.

Wartime production standardized the C-47 and R4D, but some VIP transports that appeared in 1945 were designated C-117s. Various DC-3s drafted from the airlines in 1941-42 became C-48s through C-52s, C-68s and C-84s.

After the war, some C-117s were completed for civil use as DC-3Ds. Counting the C-47s/R4Ds as the DC-3s that they really are, 10,655 DC-3s were built. Most that are still flying are C-47s converted to civil use and designated DC-3Cs. In the 1962 grouping of U.S. Air Force and Navy aircraft under a common designating system, the Navy R4Ds through -7s became C-47s while the R4D-8s became C-117Ds.

The Super DC-3 of 1949 was not a separate airplane. Douglas came up with a conversion that stretched the fuselage, put sweepback in the wings, changed the size and shape of the tail, and added bigger engines. You turned in your old DC-3, plus about $110,000 (the 1941 price of a new DC-3) and got it back as a Super DC-3. The Air Force tested one as a YC-129, redesignated it YC-47F, and then turned it over to the Navy, which ordered 98 as R4D-8s. Only five civil Supers were produced; their improved performance could not overcome the big price advantage of the plentiful and low-priced surplus C-47s.

Update — The were still 481 DC-3s on the U.S. Civil Register in January 2000, and at least that many more in other

1

2

3

4

countries.

The photographs

1. The Douglas DC-3 of 1935 was a direct development of the DC-2. It's easily recognized by longer and more pointed wings, a fatter fuselage with three rows of passenger seats instead of two, and a small dorsal fin. This DC-3A was in United Air Lines service when photographed in 1940.

2. The principal difference between the civil and military DC-3s was the large cargo doors on the left side and the

reinforced flooring. This is an Army C-47 photographed in 1945. The equivalent Navy model was designated R4D.

3. In 1951, the U.S. Navy had 98 of its R4Ds rebuilt as Super DC-3s under the designation R4D-8. Note the detail changes. In 1962, when U.S. service designations were standardized, R4D-8s became C-117Ds.

4. During the Vietnam War the docile DC-3/C-47 became a powerful aggressor. Four fixed rapid-firing guns were installed to fire out the windows and door as the pilot made pylon turns around a ground target.

The Fournier RF-4

'Powered glider' is more like an ultralight with glider features

2nd February 1974

Columnists who cover random topics are always faced with the question of what to write about next. Once in a while we luck out merely by reading the current issue of the paper. As mentioned in Dave Sclair's Touch & Go column two weeks ago, a reader wrote in to ask about the Fournier RF-4 powered glider. There's plenty of information on hand about that. Here's the story.

First off, the Fournier is not really a "powered glider" as reputed. It is more like an ultralight with glider features to improve performance on low horsepower. This status is made pretty official by the fact that the RF-4 is listed in the airplane section of the standard reference, "Jane's All The World's Aircraft," instead of in the glider section.

The RF-4 has a glide angle of 20:1 and a sinking speed of 4.27 feet per second, which is performance about equal to the "utility" airplanes of the late 1930s. It can soar, but it does a far greater amount of flying under power than the standard powered glider that uses its engine mainly for launching and flight into good lift conditions. As an airplane, the RF-4 has a top speed of 118 mph and cruises at 112. Further, it has a normal range of 410 miles and moderate aerobatic capability with its 1200cc, 40-horsepower Volkswagen engine. This extraordinary powered-glider performance is achieved by the combination of relatively long glider-type wings, extremely clean lines (including a retractable landing gear), and a somewhat bigger engine. The wingspan is 36 feet 11 inches, well under today's lowest-performance gliders (or sailplanes), and the wing loading is considerably higher.

The design of the RF-1 prototype was originated in France by Rene Fournier. Called an Avion Planeur for airplane glider, the all-wood RF-1 was built by the light-plane firm of Alpavia, S.A., and the first flight was on July 6, 1960. A novel feature was the glider-like single retractable wheel, with ground stability for taxiing provided by U-shaped skids halfway out to the wingtips. The engine on this first model could be restarted in the air by means of a unique compression release that allowed the prop to freewheel without having to dive the ship. The production models use a pull-cord to turn the engine over.

The performance of the RF-1 impressed the French government, which financed construction of two RF-2 pre-production prototypes. Those models were followed by 95 production RF-3s, which were introduced in March 1963. After three RF-4 prototypes were built in France, a new firm called Sportavia-Putzer was set up in Germany. Production began in 1966, and the German-built RF-4D is on the market today.

While aircraft that have "standard" licenses in their country of origin can usually get licensed in the United States under reciprocal agreements, there are exceptions, and the RF-4 is one of them. That converted VW engine is still a single-ignition type, which the FAA simply will not approve for standard licenses. Single-ignition antiques like Aeronca C-3s and Taylor J-2 Cubs seem to contradict this, but that's another story for another column.

So the RF-4s in the United States have to operate on Experimental licenses, which restrict their utility considerably. For one, they cannot be used commercially, as for rental. Further, it is sometimes hard to renew an Experimental license on a factory-built airplane. And what about all those VW-powered homebuilts flying around the U.S.? Yes, they fly on X-licenses too, and their owners have no trouble getting them renewed. But they occupy a special subcategory of Experimental called Amateur-built, which exists for the specific purpose of recreation and education. They are built for that purpose alone, which justifies continued renewal of their X-certificates.

Unfortunately, recreation and education is not a legitimate use for a factory-built Experimental in this country, so the RF-4 is pretty well hamstrung as a sport plane and will remain so until such time as Sportavia and the firms that modify VW engines for aircraft use come up with a licensable twin-ignition installation. One glider dealer sold his RF-4 out of the country because he couldn't use it in his commercial operation. Mira Slovak's "Spirit of Santa Paula" can be seen in the Museum of Flight in Seattle. Using extra tanks, he flew it across the Atlantic Ocean three times.

1

2

The photographs

1. The long glider-like wings of the Fournier RF-4 are evident here; however, they are considerably shorter than those of the average small sailplane. The RF-4 should be regarded as a unique light airplane, not a powered glider.

2. This close-up of the RF-4 shows the single-wheel retractable landing gear, the stabilizing outriggers under the wing, and the neatly cowled engine. Unlike some powered sailplanes, the propeller does not feather to reduce drag while soaring.

Where are the Hawks?

Those built between the world wars were never available as surplus to the public

1st March 1974

As one who is more concerned than the average person about antique airplanes and their whereabouts, I am frequently contacted by aircraft buffs who are interested in finding a particular model to restore. In some cases I have been able to help. In others, particularly those concerning pre-WWII military models, I have not.

The most sought-after models seem to be Army fighters. In order of popularity, they're the Curtiss P-6E Hawk, the Boeing P-12 biplane and the little Boeing P-26 monoplane. The would-be restorers carefully point out how many of each were built, and reason that there must still be a few around, probably stashed in old barns.

Unfortunately, this hope is based on faulty thinking. The seekers have in mind the huge surplus sales that followed both world wars, when practically any model in the military inventory could be bought surplus. What these people do not realize is that the between-wars models were never available for sale to the public when they became obsolete or wore out.

When such a plane was surveyed (Army lingo for written off the books), it might be scrapped, but it was definitely not sold. It frequently went to a service mechanics school as Class 26 (non-flying) material or was sometimes donated under a very restrictive contract to a civilian college or high school that had an aviation course.

Again, it was non-flying, and the school could not pass the plane on as a unit when through with it. It had to be scrapped or returned to the government. A few were returned after WWII to be replaced by later equipment and were scrapped before the Air Force Museum program got going. Others, fortunately, were found and acquired either by the Air Force Museum or by the Smithsonian. Many others were scrapped by the schools, and only a few random parts have survived. One complete P-12E was acquired in the 1950s by the Planes of Fame museum (formerly The Air Museum) at Buena Park, California. Officials found it at California Polytechnic College, but the red tape still applied. A private individual could not have done it, but the museum capitalized on its status and was able to work out a contract with the state to use the plane as a bona fide museum piece.

Some existing antiques seem to contradict the above. Not so; they are specific exceptions. Back in the late 1930s, the Navy turned two Boeing F4B-4s (similar to the Army P-12Es) over to the predecessor of the present FAA. The aircraft were soon declared surplus as civil airplanes and were quickly acquired by stunt pilot Jesse Bristow for air-show work. He still had one in 1947 but sold it to someone who crashed it the following year. The last owner of the other F-4B-4 donated it to the Smithsonian, which now has it out on loan to the Naval Aviation Museum in Pensacola.

Two Curtiss Hawks used by civilian stunt pilots in the 1930s (one survives today) were never military property – both had been civil-registered factory demonstrators. The surviving P-6E in the Air Force Museum is one of the school-donation ships that was fortunately saved. A P-6E "restoration" that is expected to be flying this year is more like a replica. The owner started with a single lower wing panel and built a whole new airplane to fit it.

Further exceptions are the two Boeing P-26s in the

1

2

3

United States. As WWII got underway, the Army donated the ones based overseas to the governments of the Philippines, Panama and Guatemala. Panama passed its Peashooters on to Guatemala, which managed to keep some of them going until well past WWII. The last two were ready for the scrap pile in the 1950s when Ed Maloney, curator of The Air Museum, acquired one and got it shipped to California. The Smithsonian got the other. Notice that I said *the* other. Don't go there hoping to find another. Believe me, you won't.

The photographs

1. The beautiful Curtiss P-6E Hawk, shown in color-ful markings of the 17th Pursuit Squadron, is the between-wars antique that restoration buffs would most dearly love to acquire. Unfortunately, none are available, either from the military or in old barns.

2. This former U.S. Navy Boeing F4B-4 fell into private hands in a roundabout way. The Navy turned it over to the old Civil Aeronautics Authority (CAA), which eventually sold it as surplus.

3. Two more roundabout acquisitions. These two Boeing P-26As were turned over to Panama by the U.S. Army and were then passed on to Guatamala. The Planes of Fame museum acquired one; the Smithsonian got the other.

Convair's Pogo

Vertical flight without wings or rotors became possible with high-powered turbines

2nd March 1974

Man dreamed of vertical flight long before practical flight of any kind became a reality. Helicopters, of course, were the first machines to achieve vertical flight. Experimentation began long before World War I, but the first recognized successful flight was in Denmark in 1913. While there were a few intermittent efforts between WWI and WWII that could be called successful, the helicopter was still a purely experimental vehicle in the late 1930s. It remained for Igor Sikorsky, just before WWII, to make the practical helicopter a reality.

Despite Sikorsky's success, the dream of vertical flight continued. To achieve it without wings or rotors, it was readily evident that power greater than the gross weight of the machine would be required. Not until high-power turbine development got rolling after WWII did the idea begin to become workable.

In 1950 and 1951, the Navy got interested in vertical takeoff and landing (VTOL) aircraft that could take off from small platforms on the decks of merchant vessels and warships to serve as convoy protectors. Industry got interested in the project too, and Convair and Lockheed submitted proposals to the Navy for planes that could do the job. Convair got a contract early in 1951 for what was to be a single-seat fighter designated XFY-1 (X for experimental, F for fighter and Y for Convair in the Navy designating system).

Lockheed got an order a few weeks later for its XFV-1 (V identified the Vega plant at Lockheed). The Navy, meanwhile, asked the Allison engine division of General Motors to develop a suitable turboprop engine for the new fighters.

Allison did not have anything in the works that would fill the bill, so it took two of its T-38 engines, put them together side-by-side and connected them to a common gearbox to create the 5,800-shaft-horsepower T-40A engine. Since it was obvious that such high power in relatively small airplanes would result in terrific torque problems, the engine was designed to drive two contra-rotating propellers. In case one of the two power units cut out, the other could drive both props through the gearbox; otherwise, each unit drove one of the props.

The XFY-1, which Convair named the Pogo, was finished in 1954. It was a delta-wing that rested vertically on small spring wheels at its wing and fin tips. The pilot, stationed in an amidships cockpit, faced special problems. When the ship was vertical, he still had to sit in a relatively normal position, but looking inward instead of outward. As the plane transitioned into level flight, the whole seat and control assembly rotated to position him normally for level flight. The two modes of flight also presented problems that were solved by having two pilot-ejection systems, one for level and one for vertical flight.

For its first flights, the Pogo was taken to the large Navy airship hangar at Moffett Field, California, where it made nearly 300 vertical takeoffs while hooked to a tether – just in case. Finally, it was returned to San Diego and made its first free flight and its first transition to horizontal flight on Nov. 2, 1954.

Lockheed's tail-sitter also flew, but it never took off from a full vertical position. It was fitted with a temporary bolt-on landing gear and made all its takeoffs and landings from a relatively normal attitude. It did, however, transition from level to vertical flight in the air.

The photographs

1. The Convair XFY-1 Pogo vertical-takeoff fighter, ready to lift off. Note the pilot's position and consider the problems he had in backing down to land.

2. The XFY-1 in level flight with the pilot seated in a normal position. The arrow at right shows takeoff and landing spot on Lindbergh Field in San Diego. North Island Naval Air Station is on the left.

3. The more conventional layout of the Lockheed XFV-1 makes an interesting contrast to the XFY-1. However, with the same powerplant and "tail-sitter" attitude, they had the same pilot-orientation problems.

1

2

3

Printing-press camouflage

Sky-blue and earth colors appeared when fighters began hunting observation planes

1st April 1974

Until the middle of 1916, most military airplanes were just "airplane color" – unpainted white fabric sometimes tinted with varnish to a beige or burnt amber. With the important observation planes becoming the quarry of fighters that were sent out to destroy them, protective camouflage evolved and became widely used for all combat aircraft.

In general, camouflage consisted of earth colors such as green and brown painted irregularly on top and side surfaces, and a light color like sky blue on the undersides. The French, Germans and Italians used this scheme for land planes, while the British used solid olive drab or khaki-brown for tops and sides, and clear-doped fabric underneath.

Seaplanes were also camouflaged, but in colors suitable to a marine environment. Some flying boats even went to the "dazzle" patterns used by merchant vessels and battleships.

In 1917 the Germans came up with an interesting new gimmick. Instead of camouflaging their airplanes after they were built, they printed the colors right on the fabric before covering. All that was needed for a finish was the usual amount of clear dope.

The patterns differed somewhat depending on the fabric manufacturer and the size of the airplane, but in general they consisted of five colors in either a regular hexagon pattern or irregular polygons in a repeating pattern. The colors were usually dark green, mauve, light green, fawn and pink.

In some cases, metal parts were a solid dark color while in others the basic pattern was hand-painted on such large metal areas as cowlings. Fabric was too precious in wartime Germany to lay over plywood-covered fuselages or wings, so those surfaces were either painted or clear-varnished.

The colorful printed patterns served two purposes. From a distance, particularly when viewed from above, they caused the plane to blend with the background. In the close action of combat, they broke up the lines of the planes so that the attackers had a harder time picking a specific point at which to aim.

The German navy, the first to adopt the printing-press technique, used a regular hexagon pattern. The German army soon followed, sometimes with hexagons but mostly with the irregular polygons, sometimes referred to by historians as lozenges. The famous Fokker fighters, which had an exclusive hand-painted scheme from late 1916, did not adopt the printed system until after the first D.VII fighters had been delivered in the late spring of 1918. That was well after all the other manufacturers had standardized on printed fabric.

Reproducing these patterns for latter-day restorations and replicas is a terrific job. For the Fokker D.VII in the National Air Museum of the Smithsonian Institution, the manufacturer who contributed the fabric for the restoration applied the pattern and colors with a modern silk-screen.

The photographs

1. A German naval Brandenberg W.12 seaplane displays the small three-color hexagonal pattern that was used only on fabric surfaces that were visible from above.

2. A Fokker D.VII with the four-color irregular polygon, or lozenge, camouflage. These patterns were not very evident in most old photos because the orthochromatic film of the day could not pick up the different colors.

3. A Pfalz D.XII with five-color lozenge-pattern fabric on wings and elevators. The plywood fuselage and plywood-covered fin and stabilizer were painted, so they did not show the pattern.

1

2

3

The first world flight

Four Army Air Service seaplanes departed Seattle in 1924

2nd April 1974

Fifty years ago, four single-engine Douglas DWC seaplanes of the U.S. Army Air Service were in Alaska during the early stages of an unprecedented attempt to fly westward around the world.

After nearly a full year of planning, including the construction of special airplanes and a worldwide supply operation that had been set up by the Air Service and the State Department, and supported by the U.S. Navy, the four planes and their eight crew members departed from what was then the Army airfield at Sand Point near Seattle.

The planes were named for major cities on the four borders of the country: Seattle (No. 1), Chicago (No. 2), Boston (No. 3) and New Orleans (No. 4). The corresponding crews were Major Frederick L. Martin, commander, with Sergeant Alva Harvey as mechanic; First Lieutenant Lowell Smith and First Lieutenant Leslie P. Arnold; First Lieutenant Leigh Wade and Sergeant Henry Ogden; and First Lieutenant Erik Nelson and Second Lieutenant Jack Harding. Harvey and Ogden were commissioned en route.

Weather proved to be the main headache for the early stages. It took the flight six weeks to reach Japan. The Seattle had troubles practically every flying day, including a forced landing on the way to its namesake city from the factory in Santa Monica, and further troubles that delayed the start by a day. The aircraft was also damaged during landing at the end of the first day's hop from Seattle to Prince Rupert, British Columbia. It fell behind the others with engine trouble 110 miles short of Chignik, Alaska. After a new engine was brought in by boat from Dutch Harbor, it was airborne again but never did catch up. It crashed into a mountain near Port Mellor on the Kenai Peninsula. The crew was not hurt, however, and managed to hike out in 10 days.

Command of the flight, meanwhile, had passed to Lieutenant Smith, and his Chicago became the new flagship. The flight proceeded on the selected route except for an unplanned detour to Russian-owned islands some 360 miles from Attu, the last U.S. territorial outpost. No diplomatic clearances had been obtained from Russia, and the local commandant would not let them in. In anticipation of that, a U.S. Fisheries Bureau ship had been stationed outside the three-mile limit, and the cruisers were moored to it overnight.

Upon reaching Asia, the fliers became celebrities for having flown across the North Pacific. The continuing rounds of celebrations and banquets became something to contend with while trying to maintain a schedule, particularly since they did all of their own maintenance, including engine changes.

Due to decreased lift in tropical temperatures and humidity, and greater difficulty taking off from glassy water on a hot day with full fuel, the flight schedule was revised in Southeast Asia. One of the three surviving planes was forced down by engine trouble, temporarily delaying the trip in Vietnam. After a replacement engine was hauled in 500 miles from Saigon, the cruisers continued to Calcutta, the halfway point, which they reached on June 26. There the floats were replaced by wheels for the start of the homeward half of the epochal flight.

For further details see Page 118.

The photographs

1. The special world-flight airplanes were designated DWC for Douglas World Cruiser. They were developed from the contemporary Navy Douglas DT-2 torpedo plane and could operate on wheels or twin floats. This is the New Or-

1

2

leans, presently preserved at the Museum of Flying in Santa Monica, California.

   2. The New Orleans is hoisted out of the water for maintenance at Dutch Harbor, Alaska. The aircraft's wing-span was 50 feet and its gross weight was 9,587 pounds as a seaplane. The engine was an improved version of the famous 420-horsepower Liberty of World War I. The fliers used 19 powerplants during the flight.

Steam-powered engines

The only one to make a full-pattern manned flight was the 150-horse, two-cylinder Besler

1st May 1974

Back in the days before the Wright brothers' first flight, would-be inventors of flying machines had no suitable powerplants with which to experiment. The few individuals who had progressed to the point of flying large-scale models or their full-size contraptions used steam engines. The first to achieve any degree of success was Professor Samuel P. Langley's scale-model Aerodrome, which flew for some 3,000 feet along the Potomac River in May 1896.

While steam engines produced the necessary power, they were far too heavy for flying machines, so it remained for the gasoline engine to make the airplane work. While such things were in wide use for marine, automotive and fixed operations by the turn of the century, there were no available adaptations for aircraft use. The Wright bothers had to build their own before they made the first successful powered flight in December 1903.

However, despite the gas engine's total monopoly of the airplane industry ever since, inventors have periodically considered the steam engine as the proper powerplant for aircraft. Various experimental installations have been made over the years, but none have been practical.

The most successful, and the only one to make a proper full-pattern flight, was the Besler, a two-cylinder, 150-horsepower design developed by brothers George and William Besler. The engine was installed in a Travel Air 2000 biplane and was successfully flown at the Oakland (California) Airport on April 12, 1933.

The 180-pound engine was quite light for steam, but its accessories – boiler, water, pump, condensers, etc. – increased its weight to more than 500 pounds, which actually wasn't much more than the World War I-surplus Curtiss OX-5 that had been removed from the plane. An inlet pressure of 1,200 pounds was used, and the propeller was turned at 1,625 rpm, a couple of hundred more than the old OX-5 at its best.

The steam-powered plane made only one flight, a short trip around the airport, but it did prove that steam could be used as a means of propulsion for airplanes. There is a big difference between being merely successful, however, and being competitive, and nothing more was done with the steam engine. The Beslers continued their association with the Dobel Steam Car Company of Emeryville, California, and made steam-based smoke generators for the Army during World War II.

When I last saw it, the Besler engine that was removed from the Travel Air was on display in the engine shop of the Boeing School of Aeronautics at the Oakland Airport in 1942. The Army took the school over during the war, and it was closed afterward. If the engine still exists, it should be placed in a suitable museum.

The photographs

1. The experimental 150-horsepower Besler steam engine replaced the 90-horsepower, water-cooled Curtiss OX-5 in this standard Travel Air 2000.

2. The two-cylinder Besler steam engine that went in the Travel Air had a vertical boiler and firebox immediately behind it.

3. Close-up of the steam-powered Travel Air shows the two radiators that were necessary to condense steam back into water so the supply could be maintained long enough for the plane to make a full-circuit flight.

1

2

3

Forward firepower

Synchronizers solved the problem of firing bullets through the turning propeller

2nd May 1974

When World War I began, military aviation was new and flying was essentially a sport. Allied and German pilots in their unarmed reconnaissance aircraft cheerfully waved at each other in passing.

The tactical importance of aerial observation was soon apparent, however, and stopping the enemy from observing one's own territory became a high priority. Antiaircraft gunnery from the ground was useless for the purpose. The best way to knock an airplane down was to use another.

Easier said than done. After carbines and pistols proved ineffective, the planes began to carry machine guns. The contemporary pusher designs were well suited for such missions. The gunner stationed in the nose cockpit of the pod or nacelle had a wide field of fire to the front for his flexibly mounted gun. The pushers, however, were too slow to catch their quarry. It took the fast and relatively clean tractor design to catch up, but it couldn't fire forward because of the propeller up front.

Several approaches to the forward-firepower problem were tried. First, the front-seat occupant of a conventional two-seater stood up and fired a post-mounted gun over the top of the propeller arc. The added drag of this operation largely wiped out the plane's speed advantage. Besides, as a two-seater, it wasn't as fast as the single-seat scouts.

Another radical approach was to impart the pusher's front-gunner advantage to the tractor design by installing a pusher-like nose cockpit ahead of the propeller. This was supported by struts from the landing gear and the top wing outside the propeller arc. This arrangement was actually produced in small numbers in 1915.

The first real fighter – the French called it a chasseur, for chaser or pursuit – was developed by the famous prewar French pilot Roland Garros. He took a conventional Morane-Saulnier Model N single-seater and installed a machine gun rigidly ahead of the cockpit along the line of flight. The gun was aimed by aiming the whole plane. The little problem of bullets hitting the prop was taken care of by bolting steel deflector plates to the propeller blades.

Garros' device was successful, and he knocked down several German planes whose pilots thought they had nothing to fear from a French tractor behind them. Unfortunately, Garros was forced down behind German lines by engine trouble, and the Germans learned his secret. They then made one major improvement. Instead of deflecting the occasional bullet that didn't pass between the prop blades, they developed a synchronizer that kept the gun from firing when a blade was in line with it.

The German system, developed by Fokker on direct orders from officialdom in mid-1915, used straight mechanical drive-through cams and rods. By 1916, the Allies made improvements of their own with a hydraulic system. That remained standard for everyone well into World War II, when the increased use of wing-mounted guns and eventually the introduction of the jet finally eliminated the need for the synchronizer.

The photographs

1. The standard pusher designs of the time, such as this 1915 British Vickers FB-5 Gunbus, had a wide field of forward fire, but they were too slow to catch the faster tractor types that they wanted to shoot down.

2. In the absence of a synchronizer for its own fast tractor types, Chance developed this Spad A.4 on which a gunner's station was installed ahead of the propeller. Note the wide separation of the cockpits. This ski-equipped model was used by Russia.

3. Since it took a fast single-seater to catch another, French pilot Roland Garros installed a fixed machine gun in the nose of his Morane Model L parasol monoplane and used steel plates that were bolted to the propeller to deflect those bullets that did not pass between the blades. This is a later Morane Model N that was put into limited service by both the French and British. Note the deflectors on the propeller blades.

4. The armament and powerplant from Garros' Morane set up for study in the Fokker factory. The steel rod from the deflector runs inward to the propeller hub to resist the tendency of centrifugal force to throw off the defender.

5. Anthony Fokker installed the first synchronized machine gun in an 80-horsepower Fokker M-5 monoplane. The gun is a standard infantry Parabellum, still with its stock. The headrest is to steady the pilot's head for aiming the gun.

6. Fokker and early German pilots who used his synchronized gun got carried away with its effectiveness and wanted still more firepower. This Fokker E-IV, built especially for German ace Oswald Boelcke, had three guns. Almost until World War II, two synchronized guns were standard for most fighters.

1

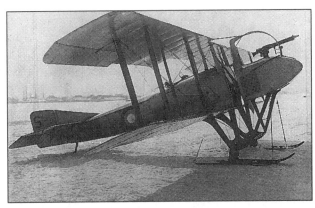

2

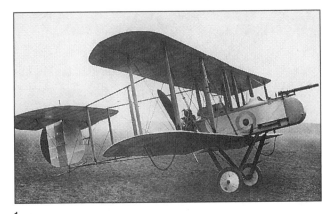

3

4

5

6

Ryan's Vertijet

Air Force X-13 is best U.S. example of turbojet VTOL aircraft

1st June 1974

The first serious efforts to develop true vertical takeoff and landing (VTOL) aircraft such as the Convair XFY-1 followed the availability of big turboprop engines that had more thrust than the gross weight of the aircraft.

The next step was to try the same thing with turbojet engines. The best American example is the Ryan X-13 Vertijet. The aircraft wasn't a fighter like the Convair and Lockheed efforts. It was strictly a research item and was therefore put in the Air Force's X-series of research aircraft.

The X-13 was a relatively conventional delta-wing aircraft that was powered with a single Rolls Royce Avon engine that delivered 10,000 pounds of thrust. Approximate empty weight of the plane was only 7,500 pounds. Operation, however, was quite unconventional.

Actually, the two prototypes built in 1955 were combination types. They had temporary fixed tricycle landing gear, so they could take off normally as well as vertically. In the interest of mobility and the ability of future military VTOLs to take off from unprepared remote bases, the X-13 was intended to operate in the VTOL mode from a truck. The vehicle had a flat bed that could be raised to the vertical position. The plane hung by a nose hook and the pilot merely had to apply enough power to enable the plane to raise itself off the hook and climb out.

The usual problem of VTOLs – control at zero airspeed – was taken care of by deflecting the jet exhaust. For forward flight, conventional controls were used. The pilot had some interesting problems when making a vertical landing back on the board. To make him more comfortable and to enable him to function in a relatively normal attitude, his seat pivoted for the VTOL mode. The board was on the opposite side of the plane, however, and the pilot had a hard time judging his distance from it for the precise job of engaging the hook. To help with this positioning problem, a long wand projected from the top of the board. The big measuring stick was painted in sections so the pilot could tell how far out he was.

The first X-13 flew on Dec. 10, 1955, and used the temporary tricycle landing gear for a normal level takeoff. The first VTOL flight was made on May 28, 1956. The second prototype was the first to transition from one mode to another, taking off horizontally on Nov. 28, 1956, then hovering vertically and reverting to level for the landing.

While VTOL aircraft like the Convair, Lockheed and Ryan worked, tests proved that they were not the proper solution to the VTOL problem.

The photographs

1. Fitted with a temporary fixed tricycle landing gear, the Ryan X-13 Vertijet takes off like a normal jet airplane.

2. The X-13, still with temporary landing gear, approaches its fully elevated truck bed for a vertical landing. Note the wand used by the pilot as a position reference.

1

2

Radical Ryans

Open cockpit and sturdy structure have made them popular war-surplus aircraft

2nd June 1974

A total of 1,123 Ryan PT-22 trainers were built for the Army during World War II. Another 100 slightly lower powered sister ships were built as PT-21s and another 100 served in the Navy as NR-1s. After the war, most went on the surplus market and became quite popular with private pilots.

Before the war, the earlier Ryan STA Sport Trainer had been popular with flying schools. After the war, the civil designs rather than the surplus military types were still favored by the schools.

With 132 to 160 horsepower, the glamour of open cockpits and a rugged structure, the Ryans have retained their popularity with the sportsmen. A surprising number are on hand today.

Taking advantage of the Ryan's sturdy structure, a few professional air-show pilots (and some brash amateurs) have undertaken sundry modifications, including an increase in power, and have made all-out aerobatic types of their Ryan PTs.

Other modifications have improved the reliability of the powerplant. The 160-horsepower Kinner in the PT-22s, for instance, has been replaced with other engines, notably the 175- to 200-horsepower Ranger six-cylinder inverted in-line. Other changes include cleaning up the landing gear or adding a canopy over the cockpits.

Five of the more extreme modifications are presented here for comparison with a stock PT-22 that I photographed in March 1942.

The photographs

1. A stock Army Ryan PT-22 with 160-horse Kinner radial engine and a wooden propeller. The PT-21 had 132 horsepower and some fairing between the forward and middle landing-gear struts. Navy NR-1s duplicated the PT-21s, which were known as Ryan ST-3KRs in prewar civilian life.

2. This PT-22 has been fitted with a 220-horsepower Continental radial engine and has had the nose shortened to keep the ship in balance. Of course, the front cockpit has been eliminated on this and similar conversions.

3. Not only has this PT-22 been hopped up with a 220 and chopped, it has been doubled. It was converted to a biplane by using another set of PT-22 wings. The late Cliff Winters used it for air-show work until a snap and a half instead of a single snap on takeoff ended his colorful career.

4. Another extreme modification was to install an in-line Ranger engine and build up the rear fuselage to fair in an enclosed cockpit. This conversion by Dick Ennis of San Fernando, California, was called the Ryan Ranger.

5. Installation of a flat-six Lycoming O-435 engine in this PT-22 resulted in a greatly revised nose. The rest of the airframe remained stock.

6. One of the simplest modifications was to build a sliding canopy over the cockpits, fair in the landing-gear struts, and add wheelpants.

1

2

3

5

4

6

No dual before solo

Non-flying trainers allowed students to get the feel of the controls

1st July 1974

How many hours of dual did you have before you soloed an airplane? Disregarding the few who learned in single-seat gliders and the current crop of hang-glider enthusiasts, you probably had around eight if you were a typical student at a typical flying school. Of course, we hear occasionally about real eager beavers who did it in four hours or even three, but they are notable exceptions.

There was a time, though, when the student went solo right from the start as part of the regular curriculum. The French used this system back in World War I. The students were started out in Penguins, relatively conventional airplanes that would not quite fly. Sometimes these "airplanes" were worn-out crates that had their wings clipped. Sometimes they merely had some wing fabric removed. In some cases they were specially built as non-fliers. The French called them Roleurs, meaning that they would roll along the ground, but would not fly.

The procedure was for the student to get the feel of the controls by charging across a wide-open field. In the process, he'd also learn how to handle the tricky engines of the day. Once he was able to get the tail off the ground and keep the ship going straight, he was ready for the next stage, which used a ship with more area and power that could actually fly.

Since the United States was so far behind the rest of the world aeronautically when it got into the war, it tried all sorts of European ideas. One was the Penguin or Roleur method of training. The big fields of Texas were considered ideal, and the Army ordered 300 examples of an American version known as the Breese Penguin. It was powered with a 28-horsepower two-cylinder Lawrence engine that proved to be one of the roughest-running mills around. Well, it soon became evident that the Penguin system wasn't suited to the American way of doing things, and 296 of the little Breeses never got out of their packing crates.

None of the oddball ideas in aviation ever vanish completely. If they are forgotten, someone soon reinvents them.

Such was the case with the Penguins. Around 1930, someone went at it in a systematic way. A non-flying device called the Cycloplane was introduced as a ground trainer. It was a very well-thought-out and functional design. It had a guard around the propeller as a safety feature and even had a nose wheel out front to keep the student from nosing it over. There were several versions, one of which had a pivoting wing that allowed the student to bank it with both main wheels on the ground.

For this next stage, the student moved on to another Cycloplane that had the advantage of being very similar but fitted with longer wings and some fuselage streamlining so that it could fly.

As a low-cost way to learn, the system made sense. However, the Depression came along just then, and the flying business took such a nose dive that even cost-cutting tricks like the Cycloplane system could not survive. The gradual disappearance of big sod fields and the advent of paved runways at most airports are a pretty good guarantee that the Penguin method will not be tried again.

The photographs

1. One of the 300 Breese Penguins that were built for the Army in 1917. Note the short wings and open rear fuselage. The ailerons were useless; the Penguin couldn't bank with both wide-track wheels on the ground.

2. This is one version of the Cycloplane ground trainer. Fitted with a 20-horsepower engine and not enough wing area to fly, it sort of defeats the "all-solo" concept by having a second seat for an instructor.

3. A single-seat Cycloplane that pivots on its landing gear so that it can be banked. Note the full-span ailerons.

4. Although structurally similar to the ground trainer, the advanced Cycloplane was a bona fide airplane. While the performance was marginal by contemporary light-plane standards, it was enough to get the solo student into the air and around the pattern.

1

2

3

4

Modified sprayers

War-surplus Stinson L-5s were converted from monoplanes to biplanes

2nd July 1974

Odd modifications are made when standard-configuration airplanes are adapted to special purposes. Some are obvious advances, while others may seem to be steps backward at the time. Converting a monoplane into a biplane, for example, seems to be the wrong way to go these days.

The plane we are talking about is the World War II-surplus Stinson L-5, one of the special low-and-slow observation monoplanes that was developed for the Army early in the war. It originally was designated O-62, but the Army dropped the O-for-observation designation in 1942 and redesignated those models remaining in production as L types (L for liaison).

The L-5 was loaded with advanced features that contributed to its low-speed performance. It had big flaps, leading-edge slots that ran nearly half the span of the wing, and ailerons that drooped a few degrees when the flaps were lowered to contribute to the overall lift. The engine was a 185-horsepower, flat-six Lycoming O-430-1 that gave a 130-mph high speed at the normal gross weight of 2,020 pounds.

After the war, a lot of L-5s found ready customers in the surplus market. Some became just private owner types, but others were put to work that capitalized on their special capabilities. Two such jobs were glider towing and crop dusting or spraying.

The tightly cowled Lycoming wasn't the optimum engine for dusting, so some operators replaced them with 220-horsepower air-cooled radial types, either the seven-cylinder Continental R-670 or the nine-cylinder Lycoming R-680. The fact that the L-5 did not qualify for a standard license with these engines did not bother the operators. They were operating on Restricted licenses as duster-sprayers anyhow.

Since it is characteristic of dusters to operate at higher gross weights than equivalent standard-license designs, some of the operators sought means other than higher horsepower to increase the payload.

The logical idea of adding more lifting surface in the form of a second wing rather than by increasing the span of the existing wing proved to be a practical idea for the L-5. The fuselage was deep enough and the monoplane wing chord was narrow enough for an efficient gap-chord ratio. Naturally, since the original wing was permanently fixed relative to the center of gravity, the new wing had to be mounted directly below it to maintain the balance. An additional benefit of the lower wing for a crop duster is the stronger downwash over the crop and the resulting improvement in distribution of dust or spray.

The photographs

1. This Army L-5 was photographed during World War II. The later L-5B cut down the rear-cockpit visibility somewhat by raising the aft turtledeck to the wing and eliminating some of the windows.

2. A Stinson L-5 with minimal modifications — it still has its original 185-horsepower Lycoming engine — is rigged for spraying. This one has an Experimental license. Most sprayers flew on Restricted licenses.

3. Another minimally modified L-5 rigged as a duster. Note the long exhaust stacks, which keep sparks away from flammable dust.

4. This surplus L-5 was converted to a sprayer with 220-horsepower Continental radial engine and an additional wing. The area of the upper wing has been increased slightly by elongating the tips and squaring them off.

1

2

3

4

Ryan's Standard

Airline's modifications were considerably different than anyone else's

1st August 1974

There were two standard primary trainers in the Army Air Service inventory during World War I: the famous Curtiss JN-4 Jenny series and the Standard Aero Corporation's Model SJ. The double meaning of the word "standard" as used here and the near similarity of the letter-type designations has been a source of confusion ever since.

The Jenny, of course, won everlasting fame as *the* trainer of WWI; meanwhile, nothing was heard of the Standard, which was actually a later design by nearly three years – and a better airplane. The Standard's opportunity for wartime fame, however, was scuttled by its engine, the 100-horsepower Hall-Scott A-7. Thanks to the A-7's chronic troubles, including in-flight fires, the Army grounded most of the 1,601 SJs that had been built. Many others that had been ordered were delivered but remained in their crates throughout the war.

About the first thing the buyer of a war-surplus Standard did to his new plane was replace the Hall-Scott with a 90-horsepower Curtiss OX-5 or a 150-horsepower U.S.-built Hispano-Suiza, also known as the Hisso. Except for the powerplant changes, which identified them either as an OX Standard or a Hisso Standard, the planes retained their standard configuration and were called J-1s instead of SJs.

Several small firms specialized in such conversions plus additional custom modifications. The best known was the Lincoln Aircraft Company of Lincoln, Nebraska. Its Lincoln Standard with the 150- to 180-horsepower Hisso and an enlarged front cockpit was a popular standard model of the early 1920s barnstorming era.

When Ryan Airlines set up in 1924 to operate between San Diego and Los Angeles, it acquired a number of Standards and did its own modification work. A bona fide passenger cabin replaced the open front cockpit and the passenger capacity was increased to four by putting the gas tank on the center section of the upper wing (on such a short route, it didn't need much gas). The resulting Ryan Standards were considerably different than anyone else's modified versions of the Standard airframe.

All the modifications added weight that cut into the performance, so Ryan added some wing area by incorporating a simple method. The company merely replaced the short bottom wing panels with longer upper wing panels. No significant rework like splicing spars was necessary; just put the underside strut fittings on the topside of the panels and add an extra bay of struts at the attach points of the old overhang brace wires.

Such modifications were easy to do in those pre-regulation days. In fact, it was *standard* practice.

The photographs

1. This Standard SJ-1, as delivered to the U.S. Army in 1917, had a unique vertical radiator, an anti-noseover wheel for the benefit of student pilots, and king-post-and-wire bracing on the upper wing overhang.

2. Ryan Airlines' 1924 conversion of the Standard was equipped with a four-place passenger cabin, a gas tank in the upper wing's center section, and an upper wing panel that was used in place of the lower, necessitating the use of an extra bay of struts.

1

2

The neglected N3N

First service primary trainer to use all-metal construction, it has an identity problem

2nd August 1974

There are 195 single-model biplanes flying around today that have a serious identity problem. Many aviation people not closely connected with them think they are Stearmans and call them such, much to the annoyance of their owners.

The planes in question are N3Ns, 996 of which were built at the U.S. Naval Aircraft Factory in Philadelphia from 1936 to World War II. Back in those days, the Navy designed and also built some of its own airplanes.

Even their designation is confusing. The first N stands for trainer in the Navy designating system that was used until 1962. The 3 means the third trainer developed by the Naval Aircraft Factory, which itself is identified by the second N. The dash number identifies the configuration as -1 for the first, etc. The contemporary N2S-1 was the first configuration of the second N-type developed for the Navy by S-for-Stearman.

The N3N was an unusual airplane for its time. It was the first service primary trainer to use all-metal construction. The fuselage featured a bolted aluminum angle frame instead of the customary welded steel tubing or the wrapped sheet aluminum that was just coming into style. It also had quickly removable side panels the full length of the fuselage for easy maintenance and repair. The upper wing was in one piece, and the whole airplane was fabric covered.

The prototype XN3N-1 used the 220-horsepower Wright J-5 Whirlwind engine that was made famous by Charles Lindbergh in 1927. The powerplant went out of production in 1929, but the Navy had a large stockpile and specified them for such new trainers as the 1934 Stearman NS-1 and the first 30 production N3N-1s out of 180 built. Most of those were eventually refitted with the later 240-horsepower Wright J-6-9 engine that was used in the N3N-3, but a few got to the end of the war with their original J-5s. The J-6-9 went out of production at Wright during the Depression, but the Navy acquired the design rights and continued to build them for years.

The N3N-1s went into service with oddly flat cowlings around their engines, but by 1941 most had been removed. The later N3N-3 with the J-6-7 (816 were built) never used a cowling as standard equipment. Principal points of recognition were tripod landing gear and a very large rudder for the N3N-1, and a single-leg gear and much smaller and more rounded rudder for the N3N-3. The single XN3N-2 was a production N3N-1 with minor improvements and enclosed cockpits. All of the N3Ns were finished in overall orange yellow and soon earned the nickname "Yellow Peril."

While all the other service biplanes were taken out of service soon after the war, the Navy kept a few N3N-3 seaplanes around well into the jet age. There was a flight of them at the Naval Academy in 1961, making the N3N the last biplane in U.S. military service. The academy probably kept them around for the same reason they had sailboats – to show its midshipmen the old way of doing things.

Surplus N3Ns were immediately in demand as dusters, and many were fitted with larger engines such as the 300-horsepower Lycoming R-680 or the 450-horsepower Pratt & Whitney Wasp Jr. Now that biplane dusters are being replaced with specially designed ag planes, the ancient N3Ns are not being scrapped; they are being reconditioned as 240-horsepower two-holers by the antiquers.

The photographs

1. The XN3N-1 prototype was photographed here in 1946 after it was modified to production standards, except for the XN3N-2 cockpit canopy. The engine is the later J-6-9 of the N3N-3 but retains the flat cowling of the -1.

2. The major production N3N was the -3, with single-leg landing gear and a redesigned tail. Duster operators usually replaced the old 30 x 5 wheels with surplus Stearman or Vultee BT-13 units.

3. The last biplanes in U.S. military service were the few kept at the Naval Academy until 1961. A few N3N seaplanes were sold surplus but are not known to have been issued standard licenses.

4. In the years immediately following World War II, N3Ns were modified and upgraded for use as dusters and sprayers. This one has a 450-horsepower Pratt & Whitney R-985 Wasp Jr. engine and a sliding canopy over the cockpit.

1

2

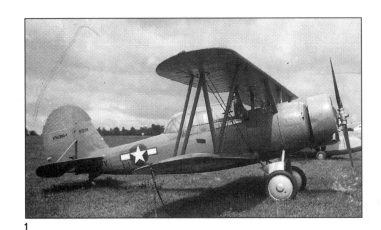

3

4

The Caproni houseboat

Eight-engine airplane got off the water (barely), but it never got off the ground

1st September 1974

There was a wide-body transport 50 years before the Boeing 747 came along, but it did not get into the history books because it never got into service. It ended up as a unique but very expensive experiment.

The Caproni firm, Italy's major aircraft manufacturer, specialized in building heavy bombers throughout World War I. One of its designs was a twin-fuselage triplane with an engine in the nose of each fuselage and a third engine mounted as a pusher in the nacelle between the fuselages. The Lockheed P-38 Lightning of World War II used the same layout without the center engine.

After the war, with visions of an air transport industry opening up, Caproni engineers came up with an ambitious transport project. Using three sets of surplus triplane bomber wings, the firm produced an eight-engine triple-tandem-wing flying boat. Unofficially, it was called the Capronissimo around the factory. Where there had been tandem-wing airplanes in the past, none had been notably successful. They all used two sets of tandem wings. Caproni was really daring in using three.

The hull, reminiscent of a houseboat, was arranged for 96 passengers in 12 rows of fixed benches that had groups of four facing each other, as on a railway coach. There were two aisles running the full length of the hull and the two pilots sat side-by-side in an open cockpit over the bow of the hull. The twin-fuselage bomber heritage was continued above the hull in the form of two boom-like structures running the full length of the ship, each with a U.S.-built 400-horsepower Liberty engine at each end. The other four engines were installed at the front and rear of two nacelles located between the booms at each end of the ship. One mechanic, controlling four engines, was seated in each of the two nacelles.

With all eight engines located at the ends of the hull and the passengers distributed the full length, contemporary technical publications described the longitudinal moment of inertia as "colossal" and questioned whether the thing could fly at all, much less under control. It did fly, however, but just barely.

The houseboat was launched for tests on Lake Maggiore in February 1921. Finally, on March 2, it made its first flight, a straight-ahead hop of about a mile. Shades of the Hughes Hercules shortly after World War II. Thanks to the dihedral, lateral stability seemed to be all right, but longitudinal control was about nil. Photos and drawings show no conventional elevators. The rear-wing ailerons might have been used for that purpose.

On the second hop, made on March 4, 1921, the aircraft got off the water, after which the flight was all down hill until it hit the water again. The pilot was unable to raise the nose, and the houseboat hit the surface slightly nose-down at flying speed. No one was hurt, but the aircraft was damaged so badly that it never was rebuilt. Alas, Caproni and the Italian nation lost the opportunity of giving the world its first wide-body airliner.

The photographs

1. Three sets of 100-foot triplane wings and a boat-like hull earned the Italian Caproni Ca-60 of 1921 the nickname "Caproni Houseboat." A WWI-era joke making the rounds about the Caproni bombers went like this: "Put a chicken between the wings; if it gets out there must be a wire missing."

2. Front view of the Ca-60 shows the generous dihedral of the nine wings. Each of the full-length booms above the hull has a 400-horsepower Liberty engine at each end. The two center nacelles each have one tractor and one pusher Liberty.

116

1

2

The first world flight, Part II

Two of the four DWCs that started actually finished the 175-day journey in 1924

2nd September 1974

Part I of this two-part story about the first world flight appears on Page 98. It covered the flight from its start in Seattle on April 6, 1924, to the halfway point at Calcutta, India, on June 26.

The major incident following departure from Calcutta was the discovery of a stowaway. A zealous newspaper reporter had welcomed the fliers to northernmost Japan and kept up with the flight the rest of the way. He had struck a friendship with the fliers, and was allowed to accompany them on the next leg, but was bumped per telegraphed orders from headquarters at the next stop. The only serious technical problem was a disintegrating engine on the New Orleans about 100 miles short of Karachi. With no terrain suitable for landing, the crew coaxed the plane into Karachi, where it got a new engine, as did the other two.

The trip through the Near East and through Southern Europe to Paris was simple compared to past adventures. In Paris, the flight encountered its normal accolade plus Bastille Day, the French equivalent of the 4th of July. After a two-day layover, the expedition made a short hop to London and then Hull, England, where it took on pontoons and new engines for the flight across the North Atlantic.

The leg from the Orkney Islands to Iceland was a disaster. The Boston and the Chicago got separated from the New Orleans while flying in fog. The Boston and the Chicago returned to the Orkneys while the New Orleans made it to Iceland. The Boston and Chicago started out again, but the Boston was soon forced down on the open sea with engine trouble. The water was rough, and when the Chicago tried to land alongside to help, it was waved off. The Boston had been damaged by the hard landing, and its crew did not want the other aircraft to risk damage. Attempts by the cruiser USS Richmond to tow the Boston were unsuccessful. When the Richmond attempted to hoist the Boston aboard, the tackle broke and the airplane sank. The Chicago, meanwhile, continued to Iceland to rejoin the New Orleans.

With their intended first landing spot in Greenland still ice-locked, the Chicago and New Orleans forged ahead with their longest leg: 835 miles. Another hop brought them to Ivigtut, where engines were changed and the ships were tuned up for the 500-mile flight to the North American mainland, which they reached on Aug. 31.

A surprise awaited them two legs further down the coast. The crew of the Boston had returned to North America by surface ship and had arranged for the prototype DWC to be renamed the Boston II and flown to Newfoundland so they could rejoin the flight. The three planes then continued to Boston, where wheels were reinstalled for the crossing of the continent.

A relatively direct crossing to Seattle was planned, but the fliers' fame and the Air Service's thirst for publicity called for a zigzag route via Washington, Dayton, St. Louis, Texas and San Diego. The actual circumnavigation of the globe was completed at San Diego, where the planes had been flown from the factory for compass swinging and other work before heading north to Seattle. The official terminus, however, was Seattle, so the three headed up the coast and arrived there on Sept. 28, 1924, 175 days after departure.

The two DWCs that actually flew all the way around the world are still in existence. The New Orleans is in the Museum of Flying in Santa Monica, California. The Chicago is in the National Air Museum of the Smithsonian Institution in Washington, DC.

Three of the crew members are also with us today. First Lieutenant Leigh Wade and Sergeant Henry Ogden, both of the Boston, and Alva Harvey, who went down with the Seattle in Alaska, are expected to be in Seattle for the 50th-anniversary celebration on Sept. 28, 1974.

The photographs

1. The Chicago gets serviced by a U.S. Navy crew while riding at anchor in Kasumigaura, Japan.

2. Pan American Airways borrowed the New Orleans from the Air Force for publicity in connection with its inauguration of scheduled around-the-world service in 1959. Pan Am flew it in 2-1/2 days compared to the DWC's 175. The 50-foot wingspan of the DWC is only four feet more than that of the horizontal tail on the Boeing 707-321.

1

2

Deliberate oil leaks

They made a convenient research tool for early-day high-performance aircraft

1st October 1974

Most pilots, especially those of older airplanes, have experienced engine-oil leaks at one time or another – and have done the usual amount of grumbling and cussing as they cleaned up the mess. Such leaks are certainly one of the major annoyances of flying.

Problems, however, can be put to good use. When they noticed that leaks followed the lines of airflow along fuselages and left a highly visible trace, engineers put oil to work on the outside of the airplane as well as inside the engine.

When really high-performance airplanes began to appear shortly before World War II, it was discovered that the shape of the nose and fuselage forward of the wing, and the wing-fuselage intersection itself, was critical. Minor changes in contour would affect the drag and consequently the performance. Considerable wind-tunnel and flight testing was done to evaluate different contours and appendage details in search of the best combination for a particular airplane. Routine oil leaks and exhaust-smoke streaks gave an indication of airflow in some of the critical areas, but not necessarily the correct ones.

The idea of using oil as a research tool was developed, and tests were made with a mixture of oil and powdered graphite or lampblack, which was applied to the nose with a paint brush just before takeoff. This system covered the desired areas all right, but had the disadvantage of being blown around by the prop and the airflow throughout all the flight attitudes from run-up to landing. Something was needed to

show airflow at specific airspeeds and trim conditions.

The problem was solved by installing special equipment: a storage tank, pump and distribution manifold with leak holes to the outside of the nose behind the propeller spinner. When the pilot was ready to test at a certain speed, he flipped the switch and the oil was pumped out. Only a small quantity was needed, and it quickly made the airflow trace for the desired condition. The stuff dried in place quickly, and the trace was not altered by subsequent airflow changes during the landing.

The photographs

1. An inadvertent oil leak is evident on this Nicholas-Beasley NB-3, powered with a British Siddely Genet radial engine. Notice how the oil has traced the airflow over the wing root. It looks as though the pilot has made just one pass with a clean-up rag before the picture was taken.

2. Deliberately leaked in this case, the oil-graphite mixture on the nose of a 1938 Curtiss YP-37 does not look very spectacular, but it's very informative. Notice that the air does now flow smoothly around the air scoop; it breaks away just aft of the lip, indicating turbulent airflow at that point and a need for redesign of the scoop.

3. More oil and a bigger mess this time. The plane is a Curtiss P-40D that was tested in June 1941. Note how the front windshield is covered, and there is evidence of a turbulence pattern on the right-hand curved panel.

1

2

3

Canadian civil aircraft markings

First it was G, then CF and finally just C

2nd October 1974

Since 1929, Canada has used the letters CF and a dash followed by three more letters as its civil aircraft registration marking. Many U.S. pilots have wondered why the Canadians are different and use letters instead of numbers. Actually, it is the United States that is different; Canada and most of the other nations of the world conform to a system that was set up by international agreement in 1919. The United States did not go along at the time and did not enforce aircraft registration until 1927. It uses the letter N to identify the country and numbers to identify the airplane. Practically everyone else uses letters throughout. Canada used the single letter G as a prefix until 1929.

CF identified Canada in the international system and the three letters after the dash identified the individual airplane. On Jan. 1, 1974, Canada dropped the CF- and used C alone as the national identifying letter. Planes that had carried CF- were then given until Dec. 31, 1983, to switch the positions of the dash and the F to come up with a registration consisting of C- and four letters. An airplane marked CF-LAT would then become C-FLAT. Airplanes on order before the end of 1973 with CF- registrations were expected to have them changed to C- before delivery in 1974.

All new registrations assigned after Jan. 1, 1974, start with the C- and then the letter G in a new series starting with C-GAAA. The new registration can be carried on each side of the fuselage or on the vertical fin in letters as large as practical but no smaller than six inches. The registration must also be carried on the underside of the left wing. No requirement exists for registration on the upper wing. With the underwing location, Canadians are ahead of the United States;

there is a lot of pressure here to have numbers under the wings so that people can identify low-flying planes for disciplinary purposes. Pilots, of course, are against this. Not that they want to avoid identification, but because of the cost and trouble of painting the numbers.

The paint problem is the reason for the generous transition period for Canadians to change from CF- to C-F. On an airplane with a coat of paint that's several years old, it would be almost impossible to get the paint to match after switching the dash and the F around, so the 10-year period is to allow reasonable time to repaint or recover.

The photographs

1. The original Canadian registration was G (for Great Britain), CA (for Canada), and two more letters for individual aircraft identification. The rudder was home to an additional G. This arrangement was used through 1928, as on this Fokker Universal.

2. In 1929 Canada adopted the new registration prefix CF, followed by three letters. The new series started at CF-AAA, so this Lockheed Vega is an early example.

3. A Stolp Starduster Two homebuilt with the new Canadian C-F arrangement. It had previously been CF-ZCK. Note the absence of wing registration letters, as allowed by revised regulations.

4. Two Cessna 150s display the two styles of Canadian registration that were allowed during the transition period. It is interesting to note that the old G-CA registrations did not have to change after the adoption of CF. They could be retained, which a few managed to do until after World War II.

1

2

3

4

A P-51 by any other name

Not necessarily a Mustang just because it looks like one

1st November 1974

The North American P-51 Mustang is probably the most famous U.S. fighter plane of World War II. There were, however, some nearly identical planes that were not P-51s.

The North American Model 73 was originally ordered by Britain in 1940. The U.S. Army wasn't very interested, but agreed to test two of the first 10 and designated them XP-51 in the P-for-pursuit series. The aircraft proved to be a lot better than the production Curtiss P-40s that were just then going into service with the same 1,100-horsepower Allison engine. A single order was placed for 150 production P-51s, indicating that the Army still did not take it very seriously as a fighter. It did, however, order 500 examples to be used as dive bombers under the designation A-36A in the A-for-attack series. The Army had other dive bombers, but using a single-seater for that purpose was something new.

In most respects, the A-36A was similar to the XP-51 and the production P-51A except for bomb racks for 500-pounders under the wings and unique dive brakes on upper and lower surfaces. Some A-36As saw action in North Africa, but there was no further development.

When the Army got its P-51s, they were different from the British models. The U.S. versions had four 20mm cannon in the wings. The A-36 had two nose guns and two more .50s in each wing.

Back in World War I, some single-seat fighters were fitted with cameras and used their speed and maneuverability to get over areas that were too heavily defended for the big and slow two-seater types to penetrate. The same problem came up in WWII, so the same thing was tried again.

At first, oblique cameras were merely installed in standard fighters with no change of designation. But as the photo equipment and controls got more elaborate, the characteristics of the airplane were altered enough to warrant a change of designation. In the case of the Lockheed P-38, the cameras went into the gun compartment, so the former P-38 airframe was no longer a fighter. Various airplane details resulted in the photo versions of the P-38 being designated F-4 and F-5 in the F-for-foto series.

In the P-51, the cameras went into the aft fuselage and did not affect the armament, but the designation was changed to F-6. This series developed in parallel with the P-51s and showed the same external and system variations. The 57 plain F-6As were redesignated from the camera-carrying P-51s and still carried their wing cannon. The 35 F-6Bs were equivalent to the P-51As, with no nose guns and only four wing guns. There were no plain F-6s. For some reason they were designated P-51-1, still with cannon.

The 91 F-6Cs were similar to the P-51B and -C. They still had the original low canopy, but they were now powered by the 1,300-horse Rolls-Royce Merlin, which was built in the U.S. by Packard. Incidentally, the Merlin installation that made such a great airplane out of the P-51 was tried in England before it was tested in converted airplanes in the United States. The two were originally designated XP-78s, but since everything aft of the firewall was identical to stock P-51s, they were redesignated XP-51Bs. The production P-51C was identical to the production -B except that it was built in North American's plant in Dallas.

Someone in authority sensibly ordered the different series letters of subsequent F-6s to match the equivalent P-51s, so the 135 F-6Ds were equivalent to the bubble-canopy P-51D and the 163 F-6Ks matched the P-51K.

In 1948 the new U.S. Air Force did away with the F-for-foto designation. F then replaced the old P-for-pursuit and became the F-for-fighter but with the same old numbers. The photo versions then became RF-51 (R for reconnaissance). Similarly, the F-9 photo conversions of the Boeing B-17 became RB-17s. The 1948 use of the R prefix should not be confused with the earlier wartime use of R on obsolete airplanes restricted from their originally designated mission, as the RP-40s that were no longer to be used for combat.

The photographs

1. Dive brakes are the most noticeable feature of the A-36A dive-bomber version of the Allison-equipped P-51A fighter. This one is undergoing testing by the Royal Air Force. Note the open brakes and the two 500-pound bombs.

2. Cannon in the wings are the distinguishing feature of the first 150 P-51s. These have the Allison engine and the original low canopy. Many were fitted with reconnaissance cameras, some as P-51-1 and some as F-6A photo planes.

3. Camera ports for oblique cameras are visible in the aft fuselage at the right edge of the insignia. This is an F-6D, with airframe and equipment other than cameras identical to the bubble-canopy P-51D.

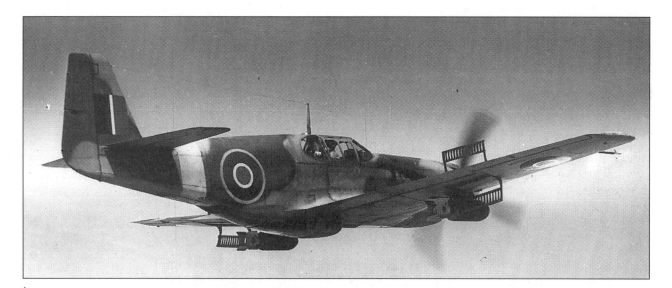

1

2

3

Doctored photographs

Wartime censorship is understandable, but emotions led to curious touch-ups

2nd November 1974

Practically anyone who has a long-term association with airplane photographs, particularly military photos, has encountered a few that have been doctored. Photos are sometimes altered simply to sharpen detail or contrast before they are used in newspapers or magazines. There are many other reasons for altering airplane photos, however. We'll illustrate a few here.

One legitimate reason is military security during times of war. The most obvious procedures are blanking out the military serial numbers on the planes and deleting background detail.

The idea behind censoring serial numbers is to keep information from the enemy. Keeping aircraft quantities secret is a priority, but several fallacies make that effort rather futile. First, for World War II at least, the serials were assigned when the planes were ordered, usually a couple of years before they were delivered. Enemy intelligence probably had knowledge of the quantities soon after the fact and did not have to wait for later photos to determine the numbers. Another fallacy was inconsistent application of the censorship policy by different censors in different areas of the country. On the other hand, deleting unit markings from combat planes in various forward or staging areas made sense in light of more immediate strategic or tactical considerations.

Deleting serial numbers goes on even in peacetime. It has long been Air Force practice to erase serials and unit markings from crash photos before releasing them to the public or to unclassified publications. This is supposedly to prevent identification of the pilot or unit.

Censoring backgrounds makes sense in wartime, particularly when it is necessary to conceal the location of a particular airplane or plant, or to cover up details of defenses around a particular factory. In nonmilitary applications, surroundings are often touched out to eliminate distractions and make the airplane stand out better. The extreme of this is to completely white out everything but the airplane, particularly on photos taken inside a cluttered factory.

Another ridiculous form of photo retouching is an at-tempt to erase bad memories. The prime example is postwar publication of German aircraft photos from 1934-45 in German books and magazines. All German planes of that period were marked with swastikas. Latter-day editors sometimes removed them without altering the rest of the marking, so it was quite obvious what had been on the plane. The swastika has been around since prehistory and is prominent in American Indian lore. Two other countries, Finland and Latvia, used it as airplane insignia before World War II, but its use as the symbol of the Nazi party made the mark itself despised. It still reminds many people of the Nazis and it is only recently that emotions have settled to the point where swastika decals are included in model kits of German WWII airplanes.

The photographs

1. A wartime censor blacked out the Army serial number on the tail of this Bell P-39Q Airacobra before the company was allowed to release it. The censor did not do a very good job. The number, 43474, is still readable.

2. No wartime censorship here; they were just suppressing details. When the second Boeing XC-97 caught fire in the air and crash landed at Wright-Patterson AFB early in 1946, officials blanked out the serial number before releasing the photo. Doing the same thing to the truck's serial number seems silly.

3. Dark camouflage paint made this 1926 experimental Boeing Model 66 fighter blend with the factory interior, so the background was blanked out. The company did not get a chance to photograph it outdoors before it was shipped to the Army. The Army bought it and designated it XP-8.

4. The German marking for civil aircraft was a black swastika inside a white circle backed by a red band. For postwar publication, the editor blanked out the swastika on this Hirth Minimoa sailplane but left the circle and band intact. The Germans deleted the band and circle on military aircraft in 1938 and used only a narrow white border around the swastika.

1

2

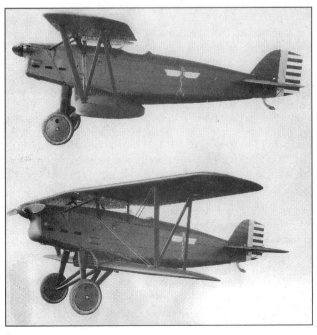

3

4

The first hang gliders

They were the earliest form of heavier-than-air human flight

1st December 1974

Hang gliding, the latest aeronautical craze, is the oldest form of heavier-than-air human flight. Its present popularity is entirely understandable. With purely recreational flying in conventional equipment rapidly being priced out of sight, a return to simple beginnings makes sense. Let's back up 83 years and see how it all got started.

Consistent manned flight began with experiments by a German engineer named Otto Lilienthal. Lilienthal studied how birds flew and he built models for 30 years before taking to the air in a man-carrying glider in 1891. During the next five years he built 18 small gliders and made approximately 2,000 flights. He gained fame and secured his place in the history books, and his name is well known to anyone with enough interest to look him up.

Not as well known is the fact that Lilienthal was also the first to build a special launch site for glider operations. Notice that I did not say airport or even gliderport, for Lilienthal's site was exactly the opposite of what we imagine an airport should be. He needed a facility that was suited to the characteristics of his flying machines, and that is just what he built: a low conical hill in an otherwise flat area. Since his gliders only descended, they had to be launched from up high. They also had to be launched into the wind. If the wind was wrong, there was no flying.

From his cone, Lilienthal could always launch into the wind and have clear ground on which to land. The earth for this private mountain came from a canal that had been dug near his home in Berlin. The details are not available, but in those days before heavy equipment, piling up that much dirt must have been a tremendous task.

Unlike many of the modern hang gliders, the Lilienthals and their successors, the Pilchers and Chanutes, did not have moveable control surfaces. Control was by body English. The pilot moved his weight to change the balance and trim of the glider.

By experiment, Lilienthal soon found that a wingspan of approximately 20 feet was all that a man could control. While more span was desirable, the inertia was too much for one man to overcome with limited movement. Lilienthal recognized the need for mechanical control, so he developed a rudder that worked with cables connected to a headband. The head was the only part of the pilot that was free to operate such a control. His legs had to swing for balance, and he needed his hands and arms to hang on to the machine. Lilienthal was testing this setup when he stalled and fell to his death on Aug. 9, 1896. It remained for the Wright brothers to establish the final workable combination for successful flight: long-span wings and three axes of mechanical control.

Lilienthal tackled the problem of getting more wing area without increasing the span by adding wings and found that the drag increased and the glide angle decreased. After the serious and organized sport of gliding and soaring got underway in Germany following World War I, wingspan became the general index of a glider's performance. The glide ratios on some of today's 60-foot spans are nearly 50:1 while the old 20-foot biplane hang gliders did well to get 2:1 or 3:1.

Comparative performances are not important to current hang-glider enthusiasts. They are out for the sheer joy of inexpensive flight. Incidentally, the term that is preferred these days is "foot-launched glider" rather than hang glider. Back when there were only hang gliders, there was no need for the term for identification. After the more modern designs with seated pilots and airplane-type controls appeared in the 1920s, and the older designs were still in use, the need to distinguish them arose. While most of the latter-day hang gliders feature mechanical control and most of the pilots are supported by slings instead of truly hanging, as in the past, it looks like the name hang glider will stick.

The photographs

1. "Body English" is demonstrated by Otto Lilienthal during a flight in one of his monoplane hang gliders sometime between 1891 and 1896. Note that the framework is not laid out in the later spars-and-ribs pattern. Lilienthal patterned his wings after those of birds.

2. The first launch facility was this 60-foot-high mound that Lilienthal built for consistent into-the-wind downhill launches of his hang gliders. He later moved on to higher natural hills.

1

2

More doctored photos

Some scenes aren't what they appear

2nd December 1974

Our previous column on doctored photos (Page 126) concerned censored markings on aircraft. This time, the photo itself has undergone major alterations to make the scene appear entirely different from what it actually was.

Back in the early days of World War II, Bell Aircraft and the U.S. Army Air Forces got a lot of publicity mileage from a spectacular photo of one of the new Bell P-39 Airacobra fighters that was firing its guns at night. As printed in the newspapers and magazines, the picture appeared to be a very close-in shot of the powerfully armed fighter in full flight with all guns blazing. The use of tracer bullets added to the effect.

Getting an actual flight scene like this would have taken some doing. A check of the perspective reveals that the camera used a normal lens and was placed quite close to the subject. If the camera were in another plane, the formation flying would have been terrifically close. It would have been tricky enough under the best of conditions, and even more difficult at night, particularly with the subject pilot firing his guns as well as holding formation.

As can be seen from the second photo, the flight was a fake and the photographer was safely on the ground. Other than the gunnery, which was real enough, all the "action" was the result of a retouched photo.

There was a lot to do, such as blacking out all of the ground details and then removing the landing gear and closing up the nosewheel doors. To get a little more action into the scene, the "flight" picture was tilted a bit.

It may be confusing to those who come across this shot in old magazines to find it credited to two sources. The manufacturer released it, with the military censor's approval, and got the proper credit lines in various publications. The Air Force made copies of the photo and released them on its own, so other prints appear as "Official Photo U.S. Army Air Force" even though it was not an original Army photo. Much can be written on the subject of incorrect photo credits.

As is to be expected from any new and successful gimmick, it was soon copied, and both Lockheed with its P-38 and Republic with its spectacular eight-gun P-47 were soon out with "night flight" shots of their own.

The Bell P-39 itself was a sensation when it went into service in 1941. In addition to its "new" feature of tricycle landing gear, it had its Allison engine located amidships behind the pilot, who was in a coupe-like cockpit with automotive-type doors on each side. The propeller was driven by a spur gear at the end of a 10-foot extension shaft, and a 37-millimeter cannon fired through the hollow prop hub.

Before they were able to mount them in the wings – a World War II innovation – forward-firing cannon on fighters shot through the prop hub, not between the blades as the machine guns did. This arrangement started with the French Spad in World War I, with the short cannon nestled between the cylinder blocks of the V-8 Hispano-Suiza engine. As on the P-39, the prop was driven by a spur gear to align it with the cannon.

The rest of the P-39's armament was heavy by U.S. standards of the time: two .50-caliber machine guns in the nose and two .30-calibers in each wing. While the P-39 did not stack up well against other fighters, particularly the Japanese Zero, and was rejected as a fighter by the British, its firepower was put to good use by the Soviets. They found that it was just great for shooting up German tanks and that it could absorb terrific punishment from enemy fire and still get home. Of 9,558 P-39s built, the Soviets got 4,773 plus a couple of hundred of the British rejects.

A very few P-39s got into civilian hands after the war and had short racing careers. Only one, Mira Slovak's "Mr. Mennen," is believed to be around today. It's expected to show up on the racing circuit again.

The photographs

1. This World War II publicity photo of a Bell P-39D Airacobra is not what it seems. The aircraft is supposed to be firing all its guns – six machine guns and a cannon – during a night flight.

2. Actually, the warbird was not flying at all. It was tied down at the test-firing range at the factory. A little artwork transferred the plane from the ground to the night sky.

130

1

2

Kondor's cut-and-try

D-VI biplane was Germany's best example of aeronautical experimentation

1st January 1975

Back in World War I days, the development of a "new" airplane was often a simple case of "cut and try" experimentation. Such things were sometimes very simple. Relatively minor modifications were made to an existing model and – Presto! – a new model.

In other cases, the better features of two successful models were combined to produce a new one that only sometimes was a distinct improvement over both of its predecessors. The outstanding example of this technique is the Curtiss JN series, notably the JN-4, which resulted from the combination of models J and N. Curtiss was the leading exponent of "cut and try" in the United States from 1910 to the end of World War I, but the company never produced another hybrid that matched the Jenny.

A good example of "cut and try" on the German side during World War I is the Kondor D-VI of 1918. The aircraft was one of several unsuccessful experimental fighters that were turned out by the Kondor Flugzeugwerke G.m.b.H. of Gelsenkirchen-Rotthausen. An earlier experimental model was a thoroughly conventional single-seat biplane that was powered with a 140-horsepower Oberursel rotary engine, which was a copy of the French Le Rhone.

One of the undesirable features of biplane fighters was poor visibility up and forward. In some cases, the problem was solved by putting a window in the center section, as on the British Sopwith Camel. In others, it was handled with a big cutout in the trailing edge of the center section, as on the French Spad. Aerodynamically, it was best to have no cutout at all, but the feature was needed for another reason: to enable the pilot to get into the cockpit.

Kondor sought to improve visibility by eliminating the center section of an established model, but the results were different than expected. While the visibility of the new D-VI model was terrific, the aerodynamics were horrible. Kondor, in those dark ages of aerodynamic knowledge, had managed to produce a biplane with six wingtips. Knowing a lot more about tip vortices, gaps in continuous spans and such things today, we can forgive Kondor for an honest but futile effort to overcome a tactical deficiency in a military airplane.

Eliminating the center section also introduced some interesting structural problems. With no spars to carry the compression loads between the two upper wing panels and no closed structure to anchor the roll wires found on conventional biplanes, Kondor had to develop rigid steel tube trusses to support the upper wings and the landing wires.

With the tail surfaces working in two wingtip vortices as well as the usual turbulence caused by the cockpit cutout and the pilot's head and shoulders, the D-VI was quickly rejected. The effort, however, was not in vain. It was now the summer of 1918, and Fokker had just broken the long-standing "monoplane barrier" and won an order from the German Army for the E-V parasol monoplane fighter that was soon to be redesignated D-VIII. Other manufacturers rushed to design new parasol monoplanes, but all Kondor had to do was develop a monoplane wing to fit onto the rigid center-section trusses of the D-VI fuselage.

The result was another new model, the E-III. Unfortunately for its manufacturer, 140 horsepower was inadequate for fighters by the time it appeared. That rendered the E-III noncompetitive against Allied models. An improved E-IIIA with a 200-horse Goebel rotary was quite successful and won a production order, but the war was over before any could be delivered.

While most postwar German fighters were scrapped or turned over to the Allies, several E-IIIAs were flown by factory pilots to Switzerland, where they were put to good use.

The photographs

1. While attempting to improve upward and forward visibility, Kondor eliminated the center section of the upper wing and unknowingly added the aerodynamic handicaps of six wingtips. This is the experimental D-VI model, which was tested in the spring of 1918.

2. Developing new models in the old days was sometimes merely a matter of substituting major components. This successful Kondor E-IIIA parasol monoplane was the result of attaching a cantilever monoplane wing to the rigid center-section supports of the unsuccessful D-VI biplane.

1

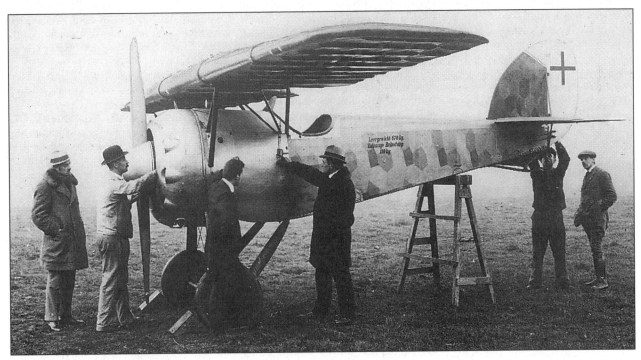

2

Japanese crosses

After the war, the rising sun gave way temporarily to an Allied-ordered insignia

2nd January 1975

Since the days of World War I, when distinctive national insignia were applied to military aircraft, the rising sun of Japan has been one of the simplest and most logical markings used. The Japanese call it the heinomaru, but Allied pilots in World War II referred to it with considerably less respect. They called it the meatball. Even American noncombatants were kept familiar with the marking through aircraft-recognition posters, security warnings, etc.

For a short time, however, some Japanese military airplanes flew with a marking that relatively few Allied personnel saw. It was a straight-sided cross that was similar to what the German Luftwaffe used, but it did not mean that Hitler had taken over Japan. The war in the Pacific was actually over when the temporary marking was used.

Why the change from a white-bordered red circle to a green cross? It wasn't originated by the Japanese, but by Allied headquarters when surrender negotiations were underway. With surface ships too slow to cover the Pacific distances in reasonable time, the Japanese plenipotentiaries came to Allied headquarters by air. Since they would be using first-line military aircraft, measures were taken to ensure that a Japanese bomber headed for the meeting place was actually carrying officials and was not a maverick with a crew of no-surrender zealots on a kamikaze mission.

For positive identification, the Allies decreed that the special airplanes should be painted all white and be marked with green crosses in place of the normal military insignia. The two Mitsubishi G4M2 bombers (Allied code name Betty) were the first planes so marked, and they were about the only ones to get their pictures in the papers.

The cross saw limited use on other planes, however, as there was a need for air transportation of Japanese officials arranging withdrawal of troops from Japanese-occupied areas on mainland China and elsewhere. As a result, some military two-seaters and light transports also got the white paint and green crosses. One oddity here was that some Mitsubishi A6M5 Zero fighters (Allied code name Zeke 52) also got the crosses but not the overall white paint. Their crosses were formed by using white squares painted over the original circles.

Since the Zeroes certainly were not needed in a defense role against Allied aircraft, I would guess that they flew escort to some of the transports to protect them from armed zealots who might want to interfere with the surrender operations and keep fighting.

The photographs

1. This Mitsubishi G4M2 bomber was used to transport Japanese plenipotentiaries to Allied headquarters for surrender negotiations at the end of World War II. The plane is all white with green crosses.

2. A Mitsubishi A6M5 Zero carries the famous heinomaru red circle, called meatball by the Allies. Note that it is backed by a white circle when used on dark backgrounds, but is not bordered when used against a light background, as on the underside of the wing.

3. Some Japanese fighters like this Zero carried the green crosses, but used only white squares as background instead of painting the entire airplane white.

1

2

3

The Seversky SEV-3

Three-seater had wheels in its pontoons, whose angles could be altered

1st February 1975

The story about the Edo Corporation's search for the Seversky SV-1 amphibian on the front page of the 1st January issue of the *Flyer* brought me a few queries.

First, a correction regarding nomenclature is in order. The plane is not the SV-1; it's the SEV-3. As the builder rather than the designer, perhaps Edo does not have accurate records of the aircraft, or perhaps it was called that around the shop when it was being built. The letters SEV stood for Seversky, and, since it was a three-seater, the plane was officially designated the SEV-3. The later SEV-1s were single-seat fighters. Production versions of that first amphibian were SEV-3M-WW for three-place military model with Wright Whirlwind engine.

The unique features of the SEV-3 were the use of wheels in the pontoons, the fact that the angle of the pontoons could be altered for flight and ground angles, the elliptical planform of the wing, and the bronze finish that was applied over the aluminum monocoque structure.

Seversky Aircraft Corporation was formed in 1931 by a group of Russian refugees that included Alexander P. De Seversky, a World War I pilot. Since they did not have a factory of their own, their first plane was built for them by Edo, the well-known pontoon builder. The letters EDO are the acronym for founder Earl D. Osborn.

After setting amphibian speed records in the prototype, which was registered X-2106 and was powered with a 420-horsepower Wright J-6-9 Whirlwind, Seversky went after military business. The Air Corps tested the X-2106 at Wright Field, but had no requirements for such an amphibian. Seversky converted it to a land plane and called it the SEV-2XA for two-place experimental Army. That configuration resulted in a milestone order for BT-8 basic trainers, the Army's first monoplane trainer and its first trainer using all-metal construction. The X-2106 was a company-owned airplane that never became Army property. After testing, it went back to Seversky and was converted back to an SEV-3 amphibian. With a new 710-horsepower Wright R-1820 Cyclone engine, it set more amphibian speed records.

The second Seversky airplane, registered X-18Y, was a near-duplicate of the SEV-2XA. It started out as a two-seat fighter with an 800-horsepower Cyclone engine. With an Air Corps pursuit-plane competition coming up in 1935, it was converted to the single-place SEV-1XP with retractable landing gear. After a change to the 1,000-horsepower Pratt & Whitney R-1830 Twin Wasp engine it eventually won the competition and a 1936 production order for 77 P-35s. The X-18Y then went back to Seversky and became a racer.

The P-35 evolved through the single XP-41 into the P-43 of 1940. A stretched version with the big 2,000-horsepower Pratt & Whitney R-2800 Double Wasp engine became the immortal P-47 Thunderbolt of World War II.

The Seversky Aircraft Corporation became Republic Aviation Corporation in 1939 as the result of a reorganization that ousted Seversky. He was on a European sales tour at the time and found that he had no job to come home to.

As for the possible existence of the Seversky prototype, it's an interesting question. According to aviation historian Kenn Rust, the X-2106 was sold to an individual in Mexico in 1938. That shouldn't be hard to check out. FAA files would show if an export license had ever been issued for it, after which a check of Mexican files should reveal the ownership and subsequent maintenance history.

If that lead is no good, rumor has it that one or more of the export SEV-3M-WWs is still airworthy in Colombia. South America has recently been a prime source of vintage expatriate American airplanes for U.S. museums and affluent collectors like the Confederate Air Force.

The photographs

1. The Seversky SEV-3 prototype flies past downtown Manhattan with Alexander De Seversky at the controls. Note that the Edo amphibious floats are trimmed to the minimum drag position. Compare the original tailwheel mounting with the later photos.

2. The prototype was converted to this two-seat SEV-2XA for evaluation by the Army Air Corps. This configuration resulted in an order for BT-8 basic trainers with the same landing-gear fairings but a greatly enlarged canopy. Note the early modified canopy and deletion of side windows.

3. The SEV-3 is shown here with its floats trimmed for takeoff and landing as a land plane. This is actually a five-point configuration, as there are small wheels in the water rudders as well as the two main wheels and the tailwheel.

1

2

3

The Thunderbird

W-14 had a tough go against the Big Four of the day

2nd February 1975

The word Thunderbird, which originated in American Indian mythology, is quite popular today. We have Thunderbird automobiles, wines, motels and airports. It would seem logical to have an airplane called the Thunderbird.

Well, there was. The Thunderbird first appeared in July 1926 when a biplane designed by Theodore A. Woolsey made its first flight. The airplane itself was as good as most of its contemporaries and better than some, but it takes more than just a good name and an average airplane to make the big time in aviation.

The Thunderbird W-14 was thoroughly conventional for its day. It had welded steel-tube fuselage, tail and wingtips, and wood-frame wings. All were fabric-covered. The airplane was a three-seater with the pilot in the single rear cockpit and the passengers sitting side-by-side up front. The original powerplant was the still-plentiful war-surplus Curtiss OX-5. With only 90 horsepower, the engine was barely suitable for bare-minimum airplanes. Its principal asset was its availability at bargain-basement prices of $250 to $500.

The Thunderbird Aircraft Company was formed to manufacture the Thunderbird, and deliveries began in late 1927. The original plant was in Los Angeles, but a move was soon made to larger quarters in Glendale, California.

If the Thunderbird had any major shortcomings, they would have to be the combination of a late entry in an overcrowded field and all the handicaps of a new and small outfit trying to compete with the establishment. When the W-14 entered the market, most of the three-seater OX-5 business was handled by the Big Four of Travel Air, Waco, Alexander (Eaglerock) and American Eagle. Next in line were Swallow, Kreider-Riesner (Challenger), Lincoln-Page, Air King and International.

Everybody recognized the shortcomings of the OX-5 and went to more power, first with the 150- to 180-horsepower Wright A, E or I engines. American-built versions of the famous French Hispano-Suiza, they were called Hissos in the States.

The Thunderbird followed right along and came out with the W-14H (H for Hisso). The boost in power did little, however, to help the Thunderbird in the marketplace. The competition was already going on to the next generation of light American radial engines that appeared in 1928: the Warners, Axelsons (Flo-Co) and Kinners. While those engines were infinitely more expensive than the water-cooled war-surplus models, their lighter weight, easier maintenance and greater reliability more than offset their price tags.

Thunderbird development stopped with the W-14H. Most of the others carried on until the Depression wiped out three-seat biplane production. Despite the more powerful models, the basic OX-5 models continued to sell into 1930, but by that time Thunderbird was no longer a significant producer.

The photographs

1. This 1928 Thunderbird W-14 was equipped with a 90-horsepower Curtiss OX-5. The factory lettering on the nose reads "THUNDERBIRD," with "The Wings Of The Wind" below. The use of the letter N in registrations of the time meant that the airplane was registered but was not licensed.

2. The Thunderbird W-14H was an improved model with the 150-horsepower Hisso instead of the OX-5. The only outward difference was the slightly larger cowling around the bigger engine, and different spacing of the exhaust stacks. Note the wire wheels without brakes.

3. This patched-up W-14H was flying without a license when it was photographed in Oregon in the late 1930s. Oregon, one of the last states where planes without federal licenses were allowed to fly, was a haven for relics that could not fly elsewhere. Old 5457, therefore, could have been the last Thunderbird in regular use.

4. This landing view of W-14 N5830 shows the unique curved shape of the belly radiator. Belly radiators on contemporary OX-5- and Hisso-powered models were rectangular.

1

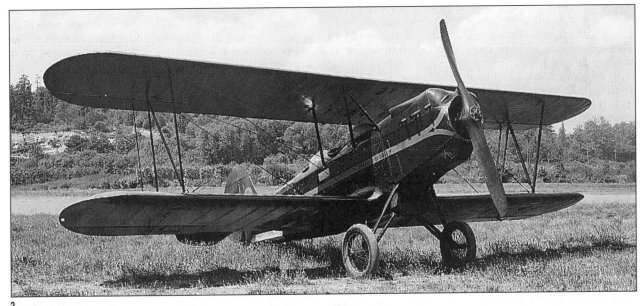

2

3   4

Elephant races

National Air Races once had several events for large aircraft

1st March 1975

Mention air racing today and most people think of hopped-up single-seaters roaring around the pylons. Until a few years ago, we also had cross-country races leading into major pylon events like the National Air Races. Cross-country races seem to be dead now, except for the annual Powder Puff Derby, which is something quite different.

Today's racing is confined almost exclusively to the pylon events and the hottest single-seaters around. There was an interesting variation back in 1970 called the California 1000 in which a four-engine Douglas DC-7 placed sixth. That event was won by a single-seater with long-range tanks. Most of the other fast single-seaters had to make stops for fuel, which gave the transport an advantage.

The appearance of a four-engine plane on a pylon course was quite a novelty at the time, but old-timers will remember when the National Air Races of the 1920s had not one but several events for the bigger ships. One of the earliest was the Liberty Engine Builders Trophy Race, which was held for several years. Sponsored by the manufacturers of the World War I Liberty engine, the race was limited to standard service observation planes. Since it was just one event in a series of U.S. races, Liberty Trophy entries were predominantly from the United States. In 1925, however, France won when it sent over a pair of Breguet observation planes.

Even the multi-engine types had their own races. There were events for military bombers and transports, as well as for civilian transports. While certainly slower than the high-powered single-seaters and even the two-seaters, the bombers and transports looked like turtles as they lumbered around the pylons. You can thank a phenomenon called "proportional speed" for that. Say a Martin NBS-1 bomber is 42 feet long and a contemporary pursuit plane is just half of that. If both are flying at the same speed, the pursuit is going twice its own length in the same time that it takes the bomber to go its own length. That makes the bigger aircraft look as if it is going half as fast as the smaller pursuit. Add in the actual difference in speed – 160 mph for a Curtiss PW-8 pursuit

and 99 mph for the Martin – and the effect is amplified. The comparison to an elephant race under such conditions is appropriate. The public must have loved it, however, for the events lasted several years.

The National Air Races of those years were quite different from today's events in other ways. They ran longer, for one thing. The nationals of 1929 lasted from Aug. 24 through Sept. 2. In addition to 35 events, including dead-stick landing and balloon-busting, they had "On To Cleveland" races from various parts of the country in which civilian pilots flew stock commercial airplanes.

There were also several pylon events that were open to anyone with stock planes in various engine-displacement categories, including events for planes powered with the Curtiss OX-5. The events died out in the early 1930s after special race planes began to dominate, and the number of pylon events dropped to a very few for the built-for-purpose racers.

It would be interesting to find out if someone could successfully hold a stock-airplane race with cross-country events and pylon events for unmodified models like Piper J-3s and Cessna 150s.

The photographs

1. The Dayton Chamber of Commerce Trophy at the 1924 National Air Races was won by the four-wheeled Martin MB-1 transport on the left. The aircraft had been built for the Post Office as a mail plane, but was turned over to the Army for use as a transport. The plane at the right is a Martin NBS-1 bomber. Both were powered by two 400-horse Liberty engines.

2. The first production model of the famous Ford Trimotor rounds the home pylon in the Detroit News Transport event at the 1926 Philadelphia races. Though spectacular, it did not win; a single-engine Bellanca took the trophy.

3. An Army Keystone LB-7 bomber practically puts a wingtip on the ground as it rounds a pylon in the late 1920s. With extra cockpits and crew, the larger airplanes provided opportunities for spectacular air-to-air photographs.

1

2

3

The Bowlus Baby Albatross

Designed by the man who built the 'Spirit of St. Louis,' it was for the Sunday soaring pilot

2nd March 1975

In the booming homebuilt airplane business, the glider category seems to have been pretty much ignored. There are plans for gliders and sailplanes that can be built at home, but they seem to be at both ends of the performance scale, not in the middle. We see plans for low-performance types like updated primaries and several high-performance "lead sled" types. There's nothing much around in the line of a relatively simple, low-cost, utility sailplane for recreational soaring.

Back in the middle and late 1930s, long before the present homebuilt trend got underway, the sport of soaring was catching on in the United States. A number of manufacturers produced good training and utility sailplanes, and plans for domestic and imported designs were available for those who wanted to build their own.

There was, however, no amateur-built category in those days, and no official recognition of homebuilts. Most of the operations with homebuilt planes and gliders were strictly bootleg.

That meant that for their operation to be legal, the amateur-built gliders as well as the airplanes had to be licensed to the same standards required for the standard production models. For the amateur who designed and built his own, the costs were prohibitive, which is why there were so few acknowledged homebuilts during that era.

There was one man who recognized the need for a recreational sailplane that did not carry the full price tag of a factory-built model. William Hawley Bowlus, famous as the shop manager who built Charles Lindbergh's "Spirit of St. Louis," had been a glider enthusiast since his youth. He developed a number of highly successful sailplanes, and he even got the Lindberghs enthusiastic about them.

In 1938 he developed a unique design known as the Baby Albatross. Built especially for the Sunday soaring pilot, the design was representative of the "floaters" of the day: long-span ships built as light as possible to reduce sinking speed for slope soaring, which was the standard technique of the day. Bowlus saved on weight and drag by shortening the traditional fuselage to a short pod and carrying the tail surfaces on an aluminum-tube boom.

Bowlus put the Baby Albatross on the market as a type-certificated sailplane that could be assembled at home and still qualify for a standard license.

Instead of a roll of blueprints and a bundle of sticks, the Baby Albatross came as a 10-unit kit-built series of components. The instructions did not show how to build a rib or hack out a fitting; they merely showed how to fasten factory-built Item A to Item B, and so on. The customer did not actually build anything. He assembled ready-made parts.

Because of the absence of this class of sailplane today, considerable interest has been shown in building something similar to the old Bowlus. As a well-known pack rat of data on old aircraft, I have gotten several requests lately for Baby Albatross plans. I do have a set, but they are no help in building a glider for the reasons I just mentioned.

Don't try to track down a set of factory layouts through the old Bowlus organization either; they don't exist. I know, because Hawley Bowlus and his son were interested in building a Baby Albatross a few years ago, and they contacted me in search of an old pod that could be pulled apart so that the rings could be used to make new patterns.

The photographs

1. A pair of Bowlus Baby Albatross utility sailplanes at the Seattle Sky Sports field. N28387 on the left is the kit-built model with molded plywood pod. N25605, owned by the author, is the third prototype. It uses a built-up plywood pod. The striped tail was a trademark of the old Bowlus designs.

2. A flight view of N25605 shows the Baby Albatross' 44-foot wingspan, the aluminum-tube tail boom and the pendulum elevators without fixed horizontal stabilizers. Now called flying tails, they have become popular on production airplanes in recent years, but incorporate tabs to impart the essential feel that was lacking in the 1930s designs.

3. N25605 takes off on an auto tow. The closed parachute ahead of it lets the 1,200-foot steel wire towline down gently as the tow car decelerates after the glider has released.

1

2

3

Linke-Hoffman's giant

Big biplane had four Mercedes engines driving one propeller

1st April 1975

Germany, more than any other nation during World War I, went to great lengths to develop very large airplanes. So numerous were its designs, in fact, that a special designation was created. It was known as the R class, or Reisenflugzeug, which meant giant airplane and identified the models by sheer size rather than military function.

The most successful designer of the R types was Zeppelin, better known for its rigid airships. The Zeppelin R types were the only ones to actually get into series production. They were also subcontracted to several other manufacturers.

One of the more unusual designs was the single Linke-Hoffman R-II, which was built in 1918 by the Linke-Hoffman Werke of Breslau. Linke-Hoffman started developing giant designs in 1916 and later got in on building Zeppelin R-VIs under license. The firm was well experienced in the field when it got underway on its R-II.

At first glance, the R-II was a thoroughly conventional biplane. It had a few obvious contradictions, however. The tail was a big biplane structure representative of the other giants and some twin-engine bombers while the front end, with a single two-wheel landing gear under the fuselage and only a single propeller in the nose, looked like a normal single-engine design.

The surprise feature of the R-II was its four engines and one propeller. From the Wright brothers forward, there have been many examples of one engine driving more than one propeller, but the opposite case, of several engines driving one propeller, is rare.

All four 260-horsepower Mercedes engines of the Linke-Hoffman R-II were installed inside the fuselage, contributing greatly to aerodynamic cleanliness by eliminating the traditional engine nacelles. The hookup to the prop was relatively simple and worked very well. Two engines on each side of the fuselage were parallel to the longitudinal axis and faced each other. Those pairs were connected to each other and the opposite pair through gear boxes. The single propeller, the biggest ever installed on any airplane, had a diameter of 23 feet (compared to 17 for a World War II B-29) and was geared down to a mere 545 rpm.

The airplane had a wingspan of 138 feet 4 inches, not quite four feet short of the B-29 (141 feet). Since it was a biplane, it had more area (3,443 square feet compared to the B-29's 1,739). Gross weight was 26,460 pounds against 105,000 for the early B-29. The top speed was only 80.8 mph, compared to the B-29's 365. It is hard to believe that such a mass could be dragged into the air with only 1,040 horsepower.

The R-II was not completed in time to see war service, but it did start its test flights in January 1919. A commercial version was planned when the bomber proved to have good performance and handling characteristics, but the Allied ban on the building of large airplanes shelved it. (The ban was not lifted until 1926.) The R-II was damaged on one of its test flights and dropped from sight. Whether that was due to extensive damage or to the scrapping edict of the Allied Control Commission is not known.

In any case, the Linke-Hoffman R-II stands as one of the world's more unusual airplanes.

The photographs

1. The Linke-Hoffman R-II of World War I was only one of numerous German experiments in the line of giant airplanes. It had nearly the wingspan of a B-29, double the wing area, and flew on only 1,040 horsepower.

2. While the boxy tail of the R-II looked like those of other big bombers, the front end with its single propeller and two-wheel landing gear made the four-engine giant look like smaller single-engine designs.

1

2

Curtiss Page Navy racer

Navy converted it from a biplane fighter to a monoplane champion

2nd April 1975

Biplanes and monoplanes are two distinct types of airplanes, but in rare cases one is converted to another. Perhaps the most famous example is the surgery performed on a standard Curtiss Hawk F6C-3 biplane fighter in 1930. Originally a standard shipboard Navy fighter, this well-known single-seater was converted to a seaplane for the 1930 Curtiss Marine Trophy Race in Anacostia, Maryland. An annual competition for military seaplanes, it was sponsored by the Curtiss Company.

The conversion for this race was nothing extraordinary. Twin wooden floats were substituted for the standard wheel landing gear. One innovation that would be copied by later racers took place, however: Many of the small gaps and joints in the cowling, etc., were carefully taped over. That gave the plane a somewhat messy appearance, but the gimmick paid off. The F6C-3, piloted by Marine Captain Arthur Page, won the race with a speed of 164.1 mph.

The airplane was strictly a stock service fighter, except for the strut roots, which were taped and streamlined with putty. The powerplant was the standard Curtiss D-12 engine, a water-cooled V-12 that put out a normal 435 horsepower from a displacement of 1,150 cubic inches.

With its victory secure, the F6C-3 was sent back to the Curtiss factory for a major rebuild. Its next challenge was the Thompson Trophy Race, which was to be held at the National Air Races in Chicago from Aug. 23 through Sept. 1. The photos here show its conversion from a biplane to a parasol monoplane, which involved more than just removing the bottom wing. Since the Hawk biplane wings were heavily staggered, it was necessary to move the upper wing aft nearly a foot to keep the hot ship balanced. Considerable weight was added up front, however, when the old D-12 engine was replaced by the later Curtiss V-1570 Conqueror. The powerplant was another stock fighter engine that normally delivered 600 horsepower. For the Thompson Trophy Race, it was hopped up to somewhere between 700 and 800 horsepower.

Other alterations included replacement of the core-type nose radiator with thin "skin" radiators built onto the upper and lower surfaces of the wings, an extensive cleanup of the fuselage lines and intersections, and reduction of the cockpit cutout. The plane, finished in time for thorough testing at the factory, did not suffer the usual rash of last-minute construction just before the race. While the full range of test data was not obtained, it was estimated that the XF6C-6, as the plane was now officially known, was capable of 250 mph on the straightaway.

Despite the new designation, the plane quickly became known as The Page Navy Racer with Captain Page flying it. The name stuck.

Naturally, the Curtiss was the favored entry in the race. It was first in the air after the starter's flag dropped, and it had nearly lapped the five-mile course when the last entry took off. Page easily maintained his lead, and was averaging 219 mph through the 17th lap of 20 when he was overcome by carbon monoxide fumes, crashed and was killed. The race was won by Northwest Airways pilot Charles "Speed" Holman, who was flying a Laird biplane that had been built in 31 days and had only 10 minutes of test time on it. Holman's time was 201.9 mph.

The photographs

1. The Curtiss Hawk F6C-3 was a stock Navy shipboard fighter in 1927-29. When the Navy standardized air-cooled radial engines for shipboard use, liquid-cooled fighters were withdrawn from the fleet.

2. This Curtiss F6C-3 on twin floats won the 1930 Curtiss Marine Trophy Race with only minor cleanup. The same plane, a stock fighter, was then rebuilt as the special XF6C-6 racer for the 1930 Thompson Trophy Race.

3. With its lower wing removed, the landing gear changed to single-strut type, and its radiator built into its wings, the suped-up XF6C-6 was the heavy favorite to win the 1930 Thompson Trophy. It was leading the field when it pilot, Captain Arthur Page, was overcome by carbon monoxide fumes and crashed.

4. Side view of the XF6C-6 emphasizes the rearward relocation of the single wing. Special race coloring, instead of the traditional Navy overall silver, was blue fuselage, tail and landing gear, with gold wings.

1

2

3

4

Sweepback and the Great Lakes

The Model 2T's snappy appearance was born of necessity

1st May 1975

One of the distinctive features of the famous Great Lakes Model 2T biplane is the nine-degree sweepback of the upper wing. Would you believe it wasn't always there?

When the airplane was designed in 1929, it was intended to be one of the new-generation sport and training biplanes that would be powered with the four-cylinder air-cooled Cirrus engine.

The Cirrus, one of the new crop that had come along in the late 1920s, was the replacement engine for the heavy Curtiss OX-5, a water-cooled V-8 that had been the standby of general aviation since World War I.

Most of the OX-5-powered ships were big three-seaters such as the Travel Air, Eaglerock, American Eagle and Waco 10. The new engines were also in the 90-horsepower range, but they were smaller, with less displacement, and considerably lighter. The Cirrus had 310 cubic inches compared to the OX-5's 505. With the lighter engines came small two-seaters. Besides the Great Lakes Model 2T, there was the well-known Fleet Model 2 that used the 90-horsepower Kinner air-cooled radial.

One feature on most of the older biplanes was the location of the front cockpit between the center-section struts. That wasn't much of a problem. The planes were big, with plenty of gap between the wings, and getting in and out wasn't difficult. For the smaller planes, however, the narrower wing gap made front-cockpit entry something of a struggle.

Great Lakes and Fleet went at the problem the same way. They put the center-section struts ahead of the front cockpit. Great Lakes did it by moving the upper wing farther ahead than was normal. Fleet canted the struts sharply forward from the wing to the fuselage. Each also put a large cutout in the trailing edge of the center section to further simplify the access-from-the-rear technique.

The system worked fine for the Fleet, but with its top wing a little too far forward, the Great Lakes turned out to be a little tail heavy. The problem could not be solved by moving the straight wing aft a bit without complicating the access problem, so a different approach was tried. The center section was left right where it was, and the outer panels were swept back just a bit over nine degrees to move the center of lift aft the required distance for good balance. An additional benefit was the distinctive appearance that the sweep gave the airplane. Only three or four Model 2Ts were built with the straight wing before the sweepback was added to make the Model 2T-1A.

While it never caught up with the Fleet in overall popularity, the Great Lakes was well received and was particularly desirable as an aerobatic trainer and air-show performer. Unfortunately, the Cirrus engine had many shortcomings and proved to be a handicap. Some owners started replacing them with other models in the 1930s. In the post-WWII years of the antique airplane boom, practically every original Great Lakes still flying used a later-day replacement engine.

The old 1929 design, put back in production this past year, uses a flat-four engine and retains the distinctive swept-back upper wing.

The photographs

1. One of the original Great Lakes 2T-1s with the straight upper wing, this aircraft has the original upright Cirrus engine and the small vertical tail.

2. Matching side view shows the change in appearance of the Great Lakes 2T-1A compared to the unswept 2T-1 model. Note the revised landing gear.

3. Flight view of the Model 2T-1A emphasizes the width of the straight upper wing center section and the sweepback of the outer wing panels.

1

2

3

The forgotten Douglas

Thanks to World War II, there was little interest in the DC-5

2nd May 1975

With the exception of the DC-1, which was a single prototype airplane, all of the Douglas DC airplanes have been built in production quantities for use by the airlines.

Again, with one exception, everything from the DC-2 to the DC-10 has had such wide exposure that it is readily identifiable to practically anyone with the slightest knowledge of recent aviation history. The exception, however, is the DC-5, also known as the Missing DC or the DC What?

The DC-5, the only high-wing DC model, was designed for a somewhat different airline market than the famous DC-3. The general structural features, however, reflected contemporary Douglas practice. Not even the nontraditional high wing or the new tricycle landing gear – first fitted to an airliner on the DC-4 prototype of 1938 – could cast doubt on its identity as a Douglas.

Unfortunately, the calendar kept the DC-5 from becoming another well-known airliner, for only 12 were built. After the company-owned prototype flew in February 1939, there were three transports built for the Navy as R3D-1s and four for the Marines as R3D-2s. KLM, the Royal Dutch Airline, got the remaining four.

The difference between the R3D-2s and the -1s was the large cargo doors on the R3D-2s' left-side fuselages. It is interesting to note that the Navy bought DC-5s before it bought DC-3s. Navy/Marine DC-3s were designated R4D-1s through -7s (the -8s were Super DC-3 conversions). The earlier DC-2s were R2D-1s.

With World War II warming up, interest in the DC-5 waned and Douglas concentrated its transport production effort on the DC-3s and DC-4s. The prototype was sold to William E. Boeing, who traded his old Douglas Dolphin amphibian for it. After the United States got into the war and the services were buying up or requisitioning needed transports, Boeing sold it to the Navy, which redesignated it R3D-3. The Navy/Marine DC-5s did not get to the war zones, but they served as trainers and transports. They were scrapped when the war was over.

The four Dutch DC-5s had somewhat more adventuresome careers. Holland was taken over by the Germans in mid-1940, before the DC-5s could be delivered, so two were diverted to the Dutch West Indies and two the Dutch East Indies. By late 1941, all four were based in Java. When the Japanese invaded Java in 1942, three of the DC-5s escaped to Australia, where they were operated for a while by Australian National Airways. In 1944 they were taken over by the U.S. Army Air Forces as C-110s. After the war, one was reacquired by the airline. It was sold to Israel in 1948, and when last heard of was an unflyable hulk.

The Japanese, meanwhile, had managed to fix up the DC-5 they captured and fly it back to Japan for evaluation and use as a transport.

Of all the DCs, from DC-1 through DC-10, only the DC-1 is definitely extinct. It was destroyed during the Spanish Civil War. The Israeli hulk of the last DC-5 may or may not be in existence. If it could be obtained, it would be a very worthwhile project for a motivated group. As a standard-licensed transport, it could be used for revenue purposes instead of a new life as a mobile museum piece like some of the nearly extinct military types that have been brought back to the United States.

The photographs

1. The prototype DC-5 with its original straight horizontal tail. The engines were 1,100-horsepower Wright R-1820-G-102A Cyclones. After certification, it was sold with these same markings to William E. Boeing. The name ROVER was added to the nose.

2. The underside view of the first DC-5 shows the wing planform, the dihedral on the horizontal tail, and the unique retraction of the main landing gear outward from the nacelles to lay the wheels flat in the outer wing panels.

3. The Marines had four cargo versions of the DC-5 that were known as R3D-2s. Three similar transports without the cargo doors were built for the Navy as R3D-1s. The single R3D-3 was the DC-5 prototype after the Navy bought it from William E. Boeing.

4. The airline DC-5 abandoned by the Dutch in Java was repaired by the Japanese and flown to Japan. Carrying the Japanese military markings, this DC-5 was photographed at a public showing of captured Allied aircraft.

1

2

3

4

The Vultee Vibrator

WWII trainer received the biggest Army order since WWI

1st June 1975

After World War II began in Europe in 1939, the United States woke up to the woeful inadequacy of its air power and began a massive program of new designs and inventory expansion. The combat planes for both the Army and the Navy that resulted from this program are world-famous, and even today they are constantly eulogized in books and magazine articles.

Far less glamorous, but still very important, are the trainer types that the combat crews used before they were checked out in their war chariots. Some were products of well-known, old-line organizations and the result of long evolutionary processes. Others were new products of relatively new firms that were developed to meet new requirements. One was the Vultee BT-13/BT-15/SNV series, which was produced by the Vultee Aircraft Corporation of Downey, California.

Vultee's background in military aircraft was about nil. Gerard Vultee had been associated with Lockheed before founding his own firm in 1933. His initial product was a single-engine transport, the V-1A. A few were sold to the airlines before a federal law was passed in the mid-1930s that banned single-engine transports from the trunk airlines.

Vultee then entered an attack-plane variation of the V-1A in a U.S. Army competition, but sold only a few examples.

With the European war imminent, Vultee went after the export-fighter market by developing a single-seater called the Vanguard. Due to an arms embargo, however, Vultee was unable to accept foreign orders. The Army took them over as P-66s and then passed most of them on to China.

When the United States announced a need for basic trainers, Vultee engineers quickly adapted the basic design of the Vanguard into a two-seater with lighter wing loading by stretching the fuselage and the wings, and fitting a 450-horsepower Pratt & Whitney R-985 Wasp Jr. engine. The Army liked the effort and placed the largest order for a single model since World War I days. The new model was designated the BT-13. The Navy was interested too, and ordered some under the designation of SNV-1.

The official name given to the whole series was Valiant, but the pilots quickly bestowed their own unofficial label of Vultee Vibrator. The name is still used today.

Production was so rapid that the airplanes were getting ahead of the engine supply, so the Army opted for a substitute powerplant. That resulted in the BT-15, which used the nearly equivalent 420-horsepower Wright R-975 Whirlwind engine. The commercial version was better known as the J-6-9.

After the engine shortage was solved, the Wasp Jr. went back into the Vultees. Structural improvements that had been made on the BT-15 were now incorporated in the later BT-13s, which were designated BT-13As. Equivalent Navy models were called SNV-2s.

Now shortages other than engines began to complicate the program. With aluminum needed for combat planes, the trainers got lower priority, so the engineers began to look around for substitute materials. One, the Fleetwing BT-12, was a stainless-steel design; Vultee tried plastic-bonded plywood for outer wing panels and rear fuselage cones. Since they were directly interchangeable parts, their use did not affect the airplane's designation.

Completely unknown today is a "different" Vultee that Vultee didn't even build. That would be the XBT-16, a duplicate of the BT-13 that Vidal Research Corp. built. It was constructed entirely of wood bonded with plastic, but nothing ever came of it; eventually the aluminum shortage dissipated and most of the firms that built trainers were able to continue with all-metal models.

After the war, the basic trainer category was dropped and all of the Vibrators became available on the surplus market. Of the 9,832 that were built, 3,499 were still on the civil register in 1947. Only 114 show up on the latest register. Now regarded as antiques, they have been painted in the old prewar blue-and-yellow Army colors, even though they might have been Navy models or the post-1942 Army models that were delivered in natural metal finish.

2000 update: The 1975 register was very incomplete. The 2000 register lists 171 BT-13s, 26 BT-15s and 24 SNVs.

The photographs

1. A Vultee BT-13A delivered early in 1942 after the Army settled on all-silver for training planes. The colorful Army tail stripes were deleted in May 1942, along with the red center of the wing insignia.

2. A typical wartime publicity photo of Vultee BT-13As. The different finish on the outer wing panels and rear fuselage sections indicates that these components are wood, not metal.

3. This all-wood version of the BT-13A, designated XBT-16, was developed by Vidal Research Corporation as a possible way to beat the 1941 aluminum shortage. Vultee used some wood substitute parts on some BT-13s, but was soon able to resume all-metal construction.

4. While most postwar civilian owners operated their surplus Vibrators in stock configuration, a few tried interesting variations. This one, the McKissick Viceroy, was reworked into a five-place cabin configuration.

1

2

3

4

Military Beech 18s

All-metal aircraft lent itself well to trainer and transport roles

2nd June 1975

When U.S. involvement in World War II became imminent, the military began a rapid expansion of its air forces. Part of this program was to take established commercial designs and adapt them to secondary military roles. A good example is the use of the Beechcraft Model 18 by both the Army and the Navy.

The twin-engine Model 18 was an all-metal light transport that appeared in 1937. A variety of engines could be used, the best known of which was the 450-horsepower Pratt & Whitney Wasp Jr. The airplane was thoroughly conventional and bore a very strong resemblance to the famous Lockheed Electra of 1934. However, it was to far out-last the Electra and establish a world record for continuous production of a single model. Would you believe the Beech 18 was in production for 30 years?

Its excellent capabilities as a light transport attracted the attention of the military, which soon placed orders. The Army's first 18s were stock transports procured in 1940 under the designation of C-45 in the C-for-transport and -cargo series. Others that followed and were slightly modified for photographic work were designated F-2s in the F-for-foto series.

The next year saw the adoption of two advanced trainer versions: the AT-7, which was essentially the C-45/F-2 with the interior arranged for navigation training; and the AT-11, a bomber trainer.

The AT-11 had notable external changes. The standard streamlined nose was replaced with a blunt transparent nose to house a student bombardier and bomb sight. Also, a machine gun turret was built into the top of the fuselage behind the wing. When the turret was not installed, it was replaced with a plexiglass blister.

The final Army variant on the Model 18 was the CQ-3, which was the late C-45F adapted to the role of director plane for radio-controlled aerial targets.

In 1951, some 900 Model 18s that were still in the Air Force were sent back to the factory for "remanufacture" as C-45Gs and -Hs. Since the ATs were all out of service by then, some of the C-45Gs were used for training under the designation of TC-45G.

The Navy also took the Model 18 aboard in quantity under two basic designations. The first was JRB-1, the JR standing for utility transport and the B for Beech. The -1 indicated the first configuration of the Navy model. By the end of the war, the designation had reached JRB-5. While most were used as light transports, some were modified with an aerial "vista dome" on top of the fuselage as a high-visibility station for a crew member who directed radio-controlled aircraft.

The other Navy designation was SNB, for scout-trainer by Beechcraft. The SNB-1 was a duplicate of the Army's AT-11 and the SNB-2 matched the AT-7. The Navy also added suffix letters to the designation for special purposes, and the SNB-2P was a photographic variant essentially the same as the F-2 since the Navy did not have a separately designated photo category. The SNB-3s and -4s were also similar to the AT-7s. A modernization program started in 1951 resulted in some SNBs becoming SNB-5s and some JRBs becoming JRB-6s.

In 1962, when the designations for U.S. Air Force and U.S. Navy airplanes was standardized, the Navy Model 18s took on Air Force designations. The SNB-5s became C-45Js. Some had a T prefix, as TC-45J, to indicate their primary use as trainers rather than transports.

The photographs

1. The Beech Model 18 lent itself easily to military trainer and transport roles. This is an AT-7 (advanced trainer) with minor cabin variations.

2. A special variant of the Navy's JRB-1 utility transport version of the Beech 18. The superstructure housed a crew member who controlled pilotless aircraft by radio. The side door was fitted with an inward-opening panel for oblique photography, the same as the Army's F-2 photographic version.

3. The AT-11 was the Army's (later U.S. Air Force's) bomber-trainer version of the Beech 18. It featured a bomber-type nose and a dorsal gun turret. In this photo, the turret has been replaced by a streamlined plexiglass dome.

1

2

3

A monoplane Camel

The Swallow never got a chance to show its capability in World War I

1st July 1975

Once an airplane has been put into production, it is not unusual for the manufacturer to experiment with various modifications in the hope of improving performance, combat effectiveness, economics or whatever.

Some of the modifications or improvements work out and are incorporated in later production versions; others are quickly discarded.

Sometimes the modifications are sufficiently major to result in a new model. Again, that may or may not be good. Presented here is a monoplane conversion of one of the best-known airplanes of World War I, the Sopwith Camel.

The Camel, named for the unusual hump in the fuselage ahead of the cockpit that covered the butts of the twin Vickers machine guns, was introduced on Dec. 22, 1916. While the new Sopwith had a reputation as a tricky ship, it actually was designed to be the most maneuverable fighter possible for its weight and powerplant, an achievement partly accomplished by keeping it as short as possible and concentrating the major masses quite close to the center of gravity. That the Camel was a good fighter is proven by the fact that it is credited with the destruction of 1,294 enemy aircraft in its combat career, more than any other World War I fighter.

Sopwith tried many modifications on the Camel. One, a set of tapered biplane wings, did not sell. Another, the result of popular demand, was a two-seat trainer for checking out green pilots. Still another was a folding fuselage, hinged just aft of the cockpit, for shipboard stowage. Apparently that was considered easier than folding the wings.

Sopwith also tried removing the bottom wing and converting the Camel into a parasol monoplane. It was more than just a process of elimination, however. The modification altered the bracing setup, so it was necessary to install a pylon above the center section to support the landing wires. Also, since the lower wing was installed considerably aft of the upper wing, leaving the upper wing straight would move the center of lift too far ahead of the center of gravity. That problem was easily solved by sweeping the single wing back so that the centers of lift and gravity lined up.

Since the new plane was so different from the Camel, it was given a new name, the Scooter. It wasn't intended as a fighter, but was basically an aerodynamic experiment undertaken in June 1918. It actually turned out to be a good airplane, with plenty of maneuverability. When a fighter version was developed, it was given a little more wingspan to counter its armament's extra weight. Called the Swallow, it first flew in October 1918 and showed promise. The war ended a month later, however, and there was no further need for new fighter designs.

The photographs

1. The famous Sopwith Camel, one of the most famous World War I fighters, has received new publicity as Snoopy's mount. This is Frank Tallman's Camel, the only one in the world that was flyable at the time of its restoration in the 1950s.

2. A matching view of the monoplane Camel to show off the differences that resulted when the Scooter monoplane was developed from the Camel. Only the wings are different. The wing here is close enough to the fuselage so that the pilot can see above as well as below it. Poor field of vision from the cockpit was one of the Camel's shortcomings.

1

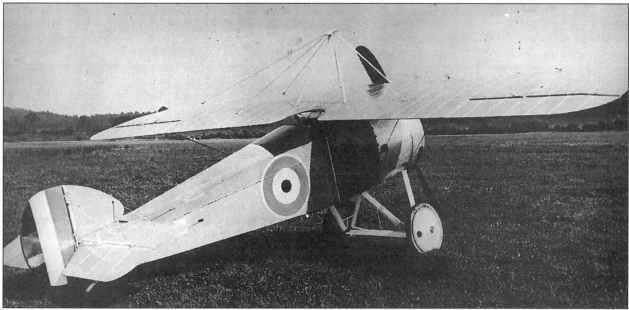

2

Tri-float seaplanes

Similar to aircraft with conventional landing gear, they rested 'three-point' on the water

2nd July 1975

Since the U.S. Navy retired the last of its pontoon-seaplane trainers in 1960, the only pontoon arrangement seen on seaplanes has been the well-known twin-float (or pontoon) arrangement.

Since getting its first seaplane in 1911, the Navy has preferred the single-float arrangement, although it did make limited use of the twin-float type. The single float under the fuselage was not inherently stable, so small outrigger floats were added under the wingtips in the manner of flying boats.

While there are plenty of hull-type amphibians around today, it seems an oddity that no examples of the single-float arrangement have ever been approved for civil aircraft.

Back in World War I days, however, there was a third arrangement that was in wide use. A three-float type, it was similar to conventional landing gear with its two main floats forward and a tail float where the tail skid would normally be located. The seaplane rested "three-point" on the water, just as the equivalent land plane would on the ground.

The main floats were considerably shorter than the corresponding single twin-type floats, and usually did not incorporate the customary step. In fact, the aft end of the float was usually located at the point where the step would be found on other seaplanes. The bottoms of the floats were flat, with an upward curve at the bow in the manner of a sea sled.

The tail float was usually more boat-like, with vertical stem and stern, and sometimes a water rudder at the stern. In some cases, three-float types with longer main floats were seen, but those used the tail float merely as a safety measure.

With their flat bottoms, the "sea sled" floats did not perform well in rough water, which put something of a limit on their military effectiveness.

However, without military requirements and rough water to consider, the old three-float arrangement might be just the thing for the present-day amateur builders who would like to convert their homebuilts to seaplanes without the difficult job of building conventional V-bottom sled-type twin floats or accomplishing the near-miracle of finding a set of ancient Edo 1070s or 1200s. Since sport flying is normally limited to good weather, the flat bottoms should not be a handicap, and the simple box construction should be a relatively easy project.

The photographs

1. The flat bottoms of the forward floats on this 1915 British Short torpedo plane show up clearly here. The Union Jack on the fuselage was the marking used by the British before the well-known tricolor circles were adopted. A design oddity (by later standards) was the aileron system. At rest, both ailerons drooped 90 degrees but "floated" level in the air. To turn, only the outside aileron moved; it was pulled down to get around the Wright patent.

2. A three-point attitude on the water is demonstrated by this U.S. Navy Thomas Morse S-5 of 1918. A seaplane version of the Army's S-4B model, it was powered with a 100-horsepower Gnome rotary engine. It is interesting to consider the starting procedure in those days. With no self-starters, the seaplanes must have been hand-propped ashore and then launched.

3. A three-floater in flight. This is a 1915 British Sopwith Baby seaplane undergoing tests by the U.S. Navy in 1918. The Navy actually used some of these hand-me-downs on active duty in France during World War I.

1

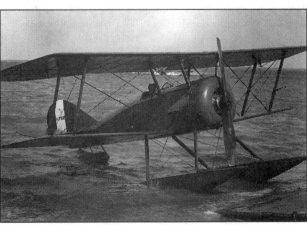

2

3

More Camel mods

Second cockpit and tapered wings showed results

1st August 1975

A recent column (Page 156) on the monoplane version of the Sopwith Camel has stirred quite a bit of interest, so I'll talk here about a couple of other modifications that went unmentioned.

By far the most useful of the various mods was the two-seat trainer conversion. The Camel earned a reputation as a tricky plane as soon as it entered service. Unfortunately, there were no "intermediate" types, something between the docile trainers that new pilots had flown and the snappy little Camel.

What could have served as good transition types were in service on the war front. The obsolete aircraft that had filtered back from the front lines to the schools were even clumsier than the trainers themselves.

There was a clear need for a plane that had the characteristics of the Camel, plus dual controls, so a two-seat Camel was developed and put into production.

No formal data on the characteristics of the two-seater is available, but it is interesting to think about the spin characteristics of a design that was already tail heavy after the two-gun armament was pulled out of the nose and a second seat was installed behind the regular one. With no longitudinal trim system, both pilots probably had to straight-arm their sticks to get the tail up for takeoff.

The other mod I want to talk about here involved another engineering experiment. This time, the standard straight-chord wings were replaced by a tapered set and the upper wing was lowered slightly. The characteristic window in the center was retained, however. This mod was evaluated for its combat potential and carried full armament. The hump through which the guns protruded and which gave the Camel its name, shows clearly in the photos.

With the decreased wing area and drag, the taperwing Camel was a bit faster than the original, but it did not show enough of an overall improvement to justify tooling up for the new wings. A production disadvantage, of course, was the fact that there were so many ribs of different sizes, which complicated the tooling situation. All of which goes to prove that improvements do not necessarily sell themselves; they have to be evaluated against the cost of adopting them as well as their effectiveness in improving the product.

Other adaptations and special uses of the Camel will be presented in a future column.

The photographs

1. Easy checkout in a tricky beast. The easiest way to check out an inexperienced pilot in a Sopwith Camel was to send him up with a check pilot. However, since the Camel was a single-seater, that called for a modification in the form of a second cockpit. The idea carried into World War II, when all major aircraft-producing nations developed two-seat trainer versions of their hot fighters.

2. New wings for an old bird. An experimental version of the Sopwith Camel fighter fitted with a set of tapered wings. Though an improvement, they didn't justify the tooling effort or slower production of the standard model.

1

2

Gotha's Boxcars

Germans led the way with troop and cargo gliders

2nd August 1975

The Germans became the first country to use gliders in military operations in early 1940. Within a year, they were also the first to convert them to airplanes by fitting them with engines.

The first military glider that saw action was the DFS-230, but it was relatively small and carried only 11 crew and troops. Something bigger was clearly needed, and the Gothaer Waffonfabric A.G. of Gotha responded with a twin-boom design that was designated the Go-242.

Gotha, incidentally, was the builder of the famous Gotha bombers of World War I. It remained in the aircraft business between the wars, but did not turn out anything memorable until the Go-242 appeared in the spring of 1941.

Other than the odd configuration, which was clearly the inspiration for the later American Fairchild Flying Boxcars, the construction of the Go-242 was conventional. The wing was built of two wooden spars and wooden ribs, with plywood covering ahead of the main spar and fabric aft. The pod was welded steel tubing with fabric covering. The landing gear consisted of two main wheels and a nose skid.

For efficiency, the rear end on the pod was hinged, allowing easy loading of bulky cargo. The production Go-242A-1 version was intended primarily as a freighter; the 242A-2 was an assault model. Side doors were added to the -2 model so troops could come out the sides as well as the rear. Normal crew was pilot and copilot, with up to 21 fully armed troops.

The Go-242 was not small. Its wingspan was 80 feet 4.5 inches, its length was 51 feet 10 inches, and it had a maximum overload gross weight of 16,094 pounds. Even though it was a heavy freighter, it was also a pretty good glider, with a glide angle of 16 to 1. It could be towed at 149 mph and could dive to 180. Speed for best glide angle was 102 mph.

The Go-242B was introduced in 1942. It differed from the A version mainly in that it had an all-wheel tricycle landing gear, the first used by European military aircraft. A C version was built for water landings, but it was never put into service.

The eternal problem with gliders is getting them back to their starting point. Gotha's solution was to install two conventional airplane engines on forward extensions of the tail booms. The engines were 700-horsepower Gnome-Rhone radials from the captured French aviation industry. The powered version was designated Go-244, and 133 were converted from existing Go-242 airframes. Only 39 were actually built from scratch as powered aircraft, and the Go-244 program came to an end late in 1942. Production of the Go-242 glider continued until mid-1944.

The British and Americans, quick to follow the Germans' lead, also made extensive use of troop and cargo gliders, particularly in the invasion of Europe in the summer of 1944. However, although they experimented with powered versions, none went into production.

After the war, one American design followed the lead of the Go-244 conversion and then went on to better things. Two Chase all-metal gliders were built as G-20s. One, fitted with Pratt & Whitney R-2800 Double Wasp reciprocating engines, was designated XC-123. The other was fitted with the inboard paired jet engines of a Boeing B-47 and was redesignated XC-123A.

That combination was a winner, and more than 300 were built.

The photographs

1. Early prototype of the German Gotha Go-242 military glider of WWII. This particular model was designated Go-242A-0. Production models had slightly deeper tail booms that projected below the underside of the wing. The main wheels could be dropped if landing on the three skids was desired.

2. Ferocious slowpoke. Shark's teeth are usually associated with fast military planes like fighters, but they were applied to this slow Gotha Go-242A. Note the raised rear section of the pod for bulk loading, and the open side door for personnel.

3. Combat gliders, German and Allied alike, often broke up after hard landings in unsuitable terrain. Note that both booms of this Go-242A have broken off. The pod survived intact.

4. The powered version of the Go-242 was designated Go-244. Several engines were tried before the Germans settled on the captured French Gnome-Rhone 14M. Note the fixed tricycle landing gear as used on the Go-242B glider.

1

2

3

4

Pull-off parachuting

It was the method of choice during the biplane days

1st September 1975

Sport parachuting is practiced all over the United States and throughout the world today. There is even international competition, and commercial support such as instruction, equipment, etc.

It was not always so. Practical parachuting has been around since the late 19th century, but it was hardly a sporting proposition then. Most of the jumping was done as exhibitions for good old money. The usual jumping platform up until World War I was a hot-air balloon, and the "aerialist" who did stunts on a trapeze suspended himself from a balloon and then concluded his act with a parachute drop. It was a fixture on the county-fair circuit.

Pack-type parachutes were developed late in World War I and perfected soon after. They made jumping from airplanes more practical than it had been with the old balloon-type chutes. Freed of the elaborate preliminaries of setting up and inflating a balloon, exhibition parachuting became more prolific. I can remember back in the late 1920s and early 1930s when itinerant jumpers would pass the hat at the local airport and then go up and jump.

The U.S. Armed Services were the first to adopt pack-type parachutes as required equipment in normal operations. Until about 1923, the use of parachutes was optional for pilots. After a test pilot was killed at McCook Field when the wing of an experimental fighter came apart, parachutes became mandatory.

Since they had the equipment and suitable jump platforms, it was natural that servicemen got a head start on civilians in exhibition jumping. The Army was doing a lot of development work with parachutes and the final proof was a live jump. Graduates of parachute-packing school had to jump in chutes they had packed themselves. A final exam like that was good incentive for paying attention in class.

With the big boxy biplanes that were standard in the mid-1920s, the preferred method of jumping seemed to be the pull-off. The jumper would climb out of the cockpit, work his way through the struts and wires to the outer struts, and then pull the rip cord. He did not have to jump. The opening of the chute pulled him right off the wing. One of the photos here shows a jumper an instant after he pulled the rip cord. In that short interval, he has put his hand back around the

strut. If he tried holding on tight with both hands, the pull of the chute would easily have him pulling the strut out of its fittings.

While the planes of the time were not cabin models, they could easily carry several jumpers. The other photo here of the Navy Douglas torpedo plane shows one man just after he was pulled off, with two more in the rear cockpit and another in the front cockpit with the pilot. It was not uncommon at the time for jumpers to be in position out on the wing before takeoff. At speeds of a little over 60 mph, it was not hard to hang on during the climb.

The pull-off jump virtually disappeared with the demise of the big biplane. Monoplanes, of course, offer nothing for wingwalking jumpers to hold on to, and today's smaller biplanes do not have as much rigging and they are not able to fly well with a proportionally greater weight out near the wingtip. It has been done recently on Stearmans and Tiger Moths, but it's still uncommon.

More on old-style jumping in a later column.

The photographs

1. Hang on! A jumper grabs hold of the strut of this Navy Douglas DT-2 torpedo plane with both hands after pulling the rip cord for a pull-off parachute jump. Note the deflection of ailerons and rudder that's needed to keep the big 400-horsepower biplane flying straight and level with the man's weight at the wingtip. This photo was taken in March 1926.

2. Another jump from the same kind of plane at a different time. With one jumper tumbling away, there are still four people aboard a plane that was normally a two-seater. Note the common practice of leaving the side cowling plates off the engine section. Fast climbs to jumping altitude apparently caused problems with overheating.

3. Pull-off parachute jumps were so commonplace at the Navy Parachute School at Lakehurst, New Jersey, that platforms were built for them on the lower wings of this Douglas DT-4.

4. The Army did pull-off jumps too. Note the platforms built on the upper wing of this de Havilland 4B, far enough outboard for the jumpers to clear the tail. The jumpers lay prone during takeoff and climb.

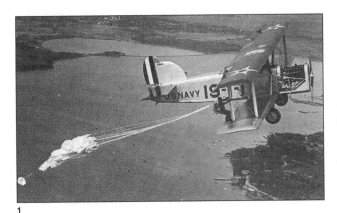

1

2

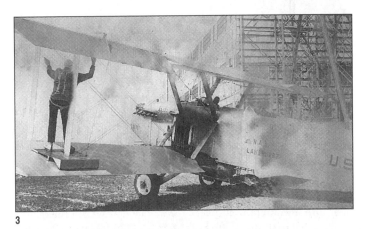

3

4

Aerial hitchhikers

Some passengers climbed aboard while the airplane was still airborne

2nd September 1975

Ever since flying became a serious business, man has had many reasons and countless occasions for getting out of an airborne aircraft, fully airworthy or otherwise, and getting on the ground. Our last column showed one variation of the parachute jump, the usual means of plane-to-ground travel.

By way of contrast, we show this time the exact opposite, with an aerial hitchhiker catching a ride in a plane that did not have to land to pick him up. While this was never expected to become a common procedure for catching the commuter plane, it did have a significant military purpose when it was developed during World War II. It could be used to pick up agents from behind enemy lines and had potential as a rescue device for downed airmen or other stranded personnel in war or peace.

The procedure was developed from the basic technique that was used by All-American Aviation in the late 1930s for picking up air-mail sacks at towns along the route that were not served by regular airlines. The plane, standardized as the Gull-wing Stinson, trailed a hook and snatched mail sacks from a harness suspended between two poles. The sack was then hauled into the plane.

It worked fine for inanimate objects, but such an abrupt snatch would not do for humans. It was necessary to make the system shock-absorbing. That was done by using a long elastic rope and an inertia reel in the plane. In initial trials conducted with dummies, it was found, as expected, that the "body" would drag along the ground before it was lifted into the air. That too was unacceptable.

The problem was overcome by using a suitable flight parameter in which the plane pulled up steeply at the instant the subject's weight tightened the rope. That, plus the resiliency of the rope, resulted in enough upward motion of the subject's body to overcome any tendency to drag on the ground as it accelerated from zero to approximately 80 mph in a few seconds. Once safely airborne, the rope was reeled

in and the subject climbed into the cabin of the snatch plane.

The procedure shown here was one of a series of tests conducted at Wright Field late in World War II. The plane is a Noorduyn UC-64A Norseman, the U.S. Army version of the famous prewar Canadian bush plane.

The subject, in this case Staff Sergeant Harry C. Conway, sat on the ground facing the Norseman as it approached. He wore a special harness that was attached to a pickup line that was suspended from a rope that was supported by two poles. The plane flew low between the poles and its trailing grapnel engaged the sergeant's pickup line just after knife blades installed on the front of the landing-gear struts cut the supporting rope. As the pickup rope was laid out, the plane was pulled into its steep climb before the sergeant's full weight tightened the rope. The 35-degree climb angle and the resiliency of the rope then lifted him safely upward.

While we do not know of any recent examples of this procedure, it would certainly have it all over ribbon-cutting as an air-show act. Most of the recent general aviation planes are not suitable for the job, but there are a few surplus Norsemans flying around. . .

The photographs

1. Up and away, especially up. This photo of an aerial pickup shows the man moving upward as well as forward from the moment the rope tightens. Using bigger pickup planes, the same technique was used to snatch gliders from the ground, but the "instant-up" factor wasn't as important because the glider could roll along the ground and be quickly airborne on its own wings.

2. The shock of the snatch pickup had no ill effect on the hitchhiker, and he was able to scramble into the cabin of this Canadian-built Noorduyn Norseman, which was designated UC-64A when the U.S. Army used it during World War II.

166

1

2

Mixed-up Hawk

From pursuit to trainer and back to pursuit again

1st October 1975

It has been customary in air forces around the world to hand down obsolete high-performance aircraft to flight schools. A rather odd switch took place in the U.S. Army in the late 1920s.

The standard pursuit planes of the time were the Boeing PW-9 and the Curtiss P-1, the latter of which was popularly known as the Hawk. When both were in production, there was no supply of older equivalent models to use as trainers. Someone in the Army then got a bright idea for supplying flight schools with fighter-trainers without waiting for the supply of first-line pursuits to become obsolete. When a plan to build a few dozen PW-9s with less powerful engines was authorized, Boeing and Curtiss were given contracts to develop prototypes.

Boeing pulled one PW-9A off the delivery schedule and replaced its 435-horsepower Curtiss D-12 engine with a 180-horsepower World War I-surplus Wright E engine. That was the famous French Hispano-Suiza built to American standards by the Wrights. Identical to the fighter except for the powerplant, the new airplane was designated XAT-3 for experimental advanced trainer, third model. The earlier AT-1 and AT-2 were two-seaters designed from scratch as trainers.

Curtiss did the same thing with one of its P-1As. With the same Wright-Hispano (Hisso) engine, the new trainer was designated XAT-4 by the Army. After testing both prototypes, the Army awarded Curtiss a contract for 40 production AT-4s in October 1926.

Before that contract was completed, it was obvious that the day of the Hisso's military service was coming to an end, so the last five airplanes were completed as AT-5s and were fitted with the new 220-horsepower Wright J-5 Whirlwind engine, the same that Lindbergh used in his famous transatlantic flight.

The Whirlwind proved to be a big improvement over the Hisso, and the Army ordered a further 31 Hawk trainers with slight improvements as AT-5As before the low-powered fighter-trainer concept had much of a chance to prove itself in the schools.

The concept suffered one shortcoming. Although carrying less than half the horsepower of the original fighters, the trainers still used the highly stressed airframes of 160-mph fighters. They were considerably overweight for their power and just did not have the zip and maneuverability that was expected. As fighter-trainers, they were pretty much a flop.

The Army then came up with another bright idea: recover the lost performance by installing the 435-horsepower D-12 engine that the Hawk had been designed to use in the first place. That was quickly done, and by early 1929 all of the former trainers were redesignated as fighters, or pursuits as they were then called. The AT-4s became P-1Ds, the AT-5s became P-1Es, and the AT-5As became P-1Fs. By this time, however, the P-1 was no longer a first-line fighter. The "new" P-1Ds, -Es and -Fs were therefore obsolete when they went right back to the advanced-training schools, where they served as fighter-trainers into the early 1930s.

The photographs

1. A Curtiss Hawk AT-4 advanced trainer, which was a standard P-1A airframe fitted with a 180-horsepower Wright-Hispano (Hisso) engine in place of the 435-horsepower Curtiss D-12 that was used in the fighter version.

2. Like the AT-4s, the AT-5s were built from fighter airframes fitted with engines of less horsepower than the fighters. This AT-5A used the same 220-horsepower air-cooled Wright J-5 Whirlwind engine that was made famous by Charles Lindbergh and other distance fliers in 1927.

3. Since fighters with low-powered engines didn't work out well as fighter trainers, the Army ordered all the AT-4s, -5s and -5As to be fitted with Curtiss D-12 engines and redesignated as fighters (or pursuits). This P-1D was originally an AT-4.

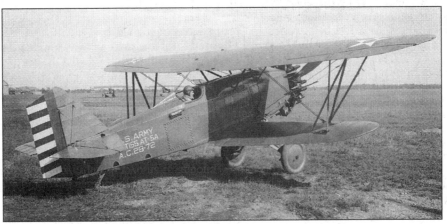

Mister 50-50

Clayton E. Henley uses N-numbers to display his affinity for the big five-oh

2nd October 1975

Henley Aerodrome in Athol, Idaho, is a real oddity among airports. The FBO there gives instruction in J-3 Cubs, and passenger hops are available in de Havilland Tiger Moths with British World War II markings. It's not the perfect grass-strip setup, but the paved runway and taxiway provide a modern touch.

A further oddity to those who keep track of aircraft markings and registration numbers is the corner that owner Clayton E. Henley seems to be getting on the registration number 5050. Three of his planes that are now flying have it, and he has another reserved for an antique that is yet to be restored.

Of course, three planes cannot fly with the same number. Henley's all-yellow Tiger Moth has N5050. Another Tiger, with camouflage on the top and halfway down the sides, has N5050C. The FAA treats letters on the end of the registration number as just another digit and not as a suffix to separate one run of numbers from another, as it did in the past. Instead of being listed on the register as N5050A, N5051A, N5052A, etc., they go N5050A, N5050B, N5050C, etc.

In the application of N5050C to his camouflaged Tiger, Henley adopted a trick used by some other restorers of old military airplanes that carry authentic markings. He applied the N and the first four digits about as small as allowed on the side of the fuselage in black so it looks about like the British military serial number of the period. The letter C was put on in a much larger size and a contrasting color to look like the unit marking of a plane within a squadron.

One of the Cubs is also a 5050, in this case N5050R. Of course, it's not the original number for the airplane. In building up his collection of 5050 registrations, Henley found that there were not many left. The current civil register shows that 21 out of a possible 25 combinations are now taken. There will never be an N5050 followed by the letters O or I for the obvious reasons that they could be incorrectly read as

a zero or a one.

Any owner of a U.S.-registered airplane who doesn't like the number it came with can get just about any available number/letter combination that meets FAA requirements. It used to be that the low two- and three-digit numbers were reserved for government aircraft, but they now are all open except for a very few, like N1, which is reserved for the head person at FAA. Numbers can be of any quantity up to four if used with a single suffix letter or three when used with two letters.

The use of two suffix letters started as a publicity gimmick for American Airlines back in the early 1950s, as N303AA for American Airlines. However, the FAA regarded it merely as N303A and did not count the second letter. Just recently, the FAA increased the number of available registrations by regarding the second letter as another digit.

It's perfectly possible, therefore, for anyone with a fleet of planes to follow Mr. Henley's example and give them all the same basic number. However, it looks like he has a head start that will be hard to overcome.

The photographs

1. Two British-built de Havilland Tiger Moths at Henley Aerodrome in Athol, Idaho. The one in the foreground is all yellow and carries U.S. civil registration N5050. The one in the background is yellow on the underside and camouflaged on top and most of the sides. It is registered N5050C.

2. A closer view of N5050C shows how the N5050 part of the registration is in small black figures while the C is larger and in a contrasting color to resemble part of a squadron marking instead of the last letter of a U.S. civil registration.

3. Clayton E. Henley, owner of Henley Aerodrome, added to his collection of 50-50 registrations by canceling the original registration of this Piper J-3 Cub and having it reregistered as N5050R.

1

2

3

'The Swoose'

It was the only B-17D in the South Pacific to survive the early days of WWII

1st November 1975

The mass-produced versions of the Boeing B-17, from the B-17E variant through the G, were among the most famous airplanes of World War II. Relatively few of the earlier models through the B-17D got into action, and their record was only fair, but a few individual aircraft put in some very spectacular performances.

The B-17 was built by Boeing as a private venture. It was a result of the company's entry in a multi-engine bomber competition announced by the Army Air Corps in 1934. The fly-off was held in September and October 1935. The four-engine Boeing Model 299 (there was no B-17 designation at the time) was running away with the show when an Army test pilot took off with the newfangled internal control surface locks engaged. The big contract was then awarded to Douglas for a twin-engine design that became the B-18. However, the Model 299 had so impressed Army officials that Boeing was given a service test order for 13 improved versions that would be designated YB-17s. That was changed to Y1B-17s a few days before the first one flew in December 1936.

Budgets were tight in those days, and a lot of controversy was stirred up over a 13-plane contract totaling $3,198,799. Some of the detractors said such big planes were too much for a pilot to handle, and the Army's chief test pilot helped their argument when he stood the first one on its nose while landing on its acceptance flight. Pressure was brought to bear on top-level Air Corps officials, and requirements for four-engine bombers were deleted from the 1938 and 1939 budgets.

Supporters of big warbirds did succeed in a limited way, however, and by late 1941 the production versions of the B-17 totaled 39 B-17Bs, 38 -Cs (20 of which were transferred to the Royal Air Force) and 42 -Ds. Only the -C and -D versions saw combat. With U.S. forces, that action was limited to the Pacific. There was a mix of 35 B-17Cs and -Ds in the Philippines, and another dozen were in Hawaii on Dec. 7, 1941. Many were put out of action in the initial Japanese air raids, as were several others that had just arrived unarmed on ferry flights from the States.

By the time the Allies were pushed out of the Philippines, Java and other Southwest Pacific Islands, just one B-17D survived from the 35 that served there. It was named "The Swoose" after the popular song of the time, "Alexander the Swoose," which had the line, "He's half swan and he's half goose – Alexander is a swoose." Since the plane was kept going by whatever spare parts that could be scrounged or cannibalized from other disabled B-17s, the name seemed appropriate. TV actress Swoosie Kurtz, daughter of one of the pilots (Captain Frank Kurtz), was named after the airplane.

It was used for any and all purposes: long-range reconnaissance, straight bombing, low-level strafing and personnel evacuation. It put in an average of 150 flying hours a month. As later B-17Es got to Australia in the late spring of 1942, General George Kenney chose "The Swoose" as his personal transport so the newer models could be used in combat. After further long-range flights around the Southeast Asia theater, Kenney brought "The Swoose" back to the States with him. Although later models, including the bona fide transports, were available to him, he kept the old "Swoose" until the end of the war, even taking it on trips to South America.

After the war, the City of Los Angeles acquired it with the intention of setting it up as a war memorial along the lines of the famous "Memphis Belle." Those plans fell through, however, and "Swoose" sat on Los Angeles Municipal Airport for several years. It was finally acquired by the National Air Museum and is now in storage there for eventual restoration and display. It marks the last example of the B-17 prewar series.

The photographs

1. A Boeing B-17D in the standard markings and natural metal finish used by U.S. Army combat planes until the Japanese attack on Pearl Harbor. B-17Cs and -Ds were the only versions of the early B-17s to see action.

2. The B-17D known as "The Swoose," upon its return to the United States. It had been silver at the time of Pearl Harbor. Its camouflage, quickly applied without proper primer coats, did not stick well and made the plane look even more battered than it was.

3. "The Swoose" on Los Angeles Municipal Airport in April 1946. During its stateside life as General Kenney's personal transport, its belly-gun position had been eliminated and its nose cone had been replaced with one from a B-17G. On the airplane's nose are flags of the countries it visited.

4. A painting of the airplane's namesake, the fictional Alexander the Swoose, was carried on the right side of the fuselage just aft of the door.

5. Close-up of the 31-flag panel that records the travels of "The Swoose." The first 10 cover the Southwest Pacific War Zone; the others cover its travels in Central and South America.

1

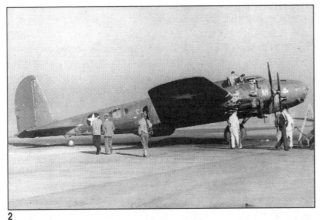

2

3

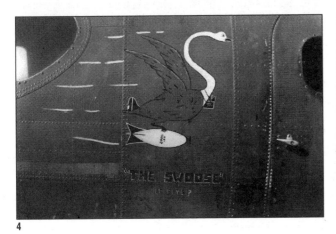

4

5

The first transpacific flight

PN-9 flew the initial 1,841 miles — and sailed the final 450

2nd November 1975

This year marks the 50th anniversary of the first transpacific flight. It was sort of an oddity among the famous distance flights of the middle and late 1920s in that it was both a success and a failure. It set a distance record for aircraft in its weight class, and the airplane did reach the island group for which it was aiming. However, it did not get all the way there by air.

Early in 1925, as part of its "achievement war" against the U.S. Army Air Corps, the U.S. Navy began preparing for a nonstop flight from San Francisco to Honolulu. Two teams and two flying boats were detailed for the task, making an intra-Navy competition of it. Team No. 1 was to use a twin-engine flying boat known as the PN-9. Built at the Naval Aircraft Factory in Philadelphia, it was essentially a World War I Curtiss F-5L flying boat with a rebuilt hull and wings, and new 475-horsepower, 12-cylinder, water-cooled Packard engines that were little more than geared versions of the wartime Liberty powerplant.

The second team was to use the Boeing PB-1, a new patrol flying boat that was designed by the Navy Bureau of Aeronautics and built by Boeing in Seattle. The PN-9 was designated No. 1; the PB-1 was No. 2.

Team No. 1 was ready first. After a battery of test flights in the Bay Area, it took off for Honolulu on Aug. 31, 1925. Commander John Rodgers, who as one of the Navy's first aviators won his wings in 1911, was in charge. Lieutenant B.J. Connell was second in command, and three others complemented the crew.

Everything went fine the first day and night. The PN-9 was on course and on schedule. The aircraft's fuel consumption, however, was higher than expected, and it ran out of gas 559 miles short of Honolulu. Since it was a flying boat, and thanks to calm seas, the PN-9 made a safe landing at sea.

When the plane was overdue in Honolulu, the Navy started an intensive search with ships and had airplanes patrol to the limit of their ranges. After 10 days, there was no sign of the No. 1 team.

Rodgers and crew, meanwhile, were not content just to sit in their boat and wait for rescue. They decided to rescue themselves.

They ripped the fabric off the bottom wings and used it to make sails. With this makeshift rig, they managed to sail 450 miles toward the Hawaiian island of Kaui, which was much closer to their landing spot than Honolulu. They got to within 10 miles of the island when they were spotted by a Navy submarine. Rodgers politely declined the proffered tow, and he and the PN-9 made it into the harbor on their own.

Despite the fact some of its fabric had been stripped, the PN-9 was not extensively damaged. After overhaul, it was used for normal duty in Hawaii before it was transferred by ship to the San Diego Naval Air Station.

The 1,841.2-mile flight that the PN-9 did make, however, was recognized by the FAI as an official distance record for Class C-2 seaplanes that stood for five years.

What about the other team? Despite the fact that the No. 1 team did not complete its flight as planned, the Navy figured it had made its point and called off the second attempt. The big Boeing, a one-only aircraft, was flown to the East Coast and used for test work at the Naval Aircraft Factory.

The photographs

1. The Navy PN-9 flying boat on a test flight over San Francisco Bay before taking off on its aborted flight to Honolulu. The PN line of flying boats was designed by the U.S. Navy, which also built the prototypes. Production of similar versions with air-cooled engines was farmed out to the aviation industry. They formed the backbone of the Navy's patrol fleet until the middle 1930s.

2. The PN-9 as it appeared on its arrival at the Island of Kaui on Sept. 10, 1925, after sailing 450 miles from the point where it was forced down by fuel shortage. Note the uncovered bottom wings. The fabric was used for sails.

1

2

Bomber into transport

Curtiss Condor was a simple conversion of the Army B-2

1st December 1975

Throughout much of aviation's history, there has been an interesting exchange of details between military and civilian airplane designs. During World War I, it was all-military, and the immediate postwar civilian designs were mostly adaptations of established military styles. The first airplanes used in Europe were straight conversions of wartime bombers. In the United States, Glenn L. Martin tried to sell a transport conversion of his famous MB-1 bomber, but with no established airlines, he had no customers.

By 1927, when significant U.S. airlines were well established, the Curtiss Aeroplane and Motor Company introduced the B-2 bomber that had been designed and built under Army contract. The Army then ordered a whole dozen of them, which was a big procurement at the time. Curtiss named it the Condor.

There was nothing spectacular about the design. It was the product of straight evolution from WWI and retained the original concept of an open-cockpit, twin-engine, biplane bomber. The only significant change from older practice was the use of a welded-steel-tube fuselage instead of wooden framework.

A unique innovation was the increased defensive firepower that resulted from putting the machine gunner in a special nest that was built into the rear of each engine nacelle.

With the airlines expanding, Curtiss realized the Condor had potential as an airliner as well as a bomber. When military restrictions on the design were lifted, Curtiss built a transport version in 1929. It was as simple an adaptation of the Army B-2 as possible. The major external changes were to move the pilots forward, enclose them in a cabin and eliminate the gunners. The nose-gun pit was removed, and the engine nacelles were merely covered over at the rear ends where the gunners had been. The engines were the same liquid-cooled, 600-horsepower Curtiss Conquerors that were used in the bomber. They were also the only liquid-cooled engines ever used on a certified U.S. transport airplane.

Internally, a cabin was provided for 18 passengers, and the pilots sat side-by-side in their separate forward cabin. The new Condor was awarded an approved type certificate in August 1929, and the first three went into service with the new Transcontinental Air Transport line, also known as TAT.

Commercial operations showed a need for some refinement of the basically military airplane, so the last three of the six that were built had some notable changes. Where the first three had the same straight-across top wing of the bomber and the same tail, the last three got additional dihedral to the top wing and redesigned the tail surfaces. The biplane horizontal surfaces were moved further apart, and the two fins and rudders were raised. The engine nacelles were extensively modified. They were now more rounded in the cross section, and the portion projecting aft of the wing trailing edge was tapered down to a point instead of being blunt. The three modified Condors went to Eastern Air Transport.

The day of the biplane transport was short, however. In addition to not being as fast as the monoplanes, the biplanes had the handicap of being unsuited to all-weather operations. All those struts and wires were ice-catchers in freezing weather and could not be deiced. The thick monoplane wings, meanwhile, could be fitted with the then-new Goodrich deicer boots.

Another column will show the reverse situation: an established commercial transport that became a famous bomber.

The photographs

1. The prototype of the Curtiss Condor Army bomber, the Curtiss XB-2, at the factory in July 1927. The basic design concept was straight out of World War I. Note the innovative machine-gun nests in the rear ends of the elongated engine nacelles.

2. In its original form, the transport version of the Condor was a simple adaptation of the Army bomber. It had no dihedral on the top wing and very slight alteration of the long engine nacelles.

3. The last three civil Condors of six built had notable alterations from the first three. This photo shows the upper wing dihedral, redesigned tail surfaces, and more streamlined engine nacelles.

4. The interior of an 18-passenger Curtiss Condor airliner. Note the overhead luggage racks as on trains, the roll-down window shades, and the galley at the rear. There is no way you could get a modern food cart down that aisle.

1

2

3

4

Transport into bomber

Swords beaten out of plowshares

2nd December 1975

Last column we showed how a standard U.S. Army bomber, the Curtiss B-2, was easily converted into a civilian transport in 1929. Less than a decade later, the reverse happened when a well-established civil transport plane became a very famous bomber that served throughout World War II.

In 1938 the Lockheed Aircraft Corporation of Burbank, California, was building the Model 14, a 14-passenger, twin-engine transport that was available to the airlines with a variety of engine options in the 700- to 1,200-horsepower range. The Model 14 was a logical enlargement of the famous Model 10 Electra that had appeared in 1934.

Just before World War II, the British Aircraft Purchasing Commission in the United States was buying military aircraft to fill imminent needs. One of its requirements was for a coastal reconnaissance bomber, but no established design was available.

Lockheed considered the requirements and thought the Model 14 could do the job. A mock-up of a revised fuselage was demonstrated in less than a month. In June 1938, the British placed an initial order for 250 military conversions of the Model 14 and identified the line as the Hudson. A total of 295 were built for Britain.

Little of the actual airframe was changed. The unique Fowler flaps, exclusive to the Model 14 at the time, were retained, along with the wing, tail and basic fuselage structure. Outwardly, there were only two notable changes: windows on each side of the nose for the bombardier's station (most of the transports already had a molded clear plexiglass nose cone) and a powered machine-gun turret on top of the fuselage just ahead of the tail. The turret was designed and built by the British; the U.S. didn't have anything like it at the time. The airline cabin was barely altered. Because of the wing location, the bomb bay was under the regular floor.

With the 18-cylinder twin-row Pratt & Whitney Twin Wasp engine or the nine-cylinder single-row Wright Cyclone, the Hudson was built in six variants – or marks, as the British called them – into 1942.

In mid-1941, the United States was awakening to its shortage of air power and began a desperate buildup of forces. One method was to requisition planes in the factories that were being built on British orders. A number of Hudsons were acquired that way. Since they were not standard U.S. Army types, they were flown under their later factory desig-nation of Lockheed 414 and retained their British serial numbers.

After Lend-Lease began, the United States paid for the British orders through Army channels, so the planes got standard Army designations. The Hudsons with Twin Wasps became A-28s in the A-for-attack series, even though they qualified better as medium bombers. The Cyclone-powered models became A-29s.

There was one major difference, however. The U.S. versions did not have the British power turrets. Those that were used on coastal patrol before, and for a while after, Pearl Harbor carried single .30-caliber machine guns in an open rear cockpit where the turret was supposed to be located. An ingenious device was used here to keep the gunner from shooting his rudders off in traverse firing: a steel tube frame deflected the gun upward when it was in line with the rudders.

The Army used relatively few of the Hudsons it drafted. In 1942 it bought 300 variants of its own, an advanced gunnery trainer that was designated AT-18. It was identical to the A-29 except for a U.S.-built Martin gun turret mounted on top.

The United States Navy requisitioned 20 Hudsons as PO-1 patrol planes in September 1941. It's interesting to note that the first submarines sunk in World War II by both the U.S. Army and Navy were from Hudsons. A classic case of swords beaten out of plowshares.

The photographs

1. The 1938 Lockheed Model 14 transport used by several airlines in the United States and abroad. This one went to Japan. Note the covered ends of the flap tracks for the unique Fowler flaps at the inner trailing edge of the wing.

2. A Hudson Mk. IV of the Royal Air Force, a highly successful patrol bomber adapted from the civil Model 14 transport. Since the Hudsons seldom poked their noses into enemy territory, the powered turret did not get much use as a defensive weapon.

3. When the U.S. Army needed patrol bombers in a hurry in 1941, it requisitioned Hudsons from British orders. Note that this one, designated A-29, has an open cockpit where the British turret was normally installed. When more suitable designs became available after the Japanese attack on Pearl Harbor, the U.S.-flown Hudsons were relegated to training and target-tow duties.

1

2

3

The Dragon

Douglas B-23 was first Army bomber to fly with a machine gunner's station in the tail cone

1st January 1976

This column was triggered by a rare sight that I encountered a few weeks ago: two Douglas B-23s taxiing on Boeing Field at the same time. On with the story.

Back in 1935 the Douglas Aircraft Corporation won a U.S. Army fly-off competition for bombers and received production orders that eventually totaled 350 airplanes known as B-18s and B-18As. They proved to be a considerable disappointment to the "better bomber" advocates, and it became quite obvious that something better was needed in the twin-engine field.

The Army held another contest, and Douglas was in there trying to win the B-18 replacement business for itself. After an intermediate design known as the B-22 never got off the drawing board, Douglas found another winner that the Army bought as the B-23. About the only feature common to the B-18 and B-23 was the wing, which was essentially that of the famous DC-3 transport. The major outward changes were the slimmer fuselage with a very short nose; the use of big 1,600-horsepower Wright Twin Cyclone engines in place of the old 950-horsepower, single-row R-1820 Cyclones; and a tall vertical tail with a long dorsal fin.

A unique feature of the B-23 at the time was a machine gunner's station in the tail cone. The B-23 was the first U.S. Army bomber to fly with one, even though lower designated B-types also used it. Tail guns were not adopted for the B-17 until the E model appeared in late 1941.

The Army ordered 38 B-23s, and they were named Dragons when the government began encouraging the use of popular names for U.S. military aircraft in 1941.

While the bigger engines gave the B-23 a big performance edge over the B-18 (282 mph to 215 for the B-18A), it was still virtually obsolete as a first-line bomber when deliveries began in mid-1939. One bomb group was equipped with the B-23, but none got into the real shooting war. Their military operations for a while after Pearl Harbor consisted of coastal patrol along with the B-18s.

The Army used some as flying test beds for new equipment and also converted 12 B-23s to transports and redesignated them as C-67s. Most of the B-23s, along with the C-67s, survived the war and were surprisingly successful on the surplus market. They were eligible for standard licenses under Group 2 Approval 2-576 awarded Nov. 28, 1945. Civilian shops converted the bombers to executive transports that could be used by business firms. Movie pilot Paul Mantz had one as "The Honeymoon Express" for couples who wanted to fly from Los Angeles to Las Vegas for quick marriages.

Update: As of January 2000, there were still six B-23s on the Civil Register. None are registered as C-67s.

The photographs

1. The first Douglas B-23, intended as a replacement for the obsolescent B-18, on a test flight from Wright Field. The tail lettering identifies it as Airplane No. 94 of the U.S. Army Air Corps Material Division, which was headquartered at Wright Field.

2. This B-23, Airplane No. 9 of the 17th Bomb Group, actually served as a bomber. The wheels were fully enclosed when retracted on the B-23; on the earlier B-18 and DC-3 they weren't. Note the single .30-caliber machine gun in the molded plastic nose blister.

3. This B-23 got diverted to transport work before it ever got going in the bomber business. The single star above the lower window in the fuselage indicates it is a staff plane for a brigadier general. Tail lettering identifies Airplane No. 63 of the 10th Air Base Unit at Chanute Field, Rantoul, Illinois.

1

2

3

Amphibious DC-3s

At 34,162 pounds gross weight, Army C-47s slowed from 220 mph to 191

2nd January 1976

The ancient and honorable Douglas DC-3 is now in its fourth decade of service. While it has been many things to many people all over the world (including both sides of World War II), few people realize that among its many configurations was a twin-float amphibian version.

The DC-3 first appeared in December 1935 and quickly became the world's most popular airliner. By a process of evolution through the earlier DC-1 and -2, it became the first airliner to show a profit for its operators without need of subsidy. Approximately 800 DC-3s through the DC-3B are reported to have been built through the beginning of World War II, when the government took over production.

Some of the models already in service with the airlines were drafted, and others that were not yet delivered were taken over right on the production line.

The Army's own workhorse version of the DC-3 was known as the C-47. It incorporated the standard DC-3 airframe with a beefed-up floor and a large two-section cargo door at the left rear of the cabin. Deliveries to the Army began in January 1942, and the Navy got duplicates as R4D-1s. An Army trooper version, without the heavy floor and cargo door, was the C-53. The various drafted civilians were C-48s through -52s, depending on engines and interior details.

The only unconventional-looking members of this DC-3 family were the amphibians. The Army diverted a standard C-47 as a test plane and redesignated it XC-47C.

The Edo Corporation, the leading float maker in the United States, started with all-metal floats in 1926. Amphibious floats it had perfected shortly before the war were its standard model with retractable wheels. The mains were just slightly behind the step and the nose wheels were up front. Takeoff and landing characteristics were the same as for the tricycle-gear planes. Brakes and nosewheel steering were, of course, incorporated.

The Army sent the XC-47 to Floyd Bennett Field in Brooklyn, New York, where Edo installed the floats. For the water tests, the C-47C was taxied down the seaplane ramps at the naval station.

The results were about as expected: The added weight and drag of the floats cut down on the performance. High speed for the standard C-47 was 220 mph, and the gross weight was 29,300 pounds. The big amphibian was slowed to 191 mph, but the gross weight went up to 34,162 pounds.

As a result of the successful tests, the Army ordered 150 sets of the big Edo Model 78 amphibious floats. Future installations, however, did not result in a change of designation for the C-47s. They remained C-47A, C-47B or whatever. While most photos show only the XC-47C prototype, there were other C-47s that were put on floats. Apparently it was as routine an installation as on civilian planes, and no one seemed to keep records on just how many were actually put on floats.

One thing is certain, however. The C-47 was the world's heaviest floatplane. (Editor's note: See Page 186.) There were others that were bigger during World War I. The German Staaken Model L, for example, was a biplane with a wingspan of 138 feet (the C-47's was 95) and four 260-horsepower engines. Its gross weight, however, was a mere 26,019 pounds.

Chalk up still another accomplishment for the venerable DC-3.

The photographs

1. The XC-47C, an Army cargo version of the DC-3 fitted with Edo amphibious floats, taxies into the water at the naval air station at Floyd Bennett Field in Brooklyn, New York.

2. The XC-47C during one of its Army tests out of Wright Field, Dayton, Ohio.

3. This is believed to be the first published photo of a C-47 other than the XC-47C. It is a C-47A-10-DK in the Philippines late in WWII. The Army bought 150 sets of Edo's Model 78 float, but no one seems to know how many were used.

1

2

3

Winged Zeppelins

Standard German bombers from 1915-18, they were once the largest airplanes in the world

1st February 1976

Although no one younger than 36 years of age has ever seen one, anyone familiar with aviation history knows what Zeppelins were. Giant rigid airships, they were a spectacular sight in the skies. The first one flew in 1900, before airplanes appeared, and the next-to-last made a spectacular exit in flames in 1937. That would be the Hindenberg at Lakehurst.

The final Zeppelin, LZ-130, was completed after the Hindenberg exploded, but it never went into service and was scrapped on Hermann Goering's orders after World War II started.

What is not generally known is that the Zeppelin firm also built giant airplanes, the biggest in the world at the time. They were not just one-shot oddities, like many other experimental giants. They were production articles and standard equipment for German bombing squadrons in World War I and were in production from 1915 to the end of the war in November 1918.

The first three were not even built by Zeppelin, which didn't have proper facilities at the time. The Gotha firm, later famous for its own twin-engine bombers during the war, built what was called the V.G.O.I for Zeppelin. It made its first flight in April 1915. Even by today's standards it was a giant, with a wingspan of 138 feet 5 inches and a length of 78 feet 9 inches. It didn't weigh much by today's standards, just 25,267 pounds. It was powered with three Maybach airship engines that delivered 240 horsepower each.

In its original configuration, the V.G.O.I Was a trimotor with one engine in the nose turning a tractor propeller and one in each wing nacelle driving a pusher propeller. It was underpowered with that arrangement, so two extra engines were added in a unique way. One was put in front of each wing's pusher engine but a little lower. It had an extension shaft that ran under the rearmost engine and tied into the propeller through a gearbox. Either or both engines could drive the prop. While this work was going on, the V.G.O.II was being completed in the original trimotor configuration. Even with five engines, the aircraft was underpowered, so the V.G.O.III came out with six. The wing-mounted engines were still in the same arrangement, but this time there were two in the nose, mounted side-by-side and hooked into the single propeller through another gearbox.

The re-engined V.G.O.I and the V.G.O.III had a unique armament arrangement. With no place in the nose to put the gunner, the forward ends of the pusher nacelles were made into machine-gun nests. That feature was retained on the later R-IV and R-VII models that Zeppelin built. The R-V turned the wing engines around to drive tractor propellers so the machine-gun nest was behind the wing on that one-only model.

The major production model of the series was the R-VI, which had four motors. Two were in each nacelle, one driving a pusher prop and one a tractor. They were 260-horsepower Maybachs, which had been developed specifically for airplane installations. The old airship-type engines were designed for reduced-throttle cruising in the airships and failed at maximum power on airplane takeoffs. Also, they did not deliver their rated power at the higher airplane cruise rpm.

The demand for the R-VI was more than Zeppelin could handle, so others were built under license by Aviatik, Schutte-Lanz, Linke-Hoffman and Albatros. A later model was the R-XIV with a fifth engine in the nose. There were near-duplicate R-XIVAs and R-XVs, but the R-XVI reverted to the four-engine configuration.

A few R-VIs were built for the German navy as seaplanes. They were identical to the other R-VIs except for the fitting of twin floats and substituting 260-horsepower Mercedes engines for the Maybachs. High speed was only 78 mph compared to a leisurely 84 for the land-plane R-VI.

Other military airplanes built into early WWII were bigger and heavier than the winged Zeppelins, but not until the Boeing B-29 went into action in 1944 did any of them achieve the status of standard military equipment.

The photographs

1. The original form of the Zeppelin-designed V.G.O.I bomber with two pusher engines and one tractor. Note the four-rudder biplane tail. This photo, taken in April 1915, seems to have started the custom of parking a little airplane under a big one to show off the new plane's size.

2. Although the V.G.O.III still had only three propellers, there were two engines connected to each. A unique feature of these early giants was the main landing gear, which was located so that the plane could rest on a tail skid or on nose wheels. Note the machine-gun nest in the front of the engine nacelles.

3. While there were three-, five- and six-engine versions of the Zeppelin giant, the version built in the greatest numbers had four engines and four propellers. This is the R-VI, which was nearly identical to the R-XVI. Note the enclosed cabin for the crew compared to earlier models. One was even fitted with the first in-service controllable-pitch propellers. Another had a 120-horsepower auxiliary powerplant to drive superchargers.

4. The seaplane versions of the R-VI for the German navy were known as Model Ls. This is the seaplane that was mentioned as being bigger than the DC-3 amphibian described in the last column.

1

2

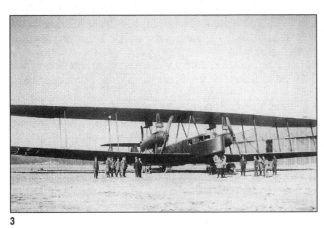

3

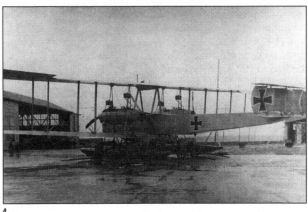

4

More heavy seaplanes

The Italian C.A.N.T. Z.511 weighed in at 73,830 pounds gross weight

2nd February 1976

The best way for a writer to learn that somebody is reading his columns is to make a mistake. The responses, although reassuring in a way, can cause considerable embarrassment.

Such was the case with my column (2nd January 1976, Page 182) on the Douglas XC-47C amphibian and the statement that it was the world's heaviest seaplane. That brought an immediate response that the Italian C.A.N.T. Z.511 weighed more. A quick check verified that the four-engine, pontoon-equipped aircraft, built as a transport by Cantieri Riuniti dell'Adriatico, outweighed the C-47. Completed during World War II, it had an empty weight of 45,012 pounds (some 11,000 more than the gross weight of the XC-47C) and a gross weight of 73,830 pounds.

Since the war canceled plans for expanding the Italian airlines, only two Z.511s were built. They were taken over by the military, and a rather unusual plan was cooked up for them. They were going to carry some of the famous Italian human-guided torpedoes nonstop from Italy to an ocean landing just short of New York City. They'd fly in low to keep under the radar screen, then land and taxi closer to the shore, where the torpedoes would be launched.

It is not known just how far the actual plans got, because both of the planes were destroyed at their moorings on Lake Trasimeno by Allied planes.

There was one other Italian seaplane that topped the Douglas. It was the single C.A.N.T. Z.509, a development of the standard trimotor Z.506 series that saw both civil and wartime military use, but weighed less than the Douglas. The slightly enlarged Z.509 grossed 35,200 pounds, topping the Douglas by only 1,038 pounds. It was built in 1937 for air-mail service to South America, but did not go into production.

Another floatplane that topped the Douglas and was overlooked by everyone was the German Blohm & Voss (later Bv) 139. Three of the diesel-powered ships were built by the Hamburger Flugzeugbau of (where else?) Hamburg between 1936-38. Manufactured for Lufthansa's transatlantic mail service, they were launched from the decks of ships by catapult. Other than their four engines and pontoons (rather than the more popular flying boats), the most distinctive feature of the Ha 139s was their inverted gull wings with the low

point at the inboard engine nacelles. In their initial civilian configuration, the Ha 139s grossed 37,412 pounds.

In 1937, Hamburger Flugzeugbau, already a subsidiary of the great Blohm & Voss shipbuilding firm, took the name of Blohm & Voss and the airplanes changed their designation prefix letters from Ha to Bv.

The coming of World War II ended Lufthansa's transatlantic operations, and the three Bv 139s were taken over by the Luftwaffe and rebuilt as armed patrol planes. They saw some action in the Norwegian invasion. The third one, designated Bv 139B, later took on an interesting modification. It was fitted with degaussing gear for detonating magnetic mines from the air. The outstanding feature of this modification was the hanging of a large electrical cable loop from the nose, wingtips and tail of the plane. The field set up by this loop and the generators that powered it would trigger the mines. With this device aboard, the airplane was designated Bv 139B-MS for minensuche (mine sweeper). Its service life in this configuration was short, however, due to a lack of spare parts for this last of three orphan airplanes. Gross weight in the Bv 139B-MS configuration was 41,888 pounds.

Now, have I missed any other pontoon seaplanes that outweighed the XC-47C's 34,162 pounds?

The photographs

1. The Italian C.A.N.T. Z.511 had a wingspan of 131 feet 2-1/2 inches, less than the Zeppelin L's 138 feet 5-1/2 inches, but it was the champ for weight at 73,830 pounds. Note the opposite-rotating propellers on the 1,500-horsepower Piaggio P.XII engines. Those on the left side of the plane have right-hand propellers, and those on the right have left-hand.

2. The single Italian C.A.N.T. Z.509 trimotor mail plane/transport of 1937 tipped the scales at 35,200 pounds gross weight. It out-grossed the twin-engine Douglas XC-C47C amphibian by 1,038 pounds. Only one Z.509 was built.

3. The German Blohm & Voss Bv 139B-MS of early World War II was also a heavyweight, but its gross weight of 41,880 pounds was less than the Z.511's empty weight of 45,012 pounds. Note the inverted gull wing and the anti-mine degaussing cable.

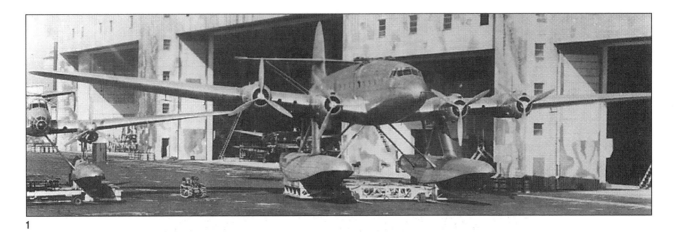

1

3

2

Modified B-17s

Taildragger configuration, load-carrying ability made it an attractive turboprop test bed

1st March 1976

Following World War II, the famous Boeing B-17 bomber embarked on a number of separate and interesting careers. One capitalized on the big ship's taildragger configuration and load-carrying ability, putting it to work as a flying test bed for the new series of turbine-propeller (turboprop) engines that were under development.

Products of Curtiss-Wright, Pratt & Whitney, and the Allison Division of General Motors, they were all in the 5,000-horsepower range, which meant that a single turboprop under test in the nose of a B-17 produced thrust that was virtually equal to four Wright Cyclone reciprocating engines. The favorite publicity photos showed the planes flying on the single turboprop with the propellers of all four Cyclones feathered.

Of the three B-17s that were converted to five-engine models, Boeing did the work on two and redesignated them as Model 299Zs (299 was the Boeing model number for the Army B-17 series). One was converted in Boeing's Wichita plant for the Army, which then transferred it to Curtiss-Wright on a bailment contract, so it remained a military airplane. The other was a surplus model owned by Pratt & Whitney, which Boeing reworked in Seattle. Since the engine builder was in Connecticut and wanted to make its own engine installation, Boeing put a long dummy nose on that one for the transcontinental ferry flight.

A notable feature of both Boeing conversions was the relocation of the pilots cabin several feet aft of its original position to make more room for the big nose engine. The Allison conversion did not have the relocated cabin.

In the late 1950s, the Air Force sold the one that Curtiss-Wright was using to that company, which continued to use it under civilian registration into the 1960s. It was then sold to a new owner who put it to work as a borate bomber in Montana. It was reconverted as far as practicable to its original B-17 configuration. The pilots cabin was left where it was, but a very short nose cap was installed that made this particular B-17 look like no other.

Pratt & Whitney donated its 299Z to the Connecticut Aeronautical Historical Association in June 1967. It now resides in that famous museum. Does anyone know what became of the Allison-powered model, Serial No. 44-85747, that Allison flew under an Air Force bailment contract?

The photographs

1. This temporary nose was built into a surplus B-17 that was intended to become a flying test bed for a 5,000-horsepower Pratt & Whitney turboprop engine. The airplane was modified in Seattle shortly after World War II, and P&W installed the engine in Hartford, Connecticut.

2. This Air Force JB-17G, used by Curtiss-Wright Corporation, demonstrates the power of its turboprop by flying with all four Wright Cyclone reciprocating engines shut down.

3. After Curtiss-Wright bought the JB-17G from the Air Force, it continued to use it as a five-engine test bed. Mounted in the nose is a supercharged Wright R-3350 as used by late-model Lockheed Constellations.

4. After it served time as a super-long-nosed model, Curtiss-Wright's B-17 acquired an extremely short nose when it was sold for use as a borate bomber. This photo was taken near Spearfish, Montana, in June 1967.

1

2

3

4

First American pursuit

French Spad had heavy influence on the U.S.-built Thomas-Morse MB-3

2nd March 1976

When the United States entered World War I in April 1917, it was three years behind Europe in the development of high-performance military airplanes. Consequently, its overseas fighting was done in planes bought from France, England and Italy.

The industry at home went all-out to develop competitive domestic designs, but only a few prototypes got into the air before the Armistice. The best of many fighters for the Army (or pursuits, as they were called) was the Thomas-Morse MB-3. This single-seater was heavily influenced by the design of the famous French Spad and was powered with a U.S.-built version of the new 300-horsepower French Hispano-Suiza engine. The firm's name resulted from the merger of the Thomas Aeroplane Company and the Morse Chain Company.

The Army ordered four prototypes from Thomas-Morse, but the first wasn't delivered until March 1919. After evaluation against other designs, the Army gave T-M an order for 50 production versions to be delivered in 1920.

For the postwar buildup of the early 1920s, the Army decided that it wanted 200 more MB-3s with various improvements, but it wasn't just a simple matter of sending T-M an additional order. Under the procurement policies of the time, the government owned the airplane design after buying the prototype. When it wanted production quantities, it put the order up for bids from the entire industry. Other firms could, and frequently did, underbid the original designer. That was the case with the improved MB-3A. The Boeing Airplane Company bid $10,175 each for MB-3As in lots of 50 and $6,617 each for the whole 200. Its total bid of $1,448,000 was $478,000 less than T-M's.

Boeing delivered its first MB-3A in July 1922 and the last in December. The aircraft went to practically every pursuit squadron in the country and remained first-line equipment through 1925. The last 50 were completed as trainers. Fitted with different tail surfaces of Boeing design, they were sent to the advanced training school at Kelly Field, Texas. Some of the remaining examples there were used to represent French Spads when the first of the great air-war movies, "Wings," was shot at Kelly in 1927.

As has happened many times with improved airplanes, the performance of the MB-3 declined as improvements (and weight) were added. The prototype MB-3 weighed 2,094 pounds and had a top speed of 152 mph in 1919. The first MB-3A weighed in at 2,485 pounds in 1922 and lost 12 mph as a result.

The main lesson that Boeing learned from the MB-3A program was that the contemporary standard of a wood-frame fuselage with wire bracing was unsatisfactory for high-powered and high-performance airplanes. The 300-horsepower Hisso engine was a particularly rough-running powerplant, causing fittings to pull loose and welded tanks to split. The German Fokkers of World War I had demonstrated great durability and fatigue resistance, so Boeing figured that steel tubing was the way to go. Where the Fokkers were gas-welded, Boeing developed an arc-welding process and introduced a new all-American pursuit, the PW-9, in 1923. The aircraft was adopted in production form by the Army and the Navy, and remained in production until 1928.

Later single-seaters kept Boeing the leading supplier of U.S. pursuits into the early 1930s.

The photographs

1. The second of four Thomas-Morse MB-3 prototypes ordered in 1918 and delivered to the Army in 1919. Heavy influence of the earlier French Spad is evident. That's the radiator up there in the center section of the upper wing.

2. The second of the 50 production MB-3s delivered by Thomas-Morse. Note the reversed tail shape, the radiator that's still in the wing, and armament of one .30-caliber and one .50-caliber machine gun. The later Boeing MB-3A had radiators on each side of the fuselage by the cockpit, a real plumber's nightmare.

3. Boeing-built MB-3As were the Army's principal pursuit planes for several years. This one was in the famous 94th Pursuit Squadron. Note the radiators on each side of the fuselage. That's an auxiliary gas tank in the center section of the upper wing.

4. Among the last 50 of the 200 Boeing-built MB-3As, this pursuit plane shows the redesigned Boeing tail. The heavier production versions did not have the performance of the lighter prototypes. Note the common practice of leaving the fabric covers off the wire wheels.

1

2

3

4

Air mail and Varney Air Lines

Swallows were converted into single-seaters with new Wright J-4 radials

1st April 1976

April 6, 1976, marks a milestone in the airline business: the 50th anniversary of the first flight of Varney Air Lines over Contract Air Mail Route No. 5, from Elko, Nevada, to Pasco, Washington. Varney is no longer in existence, and CAM-5 is long gone. However, because the original Varney organization became part of United Air Lines, United is now the oldest airline in the United States, thanks to that April 1926 flight.

United is going to celebrate the occasion by flying a restoration of a genuine 1926 Swallow biplane over the route on April 6.

In a similar commemorative activity, Western Air Lines is restoring an old Douglas M-4 biplane (which it insists on calling an M-2) to fly its original Los Angeles-Salt Lake City route, CAM-4, which was inaugurated on April 17, 1926, when it was Western Air Express. Western underwent some changes in later years that broke the corporate continuity, but not enough to disrupt its claim to a legitimate 50th anniversary this year.

A major difference between the two lines was the equipment. Varney used relatively small Swallow single-seat mail planes that were to be powered with 160-horsepower Curtiss C-6 water-cooled engines. When the engine proved unsuitable for the high desert route after the first flight, operations were shut down for two months while the entire fleet of six was converted to new 200-horsepower Wright J-4 Whirlwind air-cooled radials. No passengers were flown by Varney on that route.

Western, on the other hand, used big 400-horsepower Douglas M-2 biplanes, similar to those the Post Office Department was using on its own routes. Actually, the Douglas M models were merely civilian versions of the standard Army O-2 observation plane. Western's M-2s had a second cockpit in addition to the regular mail pit that allowed for a pay-ing passenger if room allowed.

Why were airlines so late in getting started in the United States when they had been booming in Europe since the end of World War I? The answer was government monopoly. The Post Office had been flying the mail itself since August 1918, after the Army had started hauling it on May 15. Several airlines did start up after the war, but they could not stay in business by carrying passengers alone.

The historic legislation known as the Kelly Act changed that in 1925 by arranging for the Post Office to turn the air mail over to private contractors on a number of separately contracted routes.

The turnover was to take a little more than a year and a half. It started in February 1926 and was completed in September 1927, when the last stage of the San Francisco-to-New York route was turned over to National Air Transport, which also became part of United.

The photographs

1. A historic first flight. Chief Pilot Leon Cuddybank is ready to take off on the first flight of Varney Air Lines between Elko, Nevada, and Pasco, Washington, on April 6, 1926. The line then shut down for two months to put new engines in all the airplanes.

2. One of Varney's Swallow single-seaters flying the route. The original water-cooled Curtiss engines didn't stand up under the rugged conditions and were replaced by new Wright air-cooled radials after the first round trip was completed.

3. The six Swallow mail planes of predecessor company Varney Air Lines, on the field at Boise, Idaho. Walter T. Varney wanted to get into the air-mail business so badly, and didn't particularly care where, that he bid low on the Elko-Pasco route, CAM-5. He got it.

1

2

3

North Pole fliers

An 1897 balloon attempt fell short; a non-rigid airship flight in 1926 was successful

2nd April 1976

The 50th anniversary of two nearly simultaneous flights over the North Pole will take place in May. The first was allegedly accomplished by U.S. Navy Commander Richard E. Byrd, who was already a noted flier-navigator in the arctic because of his work with the Navy-MacMillan Expedition in 1925. I use the word "alleged" because there still is controversy as to whether Byrd and Lieutenant Floyd Bennett actually reached the pole.

The other expedition was led by the famous Norwegian explorer, Roald Amundsen, who reached the South Pole in 1912.

Getting to the pole by air had long been the dream of explorers and pilots, but it did not become practical until the 1920s, when airplane performance became equal to the task.

Actually, the first aerial attempt was by the Swedish engineer Solomon Andree, who, with two companions, took off from Spitzbergen in a free balloon on July 11, 1897, in an attempt to drift the 800 miles to the pole. He was unsuccessful; the balloon came down 325 miles out. Andree and his party hiked 200 miles southward over the ice pack, but perished on a small island. Their frozen bodies and preserved photographs and records were found Aug. 6, 1930.

The first serious airplane attempt was by Amundsen in May 1925. His six-man expedition used two German Dornier Wal flying boats. After landing in open water between ice flows 136 miles from the pole to take observations, they got iced in. After three weeks and sundry misadventures, they abandoned one plane, took off from a crude runway hacked form the ice in the other, and made it back to civilization. Amundsen was to try again in 1926 with the Italian-built, semi-rigid airship that he named "Norge."

Among Byrd's backers was Henry Ford's son, Edsel, who bought the first Fokker trimotor for the expedition. The airplane was named "Josephine Ford" in honor of Edsel's daughter. Byrd and the Fokker arrived at Spitzbergen by boat late in April 1926 to find that Amundsen had already arrived with his "Norge" and had it in a crude hangar.

Tests soon revealed that the skis on the Fokker were useless and the plane could not take off. In a great display of sportsmanship, Amundsen sent his ski expert, Bernt Balchen, to the Byrd camp to help build new ones.

Byrd and Bennett took off on May 9 and completed their 1,600-mile round trip in 15 hours 51 minutes.

Byrd later hired Balchen to accompany Bennett on a nationwide tour with the Fokker. Still later, Balchen was to be a pilot on Byrd's 1927 transatlantic flight and his flight over the South Pole. Still owned by Ford, the Fokker is now on display in the Ford Museum in Dearborn, Michigan.

Amundsen took off in the "Norge" on May 11, crossed the pole and landed 2,700 miles away in Teller, Alaska. In view of the renewed hassles over the Byrd claims, maybe he really *was* the first to fly over the North Pole. . .

The photographs

1. Commander Byrd's Fokker F-VIIA trimotor at Spitzbergen before its flight to the North Pole and back. This was Plane No. 1. No. 2, in the background, is a Curtiss Oriole biplane used for local flights.

2. Amundsen's "Norge" stops off in England on its delivery flight from Italy to Norway. This is the only airship to reach the pole. The Graf Zeppelin undertook some arctic explorations a few years later but didn't get to the pole.

1

2

The Navy's baby bipes

After trying a dozen of the single-seat scouts, nothing came of the concept

1st May 1976

Military aircraft are generally regarded as high-powered and high-performance types in comparison to most civilian designs. That isn't always so, however. The services have at times come up with some very interesting ultralight midgets that would make good homebuilts today. One in particular is a little single-seater that the Navy developed in 1922.

The origins of this scout are odd by today's standards. The Navy's own Bureau of Aeronautics designed the plane and then invited bids from the established aircraft industry to build it. Wood was the standard construction medium of the time, but the Navy was interested in metal. As a result, it decided to make direct comparisons between the two structures in identical aircraft designs. Bids were sought for the two types of construction for the new scout – one wood frame and one metal frame.

Contracts were awarded to two manufacturers, the Cox-Klemin Aircraft Corporation of College Point, Long Island, for six wood-frame examples designated XS-1 (X identified Cox-Klemin in the Navy designation system of the time, and S stood for scout); and the Glenn L. Martin Company of Cleveland, Ohio, for another six metal-frame models designated MS-1. The Martin used welded steel tubing for the fuselage and two-inch aluminum tubes for wing spars, along with stamped sheet-aluminum ribs.

Because of their specialized mission, the little scouts had some interesting design features. Since they were to operate as scouts based on submarines, they were seaplanes. The Navy had already found out on other midgets that the preferred arrangement of a single main pontoon and small stabilizing wingtip floats was not very satisfactory, so the scouts used twin floats.

An air-cooled engine was mandatory for two good reasons. First, it was lighter and better suited to small airplanes. Second, there just was not any reliable, water-cooled airplane engine available in the required horsepower range. The engine chosen, a three-cylinder Lawrence L-3 radial, was the only one available.

The outstanding feature of the scouts, other than their size, was their "wireless" rigging. Instead of the traditional wires and turnbuckles of most biplanes, they were rigged entirely with rigid struts. Once adjusted, the struts not only permitted quick disassembly and reassembly, but assured that the planes ended up with the same rig each time since there were no turnbuckles to adjust and wires to tighten.

Although a dozen of the little scouts were delivered, nothing came of the concept, even though they were actually tried with subs at sea. Experimental watertight hangars were built on the decks of some subs ahead of the conning tower. After the scout was pulled out and assembled, launching was a simple matter of partially submerging and letting the plane float off the deck. One big handicap was that for such small planes, the sea had to be almost dead calm. The Navy quickly abandoned this scheme for seaborne scouts and used bigger two-seaters that were catapulted from battleships and cruisers through the end of World War II.

The scouts were 18 feet 2 inches long, had a wingspan of 18 feet, an empty weight of 650 pounds, gross weight of 1,030, and max speed of 103 mph.

The photographs

1. Glenn L. Martin built six MS-1 scouts that duplicated the XS-1s except for new experimental metal construction. The two orders were placed simultaneously, and the Martins' Navy serial numbers followed right after those assigned to Cox-Klemin.

2. The first of six Cox-Klemin XS-1 submarine scouts built from plans that were supplied by the Navy. Construction was the traditional wood framework of the time. Note the wind-driven generator under the nose to provide power for the radio.

3. The cutest little planes in the Navy may well have been the Cox-Klemin XS-1, shown here, and the duplicate Martin MS-1. Their wingspans were 18 feet. This one is on the seaplane ramp at the Anacostia Naval Air Station. Note the starting crank sticking out of the right side of the fuselage.

1

2

3

Japanese DC-3s

Nearly 500 Tabbies were built between 1940 and the end of WWII

2nd May 1976

With Douglas DC-3 transports in use by both sides of World War II, some odd aircraft-recognition problems popped up.

The principal military derivative of the famous 1935 airliner on the Allied side was the U.S. Army C-47. It was known in the Navy as the R4D-1 and by Britain as the Dakota. The Soviets also used DC-3s, including some U.S.-built models under Lend-Lease and others that they built themselves. But that's another story.

On the Axis side, Germany had a number of civilian DC-3s that had been in service since before the war, plus others that had been acquired from occupied countries such as Holland and Denmark. The German airline Lufthansa operated DC-3s on international routes and even into neutral Spain, where one was photographed alongside a civilian British DC-3 in front of an airline terminal. It is not known whether or not the Luftwaffe also operated DC-3s.

The major Axis user, however, was Japan. The Japanese not only bought a considerable number of DC-3s before the war, they also bought manufacturing rights and enlisted Douglas know-how and equipment in setting up a DC-3 factory. Two Japanese firms built the DC-3: Nakajima and Showa.

The Japanese navy knew a good thing when it saw one, and drafted some of the U.S.-built DC-3s before the war. Those aircraft became L2D1s in the Japanese naval aircraft designating system. With the increasing need for cargo-carrying transports as compared to straight passenger planes, the Japanese developed their own cargo version of the DC-3. It was quite similar to, and actually preceded, the U.S. Army C-47, including cargo door and reinforced floor. That version, designated L2D2, took on some added features not found on the C-47, such as more windows in the pilots cabin; slightly bigger Mitsubishi Kinsei engines with 1,970-cubic-inch displacement compared to the 1,830-cubic-inch Pratt & Whitney Twin Wasps of the C-47; tighter fitting engine cowlings; spinners on the propellers; and, in some cases, a machine-gun turret on top of the fuselage at the front of the cabin.

The actual manufacturers and service designations of Japanese airplanes were hard for the Allies to establish with certainty during the war, so they set up a system of easy-to-remember code names for Japanese planes. The DC-3/L2D series received the name Tabby.

Approximately 490 Tabbies are known to have been built between 1940 and the end of the war. Materials shortages were evident by the fact that items such as tail cones were made of wood. That situation got bad for the Japanese near the end of the war: U.S. technicians accompanying the occupying forces found several wooden fuselages for Tabbies in the factory. The last version carried the designation L2D5.

Some of the Japanese-built civilian DC-3s and Tabbies, plus a few prewar U.S.-built models still in service in China on V-J Day, were taken over by the Chinese and put right back to work. No further information is available concerning them, but judging by the longevity of other DC-3s throughout the world, some could still be flying.

The photographs

1. A DC-3A built under license in Japan by Showa. Note the additional small window aft of the cockpit, the base for a navigator's astrodome above it, and the fuel-dump chutes at the trailing edge of the wing.

2. The Japanese developed their own military version of the DC-3 that closely matched the U.S. Army C-47. This one has the naval designation L2D3. Allied code name for the whole series was Tabby. Note the additional cockpit windows, older DC-2-style nose cargo hatch and propeller spinners. This photo was taken in Shanghai shortly after V-J Day.

3. A Japanese L2D2 Tabby taken over by the Chinese after V-J Day and given Chinese markings. The quickly applied white paint indicates that this is one of the few Japanese military planes permitted to fly on official Japanese business during the immediate postwar surrender and occupation.

1

2

3

The Arrow Sport

Biplane had side-by-side seating and tapered cantilever wings

1st June 1976

Many of the general aviation biplanes of the late 1920s looked remarkably alike. One that stood out, however, was the Arrow Sport, which was introduced by the Arrow Aircraft Company of Lincoln, Nebraska, late in 1926.

The airplane not only looked different, it had a major structural innovation that no other U.S. biplane had ever used. First, it was a small side-by-side two-seater, a rare feature in itself for the time. Second, it had tapered wings, a feature then used only on the Boeing and Curtiss fighters for the Army and Navy.

What could be considered radical, however, was its full cantilever wings. That may have been nothing new for monoplanes, but it was rare for biplanes. The wings needed no flying or landing wires. On the prototype, they were not even connected by interplane struts. Analysis showed that the wings could take all of the applied loads with strength to spare. However, one load not considered was the psychological one. Pilots just did not trust a pair of biplane wings out there without struts, so the production articles carried steel-tube N-struts but still avoided wires.

The prototype had been fitted with a 35-horsepower French Anzani engine because there were no suitable small U.S. radials on the market. By time the Sport was redesigned for production and type-certificated in early 1929, new engines had become available. The engine of choice was the 60-horsepower Le Blond. It proved to be rather marginal for the airplane, which had a few added aerodynamic handicaps. First there was the inherent problem of all small open-cockpit two-seaters: the excessive drag of a (relatively) huge cockpit with two sets of heads and shoulders sticking up in the slipstream and messing up the airflow over the tail. Further, there was a great big cutout in the trailing edge of the wing that subtracted a sizable chunk of useful wing area in order to let the people climb in and out of the cockpit.

A later model known as the Sport Pursuit went to the 100-horsepower Kinner engine and proved to be a snappy little airplane. Unfortunately, like many others, its production life came to an end with the arrival of the Depression. Arrow survived, however, and brought out a new Sport in 1937. That one was a low-wing monoplane powered by a Ford V-8 automobile engine.

One notable user of the Sport Pursuit was Parker B. Abbott, sales manager of The Edwards Wire Rope Company of San Francisco. He not only had salesmen on the road in cars, he was also one of the first businessmen to use a personal plane. The cars had a big E painted on their roofs so Abbott could spot them from his Sport Pursuit, which was equipped with a very early two-way radio.

Out of the 71 Le Blond-powered Sports and 24 Sport Pursuits that were built, only two are known to survive.

The photographs

1. The prototype Arrow Sport of 1926, with imported French Anzani engine. Note the wire-braced, single-strut landing gear and absence of interplane struts.

2. The Arrow Sport Pursuit's distinctive wing design shows clearly here. Note also the wide cockpit, double windshields and radio antenna, and the big E on the top of the salesman's Reo Flying Cloud car.

3. A single cockpit for two makes the Arrow Sport Pursuit look like a single-seater in this side view. Note the high-pressure wheels with brakes, but no wheel on the end of the spring-leaf tail skid.

4. A later Arrow Sport Pursuit with 100-horsepower Kinner engine. Note the completely different landing gear than the prototype and low-pressure Goodyear Airwheels in place of high-pressure tires. Still no tailwheel.

1

3

2

4

The last triplane

GA-1 posted machine gunners in the forward end of each engine nacelle

2nd June 1976

From 1918-25, the engineering division of the U.S. Army Air Service on McCook Field in Dayton, Ohio, designated quite a few military airplanes and even built a number of prototypes. When it became desirable to have production versions, an order was put out for competitive bidding by the aviation industry.

One of the prototypes, tested early in 1920, was a twin-engine type known as the GAX (for ground-attack experimental). The pilots had their own interpretation of the initials: guns, armor and X for the unknown quantity, as in algebra.

Since it was a triplane, the GAX was odd from the start, but it also had other unusual features. In addition to fixed downward- and forward-firing machine guns and a 37mm cannon in the fuselage, there was a machine gunner in the forward end of each engine nacelle. The World War I Liberty engines drove pusher propellers that rotated within a cutout in the trailing edge of the middle wing.

The gunners and the two crew members in the fuselage were protected from ground fire by heavy armor plates. Instead of having their heads and shoulders sticking out of the cockpits in the conventional manner, the crew members were located well down in the cockpits and had forward visibility through viewing slots in the armor that were protected by shutters. It was blind flying before the term as we know it today was invented.

The Army asked for bids on 20 production articles to be designated GA-1s (for ground attack Model 1), and the then-little Boeing Aircraft Company got the contract. After work was well underway, the Army woke up to what a dog the overweight, unwieldy and nearly blind monstrosity really was. As a result, it cut the order to 10 airplanes.

Seattle didn't have a suitable airfield then, so the first GA-1 was trucked down to Camp Lewis, a big Army base 50 miles to the south. The first flight was made from the parade grounds in May 1921. Lieutenant Harold R. Harris, an Army test pilot who had flown the prototype at McCook

Field, was sent out to make the flight. His copilot, Holger Wictum, tells an interesting tale about it:

"Harris, being the chief test pilot, was issued the first parachute. He laid the chute on the floor of the cockpit, and it was agreed that if we had to bail out, the first one to it would strap it on and the other would go down piggyback. Fortunately, that emergency did not arrive. It was about a month after that when he had to bail out of a pursuit that he was testing at McCook Field and saved his life with that same chute, so he was the first service pilot to save his life by parachute (other than WWI balloonists)."

The GA-1s, utterly useless as tactical airplanes, were sent to Kelly Field, Texas, to be used as trainers. Another story about them comes from there. It seems that they were so unpopular with pilots that they were used for disciplinary purposes. All the commander had to do to keep exuberant young students in line was to threaten to assign them to the triplanes.

The GAX/GA-1 was certainly no feather in his cap, but designer Isaac M. Laddon went on to more famous airplanes in later years, notably the Consolidated PBY, the B-24 and the B-36.

The GAs, on the other hand, despite their oddball features, have only one legitimate claim to historical distinction: They were the world's last production triplanes.

The photographs

1. The first GA-1 attack triplane, designed by the U.S. Army and built by the Boeing Airplane Company, sits ready for its first test flight on the parade ground at Camp Lewis, Washington. Note the armored machine-gun nests in the engine nacelles. Two 420-horsepower Liberty engines gave this flying tank a top speed of 105 mph.

2. The first of 10 Boeing GA-1s was assigned to the 90th Attack Squadron at Kelly Field, Texas. The single-unit laminated-wood N-struts were often overlooked among all of the aircraft's other unconventional features.

1

2

Howard Hughes' Boeing P-12

Officially a Model 100-A, it had an extra cockpit squeezed in ahead of the original

1st July 1976

In 1929, young Howard Hughes dropped in at the Boeing plant in Seattle and ordered a special civilian version of the P-12 pursuit plane that Boeing was building for the U.S. Army.

Hughes' version was officially designated the Model 100-A, but it has usually been referred to as a P-12. It was devoid of armament and other military equipment, of course, but was structurally identical to the P-12. Further, the Model 100 was the only pursuit plane to qualify for a full approved type certificate and a standard NC license.

The 100-A had one feature that was exclusively Hughes': It was a two-seater. To squeeze the extra cockpit in ahead of the regular one, it was necessary to reduce the fuel tank and add an auxiliary tank in the upper wing. The wing tank, but not the extra seat, became a standard feature of the other four Model 100s that were built for civilian customers. Since the front cockpit was virtually a flying straight jacket, as well as hard to get into and out of, it was soon covered over, leaving the 100-A as a single-seater for the rest of its long career.

Hughes soon wanted some improvements on his plane, so he sent it to the Lockheed plant in Burbank, California, for installation of a hopped-up engine, full NACA cowling, a redesigned landing gear, fairings to round out the fuselage, a long headrest and streamline cuffs for the struts and wires. Later, a much larger vertical tail was added.

After he tired of the 100-A and went on to other things, Hughes sold it to famous stunt pilot Art Goebel, after which it was used pretty consistently for air-show work. It then had a succession of owners, one of whom replaced the Lockheed-designed landing gear with a single-strut-type taken from a Boeing-Stearman Kaydet soon after World War II.

Another owner then made further changes, covering the fuselage with metal, adding a constant-speed propeller and a more powerful version of the Wasp engine, and another vertical tail of an entirely different shape. Those changes were near the end of the line for the now-venerable bird; however, after 28 years of aerial rough stuff, the one and only Boeing 100-A shed its wings in flight in 1957.

2000 update — One of the other four Model 100s was bought by two Seattle pilots, restored as a P-12, and flown for a few years beginning in 1977 after a widely publicized "first flight." It is now displayed in the Museum of Flight in Seattle. Another has been retired to the Weeks Aviation Museum in Florida.

The photographs

1. The original two-seat configuration of Howard Hughes' Boeing 100-A as delivered on July 26, 1929. Note the streamlined fairings behind the cylinders of the 450-horsepower Pratt & Whitney Wasp engine. When the U.S. Navy took them off the similar F4B-1s, the speed increased five mph.

2. Howard Hughes shows off the early Lockheed modifications to his Boeing 100-A. Note the NACA cowling, redesigned landing gear and rounded-out fuselage. A long headrest and strut cuffs further improved the streamlining.

3. A new high tail was the most noticeable modification, along with larger wheels and wheelpants. Despite its rather extreme modifications, the Boeing 100-A still qualified for a standard license as shown by the old NC registration on the rudder.

4. Final modifications included a constant-speed propeller, single-strut landing gear, metal-skinned fuselage and a new vertical tail. The 100-A shed its wings soon after this picture was taken.

1

2

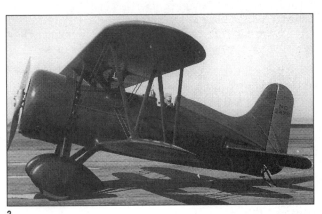

3

4

Civil Coast Guard markings

Army/Navy monopoly was broken with a Fairchild 24-R

2nd July 1976

It's popular among antiquers and sport-plane pilots to paint their vintage military trainers and suitable civilian aircraft in the colorful markings of pre-World War II. The most favored scheme is the old U.S. Army pattern of blue fuselage, chrome yellow wings (with red-center, star-in-circle insignia), and rudder stripes.

Navy markings are less popular. Some restorers even put Army colors on airplanes that were actually delivered to the Navy. No one but the ultra-purists objects when a Navy Boeing-Stearman N2S Kaydet is painted similar to an Army PT-13 or PT-17.

Further, since the colors disappeared early in the war, many restorers put those same colors on planes that were built after mid-1942 and delivered all-silver to both services. Those planes were without rudder stripes, and the red center of the star was deleted at the same time: May 15, 1942.

In the face of this strong trend toward the old Army and Navy markings, I have long pushed for someone to be a little different yet still colorful by using the old Coast Guard markings of 1936-41 on a suitable airplane. Before the war, the Coast Guard operated a number of stock civilian aircraft, many examples of which are numerous in today's antique activity.

While the Coast Guard followed contemporary Navy coloring, it had its own distinctive tail striping and marking system. Those both disappeared when the Coast Guard was taken into the Navy following Pearl Harbor. Unfortunately for antique buffs, the old markings were not restored when the service was returned to the jurisdiction of the Treasury Department after the war.

For me, a major highlight of the recent Bellingham Air Show was discovering a civilian Fairchild 24-R painted up like similar models the Coast Guard used in 1936. The Guard had four of them, two with the naval designation of J2K-1 and two with J2K-2. Fairchild lover and Coast Guard

fan Carlton W. Swickley of Port Angeles, Washington, wanted a "Coast Guard 24" and even went so far as to advertise in the Western Flyer and Trade-A-Plane in hopes that one had been surplussed after the war and was still around.

Undaunted when that road led him to nowhere, he obtained a 1946 model, which differs only slightly in external appearance from the 1936 model, and duplicated the markings of the Coast Guard's first J2K-1 (Serial No. V160). He and I both believe this to be the first antique airplane to fly with Coast Guard markings. My heartiest congratulations to Carlton, along with the wish that he garner all the trophies I feel he deserves. It's a beautiful piece of work, in addition to carrying a rare set of markings.

Other antiquers who are interested in going Coast Guard can do it authentically with such models as the Stinson SR-5, Waco EQC, Grumman Widgeon and even a New Standard D-25, a couple of which were taken over by the Coast Guard following confiscation from rum runners. The Guard also obtained four Naval Aircraft Factory N3N-3s on a trade from the Navy, left them in their original all-yellow, and added the Coast Guard rudder stripes.

2000 update: At least two antique Grumman G-44 Widgeons are flying with old Coast Guard markings.

The photographs

1. The Coast Guard's first J2K-1, a 1936 Fairchild 24-R. The guard had four, Serial Nos. V160 and V161 for two J2K-1s, and V162 and V163 for two slightly different J2K-2s. Overall coloring is silver with chrome yellow wing top and horizontal tail.

2. With all the old Army and Navy paint schemes on antique airplanes, it's unusual to see one carrying Coast Guard markings. This beautiful Fairchild 24-R was painted by owner Carlton W. Swickley to match the equivalent J2K-1 used by the Coast Guard from 1936.

1

2

First U.S. air mail

Mishaps were the order of the day for the pilot and the Post Office

1st August 1976

What with all the recent publicity about the 50th anniversary of contract air mail in the United States (April 1926), it might be interesting to check a couple of items relative to the inauguration of U.S. air-mail delivery.

The service started on May 15, 1918, when the Army flew a load of mail from New York City to Washington, DC, with a change of planes and pilots at Philadelphia.

On that day, flights started simultaneously from both ends, but it was the Washington departure that got most of the attention, including the presence of President Woodrow Wilson at Potomac Park, the temporary flying field. The New York terminal was the infield of Belmont Park race track on Long Island.

Major Reuben Fleet, in charge of the operation, personally ferried one of the six Curtiss JN-4H advanced trainers that had been modified as single-seat mail planes to Washington. The pilot selected for the actual mail flight was Lieutenant George L. Boyle. He had no experience in cross-country flying (few Air Service pilots of the time did), but he had road maps of the route to Philadelphia, located some 135 miles to the northeast. Boyle's principal qualification for the job seemed to be that he was the son-in-law-to-be of the Interstate Commerce commissioner.

There was trouble getting away on schedule. What with all the excitement, no one had fueled the airplane after Fleet had brought it in, and the engine wouldn't start.

Boyle finally took off and started in the right direction, but he quickly became lost. He landed at Waldorf, Maryland, 25 miles southeast of Washington, and put the airplane on its back. The inaugural northbound mail got to New York by train, but the southbound arrived safely by air.

There is some interesting philatelic history connected with the air-mail inauguration. A special 24-cent stamp was issued on May 14, 1918. It came in two colors: carmine and black, with the airplane in black. Good research and liaison were involved in the artwork. Not only was the picture of the airplane accurate, but it showed the correct Army serial number for the northbound plane.

Since the stamp was two-color, it had to go through the printing press twice. One sheet of 100 got reversed and the airplane was printed upside down. A sharp stamp collector bought the sheet on May 14 despite the postal clerk's

efforts to get it back because of the error. The collector sold it a week later for $15,000. Not a bad return on an investment of $24. The second owner then sold the whole sheet to the famous collector Colonel E.H.R. Green for $20,000.

One of those stamps in good condition is worth $45,000 today, and a block of four recently sold for $180,000. Now, don't rush off to the attic and search Grandma's trunk in hopes of finding one on an old letter. Green didn't put his stamps on envelopes. He broke up the sheet for individual sales to other collectors. A normal stamp of the series, however, is worth around $70 today.

The same airplane picture was used on successive single-color stamps as the air-mail rate gradually dropped to six cents by the early 1920s. Later series showed later airplanes. In 1968, for the 50th anniversary, the Post Office issued a two-color, 10-cent commemorative stamp that reproduced the original airplane picture on a somewhat larger stamp and delighted this nit-picker by correctly (probably by dumb luck) reproducing an interesting historical error.

Although built in 1917, those first mail planes carried 1917 markings, which had the red rudder stripe at the rear. The red stripe was at the front of the rudder on the 1918-19 markings.

The anniversary stamp is right in being wrong. The original stamps did not have the two colors on the airplane, so the marking error wasn't conspicuous then.

The photographs

1. The first mail plane, a U.S. Army Curtiss JN-4H Jenny, Serial No. 38262, inaugurated air-mail service on a northbound flight from Washington, DC, on May 15, 1918. The pilot got lost and landed the advanced trainer about 25 miles in the wrong direction.

2. An example of the famous inverted air-mail stamp that was issued May 14, 1918. The inversion was an accident. What's impressive is the accuracy of the airplane's detail and the fact that it carries the correct serial number for the first airplane.

3. In 1968 the Post Office issued this 50th-anniversary commemorative using the same airplane picture. The aircraft is black on a blue field. The only red on the stamp is for the rear rudder stripe. This is the wrong arrangement for the period, but it's correct for that particular airplane.

1

2

3

A Clipper 'tale'

It took three designs before Boeing got the area right

2nd August 1976

The Boeing Airplane Company won a contract in 1936 for six transoceanic flying boats plus an option for six more. The aircraft were the biggest airliners in the world in their day. The wing was almost identical to that of the experimental XB-15 heavy bomber, and the four engines were new twin-row Wright Twin Cyclones that delivered 1,500 horsepower each.

The Boeing Model 314, as it was officially designated, could be considered the first of the wide-body airliners 35 years before the term was invented. In some ways, it was more like a ship than a contemporary airliner. There was a separate flight deck for the crew, and passageways through the thick wing permitted access to the backs of the engines for in-flight maintenance. Up to 74 day passengers could be carried, and berths were available for 40 at night.

Why a flying boat? That's the way things were in those days. While there were four-engine land-plane airliners in service, they didn't have much of a payload/range combination, and there were few airports in the world that could handle heavier land planes that had range and a practical payload.

Most major cities were on or near water, however, and large flying boats that might need several miles for a takeoff run were the logical choice for the world's long air routes.

Pan Am had started with land planes for its short Florida-Cuba route in 1927, but switched to flying boats as it extended to South America. Of course, it specified boats when it started across the Pacific and later the Atlantic in the 1930s. There was an extra benefit of a flying boat that was a potent sales factor: In case of engine trouble, the flying boat could land on the sea (and did).

The first Boeing 314, named the Honolulu Clipper by Pan Am, was launched in May 1938. Despite all the design studies and wind-tunnel tests, a lot of people all the way down to kids who built model airplanes thought it did not have enough vertical tail area.

The first flight, made June 7, 1938, proved the skeptics right. Test pilot Eddie Allen had to use the engines to turn the plane in the air. Boeing quickly redesigned the tail to use two fins and rudders, and put them on the ends of the horizontal tail where they got more of the engine slipstream. That still wasn't enough, so a fixed fin the same size as the original fin-rudder combination was installed in the original center-line position.

Pan Am put nine of the Boeing Clippers into service in the Atlantic and Pacific and sold three of the later 314A models to British Overseas Airways Corporation (BOAC) for its essential wartime services. After Pearl Harbor, the U.S. Army requisitioned four and designated them C-98s. The Navy got two others but did not assign naval designations. One Army ship was returned to Pan Am in 1943, but the others were transferred to the Navy. Although owned by the military, they were operated by Pan Am crews as civilian-registered planes. Pan Am got them back at war's end, but ended its flying-boat operations on April 8, 1946. A postwar independent bought some of the leftovers but went broke in a year. The surviving Boeing Clippers were scrapped by 1951.

What ended the era of the big flying boats? By-products of World War II, primarily. The war years saw the rapid development of long-range four-engine land-plane transports and bombers, plus the simultaneous worldwide proliferation of long and heavy-duty runways that were capable of handling them. The new land planes were not only faster while carrying as much load, they could go to many parts of the world that were inaccessible to flying boats. It is significant to note that even the Navy began to de-emphasize the big boats after the Battle of Midway in 1942 and got rid of them completely in the 1960s. Progress simply left the flying boats behind. Even experiments with jet engines could not extend their usefulness.

The photographs

1. The original configuration of the Boeing Model 314 Clipper for Pan American Airways. This picture, taken on launch day (May 31,1938), shows the small single vertical tail. Note the open doors on the engine nacelles that double as work stands.

2. After the original tail proved inadequate, Boeing installed twin fins and rudders. They still weren't enough, so the original area was put back on the center line.

3. The first Boeing Clipper with its third and final tail. Other airliners, such as the Douglas DC-4E and the later Lockheed Constellation, used three vertical tails to reduce the overall height so the aircraft could fit into available hangars. Boeing used three tails on the Clipper because it needed the area.

1

2

3

The ringer

Crew of the Army's new Curtiss PW-8 tried to pull a quick one in 1923

1st September 1976

In horse racing, a ringer is a horse that is either much better than advertised or one that has been secretly substituted for a slower mount. The object, of course, is to make big money when the alleged long shot wins.

Airplane racing doesn't work quite the same way as horse racing, and the known factors are much more positive, what with specified classes, definite engine displacements, rules about supercharging, and so on.

There was one case of what could be considered an aeronautical ringer, however, and it wasn't at an out-of-the-way local meet, either. The ploy was played out unsuccessfully at the 1923 National Air Races in St. Louis.

The event was the Liberty Engine Builders Trophy Race, a pylon event for military two-seaters with top speeds in excess of 90 mph. There were no other limitations on size, horsepower, supercharging, etc. The trophy was put up by the several manufacturers who had built the famous Liberty engine for the government during World War I.

For 1923, at least, the race consisted of six laps around a 31.07-mile course. The odd mileage resulted from using the international standard course, which was laid out in kilometers. One kilometer is roughly .62 miles, and the 31-plus miles equaled 50 kilometers.

The field, with one exception, consisted of standard or new and still-experimental Army and Navy observation planes. The ringer was the first prototype of the Army's new Curtiss PW-8 (pursuit, water-cooled, Model 8), which was powered with a 435-horsepower Curtiss D-12 engine. The PW-8 had a top speed of more than 170 mph, compared to a little over 140 for its fastest competitor.

To pass the pursuit off as a two-seater, the Army Air Service cut a second cockpit in the fuselage right behind the regular one and installed a dummy machine-gun ring like those seen on the contemporary observation types. As further camouflage, the Army even changed the designation of the airplane to CO-X (corps observation-experimental).

For a while, it looked as though the Army would get away with its deception, but the Navy spotted the ringer for what it was and filed a last-minute protest that resulted in the pseudo two-seater's withdrawal from the race. The Army still won the event, however, with a Dutch-built Fokker CO-4 that it was testing at the time. Winning speed for the 300-kilometer race was 139.03 mph.

The PW-8 went on to better things than quickie two-seat conversions. Twenty-five were delivered in 1924. Powered with postwar engines, they were the first newly designed Army pursuits since World War I. The most notable feat of a PW-8 was Lieutenant Russell Maughan's famous 2,540-mile "Dawn-to-Dusk" flight of June 23, 1924. He crossed the continent from New York City to San Francisco in 21 hours 48 minutes.

No further PW-8s were built as such. The 25 were quickly replaced by the D-12-powered Boeing PW-9s that remained in production into 1928 and an improved D-12 Curtiss variant with tapered wings similar to those of the PW-9 that became the P-1 in 1925 and started the famous Curtiss Hawk line. P-1s were in production until 1929, and improved P-6s with 600-horsepower Curtiss Conqueror engines were delivered to the Army through 1932.

The photographs

1. The first of three Curtiss PW-8 prototypes delivered to the Army Air Service in 1923. Other than nonstandard silver coloring, the major oddity is the radiators on the top and bottom surfaces of the upper wing.

2. The first PW-8 after conversion to a two-seater for the 1923 Liberty Engine Builders Trophy Race. Known as the CO-X, it was withdrawn when the Navy protested the conversion of a pursuit plane to an observation type to compete with bona fide two-seaters.

3. The race was won by this Dutch-built Fokker CO-4, the second of three that the Army had bought for evaluation. The resemblance to the wartime Fokker D-VII was no accident; Fokker got a lot of mileage out of that basic configuration, and the CO-4 can be considered as a larger and more powerful D-VII.

Roland's portable Putbus

German all-metal single-seater was designed to be carried on a submarine

2nd September 1976

Every once in a while some pretty interesting airplanes are developed for specific purposes. In some cases, the airplane and circumstances click, and the combination becomes famous.

One such case that comes to mind is the little Curtiss F9C Sparrowhawk of the early 1930s. It was a washout as a carrier fighter but got a reprieve when its small size made it the only one available for hooking onto and stowing aboard the Navy's airships Akron and Macon. We'll cover those planes in a future column.

In most other cases, it seems, things don't click and the unique airplanes never get out of the prototype stage. Publicity is either nonexistent or the airplane is quickly forgotten by all except the most eager aviation buffs.

One design was a real pioneer. Even though only one was built, it introduced a number of new features, some of which were to become industry standards quite a few years later. The airplane was the L.F.G. V.19, and it was nicknamed the Putbus. The initials stood for one of those German jawbreakers, the Luftfahrzeug Gesellschaft, but the firm used the trademark name of Roland.

The Putbus was designed late in 1918 to help the German navy with its submarine campaign. The little all-metal single-seater was intended to be carried aboard a submarine and was designed for quick disassembly and reassembly as well as stowage in five steel containers built onto the deck of the sub. There were no wires to de-rig; everything was braced by struts with quick-disconnect fittings.

A small crew that knew what it was doing could dismantle the plane in 15 minutes and set it up for flight in a half-hour.

Although it was powered with a 110-horse Oberursel rotary engine, a nearly exact copy of the famous French Le Rhone, performance was not the primary object. Any airplane that could get in the air over the sub to spot potential targets or attackers was fine; a few extra mph under such circumstances was of no importance.

To keep maintenance to a minimum, the structure was kept as simple as possible. The main portion of the fuselage was simply a flat-wrapped sheet-aluminum tube without traditional longerons, a forerunner of the famous Ryan STs of the 1930s.

Also, automatic shutoff fittings were developed so that the wings, which held fuel tanks, could be removed or folded without having to drain the tanks. The floats, too, were all metal, another notable first at a time when all other floats were made of wood. The only wooden part on the Putbus was the propeller.

It was a pretty hot little performer despite all the drag of its forest of struts and its crude aerodynamic lines. With a wingspan of 31 feet 4 inches, it had a top speed of 112 mph and carried enough fuel for two hours. Empty weight was 1,056 pounds.

Why didn't the Putbus become famous? Timing, primarily. The war ended, and the need for it vanished. In the postwar disenchantment with things military, no other nations picked up that particular line of German aircraft development.

The U.S. Navy finally got around to trying some little biplanes that were built along the same lines, as shown in an earlier column, but nothing came of that experiment either.

Had a few of the little Rolands served on submarines, and especially if one or more had been successful in setting up a successful attack, you can bet that the unique Putbus would have been a famous rather than forgotten warbird.

The photographs

1. The L.F.G. Roland Putbus was developed late in 1918 to be carried on German submarines. World War I ended before the combination could be put into action, and only the single prototype was built.

2. The Putbus featured a simple structure. Its fuselage was a tube flat-wrapped from sheet aluminum, and the wings and floats were braced with struts and quick-disconnect fittings. The Putbus could be dismantled and stowed aboard a sub in 15 minutes.

1

2

The first DC-4

Douglas and five airlines worked together on new airliner

1st October 1976

The recent column (2nd August 1976) on the addition of vertical tail surface to the Boeing 314 flying boat generated a letter from a reader who pointed out that the contemporary Douglas DC-4 went the other way, starting with three tails and ending up with one.

The reader also pointed out a coincidence: The prototype DC-4 and the first Boeing 314 made their first flights on June 7, 1938.

The development of the original DC-4 was unusual. It was a joint development of the Douglas Aircraft Company of Santa Monica, California, and five airlines that had operated the highly successful DC-2. While the airlines were satisfied with the aircraft, they wanted to move up to something that offered more passenger capacity and longer range.

So, in a rare example of industry cooperation, the five lines – TWA, United, American, Pan American and Eastern – worked up their detailed requirements jointly with Douglas.

The DC-4E, as it officially became known, was a wonder when it appeared. It had provision for 40 day passengers or 28 sleepers. Powered with four Pratt & Whitney Twin Wasps that generated 1,400 horsepower on takeoff, it had a top speed of 240 mph and cruised at 200.

Wingspan was 138 feet and gross weight was 65,000 pounds. As expected, it showed strong influence from the DC-2, particularly in the fuselage lines and proportions, as well as the wing with its straight trailing edge and swept-back leading edge.

A feature new to the airlines at the time was the tricycle landing gear, which was partially responsible for the triple-tail feature. With the fuselage in level attitude on the ground, the top of the tail was higher than on contemporary models. A big single tail would be too tall and the plane wouldn't be able to get into most of the available hangars.

After factory testing, the prototype underwent accelerated customer-service testing on the airline routes. It didn't turn out to be what the airlines needed after all, so the aircraft was completely redesigned and the single prototype was sold to Japan.

The redesigned DC-4 had little resemblance to the original except for four engines and tricycle landing gear. It was smaller, with only 117 feet of span on a wing with different planform and barely 70 percent of the original area. Its Pratt & Whitney R-2000 engines had fewer horsepower (1,350 on takeoff), but state-of-the-art improvements made it possible for the new DC-4 to fly at nearly the same weight (62,000 pounds) while cruising at 239 mph.

Technically, the new plane should have gotten a new model number, but too much publicity had been given to the DC-4 to drop it.

Douglas started manufacturing 60 DC-4s without building another prototype, but the airlines didn't get them. When the United States entered World War II before the aircraft were completed, the Army took over the whole lot and future production, and designated them C-54s. Some went to the Navy as R5Ds.

The airlines that still preferred Douglas got DC-4s at war's end, either factory-new or converted military surplus as an interim model until the stretched DC-6 model became available in 1947.

The photographs

1. The Douglas DC-4E, developed jointly by Douglas and five airlines, on an early test flight. The nose wheel is just coming up after takeoff. The top row of little windows is for the upper berths of this luxury liner.

2. The original DC-4 was a good airplane but not a winner; as a result, only one was built. Note the built-in bumper under the triple tail to protect the aft fuselage structure in case of an extreme tail-low landing or takeoff.

3. This high-angle view of the DC-4E emphasizes its details, including the innovative dihedral on the horizontal tail. The small windows above the large ones are skylights for the upper berths in the manner of the contemporary Douglas DST (Douglas sleeper transport) version of the DC-3.

4. The military and airlines got this completely different production version of the single-tail DC-4. More than 1,200 were built from 1941 until the end of World War II.

1

2

3

4

Modified P-40s

A second-rate pursuit by 1942, efforts were made to improve its performance

2nd October 1976

One of the most widely produced and controversial U.S. airplanes of World War II was the Curtiss P-40.

A total of 13,736 were built, with 11,995 going to the U.S. Army and subsequent dispersal to other countries under Lend-Lease. Britain purchased the other 1,741 directly from Curtiss.

Oddly enough, the P-40 didn't start out as an original design. The prototype XP-40 had been built as a P-36A, a 1937 pursuit that was powered with an air-cooled radial engine. The airframe, the 10th P-36A, was fitted with an Allison V-12 engine because the Army was interested in using that engine in subsequent pursuit designs.

After considerable experimenting with radiator styles and positions, the design was adopted and production got underway. Deliveries to squadrons began in 1940.

With the war on in Europe, France and England were allowed to buy the latest U.S. equipment, so France ordered a block of P-40s. When Paris fell to Hitler, however, the order was taken over by Britain, which named the design the Tomahawk in keeping with the longtime Curtiss use of the Hawk designation for its fighters.

The P-40s all looked alike through the P-40C model. The D used a later mark of the Allison engine that considerably altered the nose contours. Little change was made when the British Rolls-Royce Merlin engine was adapted to the P-40F except to delete the carburetor air scoop on top of the cowling.

The P-40 was a little deficient in directional stability, so the rear fuselage was lengthened 20 inches for late-model Fs.

It was only natural that special modifications would show up in such a major series. To help pilots who trained on docile two-seaters transition into such a hot aircraft, a two-seat version known as the TP-40 was developed. After the war, others were converted to two-seaters by private owners.

By late 1942, however, the P-40 was clearly a second-rate pursuit. Though it had fallen behind the times, it remained in large-scale production. Curtiss made serious efforts to improve its performance, keep it competitive and, incidentally, keep a very prosperous Curtiss production line going.

The maximum effort was expended on three existing articles that were returned to the factory and modified as XP-40Qs. They underwent a variety of individual alterations, but the most promising arrangement consisted of a cutdown rear fuselage with bubble canopy as used on late North American P-51s and Republic P-47s. Curtiss also squared off the wingtips, and part of the cooling system was relocated in the wings to clean up the nose.

By far the most radical experiment was converting a P-40C into a twin-engine model. No special designation is known for it, and the only known information is a single photograph that turned up in the files of the National Air and Space Museum. It is not known whether the conversion ever flew.

The photographs

1. The Curtiss XP-40 was converted from a radial-engine P-36A in 1938. Note the wing's leading-edge fillet, which was used only briefly on this one airplane, as was the radiator that is partly visible behind the wing. Both features were later adopted by designers of the North American P-51.

2. The standard nose was used on all P-40s through the P-40C and British Tomahawks. The shark-mouth motif did not originate with the famous Flying Tigers; they adopted it after seeing a magazine photo of similarly marked Tomahawks that the British were flying in North Africa.

3. This is the TP-40N version, with a second cockpit added behind the regular one. The nose contours are standard for Allison-powered P-40s after the P-40C. The topside carb air scoop was used on Allison models, but not on Rolls-Royce versions.

4. This P-40N conversion, another two-seater, was a non-flying ground-taxi trainer. The nose wheel was intended to prevent nose-overs from students who hit the brakes too hard. Note the lack of sliding canopies; both cockpits had only windshields.

5. Last of the line was the XP-40Q. This is the final configuration of the third article. It was used as a racer after the war, but caught fire during the 1947 Thompson Trophy Race. The pilot bailed out successfully.

6. The most unusual modification for any P-40 was this twin-engine version of a P-40C. Since there are no top air scoops, the engines are probably Rolls-Royce Merlins. The propellers rotated in the same direction, not opposite, as on the Lockheed P-38.

1

2

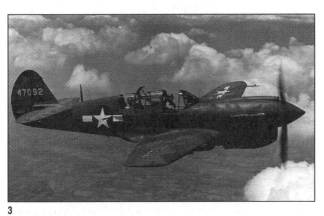

3

4

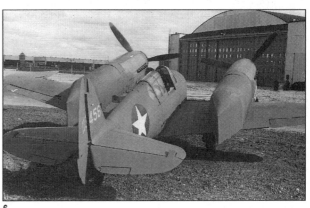

5

6

De Havilland and de Air Corps

U.S.-built DH-4s were corrected in France before they saw combat

1st November 1976

In 1916 the British introduced the de Havilland 4, a two-seat combat plane that was the wonder of its time. It could serve as an observation plane or a light bomber, and it could even hold its own against single-seat German fighters.

Its versatility extended to the powerplant department too. It could use a variety of the 200- to 350-horsepower engines that were available at the time, so it wasn't dependent on a single source, as were some designs.

The DH-4 was still going strong in mid-1917 when the United States sent a technical mission to Europe to select combat-aircraft designs for mass production in U.S. factories as America's contribution to the war effort. In its years of neutrality from 1914 to April 1917, the United States had fallen far behind Europe in aircraft design. As a result, it was decided that its aviation industry should build proven European designs rather than try to catch up with new designs.

Of several models chosen, the DH-4 was the only one to see production and to actually reach the front. The government took over the DH, redesigned it for U.S. production methods, tooling and measurements, and officially named it the Liberty Plane.

In place of the favored British Rolls-Royce Eagle engine, the United States put in the new 400-horsepower Liberty engine. Altogether, three U.S. plants turned out 4,846 DH-4s until production ended in early 1919. Of those, 1,213 went to France, but only a couple of hundred reached the front.

There were colossal scandals over the U.S. DH-4 program involving everything from contract awards to poor workmanship and materials, to shoddy inspections to featherbedding in the factories. Then there was the question of why a design approaching obsolescence was chosen for production in the first place.

None of the DH-4s that were shipped to France were sent directly into combat after reassembly. Production-line modification centers were set up to correct deficiencies and add up-to-date equipment. Even so, the plane earned itself the nickname, "Flying Coffin."

The DH-4's only notable performance in France was when it helped find the famous Lost Battalion in October 1918. After the Armistice, many of the DHs in France were not considered worth bringing home, so they were stacked and burned in a famous "billion-dollar bonfire" that contrib-

uted further to the DH-4 scandals. The bonfire obscured the fact that some 600 DH-4s were returned to the States.

After the war, the Army needed new aircraft, but the budget was tight and funds were not available. Money was available, however, for modification and maintenance, and 1,600 war-surplus Liberty Planes were rebuilt in the later DH-4B configuration. The principal change was moving the pilot behind the wings and putting the fuselage gas tank ahead of him instead of between him and the observer.

Old wooden airplanes were getting pretty creaky by 1923, when Boeing came up with a welded-steel-tube fuselage for the old DH. The Army then gave it contracts to modify a total of 180 to the DH-4M model (M for modernized). Later, the new Fokker factory, established in the United States as Atlantic Aircraft, got contracts for a further 135 DH-4M-2s. The Boeings then became DH-4M-1s.

The U.S. Marines got 30 of the Boeing models under the Navy designation O2B-1 and used some against Nicaraguan rebels in 1927. A few DH-4Ms stayed in Army service until 1932.

Only five are known to survive, and they are all in museums.

The photographs

1. The second de Havilland 4 prototype of 1916, with Rolls-Royce engine. Note that the rear cockpit is cut down to the upper longerons, and that the gas tank is between the two cockpits.

2. The U.S. DH-4 Liberty Plane as turned out by Dayton-Wright in May 1918. Color at the time was cream with khaki-brown top surfaces. The rear cockpit is in the later British configuration, with the gun ring on top of a flat superstructure.

3. The major change in the postwar DH-4B was to switch the positions of the pilot's cockpit and the gas tank. This is the standard armed configuration, with the gun ring around the rear cockpit. Insignia is for the observation squadron.

4. As DH-4Bs were assigned to noncombat roles, crew accommodations became more comfortable. The former flat aft fuselage superstructure was changed to the rounded type, and the rear cockpit was fitted with a windshield, padding and a comfortable forward-facing seat.

1

2

3

4

The Curtiss-Goupil Duck

Designed in 1896, Glenn Curtiss used it to fight the Wright patent

2nd November 1976

One of the long-running problems in the early years of the aviation industry was the patent that the Wright brothers were granted in 1906. It covered several basic features of the airplane, particularly the three-axis control system and the method of achieving lateral control.

Because of the virtual monopoly granted by this notorious document, Wilbur and Orville Wright went to court against other aircraft builders who refused to pay them the high royalties they demanded.

While others acknowledged the Wrights' pioneering work and conceded that they did indeed deserve a patent, the reaction was twofold. First, the patent was considered to be too broad; most observers felt that it should have covered only the control system. Second, the Wrights set their royalties so high that the competition could not pay them and expect to make a profit.

Even foreigners became involved in litigation with the Wrights. While some countries honored the Wright patent, others did not. Nor did some individuals. When foreign pilots came to the United States to enter races or make exhibition flights, the Wrights hit them with injunctions.

One man who fought the Wrights fiercely on their own ground was Glenn H. Curtiss, a motorcycle builder who got into aviation in 1904 by supplying light air-cooled Curtiss engines to U.S. airship builders. Largely because of his engines, he was invited to join Alexander Graham Bell's Aerial Experiment Association in 1907. That organization designed and built four successful airplanes in 1908-09 and developed many basic features of its own. As soon as Curtiss began exhibiting and selling airplanes, however, the Wrights took him to court.

The battle raged for years. Curtiss' main line of defense was that other inventors, whether their designs actually flew or not, had come up with the basics of the contro-

versial patent before the Wright brothers did. To prove prior application, Curtiss sought out, bought and restored several "flying machines" that may not have flown originally, but they did precede the Wright Flyer.

One notable example was Curtiss' restoration of, and successful flights with, the original Langley Aerodrome, which had crashed when it was catapulted from a houseboat on the Potomac River on Oct. 7, 1903 – two months before the Wrights' first flight.

A more extreme example of Curtiss' defense effort is the Duck. This design was worked up by Alexander Goupil in 1896. While Goupil never did build it due to lack of a suitable powerplant, the Duck had many features that would show up in later airplanes. The most important was the control system with its independent manual control about all three axes.

In the winter of 1916-17, Curtiss built a full-scale Duck from Goupil's drawings, updating it only enough to make it structurally and aerodynamically safe. A 90-horsepower Curtiss OX-5 installed far back in the fat body drove a nose propeller through an extension shaft. The Duck flew, both on wheels and on floats, but it didn't help Curtiss in court.

The Wright patent problem, which had shackled an entire industry, was finally resolved when the patent itself was allowed to expire in 1923.

The photographs

1. The original seaplane version of the Duck. Note the engine is far back in the body, about on the plane's center of gravity. What appears to be a lower wing is a moveable control surface similar to an aileron.

2. Because of the harsh Hammondsport winters, Curtiss moved the Duck to warmer climates in Newport News, Virginia, where he had his flight school. He continued to test the aircraft there on wheels.

1

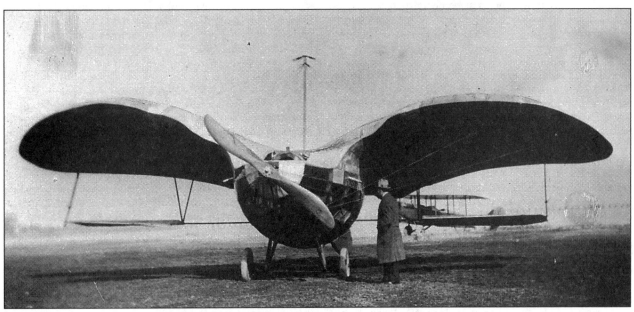

2

The Raven loses a wing

Army decided that sesquiplane could get by as a monoplane

1st December 1976

One of the relatively oddball airplanes of the early 1930s was the Curtiss Raven, an Army observation plane that was designated YO-40. It featured all-metal construction, enclosed cockpit, an air-cooled 630-horsepower Wright Cyclone engine and the new-fangled retractable landing gear, a notable "first" for Curtiss that enabled airplanes to go faster.

The really odd thing about the Raven was its wing configuration. At a time when the classic military biplane was clearly on the way out, the Raven was a cross between a bipe and a monoplane, otherwise known as a sesquiplane.

"Sesqui" means "one-half more," so the Raven was just what the term implied: a "one-and-a-half" plane.

One reason for making the lower wing so small was to minimize obstruction of the crew members' downward view. After all, the purpose of an observation plane is to observe what's happening on the ground. The less structure between the cockpits and points below, the better the view.

The upper end of the landing gear was supported by short stubs projecting outward from the bottom of the fuselage, which also provided the attach points for the lower wing. The wheels retracted inward into the flat belly.

The YO-40 first flew in early 1932 but was damaged extensively in a crash soon afterward. It was shipped back to the factory for a rebuild and reemerged with enough minor improvements and structural modifications to be called YO-40A.

Continued testing convinced the Army that the basic design was promising, so four service-test models were ordered.

Before they could be built, however, monoplanes began to really emerge, so the Army decided that the Raven could get along without a lower wing and become a monoplane with no significant redesign effort.

Consequently, Curtiss built and delivered the four aircraft under the revised designation of Y1O-40B. The 1 in the designation had nothing to do with the change to one wing; it was a budgetary designation to indicate that the airplane was procured with F-1 funds instead of the regular Air Corps appropriation. The distinction between the sesquiplane and the monoplane was in the series letter B.

With its wing still above the fuselage and supported by struts, the cleaned-up Raven was basically a classic biplane (OK, sesquiplane) without a lower wing. If the pilot didn't look down, he hardly noticed the difference.

There were significant changes, however, with the Y1O-40B. In place of the original fabric cover, the new wing was skinned with metal, flaps were added to the trailing edge, and full-span automatic slots were fitted to the leading edge.

The monoplane version of the Raven had 60 more horsepower than the sesqui, but it weighed 400 pounds more and its max speed was 5 mph less. It could, however, fly and land much more slowly, thanks to the flaps and slots. Despite the visibility and slow-flight improvements, the Army decided against the Raven, and only the single prototype and the four service-test articles were built.

The photographs

1. Wing-and-a-half is the literal translation of the word sesquiplane. This photo shows that the Curtiss YO-40 Raven Army observation plane of 1932 was just that. About all the lower wing did was provide the attach point for the struts. Note the full-span ailerons on the fabric-covered upper wing.

2. The service-test versions of the Raven appeared as true monoplanes. The similar upper wing was now metal-covered and fitted with trailing-edge flaps and leading-edge slots. On the fuselage is the insignia of the 22nd Observation Squadron.

3. This view of a Y1O-40B shows the size of the new wing flaps relative to the size of the ailerons, and the open rear of the canopy. With its lower wing, the YO-40 had a wingspan of 44 feet and a wing area of 314 square feet. The single wing of the Y1O-40B had a span of only 41 feet 8 inches and an area of 266 square feet.

224

1

2

3

Wings: Safety in numbers?

Navy was concerned about monoplane's high landing speed on aircraft carriers

2nd December 1976

In the previous column we saw how Curtiss transitioned from the classic Army observation biplane into the monoplane age via the YO-40 Raven sesquiplane that shed its half-size lower wing to become a true monoplane.

Well, the Navy saw the trend toward single-wing planes too, but it was a little hesitant about the new technology. It ordered a monoplane shipboard fighter from Curtiss in November 1932, but it soon had second thoughts.

Citing the notably higher landing speed of monoplanes and the disadvantage inherent with landing on decks of aircraft carriers, the Navy backed up a bit. It ordered an alternate set of sesquiplane wings for the monoplane that Curtiss was then building as the XF13C-1, even though the monoplane wing already had flaps.

Even as a pure monoplane, the XF13C-1 was like no other fighter seen before or since. While it had a new feature in the landing gear that retracted into the sides of the fuselage, it looked otherwise like a conservative high-wing cabin monoplane, complete with wing struts, cabin windows and doors.

Despite the flaps, the monoplane's landing speed was still a little higher than the Navy wanted. Adding wing area was supposed to take care of that problem, even though the sesquiplane wings did not have flaps.

To avoid altering the longitudinal trim, the new lower wing had to be installed with its center of pressure directly under that of the upper wing's. The monoplane wing struts were removed, and the new wing system was braced with the traditional N-struts and wires. It would seem logical to have kept the monoplane struts and just add fittings for the N-struts to secure and stabilize the bottom wing. That would

have made it capable of quick conversions.

Adding the lower wing changed the designation of the airplane to XF13C-2. The monoplane's wingspan was 35 feet and the no-flaps substitute in the sesquiplane system was the same. The lower wing spanned only 24 feet 9 inches and added 80 square feet of area.

The sesquiplane arrangement did not seem to work, however. The airplane had the lower wing on for such a short time that the designation painted on the tail wasn't even changed from -1 to -2. The two wings didn't lower the landing speed noticeably, but they did decrease the top speed by 18 mph. Actually, the sesquiplane version was test-flown first, in December 1933. Its performance was measured against the calculated performance of the monoplane, which was later confirmed by test with the single wing.

As a monoplane, the unique cabin-type fighter didn't do too well either. Some minor changes resulted in redesignation as XF13C-3, but the Navy decided to stick with biplane fighters for a while longer. Monoplane dive bombers went aboard aircraft carriers in 1938, but monoplane fighters did not go into carrier service until June 1940, long after the two-way Curtiss was forgotten.

The photographs

1. This is the original form of the Curtiss XF13C-1, designed as the Navy's first monoplane shipboard fighter in 1933. Note the retractable landing gear and the unusual cabin configuration.

2. By adding a lower wing to the XF13C-1, Curtiss produced the XF13C-2 sesquiplane. After losing 18 mph of top speed, the design was quickly reverted to a monoplane configuration.

The adaptable Navion

Production ended in 1951, but four-seater brought business to the modifications industry

1st January 1977

Back in April 1946, North American Aviation introduced the Navion, a four-place, low-wing monoplane for the general aviation market that was expected to sell well in the immediate postwar years.

Actually, the design had two purposes. In addition to getting the firm into the postwar civilian market, it served to keep the main design team together until military business could stabilize following the V-J Day cancellation of wartime contracts.

While the Navion was a very good airplane, it was too good in some ways. Its military background was a severe handicap for a civilian type. Most of the systems seem to have been developed in light of the designers' experience with military requirements. The result was a plane better suited for military standards of maintenance.

Well, as many other manufacturers besides North American found out, the postwar boom fizzled. North American found itself with a lot of unsold Navions in mid-1947 but was able to pull off a sales coup by getting the Army to buy them as liaison planes under the designation L-17A. Altogether, North American built 1,109 Navions before it sold the design rights to Ryan in 1947.

Ryan, a much smaller company with lower overhead, figured it could make a go of the four-seater despite formidable competition from the Beech Bonanza. It kept it going until military commitments for the Korean War ended production in 1951.

Ryan retained the Navion name and sold a total of 1,238, including 163 L-19Bs to the Army. A two-seat, side-by-side, stick-control trainer version that was developed for the Navy did not sell.

Ryan's principal changes were in powerplant, with a 205-horsepower Continental in place of the original C-185 in the Navion A and a 260-horse Lycoming in the Navion Super 260. The L-19B was identical to the Navion A.

The end of Ryan production in 1951 was by no means the end of the line as far as Navion development is concerned. Other firms made a business of developing and selling modifications to North American or Ryan-built airframes.

The most extreme was a twin-engine version developed in 1952 by Riley Aeronautics Corp. of Fort Lauderdale, Florida. This one was the standard Navion airframe with two 140-horse Lycomings.

Later versions had more power, as did a similar twin developed in 1953 by Camair Division of Cameron Iron Works, which used a pair of 240-horse Continentals. Temco also built the Riley version for a while.

By far the most unusual Navion modification, and one for which I have no information other than photos, is a trimotor. This one has all the features of the Riley-Camair conversions, but also has an engine in the original nose location.

The latest, and much more conservative, reworking of the old 1946 design came in 1960 when the Navion Aircraft Company was formed to update it and keep it competitive. No new airframes were built; instead, old ones were reworked. The major change was to replace the old one-piece sliding canopy with conventional cabin structure. Also, the power was increased to a 260-horse Continental. The rights were transferred to the American Navion Society in 1965.

The photographs

1. The North American Navion entered the general aviation market in 1946, but the originator ended production the following year. This is an L-19B military version built by Ryan, which took over the design in 1947 and continued production until 1951. The photograph was taken in Korea in 1950.

2. Here is a twin-engine version of the Navion as developed by Riley but built by Temco. Note the higher vertical tail. Some had wingtip fuel tanks.

3. No information available other than "Hallair" on the fin of this unique trimotor conversion.

4. Another angle of Photo No. 3, showing three engines instead of the Navion's original single.

5. The final Navion rebuild was the Rangemaster, with tip tanks and the upper fuselage built up to create a cabin. Note the open door, which replaced the original rollback canopy.

1

2

3

4

5

Bomber buildup

B-25 earned its share of glory during World War II

2nd January 1977

One of the outstanding medium bombers of World War II was the North American Aviation B-25. An entry in a 1939 U.S. Army bomber-design competition, it started out as NAA's Model 40.

The aircraft crashed during test flights at Wright Field, but a refined Model 62 was ordered into production in 1939.

The first nine of the 24 basic B-25s had wings with straight dihedral from the fuselage to the wingtips. To overcome a stability problem, the dihedral was eliminated on outer wing panels of the following planes, giving the design a noticeable gull-wing appearance.

Forty B-25As were similar except for new armor and self-sealing fuel tanks. Both the B-25 and B-25A featured machine-gun nests in the tail, with the gunner lying prone in very cramped quarters. It was crude, but it was better than no tail defense. The situation improved with the 120 B-25Bs. That design put the gunner into a Bendix power turret on top of the fuselage, just behind the wing, where he had a pair of .50-caliber machine guns. A remotely sighted turret with another pair of .50s was installed in the belly directly below the top turret.

Forward firepower was a single .30-caliber gun at the bombardier's station in the nose. By far the most famous -B models were the 16 that Jimmy Doolittle's Raiders flew from the aircraft carrier Hornet to bomb Tokyo in April 1942.

The B-25C and -D were outwardly similar to the -B but had many internal improvements and more powerful engines that permitted 5,200-pound bomb loads on short missions. A total of 1,619 B-25Cs were built at NAA's plant in Inglewood, California, and 2,290 duplicate -D models were built in a new NAA plant in Dallas. The XB-25E and -F were single experimentals that had been converted from -C models. The -E had hot-air deicing of the wing's leading edges, and the same feature was tried electrically on the -F.

A major change came with the B-25G. That one incorporated the first successful installation of a 75-millimeter cannon in the nose for direct attack of ground targets. In some cases, forward firepower was enhanced by adding four fixed .50-caliber machine guns, two on each side of the nose.

A total of 405 -Gs were built, followed by 1,000 similarly armed B-25Hs, which had the top turret moved forward and a new tail gunner's station.

The B-25 variant produced in highest numbers was the -J, which was a real flying arsenal. The initial version reverted to the bombardier-type nose of the pre-cannon models, some with nose package guns and others with guns under the wings. Other -J versions featured a solid nose containing eight .50-caliber guns in addition to the package guns. Altogether, 4,318 -Js were built in another new NAA plant in Kansas.

After the Battle of Midway in June 1942, the Navy got very interested in land-based bombers and acquired 706 B-25s from the Army contracts under the Navy designation PBJ-1, which identified them as patrol bombers (PB), the first from North American (J) and the first version.

While you might expect different versions to have different dash numbers, they did not. Similarity to different Army versions was identified by a suffix letter. The PBJ-1C was similar to the B-25C, and the PBJ-1H was similar to the B-25H.

Large numbers of the B-25 were shipped to the Soviet Union under Lend-Lease, while others went to Britain, Brazil and the Netherlands Indies. The B-25 design was removed from the bomber business as soon as World War II was over, but many hung on in the Air Force as unarmed trainers, target tugs and VIP transports. Some of the latter had very plush interiors.

The B-25s were retired from the military in the 1960s, but of more than 11,000 built, some 30 remain active in U.S. civilian aviation and are frequently seen at air shows and in war movies.

The photographs

1. One of the first production North American B-25s, showing the straight-wing dihedral and the tiny tail gunner's station. With first deliveries to the Army in 1941, the B-25s were camouflaged.

2. The B-25B lost the tail-gun position but gained a manned Bendix power turret on top of the fuselage and a remotely sighted belly turret. Notice the distinct "gulling" of the wing, a feature of all B-25s from the 10th article on.

3. The surprise feature of the B-25G, 75mm cannon, was retained on the following B-25H. B-25Gs had the top turret in the same location and, like the B through D models, behind the wing. The turret was moved forward to the leading edge of the H-model's wing, and a tail-gunner's station with two .50-caliber machine guns was added.

4. Additional machine guns were featured on the B-25J, which could use a solid nose installation or the glassed-in bombardier's nose of earlier models. Note the far-forward location of the top turret, the "sit up" tail gunner's installation and the two "package" guns on each side of the nose.

1

2

3

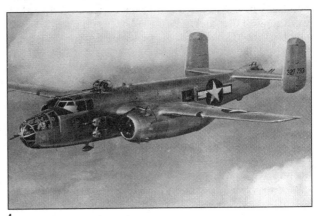

4

Duck diary

Design was already 10 years old when it went public in 1933

1st February 1977

In aeronautical jargon, the word "duck" used to apply to any amphibian – an airplane that could taxi out of the water and onto land, or vice versa. Eventually, however, the word came to identify one particular design, the Grumman JF and the nearly identical J2F.

The XJF-1, meaning experimental (X) utility (J) by Grumman (F), was introduced in 1933. The production versions through JF-3 were built until 1936, and the improved model, J2F-1 through J2F-6, was in production from 1937 to the end of Word War II.

Duck became the official name late in 1941, when the government had the services and manufacturers apply popular names to military airplanes as a security measure. In the case of Grumman, Duck was adequate identification for general public use without giving away the specific stage of model development. Duck it became, and Duck it still is for the few war-surplus models now in the hands of private owners.

Although Grumman's Duck appeared in 1933, the design concept was already 10 years old. LeRoy Grumman had worked for Grover Loening at the time the Loening amphibian was developed and offered to the U.S. Army in 1923, as described in an earlier column.

To recap, the Loening design was basically the conventional two-seat biplane fitted with a single float, but with the space between the float and the fuselage filled in to form a single unit, or hull. When the new Loening amphib outperformed contemporary Army observation land planes with the same engine, business boomed.

In 1928, Loening sold out to Keystone, which was soon absorbed by Curtiss-Wright. Grover Loening and Leroy Grumman left the firm to form new companies on their own. Grumman started business in an old garage by building amphibious seaplane floats for the Navy. The aircraft were fitted with retractable landing gear, which was a great improvement over those used on the Loenings.

Grumman then developed two fighter designs for the Navy, both of which went into production. They were followed by the JF and J2F Ducks and a line of fighters and other Navy types that continues today.

About the only easy point of recognition between the late JFs and the early J2Fs was the absence of a strut connecting the upper and lower wing ailerons on the J2F. There was a noticeable change in the J2F-5 version of 1941-42, which had a full NACA cowling around the Wright R-1820 Cyclone engine instead of the narrow drag ring.

Although designated as a utility type, some Ducks were fitted with guns and depth bombs; others had arrester hooks for landing on aircraft carriers.

The Navy still wanted Ducks in 1942, but preferred that Grumman concentrate its efforts on fighters and torpedo planes. Subsequent Duck production was turned over to the new Columbia Aircraft Corp. of Valley Stream, Long Island, which built the similar-looking J2F-6 version until 1945.

An oddity here was that the Grumman designation was retained. Usually, when a Navy model was built by another firm, a new designation was assigned. For example, when General Motors built Grumman F4F fighters, they were known as FMs.

Since it was strictly a military design, the Duck was able to qualify only for a Limited license after the war, so it was not a popular item on the surplus market. There are only about four still around today as part of the warbird movement. By far the best-known example is the one owned by Tallmantz Aviation of Santa Ana, California, that has appeared in numerous movies and is seen frequently in the "Baa Baa Black Sheep" TV series.

The photographs

1. Direct ancestor of the Grumman Duck line was the Keystone-Loening X02L-1, which was a refinement of the original Loening amphibians of 1923. This 1929 design did not get into production before the Depression wiped out Keystone.

2. The -2 version of the Grumman JF Duck was built to the specific requirements of the U.S. Coast Guard. This one was photographed at San Francisco in November 1941. Note the Coast Guard tail marking, the strut connecting the ailerons and the narrow ring cowling.

3. The J2F-1 had enough improvements over the earlier JF to justify a new Navy model number, but the only noticeable outward change was deletion of the strut between the ailerons.

4. The last Grumman-built Duck was the J2F-5, which featured a full NACA cowling around the engine. The final version was the J2F-6 (shown), which was built by Columbia under the Grumman model number.

5. The sight of a Duck these days is rare enough; two together is a major event. This pair of J2F-6s was seen at Oshkosh in 1975. Who cares that late-war J2F-6s never carried the colorful prewar markings shown? (Photo by Alice Bowers.)

1

2

3

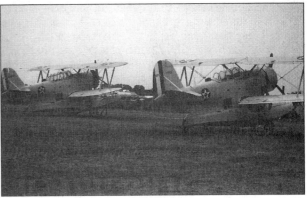

4

5

The Bull Stearman

The name is unofficial, and it should be reserved for the M-2 Speedmail

2nd February 1977

The term "Bull Stearman" has popped up again in the aeronautical vocabulary. While it seems to fit latter-day uses, it has not always been used correctly in the historical sense. How is it being used today? There are two ways.

One is in reference to special air-show Boeing-Stearman Kaydets fitted with 600-horsepower Pratt & Whitney Wasp engines. That's a major step up from the common 450-horse Wasp Jr. installations that were widely used as replacements for the original 220-horsepower Lycoming, Continental and Jacobs engines that powered Kaydets for crop-dusting and aerobatics. Some people believe all that added power qualifies the airplane as a Bull Stearman.

The other application is the considerably larger Stearman Model 4 known as the Junior Speedmail. A couple of Model 4s have been resurrected from that last resort of ancient but still-working biplanes: the duster fleet. They've been restored to mint condition and are now honored members of the antique movement.

The "Bull" label has been applied to Model 4s for pretty much the same reason as the original: It's big compared to the others Stearmans on the scene. By such standards, the Model 4 may be a "Bull Stearman" today, but it will never be *the* Bull Stearman. That distinction belongs to one model only: the Model M-2 Speedmail. Only seven of those big brutes, powered with 525-horsepower Wright Cyclone engines, were built. In 1929, Varney Air Lines bought five as single-seat mail and express carriers and acquired a sixth with a two-seat front cockpit and reduced cargo capacity. The seventh was another three-seater that went to a different customer and was fitted with a 525-horsepower Pratt & Whitney Hornet engine instead of a Cyclone. Stearman gave the M-2 the name Speedmail and advertised it as such.

"Bull Stearman" was never official. It was a nickname used by the initial operator of the plane. Varney was an early user of the original Stearman C-2 and C-3 mail planes, and it was only natural that the models have different names. Size was the most obvious distinction, so the greater dimensions and power of the M-2, plus other characteristics, just naturally generated the term "Bull Stearman."

The Bull was big, all right, with a wingspan of 46 feet and a gross weight of 5,578 pounds. Top speed was 147 mph. Still, it wasn't the biggest Stearman. That honor went to three LT-1s, which looked like the M-2 but had a four-passenger cabin ahead of the pilot's cockpit. Its wingspan was 49 feet.

The Model 4 Junior Speedmail was essentially a scaled-down M-2 with a wingspan of 38 feet and a gross weight of 3,936 pounds.

The little Model 75 Kaydet that came along in 1933 had a wingspan of only 32 feet 2 inches and a gross weight of 2,217 pounds in its standard military trainer configuration. With the current 600 horsepower, it is the most powerful of the Stearman biplanes, but a Bull Stearman it is not.

The photographs

1. This is the fourth of Varney's six Bull Stearmans. The dark coloring ahead of the cockpit and on the struts and landing gear is blue, about the shade of Chevron gas stations. The lettering was black.

2. The first Stearman M-2 delivered to Varney Air Lines as a mail and express carrier. Note the two payload compartments ahead of the cockpit. Basic color was silver; for visibility against all types of terrain, the left half of the upper wing was painted international orange.

3. The last two of the seven M-2 Bull Stearmans had two-seat front cockpits and only one mail/cargo compartment.

4. After retirement from the airline, the Bull Stearmans got new owners and kept on working. This one, the fourth, went to Alaska and was flown on skis.

1

2

3

4

The stunt

Using a pair of Jennies, this wingwalker stepped from one plane to another

1st March 1977

In the early and mid-1920s, airplanes were doing spectacular things in the name of entertainment. The "stunt," to use the generic term for one particularly noteworthy operation, involved an aerialist named Gladys Ingle who leaped from one airborne airplane to another. The airplanes were World War I-surplus Curtiss JN-4Ds, better known as Jennies. They had 44-foot wingspans, a gross weight of 2,130 pounds and were powered by 90-horsepower Curtiss OX-5 engines. With a top speed of 75 mph and a cruise speed of about 60, they were greatly underpowered by present standards.

Jennies and the very similar Standard J-1s were the principal planes in the old shows for several reasons. They had lots of struts and wires for the aerialist to hang onto, and they were slow. At higher speeds much of the aerialist's act would be impossible. Also, they were plentiful and cheap. Replacements, which were needed frequently, were easy to come by.

Just climbing off one airplane and onto another in mid-air is a considerable feat, but this particular operation involving Ingle was to be photographed at close range, which meant extra people in both planes and a subsequent decrease in performance and control.

The plane from which Ingle was transferred – let's call it the carrier – was a Jenny rigged especially for wingwalking. It had an additional set of king posts on the upper wing to provide convenient hand and foot holds. Ingle was positioned at the outer king posts on the right wing and a photographer occupied the same position on the left wing.

The receiving airplane, piloted by the famous Art Goebel, was another Jenny that was modified in the opposite direction. There were no king posts above the wing, the overhang was braced by struts instead of wires, and there was no skid under the lower wingtip (a convenient handhold on stock Jennies). Goebel's ship also carried a photographer in the rear cockpit, with a remote camera mounted on top of the fuselage just ahead of the tail. To make the photo coverage more complete, another Jenny with a photographer was flying just ahead of and to the left of the carrier.

Now consider the pilotage involved and the effect of the weight transfer on both ships. First, the left wing of the receiving aircraft had to overlap the right wing of the carrier and also be close enough to enable Ingle to get a foot onto it. That took some very precise piloting by Goebel.

At the slow speed the Jennies flew, there wasn't much of a venturi effect between the two overlapping wings. Both pilots knew to correct with aileron for any effect that arose.

The major problem was the airplanes' reactions when the weight was transferred. As Ingle's 120 pounds came off the carrier's wing at a distance of some 15 feet from the center line, that wing naturally rose. The rising wingtip was hastened by the 160-pound-plus photographer on the opposite wing. And as the wing of the carrier airplane was rising, the left wing of the receiving aircraft was dipping as Ingle came aboard. Perfect timing with aileron action – with airplanes that were famous for their sluggishness – was the only way to keep the exhibition from becoming a disaster. What a performance!

To cap it all, Ingle had to hang on to the outside of the aircraft, much like passengers on a crowded cable car in San Francisco. Goebel had to stay in the front cockpit, and the photographer certainly did not get up and give her his seat.

What a way to treat a lady.

The photographs

1. As she sets up, Gladys Ingle is ready to climb onto the left wing of Art Goebel's Jenny. Note the photographer on the left wingtip and the extra set of cabane struts on the carrier Jenny. This photo was taken by a remote camera near the tail of Goebel's ship.

2. Getting ready, Ingle reaches for Goebel's Jenny as it comes up from behind. Note that her booted legs are anchored by the king posts and wires while the photographer in the back seat of Goebel's Jenny clicks away.

3. And over she goes. Most of Ingle's weight is now on Goebel's Jenny, but her left foot is still between the king-post wires on the wing she just left. Note how far out of parallel the two planes are flying.

1

2

3

Riding piggyback

It's usually done by design, but it's been known to happen by accident

2nd March 1977

On Feb. 18, 1977, a modified Boeing 747 transport took off from Edwards Air Force Base, California, with the first Space Shuttle Orbiter mounted on its back. (Hey, sometimes we cover more than ancient history.) The event marked the first step in a new era of space travel.

Instead of launching earth satellites by means of costly one-shot boosters, several can be carried into orbit at one time by the Space Shuttle, which was built by Rockwell International. The procedure will result in a great savings in launch rockets and fuel. The Space Shuttle can also return to earth, land like an airplane, and be used again.

The 747 is used to carry the shuttle aloft, and in July it will launch the Orbiter at altitude for free-flight tests and landings. Later, when the shuttle is ready for space flight, the 747 will transport it from the big Edwards landing area to the launch site at Cape Canaveral in Florida.

All of which revives the subject of "piggyback" aircraft. A number of combinations have been tried for various purposes, and with varying degrees of success, since 1916. It's a fairly broad subject, and we'll cover different aspects of it in future columns.

One entirely inadvertent example that was "created" during World War II is worth mentioning here. That one was the functional opposite of the 747/shuttle combination. Instead of taking off locked together and separating to go their own ways, a pair of Avro Ansons took off separately and landed as a single unit. And there was nothing deliberate or planned about it. It was an accident that fortunately for all concerned had a successful ending.

Here's what happened. The Avro Anson twin-engine

trainers were on final for landing at a Canadian training center. One was below the other and, unfortunately, out of sight beneath the higher plane's nose.

The upper aircraft was on a faster rate of descent and settled right on top of the lower aircraft, which fortunately was in a position where none of the propellers could cut into the structure of the other plane. The two, now functioning in parallel as the world's only four-engine biplane, were able to keep flying.

Both pilots recognized the situation instantly and did not panic or try to pull the planes apart. Already set up for a landing, the lower pilot brought the instant biplane in for a smooth touchdown. The minor damage was easily repaired, and the Ansons were returned to service.

A further oddity of this Anson episode is that it was not an isolated incident. It happened on two other occasions with the same model, both of which are documented with photos. One was again in Canada, and the other was in Australia.

The photographs

1. A modified Boeing 747 takes off for its first flight with the Rockwell International Space Shuttle Orbiter on its back. Note the additional vertical fins that were added to the ends of the horizontal stabilizer.

2. The Space Shuttle lifts off of the Boeing 747 on an early unpowered test flight. Note that the 747 is in a shallow dive. For delivery to Cape Canaveral, the Shuttle stayed aboard the 747 for the landing and was off-loaded by a crane.

3. This pair of World War II Avro Ansons was just the opposite of the 747/Orbiter combination.

1

2

3

Unusual but 'conventional'

Quadruplanes represented the limits of responsible engineering

1st April 1977

As far as wing count, the rarest type of "conventional" airplane is the quadruplane. There have been planes with more wings, of course, but four seem to be the limit of responsible engineering.

Enough quads were built over the years to qualify them as an established type. At least one model actually got into production. Planes with five or more wings have mostly been curiosities that cannot be regarded as significant steps in aircraft development. This column is short to allow representative selection of quad photos plus long captions that treat each picture as its own story.

The photographs

1. This twin-engine British quad of 1916 had two names. It is identified both as a Pemberton-Billing for its designer, and as a Supermarine for the firm that built it. The rare feature is not the wing count, but the use of twin-row air-cooled Anzani radial engines at a time when most air-cooled airplane engines were rotaries. The four wings were intended for slow flight during night attacks on German Zeppelins. The only one built crashed during the test program. Note the left-hand propeller on the right engine, the right-hand propeller on the left engine, and how the flying wires pass through the intermediate wings.

2. After evaluation of a single prototype, at least 10 British Armstrong-Whitworth FK-10s were built in 1917. The main purpose of four wings on this military observation model was to keep the chord narrow to minimize interference with downward vision. The heavy stagger further improved the field of view and made a notable contribution to longitudinal stability.

3. The German Euler quad of 1917 started out as a direct copy of a captured French Nieuport Model 11 sesquiplane. When the triplane boom got going, Euler simply added wings to the same fuselage but didn't stop with only three. The fourth wing made no improvement, and only this single example is known to have been built. Note the absence of ailerons. The upper wing pivoted on its tubular main spar to perform that function.

4. It is doubtful whether this German Naglo fighter of late 1917 really qualifies as a quad, though it is identified as such. It was a product of the triplane boom that had a little extra in the form of what can best be described as a "winglet" beneath the fuselage that looks as though it had been put on as an afterthought.

5. Little is known of this Soviet two-seater built in the early 1920s. Although on skis, it is conventional in all respects but wing count. Considering the low power of a war-surplus rotary engine and no evidence of provisions for armament, it must have been intended as a trainer.

6. Matthew Sellers believed that the way to fly on very low horsepower was to use lots of wing area, hence a quad arrangement to get the necessary area while keeping the span short. Two of the wings were movable and doubled as ailerons. He built several ships of this general configuration from before World War I through the 1920s. He managed to fly one with as little as eight horsepower.

7. By far the most ambitious quad effort was this French Besson of the early 1920s. It had four 260-horsepower Salmson engines mounted in pairs in two nacelles that were themselves mounted on the second wing from the bottom. Its unique feature was the use of positive and negative stagger from the wings, which spanned 93 feet. Note the wartime Nieuport 11 Bebe that posed for comparison.

1

2

3

4

5

6   7

F2B or not to be

Model 69 became the first in a long line of Navy fighters that performed in air shows

2nd April 1977

The Boeing Airplane Company got into the fighter-plane business in 1921 by underbidding the rest of the industry on a U.S. Army order for 200 Thomas-Morse MB-3s.

At that time, the designers of military airplanes did not own the designs if the Army had bought them. It was a bum deal. The designer would have all the cost of developing a new model and then might see someone else get the production order.

Thomas-Morse built four prototype MB-3s and 61 production models. Boeing and five other companies bid on the later 200-plane order, and Boeing got it.

There were enough things structurally and aerodynamically wrong with the MB-3 to convince Boeing that there had to be a better way to build fighter planes. Boeing developed a new design entirely on its own, and even though it was much better than anything the Army had at the time, the Army was not interested in buying additional planes just because they were better.

Finally, after nearly a year and a half of trying, Boeing got an order for production Army fighters designated PW-9 (for pursuit, water-cooled, Model 9).

The PW-9, powered with a 435-horse Curtiss D-12 engine, remained in production until 1928, with 115 built. The Navy bought 43 near-duplicates as FBs. The major change on the principal FB-5 production model was a 500-horse Packard engine. By this time, the Navy was getting interested in air-cooled radial engines, and had Boeing try one in a variant of the production model, the FB-4.

This first radial, the Wright P-1, was a failure, so the Navy (on it own) installed a new Pratt & Whitney Wasp in the same airplane and redesignated it the FB-6. It was a great success, and the Navy asked Boeing to build production versions as FB-7s. Boeing had other ideas. It had been working on its own to develop a new model designed specifically for the Wasp and easily convinced the Navy that it would be better off with a brand-new design than a mere adaptation of a four-year-old model. The Navy went along with that and bought the Boeing-financed Model 69 prototype, designated it the XF2B-1 and ordered 32 production F2B-1s for service on aircraft carriers.

While every bit as good an airplane as the similarly powered Curtiss F6C-4 Hawk for the Navy, the F2B just did not have the glamour that went along with the Curtiss. The F2Bs earned a considerable degree of fame, however, by becoming the first of a long line of Navy fighters used in air-show maneuvers of three or more airplanes in close formation.

The F2Bs first came to public notice at the 1928 National Air Races in Los Angeles. Under the leadership of Lieutenant Tommy Tomlinson, an 18-plane fighter/bomber squadron put on an overwhelming "shoot up" of the field and grandstands in an operation that has been prohibited ever since.

The highlight of the Navy's part of the show, however, was the three-ship aerobatics that was performed by an F2B-1 team known as the Three Sea Hawks. Multiplane aerobatics were not exactly new, but something was added this time. The three planes were tied together by 25-foot lengths of rope connecting their lower wingtips. The F2Bs took off, maneuvered and then landed, still tied together. Cloth streamers were tied to the ropes at intervals so that the public could see them from the ground.

As though three planes tied together were not enough, the whole squadron flew tied together on another occasion, with each of the six three-plane elements tied. I haven't found any evidence to indicate that any other service models consistently demonstrated this trick.

The photographs

1. The Navy wanted Boeing to put the new Wasp radial engine in a four-year-old design, but Boeing easily convinced the brass that its new Model 69 would be better. The Navy bought the company-financed prototype shown here and designated it the XF2B-1.

2. The production F2B-1 showed considerable detail refinement over the prototype, noticeable here in the nose, landing gear and tail. This is one of two Model 69Bs that the Navy allowed Boeing to build for export.

3. Navy Squadron VF-1 didn't quite match the "Three Sea Hawks" by doing aerobatics while tied together by short ropes, but they did put on a good show by putting the whole squadron in the air with each three-plane element tied together.

4. Present-day aerobatic teams do a lot of tight formation flying, but this vertical arrangement, flown by Boeing F2B-1s, isn't seen in the modern repertoire. Note the variation in size and location of the wing insignias.

1

2

3

4

Jenny wing extravaganza

Modifications firms reaped JN business following World War I

1st May 1977

A question that was asked about modified Curtiss JN-4 Jennies opens up a fascinating subject that could easily fill a book of its own.

As is generally known, the Jenny was the principal primary trainer of the U.S. Army and the Canadian Air Force in World War I. Approximately 6,030 were delivered from April 1917 until the Armistice.

The Army then decided that the JN-4Ds, powered with the 90-horse Curtiss OX-5 engines, no longer fit its needs, so most of the airplanes ended up on the surplus market. Relatively few of the advanced training models (the JN-4H and the JN-6H, powered with the U.S.-built Hispano-Suiza "Hisso" engine) reached civilian hands. The Army did not retire the last of those until August 1927.

Many owners of the sluggish OX-powered models ended up putting in more powerful engines. As the most available war-surplus model, the Jenny was so widely used by barnstormers and air circuses of the early 1920s that it gave its name to the period: "The Jenny Era."

One facet of this era was the complete absence of regulation. An international system of airplane and pilot licensing had been set up as a by-product of the Treaty of Versailles, but the United States was not a party to it. Unlicensed U.S. pilots were free to conduct any type of aerial activity in unlicensed airplanes.

Under that same freedom, they could undertake any kind of modification to the airplanes that they thought would work. There wasn't much of a civilian aircraft industry in those aerodynamically depressed days. New production just could not compete with cheap war-surplus. Some firms adapted to the situation by developing and marketing various improvements for the Jenny and also selling kits or complete components.

Other than converting the open cockpits to cabins for comfort, and putting in larger engines for better performance, there wasn't much that could be done with the Jenny fuselage. The big area of improvement was in the wings.

One trick, often undertaken by owners on their own, was to increase the wing area by replacing the short-span lower wing panels with a set of uppers. Since the king posts that braced the overhanging upper wing could not be used on the underside of the lower wings, it was necessary to brace the increased span with a third set of interplane struts on each side.

Sikorsky and Sperry came out with new wings that converted the old Jenny into a parasol monoplane. A different approach was taken by another firm that stuck to the biplane configuration but single-bay panels with a later and much thicker airfoil section and shorter span. They were marketed as the ALCO High-Lift Wing and could also be adapted to the contemporary Standard J-1.

The wings on the Jenny seaplane 359W, which was operated by Alaska aviation pioneer Shell Simmons until the early 1930s, appear to be ALCO wings.

Jennies restored for movie, air-show and television work after World War II were in a different situation. It was essential to keep the wings "pure" for the sake of appearance and to provide all the struts, king posts and wires that were essential to wingwalking.

Old engines, however, were not dependable enough to be trusted when working on tight schedules. They were therefore replaced by higher powered units of WWII vintage. While the loss of authenticity was a matter of concern to airplane buffs, financial loss to a studio that had to keep a camera crew, actors and extras standing around for hours while a balky antique engine was coaxed into action was a matter of much more tangible concern.

The photographs

1. Extra wing area for this Jenny was obtained by replacing the short-span lower wing panels with a set of upper panels. Note the additional struts near the wingtips. Power has been increased by replacing the original Curtiss OX-5 engine with a 150-horsepower Wright Hispano, or Hisso.

2. This Curtiss JN-4D has been converted to a parasol monoplane with the installation of a new wing that was designed and built by Sikorsky. Lettering on the vertical fin reads "Wings by Sikorsky."

3. After its regular wings were damaged, this Alaska-based Jenny seaplane was fitted with ALCO High-Lift Wings. Like Sikorsky, the Allison Airplane Co. (ALCO) designed and built replacement wings for Jennies and other old biplanes in the early 1920s.

4. This rebuilt Jenny flew in air shows after World War II. It used a 200-horsepower Ranger engine in a steel-tube fuselage that was adopted from another airplane, but it retained the original Jenny wings that were essential to the true wingwalker's performance.

5. More engine changes resulted when even the Ranger wasn't reliable enough for air show and movie work. Authenticity really took a beating when a 220-horsepower Continental radial engine was installed.

1

3

4

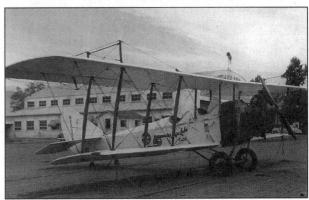

5

Lindbergh had the Spirit

But the world paid homage to the solo achievement of a remarkable individual

2nd May 1977

May 20-21, 1977, marks the 50th anniversary of Charles A. Lindbergh's epochal flight from New York to Paris, which was inspired by a $25,000 prize posted by Raymond Orteig in 1919.

By the time Lindbergh was ready to go, the ocean hop was shaping up to be a full-fledged race. One contestant had crashed on takeoff in August 1926, before Lindbergh decided to enter, and another had crashed on a test flight in April 1927.

A French contestant took off from Paris in May and vanished without a trace. The day Lindbergh arrived at his starting point on Roosevelt Field, Long Island, two other contestants were already there. They were planning to make the flight as a team. Had Lindbergh not beat them to it, the other men would have been first, but the impact would not have been the same. The world paid homage to the solo achievement of a remarkable individual, not to technology or an elaborate organization.

The major result of the Lindbergh flight was to awaken the world to the potential of commercial aviation and trigger a period of intense development and production that has since been referred to as The Lindbergh Boom.

The airplane itself was a minor miracle for the time. Named the Spirit of St. Louis in honor of its backers' hometown, but identified by Ryan, its builder, as the Model NYP (for New York-Paris), the plane was a special-purpose custom job that was designed and built in 60 days. No other firm would take the job or meet the timetable.

As a design, the NYP contributed nothing to state-of-the-art aeronautics. In the interests of reliability, it was extremely conservative in all aspects. It drew heavily on the 1926 Ryan M-1 open-cockpit mail plane and the later B-1 cabin monoplane whose construction was just getting underway when work began on the NYP.

A major change was to increase the wingspan to carry the 450-gallon fuel load for the 220-horsepower Wright J-5 Whirlwind engine. For safety, Lindbergh wanted the controls behind the main 200-gallon gas tank. That allowed a smooth nose without the drag of the windshield break. The wing ribs were the same as the M-1's and the tail surfaces were from the M-1 as well. The longer fuselage was essentially that of the B-1, as was the wide-track landing gear.

The 60-day construction period began Feb. 27, 1927, in a former fish cannery that was located some distance from a small flying field at Dutch Flats on the San Diego shoreline.

It was necessary to take one side of the wide landing gear off to get the fuselage out the door, and the extra-long wing had to come out an upstairs window. Everything was then hauled to Dutch Flats for final assembly. The first flight was made on April 28.

The tests went well but were not conducted at full gross weight. Because the field, an abandoned Army facility, was so rough, the fuel load was kept at 300 gallons. It was feared that a heavier load would damage the landing gear.

Finally, after 23 flights totaling 4 hours 15 minutes, Lindbergh headed the Spirit of St. Louis toward its namesake city as the only stop on his flight to New York and then Paris. The 1,500-mile hop took 14 hours 25 minutes, more than three times the airplane's previous total flight time. The flight to New York took another 7 hours 25 minutes.

After a few more test hops in New York, the Spirit of St. Louis departed for Paris with 465 gallons of fuel aboard. It covered the 3,610 miles in 33-1/2 hours and arrived with 85 gallons of leftover fuel.

After its stateside return by ship, the Spirit of St. Louis toured the continental United States and then South America. In April 1928 it was flown to Washington, DC, and placed in the Smithsonian Institution. In 1976 the plane was transferred to the Smithsonian's new National Air and Space Museum, where it is now on display.

Following columns will cover other aspects of the Lindbergh flight, the competitors, and the many copies of the Spirit of St. Louis.

The photographs

1. Charles A. Lindbergh and the Ryan Model NYP "Spirit of St. Louis," the most famous pilot-and-plane combination of all time.

2. The fuselage of the "Spirit of St. Louis" gets towed from Ryan's fish cannery to the waterfront airport in San Diego for final assembly. Note the mismatched wheels.

3. The "Spirit of St. Louis" on a test flight over San Diego before leaving for New York and its date with destiny. With one exception, Lindbergh was the only pilot to fly the aircraft. He let an Army friend fly it once.

1

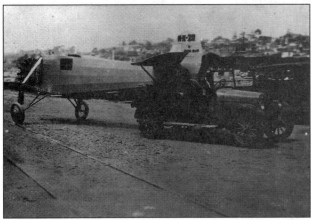

2

3

Others tried the Atlantic

Lindbergh wasn't the first to attempt it, just the first to actually do it

1st June 1977

In further honor of the 50th anniversary of Lindbergh's New York-to-Paris flight, let's take a look at the other competitors for the $25,000 Orteig prize.

The photographs

1. Rene Fonck, France's leading World War I ace, was the first contestant to actually get started on the transatlantic mission — before Lindbergh even got the idea of trying it himself. Fonck had a special Sikorsky trimotor biplane built in New York. The tests went well, and with three others in his crew he was ready to start from New York's Roosevelt Field on Sept. 21, 1926. The auxiliary jettisonable landing gear, intended to support the overload at takeoff, came loose and veered the ship off the runway. The rest of the gear broke and the plane caught fire. Fonck and his copilot escaped from the open cockpit, but the two others, trapped in the fuselage, died. Fonck immediately tried to get backing for another attempt, but eventually gave up.

2. The best-equipped contestant was Commander Richard E. Byrd of the U.S. Navy, who had flown over the North Pole in May 1926, and would later fly over the South Pole. His special Fokker trimotor, "America," cracked up on its first flight in April 1927 because Byrd stubbornly insisted on taking himself and his crew along on the test hop, which builder Tony Fokker wanted to make solo. The plane was not ready to go again until after Lindbergh completed his flight. Subsequent delays ensued while they waited for good weather all the way across because pilot Bert Acosta couldn't fly with instruments. Takeoff was finally made on June 29, with backup pilot Bernt Balchen handling all of the weather flying, which was most of it. Landfall was made on the coast of France far south of the intended point. Balchen was all for going straight cross-country to reach Paris before dark, when it was due to fog in. Byrd, however, ordered another route that lost precious hours before they got to a fog-bound Paris. There was nothing to do but head back to a clear spot on the coast and ditch offshore. The spot, Omaha Beach, was to become famous for the World War II invasion in 1944.

3. Lieutenant Commander Noel Davis of the U.S. Navy persuaded the Army to let the Keystone Aircraft Company build him a special trimotor version of the standard contemporary LB-5 Army bomber, which he named "American Legion" for his backers. With Navy Lieutenant H.S. Wooster as copilot and navigator, he made a test flight out of Langley Field in Hampton, Virginia, on April 26, 1927. The plane crashed immediately after takeoff, killing both men; the cause of the crash was never determined.

4. Another French ace, Charles Nungesser, was the first contestant to actually get away. Francois Coli was the navigator, and the plane was a converted French Navy Levasseur scout. To reduce drag, the landing gear was dropped after takeoff, and the plane was scheduled to splash down in New York Harbor. The fuselage was supposedly watertight to keep it afloat. The "White Bird," as it was named, was last seen over Ireland. No trace of it ever turned up. In one of the greatest misconceptions of all time, the U.S. ambassador to France advised his government that the French would be hostile toward any American flier arriving in Paris so soon after the disappearance of their heroes, Nungesser and Coli.

5. The Wright-Bellanca "Columbia" of 1926 was the airplane whose capabilities convinced Lindbergh that the flight was possible. He tried to buy it but couldn't. After it was equipped with long-range tanks by new owner Charles Levine, the "Columbia" set a world's endurance record of 51 hours 11 minutes on April 12-14, 1927, with pilots Clarence Chamberlin and Bert Acosta aboard. Management indecision and a fantastic game of "musical pilots" kept the Bellanca from taking off before Lindbergh; finally, with Chamberlin piloting and owner Levine as a passenger, it got underway on June 4. Since the Paris goal had been achieved, Chamberlin headed for Berlin. He came down 110 miles short, but did set a nonstop distance record of 3,905 miles.

1

2

3

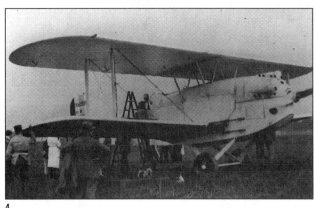

4

5

Maitland and Hegenberger to Hawaii

In many ways, it was the polar opposite of that other transoceanic flight

2nd June 1977

Every aviation journal in the country and quite a few non-aero pubs are taking note this summer of the 50th anniversary of Lindbergh's world-shaking New York-to-Paris flight.

It will be interesting, therefore, to see how many will recall a transpacific flight that came five weeks later and set records of its own.

From the standpoint of organization and equipment, the Maitland-Hegenberger flight from Oakland to Hawaii in a U.S. Army transport was quite the opposite of the Lindbergh flight.

Instead of a private individual raising his own capital and conducting an industry-wide search for suitable equipment, the Army drew on its own considerable resources to equip its project.

Instead of having a single engine, the Army plane had three.

Instead of one man flying alone without radio, the Army plane had a crew of two and carried equipment for communications and navigation.

While the timing was close to Lindbergh's, the Army was neither in a race nor after a posted prize. Further, the project was not quickly conceived and executed, as was Lindbergh's.

Ever since 1919, Lieutenant Lester J. Maitland, one of the Army's top test pilots and for a while the world's "fastest human" as holder of the absolute speed record, had a burning desire to fly from the West Coast of the United States to Hawaii. He continually evaluated available aircraft and submitted studies to his superiors that showed how it could be done, but he was always turned down.

In 1926, however, the state-of-the-art was equal to the task when the Army bought three of the newly developed Fokker trimotors for evaluation. They were built in Fokker's U.S. plant at Teterboro, New Jersey, and were to be transport-cargo planes with the Army designation of C-2.

Maitland's persistence finally paid off, and the first of the C-2s was selected for the flight to Hawaii before work was very far along. To increase its useful load, a special long-span wing was built in Fokker's Holland factory.

The engines were the dependable 220-horsepower Wright J-5 Whirlwinds, just like Lindbergh used. After completion in standard cabin configuration, the C-2 was delivered to the Army's McCook Field at Dayton, Ohio, for installation of long-range tanks and other modifications.

In tribute to its mission, the C-2 was named "Bird of Paradise." The Army's top navigator, Lieutenant Albert Hegenberger, was selected to accompany Maitland, and the airplane was ferried to the West Coast. It landed at Crissy Field in the Presidio of San Francisco.

For takeoff with its heavy fuel load, the airplane was moved across the bay to Oakland's big municipal airport, where the runway had been lengthened to accommodate it.

Takeoff was on the morning of June 28, 1927. The flight itself was uneventful, except for failure of the communications radio and navigation radio beacons, as well as the Earth Inductor Compass that had served Lindbergh so well.

The 2,407-mile flight, made entirely over the ocean, set an over-water record (Lindbergh's longest stretch over water was just more than 1,900 miles).

Maitland hit his target right on the nose by resorting to dead-reckoning navigation. He and Hegenberger landed at the Army's Wheeler Field on the Island of Oahu after 25 hours 50 minutes in the air.

Following the flight, the C-2 was returned to standard configuration and served as a regular transport on the islands well into the 1930s. It was eventually returned to the continental U.S. and set up in the Air Corps Museum at Wright Field. Stored during World War II, it was scrapped when an unappreciative colonel wanted the space.

Maitland remained in the Army through World War II. He retired as a brigadier general, served as a state aviation official in Wisconsin and Michigan, and then embarked on a new career as an Episcopalian minister.

The photographs

1. A daylight start was made by the Army Fokker C-2 trimotor "Bird of Paradise." Pilot Lester Maitland and navigator Albert Hegenberger took off from Oakland Municipal Airport on June 28, 1927. As a result of their successful flight, two streets at the airport were named for them.

2. A daylight landing marked the successful completion of the 25-hour, 2,400-mile flight at Wheeler Field in Honolulu. The com/nav aids for the flight failed, and navigator Hegenberger had to rely on dead reckoning to reach his goal.

3. A flowery Hawaiian welcome awaited the transpacific fliers at Wheeler Field. Maitland is on the left; Hegenberger is on the right.

1

2

3

The Swift that wasn't

Army had little use for interim pursuit design

1st July 1977

As the 1920s became the 1930s, the U.S. Army Air Corps began to realize that the days of the biplanes as first-line military aircraft were coming to an end.

Consequently, it expected industry to develop new single-wing designs, particularly pursuits. The only one to get a contract for design and construction of a prototype was Boeing, and its single prototype, the XP-9, proved to be a lemon.

No more development contracts for monoplane pursuits were let for several years, but a couple of new designs appeared as the result of company-funded projects. The Army helped out to the extent of providing requirements, engines and military equipment, and results of government research in structures and aerodynamics.

Further, the Army tested the company-owned airplanes on bailment contracts. The object was to develop a design that would prove suitable as an interim monoplane pursuit and help the Army transition to more advanced monoplanes with all the latest concepts.

The interim design was to be a notable mix of the old and new: all-metal structure, but fixed landing gear and externally braced wings.

The two competitors were Boeing, with its Model 248 that the Army originally designated XP-936; and Curtiss, with a somewhat larger and heavier design it called the Swift in keeping with its practice of naming its airplanes after birds. The Army gave the Swift the experimental project designation XP-934. Boeing won the competition and began producing the classic P-26 Peashooter.

The Swift, on the other hand, had a problem-plagued background. It drew heavily on the Curtiss A-8 Army attack plane of 1931 for design details, including all-metal construction, enclosed cockpit, wing flaps and full-span leading-edge slats that opened automatically at 15 mph above stall speed. Armament, advanced for the time, was a battery of four .30-caliber machine guns synchronized to fire through the propeller. Two were in troughs in the traditional nose position, and two others were in external packages on each side of the cockpit.

The Swift was designed to use the 600-horsepower Curtiss Conqueror engine, a reliable, liquid-cooled V-12 whose development roots could be traced to World War I. The Army turned down the Conqueror, correctly believing that the antiquated engine was at the end of its usefulness for pursuit aircraft. Instead, the Army insisted on and got the air-cooled 700-horse Wright R-1820F radial. Curtiss did not like the idea, of course, but had to go along with it.

The airplane, which rolled out in July 1932, quickly proved that the substitute Cyclone was not the right engine. Within a month, the heavier and less powerful Conqueror was back. The Swift's speed improved, but its overall performance was hindered by a serious overweight problem. Curtiss still had a lot to learn about all-metal construction compared to its traditional tube-and-wood methods.

After Boeing got the order for 136 P-26As, the Army bought the XP-934 Swift from Curtiss and designated it XP-31 and then ZXP-31 (Z for obsolete).

The plane saw little use. It accumulated only 287 flight hours before it was surveyed in July 1936 and assigned to an Air Corps mechanics school.

The photographs

1. The original Curtiss Swift engine was the 700-horsepower Wright Cyclone air-cooled radial. The aircraft had been designed with a V-12 in mind, but the Army insisted on the radial. Note the odd feature of wing struts attached to the landing gear.

2. The Cyclone engine proved unsuitable for the Swift, so Curtiss removed it and installed the liquid-cooled 600-horsepower Curtiss Conqueror, which was supposed to go into the aircraft in the first place. Note the experimental Army designation of XP-934 on the rudder.

3. Racy looking despite its fixed landing gear and wing struts, the Swift lost out to the Boeing XP-936 in the competition for the Army's first production monoplane pursuit. The Army still bought the Curtiss, and designated it the XP-31.

4. Though its features included the antiquated open cockpit and wire-braced wings, the Boeing XP-934 was faster and more maneuverable. It could also fly higher than the Curtiss — on 50 fewer horsepower.

1

2

3

4

The fighter with doors

P-39's novel features attracted a lot of attention when it first appeared in 1938

1st August 1977

The Bell P-39, dubbed the Airacobra, was one of the more unconventional fighters of World War II. Its 1,200-horsepower Allison V-1710 engine, housed in the center of the fuselage, turned the propeller by means of a long extension shaft. The prop was not directly on the end of the shaft; it was above it and driven by a spur gear. That made it possible to mount a 37-millimeter cannon above the shaft, where it could fire forward through the hollow hub of the prop.

Because of the increased ruggedness of new all-metal airplane structures, cannons were desirable forward-firing armament for the new generation of fighters that was developed in the years just before World War II. Unfortunately, the things could not be synchronized to fire between the propeller blades the way machine guns could, hence the complicated arrangements.

The idea of shooting a cannon through a hallow hub instead of between the blades had been tried on the French Spad XII of 1917, but it was not notably successful. On that model, the cannon was nested between the two cylinder banks of a V-8 engine in a conventional nose installation and fired through the hollow hub of a gear-driven prop. A few experimental aircraft used that arrangement between the two world wars, but it never became popular except on a small scale in World War II. Either the designers were thinking small or the airplanes of the time could not carry much weight, because the original cannon considerations were all for a single unit in the fuselage. Two, one on each wing, would have simplified the installation problems but the war was well along before the multi-cannon ships, some with as many as four in the wings, went into action.

One expected advantage of the amidships location of the engine was improved maneuverability from having the engine mass on the aircraft's center of gravity, but the overall weight problem negated that theoretical advantage.

The P-39's novel features, including tricycle landing gear, got a lot of publicity when it appeared in April 1938. The U.S. Army eventually placed orders for 8,914 P-39s through the P-39Q-30 version, and the British ordered 679. Unfortunately, however, the P-39 was pretty much a lemon as a fighter plane. The Japanese Zero overwhelmed it in early action in the Pacific, and the British soon found out it was useless over Northern Europe. In fact, the British returned some 400 to the United States, which was forced to use many in the Pacific because more effective models were not yet in large-scale production. The rest of the British models went to the Soviet Union.

In fact, the only military outfit that really liked the P-39s was the Soviets, who found that they were adept at busting German tanks. After the United States acquired state-of-the-art aircraft in quantity, many of the older P-39s, and much of the model's late production articles, were sent from the factory in Buffalo to the Soviet Union via Alaska. The route became virtually paved with wrecked P-39s.

Despite its obvious shortcomings, the P-39 was kept in production through 1944, a fact that brought considerable criticism in the "Truman Report." The P-39 was out of the picture as a U.S. Army Air Force combat type by the end of 1943, and all examples in the United States had become surplus by the end of the war.

Even in the postwar racing scene the P-39 did not do well, with the exception of a spectacular victory in the 1946 Thompson Trophy Race. Tex Johnston flew a factory-modified model in record time that year, but that was to be the Airacobra's only major racing triumph.

Some derivatives of the P-39 will be covered in a future column.

The photographs

1. The XP-39 in its original form. It was extensively modified after tests in the NACA full-scale wind tunnel and redesignated XP-39B.

2. A Bell Airacobra for England, equivalent to the U.S. Army P-39D model. Armament was 20mm cannon, two .50-caliber machine guns in the nose, and a pair of .30-caliber guns in each outer wing panel.

3. Final production version of the P-39 was the Q model, with the same nose armament save for the four wing guns, which were replaced by a single .50-caliber gun mounted under each wing.

4. Tex Johnston won the 1946 Thompson Trophy Race with this hopped-up P-39Q. Note the automobile-type door on all the P-39s, and the installation of the pitot mast in the hub of the gear-driven prop. Johnston won the 10-lap, 300-mile race with an average speed of 373.9 mph, beating the prewar record by 90 mph.

5. The last flying Airacobras are these two, according to the Confederate Air Force. This photo was taken at the CAF's 1976 air show at Harlingen, Texas. The P-39 closest to the camera sports Soviet markings.

1

2

3

4

5

The Curtiss-Wright Junior

Simplicity was the key to keeping its price at $1,500 new

2nd August 1977

The distinctive Curtiss-Wright Junior is one of those airplanes that managed to become a classic without doing anything particularly notable. Thanks to a combination of design philosophy, timing and its unique pusher configuration, it made its mark in aviation lore.

The Junior was a Depression baby. In the prosperous year of 1929, giant Curtiss-Wright had taken over the well-known Travel Air firm in Wichita, Kansas, to expand its product line. Walter Beech, then president of Travel Air, became a vice president at Curtiss-Wright. Soon after, the Depression hit.

Sales of Travel Air's big three-seat biplanes and large cabin monoplanes fell to almost zero, so the firm quickly designed and built a smaller line of biplanes. When those didn't do well either, Curtiss-Wright closed its Wichita plant and moved its remaining employees into its Curtiss-Wright plant in St. Louis.

Beech also moved to St. Louis and gave designer Karl White a tough assignment: Design a two-seat sport trainer that would sell for $1,500, which he figured was about as much as your typical private pilot could pay for a plane at the time.

After drawing several layouts, White came up with a two-seat, open-cockpit pusher that was based on a homebuilt light plane called the Buzzard that a couple of test pilots owned. The final result was officially designated CW-1 (for Curtiss-Wright Model 1) and was marketed as the Junior.

Simplicity was key to keeping costs down. The Junior's engine was the 45-horsepower Szekely SR-3, a rough-running, three-cylinder, air-cooled radial that had a bad habit of shedding parts. The aircraft had no brakes, and only a tail skid.

The airspeed indicator, which wasn't FAA-required equipment at the time, was a flat plate on the end of a wire spring that was pushed back by air pressure and read against a calibrated scale. The fuel gauge was a Ford Model A indicator mounted in the front of the 10-gallon fuel tank that formed the forward part of the engine nacelle (as if it really deserved to be called a nacelle).

The airplane was virtually a powered glider, with 176 square feet of wing area and a gross weight of only 975 pounds. Top speed was a whopping 80 mph. Despite its low cost, the Junior did not save the St. Louis plant. It shut down late in 1931 after 261 examples were built.

The Junior soon fell into disfavor, mainly because of its cranky engine. A few owners installed bootleg engines of higher power and operated in areas where FAA inspectors were not expected.

Because of its configuration, the Junior was terrific for hunting coyotes, particularly with a shotgun mounted on a swivel post ahead of the front cockpit. With its slow landing speed and soft Goodyear Airwheels, the Junior could land in rough open country to pick up a kill.

A few Juniors survived through World War II, and the last significant gathering was at the 1949 National Air Races in Cleveland, where a special race was held for them. About a half-dozen showed up, mostly stock versions with the Szekely. A couple were used for comedy routines in postwar air shows, and one had a more powerful engine installed and operated on an experimental license.

Those that survive are in the hands of dedicated antiquers, who have had their problems with the plane. Parts for the orphan Szekely are not available, and the engine is not reliable, so owners have turned to latter-day flat-four engines like the Continental A-65. That, however, brings up all sorts of engineering and recertification problems with the FAA, but the troops are persevering and getting results.

Perhaps the ultimate compliment to the 1930 Karl White design is the fact that it has been fairly well duplicated in the form of the Woody's Pusher homebuilt, which pilots who cannot get hold of a genuine Junior are turning to.

The photographs

1. A 1931 Curtiss-Wright CW-1 Junior in standard configuration. It was used in a late-1930s air-show clown act. As built, the Junior had no brakes and only a tail skid.

2. A stripped-down Junior that was used in a "Grandma Snazzy" act in a 1947 air show. The original struts have been replaced by wires and a king post, but the old Szekely has been retained. The pilot at one time did an aerial strip tease in other light airplanes, but she couldn't in the Junior because her garments would have been sucked into the propeller.

3. A standard-configuration Curtiss-Wright Junior photographed at the National Air Races in 1949. This one has the FAA-required modification of a steel cable around the engine cylinders to keep the jug in place if the flange cracked. It was a common occurrence with the Szekely's cast-iron cylinders.

4. Modern powerplants like the 65-horsepower Continental A.65 are used in the few Juniors that antiquers fly today. One Junior with a new engine earned its keep by serving as a slow-speed camera plane for movie pilot Frank Tallman.

5. Woody's Pusher was a post-WWII reproduction of the Junior, with powerplant, landing gear and structural upgrades to meet modern requirements. That's your author ready for a flight at the 1968 EAA Convention in Rockford, Illinois.

1

2

3

4

5

Lopsided Luftwaffe

German Blohm & Voss BV141 set two-man crew off to the right of its fuselage and engine

1st September 1977

Special-purpose airplanes have been with us almost since the Wright brothers, but for the most part the features that helped accomplish their particular missions have been rather conventional, such as making an airplane bigger to carry more bombs or adding windows to the cabin to improve observation. Some mission-oriented designs are more extreme, like going to twin fuselages.

One distinction that almost all airplanes share regardless of their basic layout is symmetry. As viewed in plan form, the right side is almost always a mirror image of the left side, and with very good reason. The drag of the airplane, and the thrust if it's a multi-engine type, has to be kept equal on both sides of the center line.

Any multi-engine pilot knows the trim problems that arise when he loses power on one side. As a result, there have been very few airplane designs that deliberately departed from the tradition of symmetry. Those that did were striving so hard to accomplish a special purpose that the problems of trim resulting from asymmetric configuration were considered secondary. The only airplane with such a design philosophy to reach near-production status was the German Blohm & Voss BV-141 that appeared in 1938.

During the big buildup of the Luftwaffe that preceded World War II, the German Air Ministry issued a requirement to a few German manufacturers for an observation and ground-attack airplane, with special emphasis on the need for a superior field of vision for the observer.

The specification was not sent to Blohm & Voss, but their chief engineer heard about it and convinced the company to build a privately financed prototype according to some different ideas that

1

he had. The company not only built such an airplane, but was able to sell it to the Luftwaffe.

The major departure from conventional layout with the BV-141 was to set the two-man crew off to the right side of the fuselage and its single engine. The three civil prototypes and five military BV-141A-0 models that followed had conventional symmetrical horizontal tail surfaces, but the later BV-141B models went asymmetric on the tail too, carrying stabilizer and elevator only on the left side of the fuselage to reduce interference with the observer's field of view.

On the first article, which was later designated BV-141V-1, the pilot sat under a canopy that projected above the lines of the crew nacelle, but he was soon moved forward in

an all-glass nose. This was before the advent of molded plexiglass noses, so all the glasswork was made up of individual flat panels.

For the prototypes and A versions, power was supplied by an 865-horsepower BMW 132N, which was the U.S. Pratt & Whitney Hornet built under license in Germany.

The landing gear, attached to the wings just outboard of the fuselage and nacelle, retracted outward. The rest of the structure was entirely conventional all-metal stressed-skin monocoque type.

Because of its strange appearance, it was natural that the BV-141 would be viewed with skepticism by conservative officialdom. All sorts of objections were raised.

However, further B versions were authorized. Major changes included a slightly lengthened wingspan, more forward taper on the wing's trailing edge, the left-side-only horizontal tail, and a more powerful BMW 801A engine that delivered 1,560 horsepower for takeoff. The extra horses gave the BV-141B a top speed of 229 mph at sea level and 272 mph at 16,000 feet.

The B models did not get to the Luftwaffe testing center until early 1941. By that time, prejudiced officials were saying that its intended mission was already covered by other models in service, and the full production order for squadron service was canceled after only 28 BV-141s had been built.

The photographs

1. Original wing shape of Blohm & Voss BV-141s through the A version had heavy sweepback on the leading edges and straight trailing edges with very slight forward taper to the ailerons. This is the second built, but it was designated BV-141 V1.

2. An offset crew nacelle is the outstanding feature of the BV-141. This is the first one built, and it later was designated the BV-141 V2. Note the conventional horizontal tail used on the prototypes and A versions.

3. The third prototype carried civilian markings at first but was soon repainted in full Luftwaffe colors and markings. Note the details of the glassed-in nose and the outward-retracting landing gear.

4. A flight view of the BV-141B shows off the asymmetric features of the Blohm & Voss design. Armament was two fixed forward-firing machine guns, two flexible rear-firing guns and four 110-pound bombs.

2

3

4

The seven 'Spirits of St. Louis'

The first replica was built for a Japanese newspaper, the most recent by EAA

2nd September 1977

As part of the 50th anniversary of Charles Lindbergh's transatlantic flight of 1927, a replica of the Spirit of St. Louis is touring the United States. Beyond all doubt the world's most famous airplane, the original has been on display in the Smithsonian Institution since 1928.

Replicas of the Spirit of St. Louis have been built in surprising numbers, but before we get into details let's discuss a small problem of semantics. There was only one *replica* of the Spirit of St. Louis, but it did not carry the name. All the others, with the same name, number and coloring, are *reproductions*. Louis Casey, curator of aeronautics at the National Air & Space Museum, pointed out a few years ago that only the original builder can make a replica. Those built by others, no matter how accurate, are correctly called reproductions. However, just as there ain't no such word as ain't, the public calls reproductions or facsimile airplanes "replicas" despite Mr. Casey and his dictionary. So will we.

The original Lindbergh airplane was identified by the builder, Ryan Airlines of San Diego, as Ryan Model NYP, which indicated that its intended purpose was to fly from New York to Paris. Shortly after that flight, Ryan got an order from a Japanese newspaper syndicate for an exact duplicate. Ryan built it in the summer of 1927 and called it NYP-2. The firm then went on to build production cabin monoplanes that were structurally quite similar to the first NYP except for slightly shorter wings, a slightly larger tail and, of course, the commercial appointments.

The principal model that sold was the B-1, which used the same 220-horsepower Wright J-5 Whirlwind engine of the NYP, as well as its distinctive propeller spinner.

Nothing more was done with replicas of the Spirit of St. Louis until a movie was made of Lindbergh's 1954 book of the same name. It was released on the 30th anniversary of the flight in 1957 and involved not one but three replicas of the Spirit, plus restorations and replicas of other aircraft.

All three Spirit replicas were created by modifying existing Ryan B-1s – antique J-5 engines and all – to the peculiar configuration of the original. An easy change was to extend and square off the wingtips, but the "solid" nose took some doing since the controls of the B-1 were at the front of the cabin while Lindbergh sat well aft in his single-seater with no forward visibility. Relocating the controls of a B-1 would be a major job, as well as complicating the piloting problem, so they were left where they were. The "solid" nose was built up so that the top center and side panels were removable but covering conventional windows.

For pilot visibility other than on filming flights, the panels could be removed. When flying for the cameras, only the side away from the camera was uncovered.

Two of the movie replicas were worked up by Paul Mantz, who was then the leading supplier of airplanes for the movies. The other was turned out by aviation associates of actor Jimmy Stewart, who played Lindbergh in the movie.

Ten years later, another replica was built almost from scratch by Frank Tallman, Mantz's successor, for the 40th anniversary celebration in Paris. It flew the Atlantic inside a cargo plane, not on its own, even though it had authentic tank capacity and could have gone the distance. Tallman had the controls aft, too. The most recent replica is the one built by the Experimental Aircraft Association.

To avoid the difficulties of identifying all of these replicas by builder, such as "Jimmy Stewart's" or "Mantz No. 2," we have the handy-dandy Bowers system of Replica Ryan identification, based on Ryan's own procedure. Ryan officially designated the airplane built for Japan as NYP-2. Why not carry that on and number the others the same way, and in sequence? That makes the EAA replica the NYP-7 and leaves the door open for any subsequent replicas that might come along for other movies or anniversaries.

The photographs

1. NYP-2 was built by Ryan for a Japanese newspaper in 1927. Japanese registration was J-BACC, and the Ryan serial number was 36, only seven units later than Lindbergh's.

2. NYP-3 was originally Ryan B-1 NC7209, Serial No.

5

3

2

6

4

1

156. This, the Jimmy Stewart conversion, is now in the Henry Ford Museum in Dearborn, Michigan. Note the pilot's windows, usable when overlying solid panels are removed. The famous N-X-211 is just for show; the conversions were registered under the same numbers issued to them in 1928.

3. NYP-4 (Serial No. 153, Registration No. N7206) is the first of two Ryan B-1s modified by Paul Mantz for the Lindbergh movie of 1957. The right-hand solid nose panel is in place, but the center and left-hand panels have been removed for a ferry flight to an air show. This one now hangs in a St. Louis airline terminal.

4. NYP-5, Serial No. 159, is the second Mantz conversion. Note the original 1928 Registration No. 7212 at the top of the rudder. It was owned for a while by antiquer Dave

Jamison and appeared at air shows and in the EAA museum. It's now in the Nassau County Museum, where Roosevelt Field, Lindbergh's launch site, was located.

5. NYP-6 was built from scratch with an antique J-5 engine, not converted from an existing Ryan B-1. Registration 1967T indicates the year it was built, and the T stands for builder Frank Tallman. It's now in the San Diego Aerospace Museum with nose lettering proclaiming it "Spirit of St. Louis II."

6. NYP-7 is the EAA-built replica. The wings are a little shorter than the original, and it was built in two halves for convenience. Its engine is a seven-cylinder Continental R-670 instead of an antique J-5. N-X-211, loaned to EAA by the holder, is the actual registration.

Fairchild's folders

Folding-wing monoplane stunned the aviation industry

1st October 1977

Sherman Fairchild surprised the aviation industry when he developed his FC-1 (for Fairchild commercial) cabin monoplane in 1925 to provide a mount for his aerial-mapping cameras. For one, his new airplane was a monoplane at a time when practically every other production ship was a biplane. For another, it was efficient enough to operate successfully on the 90-horsepower, war-surplus, water-cooled Curtiss OX-5 engine. For a four-place airplane of the Fairchild's size and weight, that was phenomenal.

A bigger surprise, however, was the folding-wing. The object was to reduce the wingspan of the airplane for hangaring in smaller buildings or squeezing more airplanes into an allotted space. Many publicity photos of the time show Fairchilds being towed with their wings folded, as though that was the purpose of the feature. While it was a convenience, it was not the primary reason.

The details of the folding mechanism varied on different versions of the airplane. The prototype, which had a razorback rear fuselage that thinned down to a single top longeron aft of the cabin to form a triangular cross section, had a portion of the cabin roof hinge upward to allow the root portion of the wing aft of the rear spar to swing inward without interference. With the hinge point that far ahead of the trailing edge, the trailing edges would hit each other before the wing was fully folded back. As a corrective measure, the ailerons were extended to match the length of the wing panels themselves. Before folding the wing, the ailerons were disconnected and folded forward over the top of the wing to provide the needed clearance. The wing hinge was at the rear spar-fuselage joint, and the pivot point for the struts, which had to be in direct line with it, was directly below at the lower longeron.

Another special feature to adapt to the folding wing was incorporated here. Where the few other strut-braced high-wing monoplane designs used parallel struts from the fuse-

lage to the wings, Fairchild brought the two together at the fuselage to form a V. That served several purposes. It gave him a single pivot point without the need for disconnecting the forward strut, and it maintained the rigidity of the system with the wing folded.

The front spar was locked to the fuselage by a pin that could be moved into or out of position with a hand lever, the fastest single operation of the whole folding procedure.

There was room for improvement in some of the details, so production FC-1s and subsequent models were outfitted with a different wing-panel arrangement. Full-span ailerons did not prove to be desirable, so conventional lengths were used.

Instead of folding up the center portion over the fuselage as before, the trailing edge of the wing inboard of the ailerons was built in the form of modern flaps. They were unlocked and folded up and forward to give the necessary center clearance. The smaller ailerons had only to be raised to a near-vertical position for the wings to fold completely. That arrangement was retained through succeeding Fairchild cabin models through the Model 71 of 1929-30.

As would be expected, the original OX-5 engine was marginal for high-altitude photo work, so it was quickly replaced in the prototype by a 200-horsepower Wright J-4 Whirlwind air-cooled radial.

Some production FC-1s used the water-cooled 160-horsepower Curtiss C-6, but the FC-2 model used the later 220-horsepower Wright J-5 Whirlwind.

Seaplane and far-north bush operations called for still more power, so the 420-horsepower Pratt & Whitney Wasp engine was used in an improved FC-2 version known as the FC2-W (W for Wasp). That model also dropped an established feature (the razorback fuselage) and went to four longerons for the full length.

While a lot of other cabin monoplanes appeared on the scene from 1926-29, hardly any made use of folding

1

2

3

wings. The space-saving feature was not worth the effort involved in the folding operation, even though it was advertised to be quick and easy.

One aftereffect presented somewhat of a problem. With several hundred pounds of center of gravity moving aft about 12 feet as the wings folded, a lot of additional weight went onto the tail skid or tailwheel. That made lifting the tail onto a dolly or truck bed, or even just pushing the airplane around on the ground, a much harder job. With the wings in the normal position, two men could lift the tail.

The photographs

1. The first Fairchild cabin monoplane was powered with a 90-horsepower Curtiss OX-5 engine and featured a much neater radiator installation than most of its contemporaries. This view shows the two positions of the wings and the triangular aft portion of the fuselage.

2. Rear view of the later FC-2 Fairchild with revised wing-folding details. Ailerons are now standard size and "reverse flap" structures inboard of the ailerons fold up and over the wing to give clearance and increase headroom in the back of the cabin. Note the skylight.

3. The FC-2W featured a 420-horsepower Pratt & Whitney Wasp engine and a four-longeron rear fuselage. This publicity photo shows how easily a folding-wing airplane can be transported along a road.

Overhead airports

Take off by flying downward, and land by flying upwards

2nd October 1977

For as long as the airplane has been practical transportation, sport and war machine, its owners have been faced with finding suitable areas for taking off and landing. For short-range airplanes, the need for their base to be close to the area of operations was critical.

In the old days, it didn't take much effort to convert most any piece of flat ground with clear approaches into a usable flying field. There was no need to lay concrete for runways; the planes rolled on the turf with large wheels. With no brakes and only a fixed tail skid, there was not much taxiing either. If there were hangars, they were usually at midfield. The planes were rolled out, headed into the wind, and the takeoff run started from the point where the propeller was swung (no starters either). With the light wing-loading of the old airplanes, the takeoff run was sometimes only a couple of hundred feet at most, but the climb angle was pretty shallow. A clear departure path over a long distance was actually more important than the length of the field itself.

The landings were usually set up so that the plane rolled to a stop fairly close to the hangar or the flight line, and the ground crew pushed it in after the engine was switched off (some of the old engines did not have a setting for idle; they had two speeds: wide open and off).

Since the old aircraft didn't have much range, it was essential that the airfield was close enough to where the plane was put to work, particularly in the case of military types. Unfortunately, the military did not confine its activities to flat ground where it was easy to set up bases; a mountain area that was to be scouted could easily be beyond the airplane's operating radius from the nearest suitable flat ground.

French aviation pioneer Louis Bleriot, the first man to fly across the English Channel, recognized that problem and set out to do something about it. His approach was not to extend the range of the airplane but to base it nearer to the target area despite the absence of suitable terrain for conventional air fields. That called for modifying the airplane with a "landing gear" on top and revising the pilot technique to land *upward* and take off *downard*.

The "air field" was not on the ground; it was a stout cable stretched tight along the center line of a rectangle formed by four posts that resembled telephone poles. To resist the inward loads that resulted from the weight and tension of the cables, and the weight and impact load of the airplane, each post was braced on the outward sides by a couple of dozen cables that were fastened to stakes in the ground.

The operational concept was simple. The airplane would approach the cable from the open downwind end and slightly below, then fly up until the open hook of the "landing gear" contacted the cable. The hook was then snapped shut, and the engine was shut off. Takeoff was done in reverse. Get up to speed while hooked on, unhook when flying speed was reached, and then drop down slightly and fly on out.

It worked, as the photos show, but there is no evidence that it was very practical, at least to the point of encouraging other installations. The performance of the single cable would make crosswind operations virtually impossible for the marginally powered ultra-light planes of the day, even though the arrangement could be taken down fairly quickly and set up again, much like a circus tent.

The old 1911 overhead cable technique was reintroduced during World War II and saw limited applications as "The Brodie Device," in which light liaison planes in the Cub category hooked on to longitudinal cables stretched outboard from ships. Unlike the 1911 arrangement, the later versions allowed for aligning with the wind and using the ship's speed to reduce impact with the cable. Shore-based installations had the same wind-direction disadvantages as the 1911 model.

The photographs

1. Descent after takeoff is the piloting technique here. This experiment, conducted in 1911, tested the feasibility of operating airplanes in areas where the ground was not suitable for conventional flying fields.

2. Fly up to "land" was another procedure that was tested in this 1911 photograph. An overhead cable was used for launching and retrieving airplanes.

3. A U.S. Army Piper L-4B suspended from the Brodie Device, with its cable running the full length of the ship.

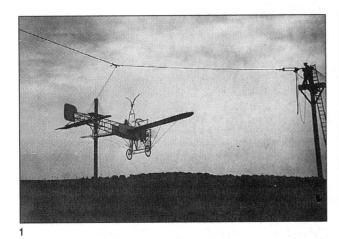

1

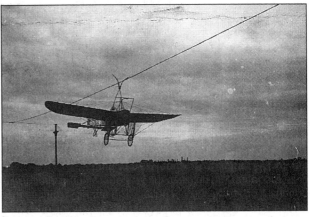

2

3

A wing of beauty

Supermarine Spitfire's production run lasted from 1938 to 1947

1st November 1977

Of all the world's military airplanes, the British Supermarine Spitfire is just about everyone's choice as the most graceful. That elliptical wing beneath a slim fuselage and closely cowled engine gives truth to the old statement, "If it looks right, it is right."

The Spitfire was more than just a good-looking airplane, however. It was also a great and very versatile fighting machine. In addition to its original role as a short-range interceptor/fighter, it became a high-altitude photo-reconnaissance aircraft, a long-range escort fighter and a ground-attack bomber, and was also fitted with folding wings for duty on aircraft carriers. After the war, it was even fitted with a second cockpit as a two-seat transition trainer. Some of the wartime high-altitude versions had pressurized cockpits, and late models joined the trend toward bubble canopies. It was even tried as a twin-float seaplane, but was not put into service in that configuration.

The prototype flew on March 5, 1936, and the first Mark Is began rolling out of the factory in May 1938. The Spit had the distinction of being the only British pre-World War II fighter to remain in production throughout the war. In fact, the last of the 20,334 built was not delivered until October 1947.

The Spitfire's graceful curves were supported by a complex structure that made for slow production, so the Supermarine was not on hand for the Battle of Britain in as great a number as the rag-and-tube Hawker Hurricane.

The outstanding recognition feature of the Spit was the elliptical planform of the metal-skinned wing, which spanned 36 feet 10 inches. On the earlier Marks, the wing completely enclosed a battery of eight .303-caliber machine guns. Later Marks went to cannon armament that projected well ahead of the leading edge of the wing.

Elliptical wings were not common to all Spitfire Marks, however. As the variety of missions assigned to the airplane increased, design changes were in order. For low-level fighting and grand-attack work, it was found advantageous to remove the sharply rounded wingtips and cap the end rib. That reduced the wingspan to 32 feet 7 inches and resulted in an obvious clipped look.

The tips were to be found on most, but not all, Mark V variants, plus the Mark XII and the Mark 22 (Britain switched from Roman to Arabic numbers near the end of the war).

The opposite approach was also taken, and the wingtips were extended to 41 feet 2 inches on high-altitude Mark VIs and VIIs. Those tips, too, had a noticeable "afterthought" look, with straight leading and trailing edges that clashed with the original graceful curves.

Naturally, the Spitfire's long production life involved other changes, including the previously mentioned bubble canopy that was found on the Mark XII, XIV, XVI, 22, 24 and Seafire 47 variants.

The 1936 prototype had a 900-horsepower Rolls-Royce Merlin engine driving a fixed-pitch two-blade wooden propeller. The engine gradually worked up to 1,720 horsepower in some Spitfires. With the Merlin boosted as far as it could go, the next logical step was to a bigger engine, the Rolls-Royce Griffon that started at 1,735 horsepower in the Spit XII and went to 2,050 horses in the Mark 22. Some of the Griffon versions used five-blade propellers while others went to two counter-rotating three-bladers on the same shaft.

The changes through many Marks may have been many, but the original Spitfire's overall design was still there as one of the aeronautical beauties of all time.

The photographs

1. The prototype Supermarine Spitfire in 1936. Note the fixed tail skid and two-blade wooden propeller.

2. Elliptical wing of this cannon-equipped Spitfire IX shows up clearly in this bottom view. Note the outward-retracting landing gear and a fixed tailwheel replacing the earlier skid.

3. Long, pointed wings are featured on this Spitfire VII high-altitude fighter. The tailwheel on this one retracts.

4. Clipped wings show up on the Spitfire XII, which used a Rolls-Royce Griffon engine in place of the original Merlin.

5. The final form of the Spitfire was the ship-based Seafire 47 with Griffon engine, coaxial propellers, bubble canopy and a revised vertical tail.

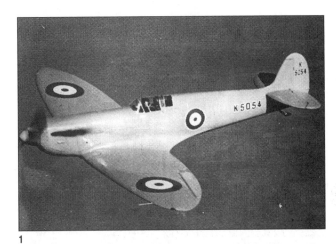

1

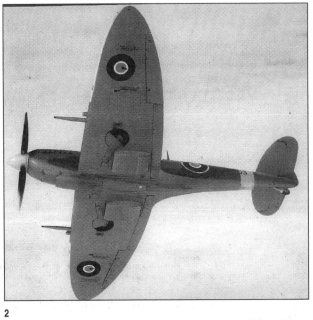

2

3

4

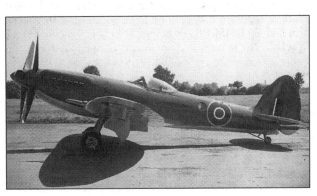

5

Boeing bomber boat

XPBB-1 combined the latest hull technology with an efficient high-aspect-ratio wing

2nd November 1977

The last large-scale use of flying boats by the U.S. Navy was during World War II. Early in that conflict the big boats were the mainstay of the Navy's patrol and bombing forces. Actually, the two functions were combined under a single designation (PB for patrol bomber), and the same airplane was used for both missions.

By far the best known of the Navy's flying boats was the Consolidated PBY, which started in 1934 as an experimental patrol plane, the XP3Y-1, but was soon redesignated XPBY-1. A further word about the naval designations here: The letter Y before the dash identified the builder, Consolidated Aircraft. Why not the more logical letter C? Because Curtiss had been using that one long before Consolidated came along.

The figure 3 in XP3Y meant that the design was the third P-model that Consolidated had developed for the Navy. The absence of a number in the PBY designation meant that it was the first PB-model for the Navy by Consolidated; its next one was the PB2Y-1. The PBYs were developed to the PBY-6A (A for amphibious).

The British bought some PBYs before the United States got into the war and designated them Catalinas in their own system, which used names instead of numbers and letters. When the U.S. government encouraged the use of popular names in addition to the numbers late in 1941, the PBY picked up the name already in use by Britain.

With war imminent, the Navy encouraged the industry to step up flying-boat development. Martin came through with the graceful gull-winged PBM Mariner series (M for Martin), which saw relatively large-scale production and served until the early postwar years. Boeing, which had built the famous Clippers for Pan American Airways, went to work on a patrol-bomber boat for the Navy under the designation XPBB-1, for experimental patrol bomber by Boeing. It combined the latest hull technology with the very efficient high-aspect-ratio wing that was then under development for the Army's four-engine, long-range B-29 heavy bomber.

Although it had the same wingspan as the bomber (139 feet 8 inches), the big boat had only two engines instead of four, making it the largest twin-engine flying boat ever built, and possibly the largest twin-engine design ever. The engines were the same 2,000-horsepower Wright Duplex Cyclones that were used in the B-29.

Since endurance on station, rather than high speed and altitude, was the desired characteristic, the weight of extra engines was converted to additional fuel capacity. The XPBB-1 had a theoretical endurance of 72 hours on 9,575 gallons of fuel. The speed wasn't much, just 219 mph max and 158 cruise. Gross weight was 101,000 pounds and it could carry up to 10 tons of bombs.

The Navy liked the results of the performance studies and placed an order for 57 production PBB-1s long before the prototype made its first flight on July 9, 1942. It was named the Sea Ranger, and the Navy financed the building of a new production factory at Renton, Washington, on the south end of Lake Washington. The prototype was built at the old Boeing Plant I, loaded on a barge and floated down to Renton for final assembly in the new plant.

As a Navy flying boat, the 10-place XPBB-1 was everything that it was expected to be, although it was never tested for its maximum endurance. The Battle of Midway in June 1942 changed the tactical situation in the Pacific, however, and the Navy decided that it did not need more flying boats. What it needed then was long-range land-plane bombers as the Army was using. So the PBB-1 contract was canceled and the Navy traded its new Renton plant to the Army for a factory in Kansas City that was already building North American B-25 Mitchell bombers. The Navy then put B-25s in service as PBJ-1s (J for North American, a carryover from a predecessor company called Berliner-Joyce).

The Navy also adopted Army Consolidated B-24 Liberator bombers as PB4Y-1s and developed a variant to more precise naval requirements as the PB4Y-2 Privateer. That left the XPBB-1 as a one-only, which soon caused it to be nicknamed the Lone Ranger. It remained at Boeing for more than a year for various tests and was flown away by a Navy crew in October 1943. It went first to San Diego, was then used for tests on the USS Salton Sea, and then flew nonstop across the United States to the Naval Test Center at Patuxent River, Maryland. After various test programs and use as a crew trainer, the Lone Ranger was scrapped in the early 1950s.

As for the Renton factory that the Navy had built, Boeing used it to build B-29s for the Army. When that work was finished after the war, the Navy used the space for airplane storage.

When the new U.S. Air Force wanted new Boeing C-97A transports and had obsolescent B-29s converted to aerial tankers in 1949, the Navy planes were moved out and the plant was restored to aircraft production. Boeing later bought the plant and still uses it for jet-airliner production.

The photographs

1. The XPBB-1 Sea Ranger was built in the old Boeing Plant 1, but final assembly was done in the new Navy-owned factory in Renton, Washington. Here the big flying boat is being launched for its initial taxi tests in July 1942.

2. The XPBB-1 on a high-speed taxi test on Lake

1

2

3

Washington in July 1942. Note that the hatch above the pilot's compartment is open, and that someone is standing up in it.
 3. The Lone Ranger, the Boeing XPBB-1, during a test flight in the summer of 1943. The exact date of the photo is not known, but the short-lived red border around the insignia gives a clue as to the general time frame. The border was soon changed to blue. Note the formidable defensive armament of the bow, side and tail-gun turrets.

Long live the Skyhawk

Twenty-five-year production run for the Navy's Douglas A-4

1st December 1977

In bygone years, the production life of military airplanes was usually short. For some models in the World War I years and the 1920s, it was sometimes only a few months or a year at most.

One, the Curtiss Hawk biplane, had what was then a phenomenal run from 1925-37. As airplanes became more complex during World War II, the production life of the most successful models was extended for as long as the design could be updated to remain competitive.

A longevity record is about to be set by a U.S. Navy model, the Douglas A-4. In 1978 this single-seat carrier-based model will have been in production for 25 years. At present, the line is scheduled to shut down when the current contract ends next year, but there is a possibility that the Navy will order additional A-4s.

Just as a number, 25 years doesn't seem like much, but in terms of aviation history it goes one-third the way back to the Wright brothers' 1903 flight at Kittyhawk.

The A-4 design originated in 1952 in response to a U.S. Navy requirement for a carrier-based attack plane. Although the Navy had advised the industry as to what it wanted, a heavy (more than 30,000 pounds) subsonic jet successor to the famous Douglas AD Skyraider, Douglas was getting concerned about the increasing weight and complexity of the naval aircraft of the time.

Douglas was able to convince the Navy that what was really needed was a single-engine model that weighed barely half as much as the Navy's specifications called for.

The Navy accepted the Douglas proposal and on June 21, 1952, it awarded the company a contract for an experimental prototype and several pre-production models. The naval designation at the time was A4D-1, which identified it as an attack (A) plane, the fourth of the type developed for the Navy by Douglas (D). The -1 indicated the initial configuration. As an experimental, the first article had an X preceding the designation.

Under construction in 1953, the XA4D-1 first flew on June 22, 1954. In comparison with contemporary jets, the A4D, which Douglas named Skyhawk, was unique. It had a delta wing like the tailless Air Force Convair Delta Dart, but it also had a conventional horizontal tail.

It was also a real midget, smaller than any single-seat fighter that the Navy had in service at the time. Because of its structural simplicity and light weight, it was known around Douglas as Heinemann's Hot Rod for its designer, Edward H. Heinemann, chief engineer of Douglas' El Segundo division.

The initial powerplant was the Pratt & Whitney J-65-W-2 that delivered 7,200 pounds of thrust. That was increased to 7,700 pounds in the early production models.

An improved A4D-2 version appeared in March 1956. The -2s served as first-line combat types until 1965, when they were redesignated as trainers. A night-flying version, the A4D-2N, appeared in 1959. A change to the 8,500-pound Pratt & Whitney J-52 engine resulted in the A4D-5 version in 1961.

In 1962, the Air Force and Navy adopted a common aircraft designating system. Most Navy types acquired new designations and the A4D became the A-4 in the new system. The A4D-1 became the A-4A, the A4D-2 became the A-4B, the A4D-2N became the A-4C and the A4D-5 became the A-4E.

In 1964 the Navy had Douglas develop a two-seat trainer version of the A-4. Designated the TA-4E, it had a 9,300-pound-thrust J-52-P-8 engine. The production versions were TA-4Fs and later stripped-down versions were TA-4Js.

A switch was pulled when the two-seater was reverted to a single-seater and produced as the A4J. Subsequent variations, with designations to A-4S, are too numerous to detail here.

At their peak of service, the Skyhawks equipped some 30 U.S. Navy and Marine Corps attack squadrons, and more than 2,900 have been built to date. Not bad for a design that the Navy had to be told that it needed.

The photographs

1. External ordnance is a feature of the diminutive Skyhawk. It can carry just about as much as can be hung on it. Note the drooped leading edge of the outer wing panel and the 20mm cannon in the wing root.

2. The Douglas Skyhawk's delta wing is evident in this formation shot from April 1960. The planes are A4D-2s

1

2

3

4

5

from the USS Forrestal. The long tubes projecting from the right side of the nose are probes for hose-and-drogue-type aerial refueling.

3. A two-seat development was originally the TA-4E, but it went into production as the TA-4F, as shown here, and later as the single-seat JA-4J. When the contract runs out in 1978, the Skyhawk will have been in production for 25 years.

4 & 5. In addition to refueling from standard Navy tanker aircraft, Skyhawks could be refueled from each other by what was known as The Buddy System in which a similar model carried external fuel tanks and a retractable hose and drogue.

The nifty Navy midget

Structurally simple SA-1 was designed for duty aboard battleships

2nd December 1977

Honors for one of the lightest airplanes ever flown by the U.S. Navy must go to the little SA-1 Ship Airplane of 1918-19. An ultra-light aircraft, this fresh-air single-seater was an oddity in configuration and its intended application.

The basic design can be traced to the little French Santos-Dumont Demoiselle of 1908, a monoplane in which the pilot sat under the high wing and the engine was just ahead of the leading edge. On landing roll, the pilot sat close to the ground and applied braking by reaching out with a gloved hand and grabbing a wheel.

Santos-Dumont produced Demoiselles as sport planes for several years, and the German Hans Grade adopted the design and produced it in Germany almost until the start of World War I.

The U.S. development was designed by the Navy, and two prototypes were built at the Naval Aircraft Factory in Philadelphia. The idea was to develop a small plane that could be carried on battleships and take off from a platform that would be built on top of a set of turret guns to do a little scouting. (The Navy had no aircraft carriers then, and shipboard catapult planes were several years in the future.) Landing back aboard was out of the question; it was a case of making it to shore or ditching at sea. The war ended before the prototypes flew, so the design never became operational.

As an airplane, the SA-1 was just about the most structurally simple flying machine that could be built. The wooden fuselage, a triangular frame with three wire-braced wooden longerons, was not even covered. The two lower longerons projected ahead of the rest of the structure to form crude anti-noseover skids, and the wheels were on a straight-across axle that was laid on top of the lower longerons.

The cockpit, if it could be called that, was formed of two vertical A-frames that started at the lower longerons and projected well above the upper, where they converged to form pylons that anchored the upper ends of the landing and control wires.

The vertical tail had a very low aspect-ratio fin-and-rudder combination, but the horizontal tail was what came to be called the "flying tail" type with only elevators and no fixed stabilizer. The powerplant was the fine little 60-horsepower Lawrance L-3, a three-cylinder, air-cooled radial.

The wing was as light as possible, and it was wire-braced from the top of the pylons and from the lower longerons. The aerodynamics were very poor, however, because of relatively low aspect ratio and the large gap where the two panels joined the fuselage.

A rather odd feature for the period was the use of wing-warping instead of ailerons for lateral control. Warping started with the Wright brothers and was still used on some first-line combat designs that were built as late as 1916, but it was pretty much a forgotten item by 1918. On the SA-1, warping was used for its weight-saving advantage. The front wing spar was held rigid by wires that were anchored to the pylons, the lower longerons and the two attach points on each spar. The rear spar, pivoting at the fuselage attach point, could be pulled up or down at the two wire-attach points to alter the angle of attack of each panel in opposite directions simultaneously. The lower, or "flying," wires were connected directly to a quadrant on a torque tube rotated by sidewise movement of the stick and moved with it.

That arrangement gave the wires the dual function of carrying the rear-spar flight loads and serving as control wires. The upper, or "landing," wires were actually single wires that ran from the attach points on each rear spar over two pulleys at the top of the rear pylon to the same points on the opposite wing to serve as carriers of the landing loads and as control "balance" wires. The system worked fine, but had the sluggish feel that was common to all wing-warpers. Lateral stick forces were relatively high, not so much because of the flight loads on the control wires but because of the physical effort required to twist the wing structure.

The SA-1's wingspan was 27 feet 8 inches, its length was 21 feet 8 inches, its wing area was 144 square feet, its gross weight was 695 pounds, and its top speed was a terrific 65 mph. Certain features of the SA-1 showed up in later designs, most notably the Roche light plane of 1925 that was produced as the Aeronca C-2 in 1929.

This little aeronautical oddity has been presented here because of recent interest in its potential as a homebuilt semi-replica. It could certainly use a modern engine, and some structural and aerodynamic refinement without losing too much of its antique appeal. One builder has already done that with his 1965 Scooter, but he covered the fuselage, lowered the landing gear, and made a much more modern design of it. Others are more interested in retaining the oddball antique characteristics of the original SA-1.

The photographs

1. The SA-1 had no ailerons. Lateral control was by wing-warping. Those wires attached to the rear pylon served as conventional "landing" wires and as the control system's balance wires.

2. The Navy's little 60-horsepower Ship Airplane of 1918-19. Note the pilot's exposed position and the high location of the rudder pedals relative to the seat.

1

2

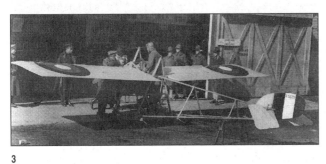

3

4

3. The pilot standing on the seat and people standing nearby provide a good indication of the SA-1's size. Color was overall light gray, the Navy standard of the time.

4. This rearview shot shows the large gap between the wings at the center section and the absence of a horizontal stabilizer. The circles on the wing are the U.S. military insignia as used from January 1918 through August 1919, with a couple of years for phaseout after that.

Spad for two

Its single-seaters were more famous, but French firm also built two-place models

1st January 1978

The little French Spads are probably the best-known Allied fighters of World War I. They were also used by Britain, Belgium, England, Italy, Russia and the United States, and led all the others as subjects of the popular air-war fiction of the 1930s.

First, however, a word about the name. There was no Mr. Spad. The name is an acronym for Societe Pour Appariels Deperdussin, a noted prewar builder of high-performance airplanes that set a world's speed record of 120 mph in 1913. After changing its name to Societe Pour Aviation et ses Derivees in 1915, the firm survived into the 1930s as a subsidiary of the Bleriot organization.

While the fame of the Spad line was earned mainly by the single-seat models VII and XIII (the model numbers were officially in Roman numerals, but are often seen in latter-day publications in Arabic), there were several two-seaters that never seemed to get out of the shadow of their illustrious little brothers. Actually, the first Spad to enter service under that name was a two-seater, but it was a push-pull model that was produced in very small numbers.

The first Spad two-seater to hold its own with its contemporaries was the Model XI of 1917. The full military designation was SXIA-2, meaning Spad Model XI, a Corps d' Armee (observation) type (A), and a two-seater (-2). The powerplant was the well-known Hispano-Suiza converted to a geared model that normally delivered 220 horsepower but was hopped up to 235 horses for the two-seater.

Geared powerplants were unusual in single-engine types of the time. The object was to turn the propeller at an efficient low speed while the engine developed high power for its displacement by turning at high speed. This gearing proved to be a source of constant trouble for those Spad models that used it.

The Model XI was essentially an enlargement of the Model VII with some notable changes, mainly in the wings. An oddity here was that the spars of the upper wings were closer together than the spars in the lower wings, which had the same chord. That difference resulted in non-parallel struts connecting the two wings.

Further, since the upper wing was quite close to the fuselage, it would have been very difficult for a pilot to get into a front cockpit directly under the wing as on most other conventional two-seaters. That problem was solved by seating the pilot a little further aft, under a large cutout in the center section, and then sweeping the wings back a bit to bring the center of lift in line with the airplane's center of gravity.

The French put the Model XI into production in large quantities, and 15 French squadrons and three Belgian squadrons used them at the front in 1917 and '18. The American Expeditionary Force (AEF) acquired 35 XIs but used them mainly for training. Unfortunately, the geared Hispano engine was a real lemon, so the French withdrew their Spad XIs from service in July 1918. Spad, meanwhile, had developed a replacement model, the XVI, that was identical to the XI except for a direct-drive Lorraine engine of 250 horsepower.

The only way to tell the XVI from the XI was by the appearance of large cylinder bank covers on the nose of the XVI. The AEF got six of those, and General Billy Mitchell used one as his personal plane. It eventually went to the National Air and Space Museum in Washington, DC.

The original Spad designer, Louis Becherau, left the firm to form his own company, so the next Spad two-seater, the XVIII, was designed by Andre Herbemont. That airplane was entirely different in structure and layout. It had a laminated wood veneer fuselage instead of the traditional wire-braced wood frame, sweepback in the upper wing only, I-struts, and the new 300-horsepower Hispano-Suiza engine buried in such a short nose that the engine was almost entirely underneath the upper wing.

The 300-horsepower Hispano was normally a direct-drive engine, but the special geared model used in the XVIII was a Moteur Cannon based on earlier engines used in Spads armed with forward-firing cannon rather than machine guns. The cannon rested in the V between the cylinder banks and fired through the hollow shaft of the propeller, which was raised above crankshaft level by the spur gears. Only one

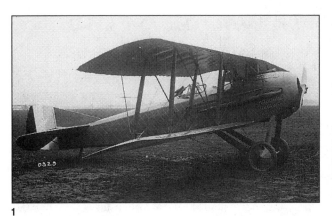

1

2

3

4

Model XVIII was built, and the cannon idea was dropped. Production orders were placed for the near duplicate Model XX with direct-drive engine and conventional armament, but relatively few were built when war's end eliminated the need for them.

The photographs

1. The prototype Spad XI. Note how the spur gears raise the propeller hub nearly to the level of the exhaust stacks on the low-mounted Hispano-Suiza engine.

2. Engine trouble forced this French-operated Spad XI down in German territory. Note the non-parallel align-ment of the struts due to the different spar spacing of the upper and lower wings.

3. General Billy Mitchell used this Spad XVI, which was identical to the XI except for a direct-drive Lorraine engine. Note that the Lorraine is mounted higher in the nose than the Hispano-Suiza and that the cylinder banks project outside the nose contours.

4. Andre Herbemont designed the later Spad two-seat-ers. This is the Model XX with a 300-horsepower, direct-drive Hispano-Suiza engine and conventional armament. The earlier Model XVIII used a geared engine and was armed with a small cannon firing through the hollow propeller hub.

Flying formation with itself

Depending on the angle, North American P-82 often looks like a pair of P-51s

2nd January 1978

Appearing from some angles to be two P-51s flying in very close formation, the North American P-82 was very nearly that. First flown in 1945, it was the result of a rush program to produce a long-range, twin-engine escort fighter for use in the Pacific. Rather than develop an entirely new model from scratch, North American found that it could meet the requirements by joining two standard P-51 fuselages with a new center section and horizontal tail.

Actually, the concept was not new; similar twins had been developed from single-engine models as far back as World War I.

World War II ended before the delivery of production P-82s began; 480 of the 500 ordered were canceled during the huge cutbacks that came after V-J day. However, 250, with designations to P-82G, were reinstated by 1946 orders.

As far as structure and systems went, the P-82 was very similar to the well-known P-51. A minor change was made in the Packard-built Rolls-Royce Merlin powerplants to have the right-hand propeller turn clockwise while the left-hand propeller turned counterclockwise to simplify the airplane's trim, as was done on the twin-engine Lockheed P-38.

The standard armament was six .50-caliber machine guns in the wing-center section. They could be supplemented by a detachable pod under the center section that carried a variety of machine gun or cannon arrangements.

Hard points were built into the wing to support a variety of external stores such as bombs, rockets or auxiliary fuel tanks.

Because the U.S. license to build them and use them in U.S. military aircraft expired at the end of the war, only the two prototypes and the P-82Bs used the Merlin engine.

A third prototype, the XP-82A, was fitted with the American Allison V-1710 engine that was used in the earlier P-51s and the P-38, and all the subsequent P-82 variants used it, still with the opposite-rotation feature.

The first production version of the Twin Mustang was the P-82B, which by a quirk of paperwork procedures had an Army serial number range lower than that of the three prototypes.

The 20 P-82Bs were built to the original concept of a long-range escort fighter. Two were converted to prototypes of night-fighter versions designated the P-82C and -D, with radar housed in a large pod under the center section and a radar-armament operator instead of a copilot in the right seat.

The next 200 were divided equally between 200 P-82E escorts and 200 P-82F night fighters. The final 50, still night fighters, were designated P-82Gs. Fourteen F and G models winterized for operations in Alaska were redesignated P-82Hs. The two-seat all-black P-82 night fighters replaced the twin-boom, three-seat Northrop P-61s that had entered the Army inventory in 1944. The P-for-pursuit designation was changed to F-for-fighter in June 1948.

While it missed out on World War II, two examples of the little-known P-F-82 achieved a degree of fame. Festooned with no less than four drop tanks, the P-82B "Betty Jo" flew nonstop from Hawaii to New York, a distance of 5,051 miles, in 15 hours 33 minutes in February 1947.

An F-82G of the 68th Squadron, 8th Fighter-Bomber Wing of the 5th U.S. Air Force scored the first USAF kill of the Korean War.

Two P-82s survive today. "Betty Jo" became a non-flying display at the Air Force Museum in Dayton, Ohio, and a B model went on to fly with the Confederate Air Force in Texas.

The photographs

1. The second XP-82 Twin Mustang over Southern California. Props rotate in opposite directions to cancel torque.

2. The first North American XP-82 Twin Mustang with Packard-Merlin engines and an eight-gun armament pod under the center section. Note the opposite settings of the propeller blades on the two engines.

3. This view of the P-82B "Betty Jo," starting its nonstop flight from Hawaii to New York, really makes the airplane look like two P-51s flying in close formation. The two drop tanks under the right wing are not visible here.

4. The single P-82D was converted from a P-82B to serve as a prototype for subsequent night fighters. Note the all-black coloring. The center radome contains APS-4 radar. Hard points are under the wing for external ordnance.

1

2

3

4

The speedy Curtiss Hawks

PW-8A placed third in the 1924 Pulitzer Trophy Race against pure racing designs

1st February 1978

Back in 1923 the Curtiss Aeroplane and Motor Co. brought out a new pursuit plane at its own expense. The U.S. Army was not officially interested in new pursuits at the time, but eventually bought the new Curtiss and two additional prototypes. They were designated PW-8s for pursuit, water-cooled and eighth model in the PW series. The third prototype, a test platform for a revised wing and radiator design, was designated PW-8A. Before it was delivered in September 1924, however, Curtiss was given a contract for 25 production PW-8s based on the second prototype. They were powered with the 435-horse Curtiss D-12 engine (also identified as V-1150 for a V-type with 1,150 cubic inches of displacement) and had thin wings braced with two bays of N-struts on each side.

A most unusual feature of the PW-8 was the use of radiators in the upper and lower surfaces of the upper wing. Curtiss had introduced them on high-powered racers in 1922. They were a military liability, however, and a plumber's nightmare, but they made for good streamlining.

The PW-8A, with wings of similar planform but a thicker airfoil, needed only one bay of struts. The surface radiators were replaced by a less vulnerable core-type that was built into the center section of the upper wing. That proved to be inadequate for cooling, so a "tunnel" radiator similar to what was introduced on the contemporary Boeing PW-9 was installed.

Using the same D-12 engine, the PW-8A placed third in the 1924 Pulitzer Trophy Race against pure racing designs. Its time around the closed course was 167.95 mph, which was not bad at all under the circumstances. The winning speed was 215.72 mph by a Verville cantilever monoplane that had retractable landing gear.

A further Boeing-inspired change was then made to the PW-8A. A new set of tapered wings was built and installed, and the airplane became the PW-8B. As such, it was the prototype for the long and famous line of Curtiss Hawks and won an initial Army order for 25 P-1s in 1925. (The old PW system was dropped and pursuits started a new series at P-1.)

The last five P-1s were fitted with later 500-horsepower Curtiss V-1400 engines and were redesignated P-2s. No production P-2s followed, but there were 25 P-1As, 25 P-1Bs and 33 P-1Cs.

By 1927 the Pulitzer Races had folded, but there were still events at the annual National Air Races for fast high-powered airplanes, and the Army and Navy still participated. By that time, Curtiss had come out with a later development of the old D-12 known as the V-1570 Conqueror that delivered 600 horsepower at 2,400 rpm. The Army ordered a stock engine installed in one of the P-2s and redesignated it XP-6 because of the engine change. In this form it became the prototype of the later and very famous P-6 series.

For the 1927 races, held in Spokane, Washington, the Army had Curtiss convert the 20th P-1A to an all-out racer under the designation of XP-6A. A special Conqueror engine hopped up to 730 horsepower at 2,600 rpm was installed, the standard tapered wings were replaced with the old straight wings of the PW-8A, and the still older PW-8 surface radiators were installed on both wings.

The XP-6A ran away with the race at 201 mph, and the XP-6 came in second at 189.6. The also-rans were stock Army and Navy pursuits from the squadrons. There were no competitive civilian racers at the time, nor would there be for two more years. Their appearance at the 1929 National Air Races started the military on its way out of the racing game.

The photographs

1. A Curtiss PW-8 production pursuit plane of 1924, showing thin wings with two bays of struts and the unique Curtiss surface radiators built into both sides of the upper wing.

2. The third PW-8 prototype was completed as the PW-8A with thicker wings and a single bay of struts. It originally had the same nose as the PW-8 and a core-type radiator in the center section of the upper wing, but it was modified to the tunnel type under the nose as shown here.

3. Tapered wings on the PW-8A turned it into the PW-8B, which became the prototype of the long line of Curtiss Hawks, starting with the U.S. Army P-1s of 1925.

4. The first production Curtiss P-1 became a test bed

1

2

3

4

5

for the 420-horsepower inverted air-cooled Allison V-1410 engine. Despite its low horsepower as compared to other Curtiss Hawks, it was entered in the pursuit-plane event of the 1926 National Air Races.

5. The XP-6A racer of 1927 was the 20th P-1A. It got the larger Curtiss Conqueror engine, the old PW-8A wings and surface radiators on both wings. The combination was a winner at 201 mph.

P-12 movie magic

Turning a single-seat Boeing 100 into a two-seat Helldiver

2nd February 1978

Antique airplanes that are used in the movies have fallen into several categories over the years:

✓ Authentic restored antiques that accurately represent the planes of their period.

✓ Excellent to mediocre replicas.

✓ Latter-day stock models with minor modifications or sometimes only a little paintbrush work to place them in an earlier era.

✓ And a few valiant efforts to modify an existing airplane to make it look like an entirely different model.

Some of these latter efforts have been very good, like the Vultee BT-13/North American T-6 combinations that became Japanese Kate torpedo-bombers in "Tora Tora Tora" and the T-6s that became very realistic Zeroes for the same film and then in the "Baa Baa Black Sheep" television series.

An earlier attempt to convert one model into another took place in 1948 when the late Paul Mantz, principal supplier of antique airplanes for the movies, converted a non-flying Boeing Model 100 single-seater into a two-seat Curtiss F8C Helldiver for the Gary Cooper movie "Task Force."

The success of the project depends on your point of view and attitudes in the matter of movie fakery and the adulteration of antique airplanes. It was either a great success as a Helldiver replica or a terrible thing to do to a classic Boeing.

Mantz had owned and extensively used a Boeing Model 100 since 1935. It was and still is a civilian counterpart of the Army P-12 and the Navy F4B-1 that went into service in 1929. In 1948 he acquired the unairworthy remains of another Boeing 100 and set about converting it into a Helldiver for the movie.

The Boeing had a straight one-piece upper wing while the Curtiss had a center section and noticeably swept-back outer panels. Since the Boeing wing was damaged and unairworthy, it was cut and re-spliced with the proper degree of sweep.

The fact that the Helldiver had ailerons on both wings while the Boeing had them only on the upper was taken care of by painting a set on the lower wing of the fake Helldiver. Since the Curtiss was a two-seater, an extra cockpit was installed ahead of the regular one on the Boeing, which put it up between the center section struts even though the pilot was considerably further aft in the original Helldiver.

The Helldiver had an entirely different landing gear

than the Boeing, so a suitable one was either acquired or concocted and installed. Also, a dummy vertical tail similar to that of the real Helldiver was built and installed. It was wire-braced as on the Boeing instead of strut-braced as on the Curtiss.

Altogether, it was a good enough representation for a fairly knowledgeable antique airplane buff to tell what airplane it was supposed to be. The experts could accept most of the inevitable technical inaccuracies, but one obvious marking was downright puzzling. The production Helldivers that operated from the carriers around 1930 were designated F8C-4s, but the movie ship was marked F8C-2. The two XF8C-2s were prototypes only, with X designations. They never flew with regular squadron markings. There was just no excuse for a goof like that. Nitpicking aside, the "Boeing Helldiver" looked good on a real carrier deck in the movie.

One still wonders, however, why one of the plentiful and bona fide two-seaters that were available was not chosen for conversion to the Helldiver role instead of going to all that trouble of reworking a single-seater into something that was supposed to be bigger. Ah, the mysterious ways of Hollywood.

What happened to the Boeing after the movie was shot? It was stored, then sold at auction as a basket case in 1968. An airline pilot living in Florida bought it and got it mostly restored to its original configuration, going so far as to build completely new wings. Lew Wallick and Bob Muckelstone of Seattle acquired it in 1977, finished the job, and flew it in the colors and markings of a 1929 U.S. Army Boeing P-12.

The photographs

1. A brand new Boeing 100, photographed at the factory on July 3, 1929. This model is the civil counterpart of the contemporary P-12 and F4B-1 fighters. Although the Model 100 was awarded an approved type certificate (ATC), NX872H was delivered with an Experimental license because the customer, Pratt & Whitney, was to use it as an experimental engine test bed. The Model 100 was the only U.S. fighter to receive an ATC.

2. A Curtiss F8C-4 Helldiver of U.S. Navy Squadron VF-1. Also known as the High Hats, the squadron operated the F8C-4s from the USS Saratoga in 1930 and '31.

3. *Action!* The fake Helldiver, old NX872H, simulated the start of a takeoff run. The plane was incapable of flight and was seen moving only with its wheels solidly on the carrier's deck.

1

2

3

4

5

4. The bogus Helldiver taxies on the deck of a real carrier for the movie. Wooden tracks for the camera dolly are in the foreground.

5. On Sept. 15, 1977, N872H — with new wings, a 450-horsepower Pratt & Whitney R-985 Wasp Jr. engine, constant-speed propeller, tailwheel, modern radio equipment and standard license — got back into the air. It has since been retired to the Museum of Flight in Seattle.

The Rearwin Sportster

Tandem-seat monoplane found a niche between the Monocoupe and the trainer market

1st April 1978

Rearwin Airplanes, Inc., of Kansas City, Kansas, was one of the relatively few airplane manufacturers that survived the Great Depression and stayed in business to help launch the post-Depression era of light airplane manufacture.

In 1929-30 Rearwin had only one design on the market – a thoroughly conventional three-seat biplane designated the Model 2000 that was marketed as the Ken Royce. The name was in honor of this two sons, Kenneth and Royce, who later became partners in the firm.

The Depression wiped out the market for that type of airplane, so Rearwin brought out a bare-minimum quickie trainer, the 45-horsepower Junior. An open-parasol monoplane with a single "bathtub" cockpit for the two occupants, it was a dead ringer for the contemporary American Eaglet, a product of the American Eagle Aircraft Co., also of Kansas City, that had just shut down. The resemblance was no accident; former American Eagle engineers came to work for Rearwin. Sales were slim, but enough to keep the firm going.

Things were looking better in 1935, so Rearwin introduced a new design, the Model 7000 Sportster. It was aimed at a new market considerably above the 36- to 45-horsepower trainers that were typified by the Aeronca C-3, the Junior and the Taylor E-2 Cub, but it was below the much more costly 90-horsepower Monocoupe.

The tandem-seat Sportster started with the reliable five-cylinder, 70-horsepower, air-cooled LeBlond 5D radial engine. Sales were good, and an improved Model 8500 soon appeared with the 85-horsepower LeBlond, more luxurious accommodations and more options.

The final versions of the Sportster were the Model 9000, which was available with the 90-horsepower Warner Scarab Junior, another five-cylinder radial that had been developed to compete with the LeBlond; and the 9000L, which used the 90 LeBlond.

The 9000L soon became the 9000KR, however, because Rearwin bought out the LeBlond Aircraft Engine Corp. of Cincinnati and moved it to Kansas City, where it became the Ken Royce Division of Rearwin Aircraft and Engines, Inc.

The same basic engine was then marketed as the Ken Royce in the manner of the 1929 biplane. The 9000KR was the deluxe model of the Sportster line and was easily recognized by the full NACA-type cowling that faired neatly into revised forward fuselage contours. Altogether, 260 Rearwin Sportsters were built from 1935 through 1941.

The photographs

1. The Rearwin Model 3000 Junior was a dead-ringer for the earlier American Eaglet. Note the single "bathtub" cockpit for the crew. It also had a 45-horsepower Szekely engine.

2. The first Sportster was the Model 7000 with a 70-horsepower LeBlond radial engine. It received its approved type certificate in June 1935.

3. This float-equipped Sportster was the Model 8500 with an 85-horsepower LeBlond and extras like an anti-drag ring around the engine. Note the increased fin area for seaplane operations.

4. The last and most luxurious Sportster was the 9000KR with a Ken Royce engine and revised nose contours.

1

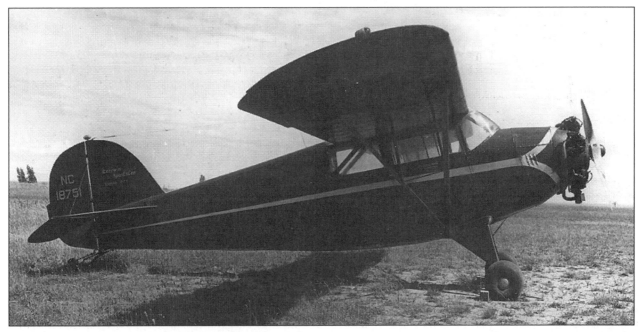

2

3

4

Story of a homebuilt

Recreational pilots can thank the Bogardus Little Gee Bee for the Amateur-Built category

2nd April 1978

The Bogardus Little Gee Bee isn't exactly an original design, and plans for the airplane have not sold by the thousands. It isn't a spectacular performer at air shows, and it doesn't have many flying hours. It doesn't get around to a lot of fly-ins, so it doesn't see much exposure. With so many negative factors, what's so special about the Little Gee Bee?

Well, the airplane is not famous for what it *is*, but it should be honored by all EAA members and homebuilders for what it *did*. Let's go back a ways.

The airplane itself is a pre-World War II design that was built in Beaverton, Oregon, by Tom Story. It was a development of an early-1930s design by Les Long that was known as the Wimpy. So, you say, just another homebuilt airplane. Yes, it was a homebuilt, but what many people do not realize is that in those prewar years homebuilts were illegal in most places. The federal regulations did not recognize them. Airplanes had to be licensed, and to be licensed they had to pass very involved and expensive engineering, flight and sometimes static testing. That put recreational designs out of reach for most of people who were interested in such things.

They were not illegal everywhere, however. Oregon, for one, had not adopted the federal regulations, so planes based there could fly without federal licenses. Such airplanes included odd modifications of standard models, pre-license-era types that were never licensed, and homebuilts. Thanks to freedom of government interference, eager builders like Les Long actually moved to Oregon so they could pursue their hobbies.

Well, George Bogardus of Troutdale, Oregon, was one of those believers in homebuilt airplanes. Unfortunately, Oregon eventually fell in line with the feds, so when World War II was over, homebuilts were illegal throughout the state. The prewar homebuilts were, for all practical purposes, grounded. True, they could be granted Experimental licenses, but only for specific purposes like demonstrations and testing. Such licenses were often for very short periods, and there was a problem in renewing them. Recreation was not viewed as a legitimate reason to issue an Experimental certificate.

Bogardus decided to do something about that. Since the only place anything could be done was back in Washington, DC, he took his case there in a way that grabbed attention. He obtained a 90-day Experimental license on the prewar Story, an aircraft he had modified with a 65-horsepower Lycoming engine and named with his initials, G.B. He headed east in August, made his pitch to the powers-that-be, and got back to Oregon in October.

There were no immediate results, but the flight and Bogardus' impassioned appeal eventually bore results. In 1948 a new Amateur-Built aircraft category was established as subcategory of Experimental. For the first time, amateur builders and fliers were "official," and they had regulations under which they could operate. Thanks to George Bogardus and his Little Gee Bee, we have our special category for recreation and educational purposes.

2000 update: The Story Flying Club is still alive with the same airplane. More than 500 Fly Babys have been built.

The photographs

1. The landing gear on George Bogardus' Little Gee Bee was rugged and simple. Note how the flying wires are anchored to the rigid structure behind the wheel. There were no shock absorbers; the fat tires of the Goodyear Airwheels did that job. The tailwheel was not steerable; there was just a spring-leaf tailskid.

2. The Little Gee Bee was quite a modern airplane for its time, with welded steel-tube fuselage, enclosed cockpit and a 65-horsepower Lycoming engine. The landing gear was rigid to support the flying wires in the mannzer of the famous Ryan S-T of 1934.

3. Tom Story continued the basic design of the Little Gee Bee into the new era and built several examples known as the Story Specials in the early 1950s. This one, with a 65-horsepower Continental, has been the property of the Story Flying Club in Seattle since the mid-1950s.

4. The basic design of the Wimpy and Little Gee Bee flies on, this time in wood. The Fly Baby was built by the author in 1960. Plans have been on the market since it won the Experimental Aircraft Association's 1962 design contest.

1

2

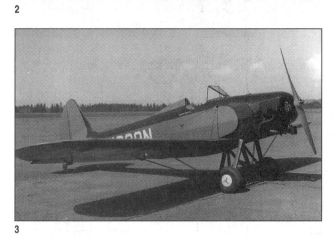

3

4

Devastator diary

Maligned Douglas TBD-1 brought the Navy into the monoplane age

1st May 1978

The Douglas TBD-1 (TB for torpedo bomber, D for Douglas) is one of those airplanes that is more famous for its shortcomings than for its accomplishments. Actually, it is more significant to aviation history for having brought U.S. naval aviation into the monoplane age than for any subsequent military accomplishments.

Beginning in the early 1920s, single-engine U.S. Navy torpedo planes were standardized as large three-seaters that could operate on twin pontoons or on wheels from aircraft carriers or shore bases. Powered with the same engines that were used by smaller and lighter two-seat scout-observation types and dive bombers, the torpedo planes were notoriously slow and clumsy.

The TBD carried on the torpedo plane tradition as far as size and seating went, but its basic design was updated with a single wing fitted with flaps and the adoption of clean lines, including enclosed cockpits and a retractable landing gear. Those features, plus a new 900-horsepower Pratt & Whitney Twin Wasp engine, increased its speed considerably over the biplanes. All-metal construction was a further advance.

Because of their size, it was necessary to fold the wings of the torpedo planes for stowage on the carriers. In the biplane years, that type of operation was accomplished manually by the deck crews; on the TBD it was done hydraulically by the flick of a switch in the cockpit.

The prototype XTBD-1 first flew on April 13, 1935. After successful tests that eliminated competing designs, plus a few minor modifications, a production order for 129 TBD-1s was placed on Feb. 3, 1936. Four torpedo squadrons in the fleet were fully equipped with the new model by mid-1938. The name Devastator was applied late in 1941 when the government decided to adopt "popular" names for its warplanes in addition to their regular alphanumeric military designations.

The wartime fame of the TBD rests almost entirely on a major failure: the torpedo attacks on the Japanese fleet during the Battle of Midway on June 4, 1942. By that time the TBD was thoroughly obsolescent. Also, warship antiaircraft firepower had increased enormously in quantity and accuracy since the unarmored TBD first appeared in 1935. The slow Devastators were sitting ducks for the Japanese gunners as they made their low and straight runs to drop their single torpedoes.

Unable to maneuver, the unescorted planes were picked off easily by the ships' guns and by defending Zero fighters. Of 41 TBDs launched on June 4, 39 were shot down and none scored hits. Torpedo Squadron 8 was wiped out completely, and only one man, Ensign George H. Gay, survived. He was picked up from the sea the day after the battle.

To offset this negative fragment of history, it should be pointed out that the TBDs scored some notable successes earlier in the year under more favorable circumstances, starting at Kwajalein and Wake Island in February and moving on to Marcus Island in March. The high point of the TBD's career was at Lae on March 10, when 10 Japanese ships were sunk at a cost of two TBDs. They also scored against Japanese carriers in the Battle of the Coral Sea on May 7-9, and should be credited with a strong assist at Midway since they drew the defending Zeroes down to a low level and enabled the U.S. Navy's dive bombers to sink three carriers without aerial interference.

The credit due to the TBD in these earlier successes was pretty well ignored in the news at the time, but the faith-

1

2

3

4

ful bird's disaster at Midway made history and saddled a true pioneer that lived beyond its time with an unjust label as a military failure.

The photographs

1. The Devastator prototype was the Douglas XTBD-1 of 1935. Instead of a torpedo, this one is carrying two 500-pound bombs on streamlined racks. Note the projecting wheel of the retracted landing gear.

2. A pontoon version, designated the TBD-1A, didn't pan out. While common in the past, it was the Navy's last attempt at a twin-float torpedo plane.

3. The TBD's wings folded hydraulically to simplify storage problems aboard carriers. Note how the ailerons cover the full span of the folding portion of the wing, which was covered with corrugated aluminum. The rest of the metal skin was smooth.

4. This view gives a good idea of the low altitude that torpedo planes had to fly when dropping their "fish." The aerodynamic cleanliness that allows high speeds doesn't do much good here because the plane has to slow down for its drop.

Early fire patrols

Despite congressional stinginess, the Air Service found ways to make itself useful

1st June 1978

When World War I ended, the war-trained Army pilots who were still in service had little to do. With the "War to End All Wars" complete, who needed armies and, in particular, an Army Air Service?

Despite the dearth of military missions, some pilots soon found themselves busy with a new and previously unforeseen activity. In June 1919, Colonel H.H. Arnold still held his temporary wartime rank and was the commanding officer of March Field in Riverside, California. He was approached by the district forester of the U.S. Forest Service with an interesting question: Could airplanes be used to patrol mountains to spot forest fires?

Arnold thought they could, and mindful of the reduced scale of flying activity at Army fields and its effect on pilots' morale, he was glad to have something for his pilots to do. So he set up regular patrols and put flight crews and mechanics to work from Mount Lassen in Northern California to the Mexican border.

Soon after his operation got underway, Arnold was bumped to his permanent rank of captain but was almost immediately promoted to major, a rank that he held into the 1930s in the slow-moving peacetime Army.

While the fire patrols were notably successful, Congress had a tight grip on the purse strings, and money for such extra activity was hard to come by. Between them, the Army and the Forest Service could obtain only enough funds to patrol California in 1920. By late season, however, the fire situation was so bad in Oregon that funds were allocated for additional patrol areas.

During its 1920 operation, Army pilots discovered 1,632 fires, 818 of which they reported before the regular sources. The 37 airplanes involved, all modified versions of the two-seat wartime de Havilland 4 observation plane, put in 2,779 flying hours and had only 13 forced landings.

For 1921, the Air Service put its accumulated fire-patrol experience into a manual and set up a six-week training course at Mather Field in Sacramento, California, for the joint instruction of Army pilots and observers, plus Forest Service personnel.

New techniques were also introduced. The DH-4s were now equipped with electrical systems and radios to replace the message-drop containers and carrier pigeons that were used previously for communications.

To the detriment of the patrol's effectiveness, Congress remained tight with the purse strings in 1921, and the opera-tion actually had to shut down for three weeks at the height of the July 1-Oct. 15 season when there was no money to purchase fuel. Pressure from foresters, who could convincingly argue that discovering fires early saved money, resulted in new funds.

Still, there was no appropriation in 1922, so the Army continued to patrol under the camouflage of "training missions" and other subterfuges. From 1923 on, the activity was scaled to what could be accomplished on an annual budget of $50,000.

Some thought was given in the early 1920s to turning over the job to private individuals, and a few actually tried it. However, there was no established civil aviation then, and the problems of finding enough individuals with the right kind of equipment, plus the problems of administering a lot of separate little contracts, killed the idea. The Army carried on into 1927.

By that time, the patrols were operating from permanent bases at Spokane and Vancouver, Washington; Eugene, Oregon; and Sacramento and Griffith Park, California. Seattle was used on a part-time basis. The airplanes were still the ubiquitous DH-4s, and the Army pilots by now were mostly reservists.

The Army's forest-fire activities came to an end in 1927, when the Forest Service took over and operated a fleet of old DH-4s that had been transferred from the Army. It also obtained other aircraft from the recently deactivated U.S. Air Mail Service.

The photographs

1. This de Havilland 4B of the 91st Observation Squadron was used on the Army Air Service's forest-fire patrols. Note the two wind-driven generators on the landing gear and the spare wheel on the bottom of the fuselage. The wartime DH-4 was the mainstay of the fire patrols until 1928.

2. This former DH-4 mail plane was turned back to the Army after the U.S. Mail Service was replaced by private contractors. The plane, given an Army serial number that was derived from its old Post Office number, was put to work on the forest-fire patrols without any Army markings.

3. This DH had the new Army tail stripes that were developed in November 1926. The 1927-style lettering on the fuselage identifies it as a Boeing-built DH-4M-1. The M models were rebuilt wartime aircraft that used Boeing-developed steel-tube fuselages. The Ms and M-1s were built by Boeing. The M-2s were built by Fokker.

1

2

3

Numbers game

The unusual tale of the Boeing Model 40A

2nd June 1978

Those of us who fly today generally take the registration numbers on our airplanes for granted. They were on there when we bought the plane, and the same numbers are still there when we sell it. Except in those cases where an owner wants a special number for personal reasons, why change the number on a U.S.-registered airplane once it has been issued?

Well, sometimes there are very good reasons, and the following piece of history can be considered a somewhat extreme example.

Back in 1927, when the registration of U.S. civilian aircraft began some eight years after the rest of the world adopted the practice, the Boeing Airplane Co. built a fleet of 25 Model 40As. They were combination mail and passenger planes for Boeing Air Transport, an airline that Boeing had set up after it was awarded the contract air mail route (CAM-18) from San Francisco to Chicago.

Boeing took over the route on July 1, 1927. It later acquired other airlines and their routes that continued to operate under their own names as divisions of an organization now known as United Air Lines.

The 25 Model 40A biplanes were given a solid block of consecutive registration numbers, 268 through 292. The numbers were painted in the standard locations of the time: the upper right and lower left wing surfaces, and each side of the rudder.

The numbers were to be preceded by the letter C to indicate a full commercial license. The national identification letter N, assigned to the United States by an international treaty in 1919, was not used on the Boeings because there was no need for the planes to fly outside of the country.

However, someone goofed and the registrations were not applied correctly. Instead of C268, for example, it came out 3268. That was much more noticeable on the rudder than on the wing because the 3 was above the registration number on the tail while it was the first figure in a straight line on the wings.

The error was soon corrected, and it has not been repeated on a Boeing airplane since. Apparently the painter heard verbal instructions to paint the C as a 3. That mistake may have been responsible for the footnote seen on Boeing memo pads for many subsequent years: "Verbal orders don't go."

By the early 1930s, it had become common practice to use the national letter N in front of the status letter, whether the planes were to fly out of the country or not. There was C for the commercially licensed model, X for the experimentals, R for restricted types, and S for state-owned planes. The Boeings went along.

One more change was still to come for that particular batch of Boeings. The government has reserved some of the lowest numbers for use on its own fleet of planes. As the bureaucracy expanded, it acquired more planes and therefore needed more low numbers. The fact that some were then in use by nongovernment planes was no problem. It simply made their owners get new numbers. For the Boeings, that was done two ways. In one case, the registration C (or NC) 217 was replaced by an entirely new four-digit number, 7471. In the other, NC270 became a different number by adding an H. Including the painting snafu, 270 carried four variations on its original registration: 3270, C270, NC270 and NC270H.

Incidentally, those suffix letters came in late 1928, when registration numbers passed 10,000. The powers-that-be figured that a five-digit number was too much, so they started again with numbers to a maximum of three digits to be followed by a suffix letter. The first suffix was E, followed by H, K, M, N, R, V and W. After those series were filled out, the numbers went to five digits and reached the high 30,000s by World War II.

Suffix letters were adopted again with up to four digits after the war, and many more letters were used.

The photographs

1. A painter made a mistake when he painted a 3 above Registration No. 270 on this Boeing 40A. His instructions were to paint a C. This, the third of 25 Boeing 40As of 1927, also carried the insignia of the new Boeing Air Transport, Inc.

2. Following the necessary correction, the 3 is replaced by the C of a commercial license. When this photo was taken in 1929, the plane had been converted to a 40B by changing the original 420-horsepower Pratt & Whitney Wasp to a 525-horsepower Hornet. The plane was back at the factory at the time for use in experiments with engine cowlings and re-

1

2

3

4

vised fuselage contours.

3. No longer an airliner, old 270 was being used by United Air Lines as a trainer by 1935. United had evolved from Boeing Air Transport. Note the second cockpit that was installed ahead of the original. The aircraft's registration number was preceded by the letters NC. This photograph

was taken by Boardman C. Reed on Nov. 4, 1936.

4. By time it was privately owned, 270 had the second cockpit replaced by a pair of extra seats at the rear of the enlarged cabin. Since the government had added numbers in the 200 range to its own reserved block of low numbers, the original 270 was altered by adding H as a suffix.

The 'Southern Cross'

Fokker trimotor made the first flight from the United States to Australia

1st July 1978

June 9, 1978, was the 50th anniversary of the first U.S.-to-Australia flight, the most notable over-water journey since Lindbergh crossed the Atlantic on May 20-21, 1927. The Australian flight was made in an airplane that was a year older than Lindy's Spirit of St. Louis. It was also a trimotor, the type that everyone had urged Lindy to use.

The trimotor, the second Fokker F-VII/3M built, was ordered by Australian arctic explorer George Hubert Wilkins for distance flying. As a result, it had longer wings and more tankage than the prototype, which had been developed for the 1925 Ford Reliability Tour and was subsequently used by Admiral Byrd for his North Pole flight of May 1926.

Wilkins took two F-VIIs to Alaska in 1926. One was the "Detroiter," a trimotor named in honor of his backers in Detroit. The other was a single-engine version that he named "Alaskan." Both were wrecked on test flights in Alaska by an expedition pilot who was on leave from the Army Air Corps.

Some exploratory flights were done by putting the Detroiter's wing on the Alaskan's fuselage, but that hybrid arrangement did not fulfill the objectives of the expedition. Wilkins sold the damaged and engine-less trimotor in 1927 to fellow Australian Charles Kingsford-Smith, a World War I pilot who had a longtime desire to fly the Pacific from the United States to Australia. No suitable airplane was available at a reasonable price until Wilkins began looking to unload his trimotor in order to finance another expedition.

Kingsford-Smith got the big Fokker for $15,000 and had the Boeing Airplane Co. repair it and replace the 200-horsepower Wright J-4 engines with new 220-horsepower J-5 Whirlwinds. It was then flown to the Douglas factory in Santa Monica, California, where additional modifications were made and the new name "Southern Cross" was painted on the fuselage.

With his plane now based in San Francisco, Kingsford-Smith was having problems financing the flight and keeping up the payments on the Fokker. For publicity and to obtain further backing, he made two attempts to break the world's endurance record of 52 hours 22 minutes, but failed both times. He was on the verge of giving up his transpacific dream and selling the plane when he obtained the support of G. Allan Hancock, a California oil tycoon. Now the flight was on for sure.

With another Australian, Charles Ulm, as copilot, and Americans James Warner as radio operator and Harry Lyon as navigator, the "Southern Cross" took off from Oakland Airport on May 31, 1928. Twenty-seven hours and 20 minutes later it landed at Wheeler Field, Hawaii, the fifth airplane to complete the 2,400-mile flight.

Wheeler was too small for the big ship to take off with the fuel load it needed for the 3,713-mile flight to Suva in the Fiji Islands, so Kingsford-Smith flew it to the long Barking Sands beach on the island of Kauai and fueled up there.

The Suva leg involved some of the worst flying weather ever encountered at the time, but Lyon's navigation was excellent and the "Southern Cross" reached Fiji in 34 hours 50 minutes. Since there were no airplanes on the islands and, consequently, no airports, the "Southern Cross" landed on a race track. It then had to fly 20 miles to Naselai Beach for the overload takeoff. This time the leg was 1,737 miles to Brisbane, Australia. It was complicated by more violent weather and malfunctioning navigation instruments. Flying time for the 7,800-mile flight was 88 hours 30 minutes over a period of 10 days.

After some notable local flights, including the first flight across the Tasman Sea from Australia to New Zealand, Kingsford-Smith and a different crew flew the "Southern Cross" westward to Europe. It was refurbished at the Fokker plant in Holland in 1930, after which Kingsford-Smith and yet another crew continued westward to Oakland to complete a flight entirely around the world. Some claim that this was the first true around-the-world flight because it crossed the equator. None of the preceding flights did.

Rather than push the luck of the faithful old trimotor with another transpacific flight, Kingsford-Smith returned the "Southern Cross" to Australia by ship. After further flying adventures, including more flights to New Zealand and the starring role in a movie about its remarkable career, the second Fokker trimotor was enshrined in a display building at Eagle Farm Airport in Brisbane, the site of its first triumphal landing in the continent.

The photographs

1. Arctic exploration was the original purpose of the Fokker trimotor that made the first flight across the Pacific. Here it is being christened "Detroiter" for George Wilkins' arctic expedition of 1926. Builder Tony Fokker, a great believer in advertising, liked to make flying Fokker billboards of his airplanes whenever possible.

2. Owned by Charles Kingsford-Smith, the decorated Fokker "Southern Cross" prepares to take off from San Francisco on its first unsuccessful attempt to break the world's endurance record. Kingsford-Smith is pulling on the left landing-gear strut while copilot George Pond brings up the rear. The plane carries the secondary name "Spirit of California" and the names of several sponsors.

3. The famous trimotor was refurbished at the Fokker factory in Holland in 1930. The original U.S. registration

1

2

3

4

number, 1985, was changed to the Australian registration G-AUSU after the Pacific flight. The Australian registration itself was changed to VH-USU in 1929 when the registrations of many countries were revised.

4. The "Southern Cross," with its 1928 U.S. colors and registration number restored, is now on display in a museum at Eagle Farm, Australia, where it ended its historic transpacific flight.

More Fokker fables

F-VIIB-3M carried Amelia Earhart to fame as first woman to fly the Atlantic

2nd July 1978

Amelia Earhart achieved sudden and everlasting fame on June 18, 1928, when she became the first woman to cross the Atlantic Ocean in an airplane. While she was a licensed pilot, a prime reason for making the flight, she was strictly a passenger. No matter; in the eyes of the press and the public, it was "her" flight, and pilot Wilmer Stultz and copilot-mechanic Lou Gordon were relegated to the background.

If it had not been for the strenuous objections of her family, another woman would have made the flight, and aviation history would have been slightly different. The story goes back a ways.

Already a noted navigator, U.S. Navy pilot Richard E. Byrd hit the big time in 1926 by making the first flight over the North Pole. In 1927 he got in on the race to fly from New York to Paris. He made it across after Lindbergh, with a disastrous finale, and he soon set his sights on becoming the first man to fly over the South Pole.

Toward that end, he bought a Fokker F-VIIB/3M trimotor, a long-range version of the one he had used in 1926 and very similar to his ill-fated 1927 model. He was, however, unable to use the Fokker for the flight to the South Pole because one of his major backers was Henry Ford, who was building trimotor airliners himself and would not stand for Byrd using a competitor's airplane. Byrd then had to sell his Fokker and use the relatively unproven Ford.

His customer for the rejected Fokker was a wealthy woman named Mrs. Frederick Guest, who planned to use it for another transatlantic flight to promote international friendship and goodwill – and, incidentally, make herself the first woman to fly the ocean. For that purpose, she named the Fokker "Friendship." As a safety factor, it was also converted to a seaplane.

Her family supported the flight, but objected emphatically to the idea of her going along, pointing out that four women had already been lost trying it. They didn't mind a woman riding along per se, as long as it wasn't Mrs. Guest.

George Putnam, a publisher who was a consultant for the family, was told to find a qualified woman for the job, and his agents soon found and recommended Earhart. She passed the interview with the Guest family and didn't do too badly with Putnam either, for she later married him.

The "Friendship" flight wasn't to be a spectacular nonstop affair from New York to Europe in the manner of previous flights. It was much shorter, from Newfoundland to the British Isles. Following their arrival at Treppassy Bay, Newfoundland, bad weather caused long delays. Then the Fokker couldn't get off the water with a full load of fuel, so the tanks were drained almost to the point of danger. When it was finally time to go, Stultz handled the tricky takeoff and then the 20-hour 20-minute flight. Earhart was supposed to spend some time at the controls, but Stultz was so busy fighting turbulence and instrument conditions that she didn't get a chance. When land was finally sighted, no one knew where they were. They just followed the unidentified coast line southward until they found a suitable harbor to put down in. It turned out to be Burryport, Wales.

Earhart was the hero of the day. After writing a book about the flight, she gave up a career in social work and got into aviation full time. She was in the headlines almost continuously thereafter, with a solo flight from Hawaii to the United States, another from the States to Ireland, plus racing and other achievements. The biggest headlines of all, however, came with her mysterious disappearance in the Southwest Pacific Ocean in the closing stages of an around-the-world flight in July 1937. Her body, and that of navigator Fred Noonan, were never found, and rumors of their demise have never gone away.

The photographs

1. The Fokker F-VIIB/3M that became Amelia Earhart's "Friendship" was originally intended for Byrd's antarctic expedition. Here it is with Byrd's pilot and copilot, Berndt Balchen and Floyd Bennett, who are standing under the left engine.

2. For the transatlantic flight, the "Friendship" was fitted with pontoons as a precaution. After the flight, it was converted back to a land plane and eventually ended up in the hands of South American insurrectionists.

3. In addition to pontoons, the Fokker "Friendship" was also fitted with metal propellers instead of wood. That's Earhart looking out the cabin door.

1

2

3

Tail-boom pushers

Not as common as tractors, their basic configuration perseveres

1st August 1978

By the time World War I started in 1914, airplanes had developed to the point where they fell into two distinct categories: pushers and tractors.

For the single-engine types at least, the tractors had a full-length fuselage, with the engine and propeller in the nose (where the installation was called a tractor because the combination "pulled" the airplane), then locations for the crew and passengers, attach points for the wings, and the tail surfaces at the rear.

The pusher, on the other hand, had a relatively short structure called a nacelle (in later days a pod) that contained the crew and supported the wings. The engine and prop were installed in the rear of the pod or nacelle. Since they were behind the main mass of the airplane, they were considered to be "pushing it along" instead of pulling it as in a tractor type. The tail surfaces were supported by paired booms spaced far enough apart laterally to clear the prop.

At the start of the war, most airplanes were such high-drag structures that there wasn't much performance difference between them. However, to meet the requirements of subsequent military operations, the tractor designs were capable of great detail refinement and gained a big performance lead over the pushers, which became a relatively rare type.

However, the pushers did retain certain advantages that kept them from dying out completely. Designers did all they could to overcome the drag disadvantages of the boom and succeeded well enough to assure the basic configuration continued to the present day.

1

The photographs

1. The typical pusher of 1914 had the crew sitting in an enclosed nacelle or pod, with the engine in the rear. Because of the location of the propeller, it was necessary to carry the tail surfaces on the ends of widely spaced booms. Minor refinements of this French Farman were used as trainers throughout WWI.

2. Pusher designers cleaned up their boom installations as the inherently cleaner tractor designs made big gains in performance. In this 1915 German Ago, the traditional four booms with wire bracing have been replaced with two laminated wood veneer booms that are essentially extra skinny fuselages. The elimination of aerodynamic drag in this case was largely offset by the greatly increased weight of the new streamlined booms.

3. The Italian Savoia-Marchetti S.65 was built for the 1929 Schneider Cup race by adopting the tail-boom pusher configuration for a seaplane and adding a second engine in the nose to create a 2,000-horsepower single-seater. This one had so many bugs that two years later it still wasn't ready to race.

4. Practically extinct during the 1920s, the tail-boom pusher made a comeback in the 1930s in the form of the Stearman-Hammond Y, a 150-horsepower two-seater that won a U.S. government design contest for "Everyman's Safe Airplane" in 1935. In its production form, the tricycle ship was supposed to sell for $700, but ended up coming close to $7,000. Only 25 were built.

5. The Dutch Fokker D-23 of 1939 revived the tandem-engine concept for a tail-boom design with a lot of power in a short-span airplane, but it didn't get into production. Actually, the configuration, seen today in the Cessna Skymaster, was nothing new to Fokker. He had beaten Marchetti and others to it by introducing a similar design in 1915.

6. Developed during World War II and powered with a Swedish-built version of the 1,475-horsepower German Daimler-Benz DB-605 engine, this Swedish Saab 21A car-

2

3

4

5

6

7

ried on the old prop-behind-the-pod tradition and was the fastest of the breed at 398 mph. The pilot's problems in case of having to bail out ahead of that whirling prop were solved by the designers, who developed one of the first ejection seats just for the purpose of getting him safely clear.

7. Tail booms survived into the jet age. The British de

Havilland 100 Vampire is typical. With a 3,000-pound-thrust de Havilland Goblin jet instead of a propeller, boom spacing was determined by the span of the horizontal tail and the track of the main wheels of the tricycle landing gear. Except for the reduced ground clearance allowed by the jet, the Vampire could easily pass for one of the older prop designs.

Dirigible dirge

Shenandoah, America's first rigid airship, was more famous for breaking up

2nd August 1978

The U.S. Navy started a rigid airship program in 1916, but it was not until 1923 that it got one into the air. Two years into the program, the Navy obtained a set of drawings for the German Zeppelin L-49, a ship that had been forced down in France the previous October. So advanced was the L-49 in comparison to the Navy's first design that a complete overhaul of its ZR-1 was ordered. Z was the Navy's symbol for lighter-than-air craft, and the R indicated the rigid type.

The final design was approved on Oct. 31, 1921, for a ship similar to the L-49 that was stretched 46 feet. It was equipped with six engines instead of five, and incorporated some structural and aerodynamic improvements of the later German Zeppelins. The components were built in the Naval Aircraft Factory in Philadelphia and trucked to the naval air station at Lakehurst, New Jersey, for assembly in a new 804-foot-long double hangar.

Flown on Sept. 4, 1923, the $3 million ZR-1 was 680 feet long and 78 feet in diameter. Its capacity was 2,115,174 cubic feet distributed in 20 cells of goldbeater's skin instead of the L-49's 1,970,300 cubic feet in 18 cells. The ship was driven at a top speed of 60 mph by six 300-horsepower Packard engines. Normal crew was 25.

After a number of test and publicity flights, the ZR-1 was christened Shenandoah (an Indian name meaning Daughter of the Stars) on Oct. 10.

Its performance wasn't up to expectations, but there was a good reason. The ship had been designed to use flammable hydrogen gas, but it instead flew on nonflammable helium, which has only 90 percent the lifting capability of hydrogen. The cost of helium was exorbitant too: $120 per thousand cubic feet in 1922 compared to about $2 for hydrogen. The price came down to $55 per thousand by 1924, but supply was short. When the Navy's new ZR-3 was received from Germany in October 1924, the Shenandoah was laid up so that its helium could be pumped into the ZR-3 (later called the Los Angeles). The Shenandoah did not get its gas back until June 1925.

The cost of helium further reduced the ship's performance. To avoid valving gas, as was commonly done to con-trol altitude and to compensate for the weight that was lost as fuel was consumed, the Shenandoah was fitted with a water-recovery system on each engine to recover vaporized water from the engine exhaust. At nearly 500 pounds apiece, those units were so heavy that the forward center-line engine had to be removed to save weight.

To avoid loss of helium due to expansion from solar heating, the ship's fabric covering was doped silver (the first rigid airship so treated) and some of the safety valves in the gas cells were removed.

In its short career, the Shenandoah made only 57 flights. The end came during a tour from Lakehurst to Detroit via St. Louis and Minneapolis on Sept. 2-3, 1925. On the first leg, near Ava, Ohio, the ship ran into a violent storm at dawn and broke up in the air. Fourteen of the 43 people aboard were killed. Most of them were carried down in the control car and the engine gondolas as they ripped loose. Others fell out of the hull where it broke apart. The survivors were all in the two sections of hull that became, in effect, rigid free balloons.

The crash touched off a terrific political struggle that made the Shenandoah more famous for its disaster than for its place as America's first rigid airship. The loss of the ship itself and the key personnel aboard, plus the political hassle, set the Navy's airship program back even though the ZR-3 Los Angeles went on to become one of the safest and most successful rigids in history. Only seven other rigid aircraft took to the air after the crash of the Shenandoah: the two Graf Zeppelins and the Hindenberg in Germany; the R-100 and R-101 in England; and the Akron and Macon in the United States.

The photographs

1. Most of the details that went into the U.S. Navy's first rigid airship were obtained from the L-49, forced down here in the woods at Bourbonne-Les-Bains, France, on Oct. 20, 1917. A French farmer armed with a pitchfork kept the captain and his crew of 18 from setting fire to the crippled ship.

2. The ZR-1, during one of its first flights. After the

1

2

3

ship was christened "Shenandoah," the name was painted on the tail and replaced the ZR-1 on the nose.

3. The USS Patoka was fitted with a mooring mast and served as a seagoing airship base. This photo shows one of only seven moorings that the Shenandoah made to the Patoka during its short career.

Floating gliders

Light weight and large 'sail' area make them difficult to control on water

1st September 1978

Until recent years, most of the soaring that was done in conventional gliders and sailplanes was accomplished with the aid of up-slope winds. The wind blowing against a cliff or a hill is deflected upward. If the vertical velocity component of the wind is equal to the sinking speed of the glider, the ship stays up.

The proper combination of geography and steady winds led to a number of famous soaring sites. Since many were at seaside or lakeside locations, the occasional glider found itself in the water when the wind died and was unable to make it back to a landing area. That situation, plus the possibility of opening up new soaring sites at places where there were no suitable open areas for regular land-type operations, led to a short period of experimentation with waterborne gliders.

Some of the designs of the time — around 1930 — were naturals for conversion to flying boats. Their wooden slab-side fuselages under a high wing could easily be waterproofed to serve as a hull. The landing skid was no problem, and the additional drag of the stabilizing wing floats was not much of an aerodynamic handicap to the high-drag designs of the period.

Even designs that could not be converted to boats, like the open-frame primaries, were given a try on the water by adding a boxy set of wooden floats in the standard airplane position.

As seaplane gliders, the waterborne designs performed all right when towed off the water by a motorboat. Landings were adequate, too, but then the problems began. If there was enough wind to produce good slope-soaring conditions, there was entirely too much wind for managing the glider on the water after it came down. With its light weight and large "sail" area, the glider was completely at the mercy of the wind.

Nothing the pilot could do would prevent it from weather-cocking into the wind and drifting straight downwind to the shoreline. Seldom would that shore be a nice wide-open beach that the ship could safely drift onto.

That problem alone kept the free-flying water glider from becoming a popular part of the soaring movement. Waterborne types did not die out completely, however. The free-flying concept was dropped, and a few primaries and other low-performance types were flown on relatively continuous tow with short ropes behind motorboats. Some released the tow line before landing; others landed while still on tow.

In recent years, some low-performance designs that could hardly be called real gliders have been developed for continuous-tow flying from water. The FAA regards this kind of activity as kiting, not true flying, and does not require licensing of either the pilot or the machine as long as the entire flight is on tow. Releasing even for a quick landing from low altitude calls for a license. The basic problem of getting the ship safely ashore with any significant wind is still a major handicap.

History repeats itself, and now that hang gliders have come on strong and revived slope soaring, we see some of these "kiters" trying their specialized art on water skis. They are either towed off the water by a boat or they can start from land for a deliberate descent onto water.

A novel idea that was tried briefly in World War II was a water-based cargo glider that was to be towed by a seaplane. It was a relatively conventional glider that used its fuselage as a hull. However, instead of having the customary wing floats, the two experimental designs that the U.S. Navy tried had low wings with watertight roots. Those portions of the wings were in the water and served the function of the wing floats without their drag.

Nothing came of the Navy's wet-glider program, but the float-wing concept is very much in evidence today. Molt Taylor, who was involved in the Navy program during the war, adopted the float-wing concept for his popular and award-winning Coot homebuilt amphibian.

The photographs

1. The Germans designed gliders for boat-towing in 1920, and American designer Glenn Curtiss picked up on the idea with this short-hulled flying boat in 1922. It was the last aircraft he designed before he retired from aviation.

2. Waterproofing the fuselage of this 1930 German Prufling secondary glider and adding wing floats turned it into a flying boat. The major handicap to such an operation was getting the ship safely ashore when winds were blowing.

3. Pontoons were also used to make seaplane gliders out of designs that didn't have a conventional fuselage that could be converted to a hull. This is a Detroit Gull primary, which in 1930 became the first U.S. glider to receive an approved type certificate.

4. Seaplane gliders were flown mostly on continuous tow behind motorboats when they proved impractical for

300

slope-soaring operations. This two-man operation using a Waco primary is representative of some of the monkey business that could be attempted.

5. One Navy wartime experiment involved a flying-boat type of cargo glider that used watertight wing roots to provide lateral stability on the water. Military gliders are long

gone, but the novel float-wing concept is still around in the Coot homebuilt amphibian. This is an Allied XLRA-1.

6. The boat-towed Skilar Aqua Glider is a flying boat in that the buoyancy of its hull keeps it afloat when motionless. When it has forward speed for takeoff and landing, it is supported by the hydro-skis beneath the hull.

Peashooter progress

The P-26, the Army's first monoplane fighter, served as a transitional design

2nd September 1978

Back in the years before World War II, the U.S. Armed Forces did not have popular names for their aircraft as they do today. One model, however, the Boeing P-26, earned a moniker for itself. It's fondly remembered as the Peashooter.

As a military airplane, the P-26 was distinct in several ways. The transition model between two distinct eras of U.S. Army fighter design, it was the Army's first monoplane fighter (they were called pursuits then; the letter F was substituted in 1948 without changing the numbers) and the Army's first all-metal fighter. It was also the last open-cockpit fighter and the last to use fixed landing gear.

The use of wire bracing for the low wing was an anachronism that hadn't been seen on a fighter since early in World War I. With only 550 horsepower, it was also the last fighter in the 400- to 600-horsepower range that had been standard since 1924. The following production pursuits, the Seversky P-35 and the Curtiss P-36, started at 1,000 horsepower.

The development and procurement of the Army's smallest fighter (27-foot wingspan and only 150 square feet of area) was also unique. It was not designed to a published Army requirement under a War Department contract. Instead, the new airplane, known then only as the Boeing Model 248, was designed and built as a private Boeing venture as the result of unofficial talks between Boeing and the Army Fighter Branch.

Since it was not an official Army program, subject to prevailing (and obsolete) military specifications and the usual Army in-plant inspectors, Boeing was able to work out some of the details in its own way and take some short cuts. The Army agreed to loan Boeing such military property as engines and armament, and to test the airplanes on a bailment contract.

Work stated in September 1931, and the first of three hand-built prototypes was flown on March 20, 1932. The Army designated the experimental project the XP-936. Two were used for flight testing, one at Wright Field, Ohio, and the other by the service pilots of the First Pursuit Group at Selfridge Field, Michigan. A third article was static tested at Wright Field.

Later, the Army decided to buy the little fighter prototypes and assigned Army serial numbers and the official designation XP-26. The designation was soon changed to Y1P-26 when the aircraft were transferred to service-test status. After testing was completed, the pair became plain P-26s.

Production models were wanted too, so the Army placed an order with Boeing for 111 P-26As. They incorporated enough changes over the prototypes to rate a new Boeing model number: 266. The first P-26A was delivered in January 1934, the last in June. The unit price, less such government-furnished equipment such as engines, propellers, armament, radio and instruments, was $9,999.

The P-26As were followed by two P-26Bs and 23 P-26Cs. Unlike the A, the B had a fuel-injected engine and wing flaps. The Army had already expressed dissatisfaction with the high landing speed of the P-26As and eventually sent them back to the factory for flaps, which reduced the speed to 72 mph. The P-26Cs had minor fuel-system variations from the A models, but all were eventually modified to B standards without a change of designation. The last P-26C was delivered on March 7, 1936.

In another departure from standard practice, the Army ordered transition fighters from Boeing only. At the time, the Army was buying major production models from two sources as Curtiss P-6 and Boeing P-12 fighters; and Curtiss O-1 and O-39 observation models in parallel with Douglas O-25s and O-38s.

The P-26s served the Army in the Continental United States and overseas until just before Pearl Harbor. One that was given to the Philippine air force late in 1941 is credited with shooting down the first Japanese plane to fall in the islands. It was the only time that P-26s as such saw combat. Eleven of the 12 export equivalents designated Boeing Model 281s went to China in 1936 (the other went to Spain).

Two P-26As survive today. One is on static display in the National Air and Space Museum in Washington, DC, and the other is a flyable example at the Planes of Fame in Chino, California. Both are former Army models that had been transferred to the Republic of Panama in 1941 and were later passed to the Guatemalan Air Force, which operated them into the 1950s.

The photographs

1. The first Boeing Model 248 with the unofficial Army designation XP-936 on the tail. The prototypes differed from the production models. They had less dihedral, more rounded wingtips, and wheelpants that projected aft of the landing-gear-strut fairings.

2. Top heavy and with a narrow landing gear, many P-26s ended up like this. Early Peashooters were sent back to the factory to have their original low head rests replaced with higher and stronger units. Their effectiveness is show here.

3. The P-26As of the First Pursuit Group, based at March Field in Riverside, California, had very unusual markings for the time. Each of the three squadrons used a different striping and color arrangement. This one carries the Thunderbird insignia of the 34th Pursuit Squadron.

4. Due to their high landing speed, two P-26Bs were delivered with wing flaps, the first for a U.S. Army pursuit. They worked well enough to justify sending all of the earlier P-26As back to the factory for flaps. The P-26B's top speed was 235 mph; service ceiling was 27,000 feet.

1

2

3

4

Going the other way

Eleven months after Lindbergh's flight, a Junkers W.33 crossed the Atlantic east to west

1st October 1978

When Raymond Orteig established his $25,000 prize for a transatlantic flight in 1919, he issued no requirements about direction. After Lindbergh copped the marbles with his eastward flight from New York to Paris (3,600 miles in 33 hours 29 minutes) in May 1927, the challenge of an east-to-west flight remained. Actually, that was much harder to accomplish because it was against the prevailing winds.

The first successful westward crossing was made April 12-13, 1928, after others had tried and failed. The airplane was a German Junkers W.33 that was built especially for the flight and was named the Bremen. Actually, two were built for a dual flight. The other W.33 was named the Europa. Both were fitted with extra fuel tanks in the fuselage and outer wing panels and, in anticipation of a descent at sea, were fitted with flotation tanks in the wings.

All-metal, low-wing, cantilever monoplanes, both aircraft were somewhat novel for the time. Junkers had pioneered the configuration and the corrugated aluminum covering back in World War I, but except for his own subsequent designs it hadn't influenced other designers except an American named William B. Stout who adapted the techniques to designs of his own that evolved into the famous Ford Trimotor.

Originally, the Bremen-Europa flight was to be nonstop from Dessau, Germany, to New York City. They first took off on Aug. 14, 1927, but encountered such bad weather after passing Ireland that they turned back. The Europa later tried an eastward distance flight but had an accident that left the Bremen alone to make the second Atlantic attempt. The only one to get a second chance at it, the Bremen was unique among the transatlantic contenders.

The three-man crew of Herman Kohl, Baron Guenther von Hunefeld and Arthur Spindler decided to cut down on the head-wind disadvantage by moving the starting point westward to Baldonnel Airdrome in Ireland. After arriving there on March 26, Spindler had a disagreement with the others and returned to Germany. A captain in the Irish air force, James Fitzmaurice, who had recently returned from an unsuccessful transatlantic attempt of his own, gladly accepted an invitation to take Spindler's place.

After the usual weather delays, a risky takeoff was made on April 12. All went well for a few hours, but then things got complicated. After dark, the lighting system failed and the pilots had to check their instruments by flashlight. A fuel line running through the cabin broke, but Fitzmaurice was able to fix it with tape. Next, the compass failed, and to make matters worse the weather was now zero-zero. When they finally broke out of the soup they found themselves over land but did not know where they were. They backtracked to the coast and then followed it south. Kohl landed alongside the first sign of civilization, a lighthouse on what proved to be Greenly Island on the coast of Labrador.

The ice on the frozen sea looked too rough for a safe landing, so Kohl put the Bremen down on a tiny frozen lake on the island, breaking the landing gear and propeller in the process. The flight time was 36 hours — 2-1/2 hours longer than Lindbergh's flight even though it was 1,500 miles shorter.

Word of the long-unreported airmen was quickly flashed to an anxious world. Though they were safe and uninjured, their situation triggered a virtual comic opera of unnecessary "rescue" attempts, one of which had tragic results.

Byrd's North Pole pilot, Floyd Bennett, left a sickbed to fly one of the rescue planes and died of pneumonia as a result. Von Hunefeld, who was sickly at the time of the flight and knew that it would be his last, died of cancer the following February.

The Bremen was ferried out by boat and brought to the United States, where it eventually ended up at the Ford Museum in Dearborn, Michigan.

The photographs

1. The Junkers W.33 Bremen with a 310-horsepower Junkers L-5 water-cooled engine. Note the full-cantilever wing and corrugated aluminum covering. Those wheels under the tail are not a common ground-handling dolly; they hold the plane level and help give it a rolling start for takeoff.

2. The Junkers W.33 used aluminum tubes for wing spars. The corrugated metal items in the wing are the extra fuel tanks; the smooth ones are emergency flotation bags.

1

2

3

4

3. The wheels of the Bremen are just leaving the runway at Baldonnell on April 12, 1928. The tail dolly, which was also used by some other long-distance fliers of the time, is still attached.

4. The triumphant crew of the Bremen got a big (and refreshing) welcome at Munich. Left to right, Herman Kohl, Captain James Fitzmaurice and Baron Guenther von Hunefeld.

Boom time for booms

As they were enlarged, they began to accommodate engines and landing gear

1st November 1978

A presentation on Page 296 shows how the old bamboo-and-wire tail booms of the ancient pusher designs gradually evolved into structures that resembled thin fuselages. They served only the boom function of supporting the tail surfaces.

Here we show how some of those booms were enlarged and beefed up to contain engines and landing gear as well as anchor the tail. A future presentation will show further enlargement to house passengers and crew.

The photographs

1. In 1915 engineers enlarged the Caproni Ca.3, a classic single-engine pusher, to a trimotor by putting an engine in the forward end of each fuselage-like tail boom. The design also marked the end of the first era of the tricycle landing gear. Note the use of tail skids as well as dual nose wheels.

2. The American Gyro Crusader of 1935 carried the Caproni concept on a light pod-and-boom twin. An oddity of this design was the location of the tailwheel at the rear end of the pod instead of under the tail.

3. The Blohm & Voss BV-138 marked one of the few applications of twin booms to a flying boat. This German patrol bomber of World War II featured a pod-like short hull, an engine in the front of each boom, and a third engine in a nacelle above the hull.

4. The most famous pod-and-boom design of the World War II years was the Lockheed P-38 Lightning with the main units of the revived tricycle landing gear retracting into the booms. With the P-38 came the revival of another feature of twins that had been used in World War I: opposite-rotating propellers.

5. The Focke-Wulf 189, a German reconnaissance plane that was used early in World War II, preceded the P-38. Since its design did not include tricycle landing gear, a single retractable tailwheel was installed in the middle of the horizontal tail instead of separate units on the ends of each boom.

6. The postwar Fairchild C-82 was also known as the "Flying Boxcar." Cargo doors and a retractable ramp at the rear of the pod permitted drive-in loading to a point beneath the pilots' station. An improved version with larger engines served the U.S. Air Force as the C-119, and the Navy and Marines as the R4Q. This particular C-82A is testing an experimental track-type landing gear.

7. Improving a good design like the C-82 and C-119 was inevitable. The British Armstrong-Whitworth Argosy went to four turboprop engines by adding two outboard of the booms. The major improvement over the "Flying Boxcar" was another cargo door in the nose that permitted straight-through loading and unloading.

1

2

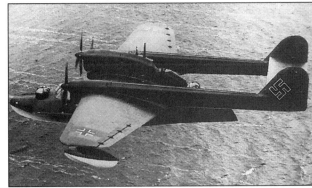

3

4

5

6

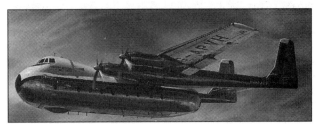

7

Wright reproductions

EAA's 1903 Flyer is the only one to duplicate an authentic operating engine

2nd November 1978

It's an awfully minor thing of nit to pick about, but I can't help it. A recent EAA announcement describes the unveiling of its newly built replica of the 1903 Wright Flyer. According to EAA, "The occasion marks the first time a Wright Flyer has stood ready, engine running and props twirling and poised for flight in 75 years."

That would imply that the Wrights never flew again. Actually, they built several other Flyers before going into production with letter-designated models: A, B, C, etc. The production of original Wright airplanes, still twin-propeller designs with chain drive from a single engine, lasted until 1914. By 1917 they were all out of regular service. Unfortunately for the Wrights, their pioneering technology had remained relatively static and other designers quickly surpassed them. In fact, Orville's one attempt at a direct-drive single-propeller tractor design in 1913 was a failure.

Although Wright planes (not to be confused with the later Dayton-Wright model) were out of service by the time the United States entered World War I, one original that had escaped consignment to a museum survived and was flown briefly many years later. That was the Wright B, a model that was owned by a wealthy young man named Grover Cleveland Bergdoll. He became famous, not as an early private pilot, but as America's most publicized draft dodger of World War I.

Bergdoll's ship was preserved, then overhauled and made ready for flight in 1934. In order to get a certificate of airworthiness for a single straight-ahead flight down a long runway, it had to have a civil registration number. Further, the number had to be displayed in the standard position of the time. After a single hop to Camden, New Jersey, the last "real" airworthy Wright model went on permanent display in the Franklin Institute in Philadelphia.

Since then, quite a few replicas (or, more correctly, reproductions) of Wright aircraft have been built. The first, a duplicate of the 1903 model, was built in England as a stand-in for the original, which had been on display in the Science Museum in Kensington since Orville sent it over there in the late 1920s. During the war years, the original was stored in the country for safekeeping, and the replica was displayed in the museum. When the original was returned to the States after the war, the copy again took its place.

Several other reproductions of the 1903 model, all non-flying and with dummy engines, have been built since the war, mostly for display in museums. The EAA example is the only one to go to the extreme of duplicating an authentic operating engine.

The Air Force Museum has a built-to-order copy of the 1909 Model A (the Army's first airplane), and several replicas of the 1902 Wright glider have been built by various individuals. Nothing, however, is known of any successful manned flights with them, though some are known to have been flown as kites the way the Wright brothers first tried theirs.

The 50th anniversary of the first transcontinental flight, made over a three-month period in 1911 by Calbraith P. Rogers, prompted the building of two replicas of the Wright Model EX that was named Vin Fiz after his sponsor's soft drink. Both aircraft departed from the true EX configuration in various ways but still captured the spirit and technology of the time.

One was built by Andy Anderson of Mansfield, Missouri. It had a modern Continental A-65 engine that had to go through two stages of speed reduction to drive the big pusher propellers through authentic chains. This hookup was almost totally unworkable, and while the airplane never flew, it did taxi.

The other was built by the author, who flew it several times on tow as a glider. It too was intended to use the A-65 engine, but Anderson's experience with that engine proved that only a slow-turning old-fashioned engine would be suitable. A Ford Model T engine was adopted for the job, but the airplane was sold before the installation was complete. The new owner never got it going before he retired it to a museum near Minneapolis. It is now in the San Diego Aerospace Museum.

Two other Wright replicas, both of them flyable, were completed in 1978. One is a 1902 glider, and the other is a 1903 Flyer that's powered by a Ford Model A engine.

The photographs

1. The last "real" Wright airplane to fly. This Model B, formerly owned by Grover Cleveland Bergdoll, made one straight-ahead flight along the length of a runway in 1934. It was then put on display in the Franklin Institute in Philadelphia.

2. One of the earliest reproductions of the 1903 Wright Flyer is this example, built for the Institute of the Aeronautical Sciences in 1953. The drooping wings are not indicative of weak construction or sloppy assembly; the original was intentionally rigged that way.

3. Andy Anderson's replica of the Vin Fiz, as completed in 1961. The wing curve was traced from an original

1

2

3

4

Wright Model B rib. The chord was a foot longer than on the EX, so the gap-chord ratio was notably different. This replica taxied but did not fly.

4. The author's replica of the Vin Fiz, also built in 1961.

Flown as a glider without the engine installed, it was converted to a tail-first 1909 Model A before the engine hookup was completed. Now in the San Diego Aerospace Museum, it has never flown under power.

Wright planes after Kitty Hawk

From 1904-10, Orville and Wilbur did the bulk of their work in Dayton

2nd December 1978

It should hardly be necessary to remind anyone connected with aviation that Dec. 17 was the 75th anniversary of the first controlled flight of a powered man-carrying aircraft. It was accomplished by Orville Wright at Kitty Hawk, North Carolina. No need to go into further detail other than to point out that the Flyer, as the brothers called their machine, was unconventional by today's standards. One reason was that the elevators were in front instead of behind, or what we today call a "canard" type.

Most of the current publications have concentrated on Kitty Hawk. What went on afterwards? Well, the Wrights did most of their remaining work back in Dayton. With their improved 1904 machine they conducted more than a hundred flights on Huffman Prairie, now the site of the giant Wright-Patterson Air Force Base, and made the first circular flight.

With their 1905 model, they made some significant changes. The control system was revised to allow separate manual operation of the rudder and the wing-warping, and the control levers were rearranged so that the pilot could sit upright instead of lying prone as he had done since the first manned flights in the 1901 glider.

The 1905 model could carry a passenger, but despite their close collaboration in the development of their Flyers, Wilbur and Orville Wright took a plane designated the Model A to Europe for a triumphal demonstration tour. Practically every flight set a record simply by exceeding the performance of the preceding one. There was no competition. Despite the published accounts of the Wrights' early work and photos of their machines, the first flight by a European design was not made until September 1906, and that was only an eight-second straight-ahead hop.

A setback took place in September 1908. The two-seater the Wrights built for the U.S. Army crashed on the final acceptance flight. Orville was hurt and Lieutenant Thomas Selfridge was killed. It was aviation's first fatal accident. A new plane was built, and the world's first military airplane was accepted for service in June 1909. Throughout that year, each of the Wright planes took off from a dolly that ran on a wooden monorail laid on the ground. Since late 1904, the plane got a boost-start from a cable that was pulled by a falling weight. In 1910 the Wrights followed the lead of other builders – who by then were making their presence felt in aviation – and put wheels under their new Model B.

The B was a milestone for the Wrights, for it was laid out in reverse of the earlier models. Before building the B, they had taken another idea from their new competition and put an elevator at the rear of one of their Model A aircraft in addition to the pair in front. When they found that the controls worked better there than they did up front, they eliminated the front set.

The Wrights' significant technical contributions concluded in 1910 when other innovators caught up and rapidly passed them. The Wrights did go on to found a flying school, however, a pioneering effort in that area.

Wilbur died on May 30, 1912, at the age of 45. Orville developed some later designs, but was so hopelessly behind the competition that he quit building in 1914.

They may have hit a technological wall in 1910, but the Wrights scored many notable aviation firsts besides their famous flight in December 1903. They were the first to build successive flying machines that were capable of duplicating or exceeding the original performance, the first to achieve circular flight, the first to carry a passenger, the first to stay up over an hour, the first to fly cross-country, and perhaps the most important, the first to teach others to fly.

Wilbur and Orville, we thank you.

The photographs

1. The canard configuration was standard for all Wright Flyers through the A models of 1908-09. The elevators were ahead of the wing, not behind it, even though the rudder was back there. There was a good reason for such a setup on the early models, which sat level and low to the ground: The tail would drag on a slow landing. With a vertically aligned surface-like rudder, that was no problem; the rudder booms were pivoted so the rudder could be moved upward.

2. The transition model was one of the last Model As. This one still had the standard forward elevators, but the Wrights added another behind the rudder on booms that were much longer than those on the regular Model A.

3. The production-model Wright B was arranged the way most airplanes have been ever since, with the elevators behind the wing. By late 1910 the Wrights had also gotten rid of their monorail takeoff system and had begun to use conventional wheel landing gear. The following R, EX, C, D and E models were basically similar.

1

2

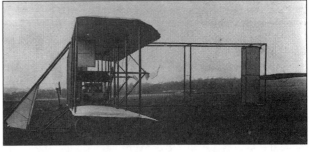

3

4

4. Old and new features were combined in the Model H of 1914. It still used a chain drive to two pusher propellers, but the booms were replaced with a fuselage. This one started out with the Wrights' controversial wing-warping system for lateral control, but ended up using ailerons between the wings as on competing Curtiss designs.

B-17s that weren't B-17s

Many of the famous bombers ended up flying under different designations

1st January 1979

The Boeing B-17, one of the most famous airplanes of World War II, was so distinctive in size and shape that anyone with any aircraft-recognition capability could easily identify one as it flew overhead. Or could they?

What appeared to be a B-17 may have actually been any one of a significant number of airplanes that were built as B-17s but converted to other purposes following delivery. Let's take a brief look at them here. Some will be treated in more detail in future columns.

XB-38. This was the first B-17 to get redesignated. Late in 1941, when the Army wanted more B-17s than Boeing could build, Douglas and the Vega division of Lockheed formed a pool to build them. It was called the "BVD Pool" for Boeing, Vega and Douglas.

Well, to get things going at the other plants, Boeing delivered examples of the current B-17E model to Vega and Douglas. After tooling up for its B-17s, Vega got an Army contract to try Allison V-1710 liquid-cooled V-12 engines in a B-17 as a backup to the standard Wright Cyclone air-cooled radial. That resulted in so many changes to the airframe that a new designation was justified. The redesigned model became the XB-38. Lockheed converted the sample that Boeing had sent them, and was supposed to convert two that it built, but the program never got that far.

The first one caught fire in the air after a total of only 12 flight hours. The crew bailed out and the first and only XB-38 was lost. The contract for the other two was canceled.

XB and YB-40. Again, these aircraft were built as B-17s but were converted for other purposes. Late in 1942, the B-17s were raiding targets far beyond escort fighter range. Someone got the bright idea to make "real" Flying Fortresses out of some of the B-17s. They had the range, so why not use them as defensive fighters? Two extra power turrets, plus double-powered side guns were added, along with heavy protective armor and 19,000 rounds of ammunition. The prototype, designated XB-40, was worked up by Lockheed.

While the additional side guns and even the extra top turret were not particularly noticeable, the most prominent feature was the new "chin" turret under the nose. It was under development at Boeing, but the XB-40 was the first to use it in service. It later became the distinguishing feature of the B-17G model.

After the Army tested the XB-40 and decided that the idea would work, Douglas was given a contract to convert 13 more as YB-40s. That contract was later increased to 20. Well, the idea did not work as well in practice as in theory.

The B-40s kept right up with the B-17s on the way to the target, but the return trip was something else. The B-17 bombers unloaded their several tons of bombs and flew home light. The B-40s, however, still had all their extra guns and armor and had a hard time keeping up. It wasn't long before they were taken off the bombing runs.

XC-108. This one got entirely out of the bomber business. By mid-1943, with the B-17G in production, many of the older models were diverted to other purposes. A former B-17E became General Douglas MacAruthur's personal transport "Bataan" under the designation XC-108. The aircraft's interior was stripped and converted to office and living quarters.

The XC-108's armament was rather illogical. It had a single .50-caliber machine gun in the nose when a tail gun made more sense. Another was converted for another general as a YC-108. One with a cargo door cut in the side was designated XC-108A, and a fuel transport became XC-108B.

F-9. The B-17's range suited it to some photo-reconnaissance missions that the other F-for-foto models could not undertake, so more than 50 were fitted with special cameras and redesignated F-9 through F-9C. Later, the F designation was dropped and the planes were known as RB-17s. The prefix R identified a special-purpose conversion of a basic B-17. It simplified maintenance and supply problems.

BQ-7. Approximately 25 war-weary B-17s were modified in England late in World War II for use as radio-controlled flying bombs against heavy German installations like missile-launch sites and submarine pens. Everything was stripped out and the planes were loaded with up to 20 tons of Torpex, an explosive. Two pilots took off in them and got them on course. With the planes under control from a "mother ship," the pilots parachuted out (their compartment had been converted to an open cockpit to simplify the process), and the mother ship flew the four-engine bomb into the target. Sorry, no photos.

PB-1. At the end of the war, the U.S. Navy took over 48 new B-17Gs and gave them the naval designation PB-1 (P for patrol, B for Boeing). They were not used as bombers, but were used first as antisubmarine patrol planes with radar search equipment in a big belly radome under the designation PB-1W.

Later, the Coast Guard used B-17s as PB-1Gs for air-sea rescue. The aircraft carried lifeboats that could be dropped to downed crews and others in distress. The Air Force used

1

2

3

4

5

similar models as B-17Hs and SB-17Gs.

The photographs

1. Lockheed's Allison-engine conversion of the Boeing-designed B-17E was identified as the XB-38 because of the major differences. The test program was not successful, so Wright Cyclone radials remained the standard engine for B-17-type bombers.

2. The real Flying Fortress was the B-40 series, with an extra power turret on top of the fuselage ahead of the fin and another under the nose. This is the single XB-40 modified from a B-17F by Lockheed. Douglas converted 20 others as YB-40s. After withdrawal from bomber-escort service, some became TB-40 bomber-trainers.

3. General MacArthur's personal transport was a former B-17E that was redesignated XC-108. Named "Bataan," it had an early form of the drop-down entry door with built-in steps, and was even equipped with a bathtub. Note the single nose gun and the faired-over tail-gun position.

4. A photo-reconnaissance version of the B-17 was designated F-9. This one was used as a VIP transport in early postwar years. Note the curtains on the former side-gun windows. All B-17s went out of the bomber business at the end of the war. The turrets were stripped off, and many became transports. Various conversions remained in service until 1960.

5. The U.S. Navy used B-17s for antisubmarine work as PB-1Ws. Note the big radome. Navy color at the time was overall dark blue. Armament was removed, and the PB-1s became patrol planes.

The Gold Bug

Merle Replogle had 26 horsepower — total — in the world's first homebuilt trimotor

2nd January 1979

One of the appealing features of the homebuilt airplane movement is the great variety of highly individualistic designs. While the majority of homebuilders prefer to build from plans, some true experimenters are capable of producing some very unusual designs.

My nomination for the all-time tops in conventional design with a difference is Merle Replogle's Gold Bug. The aircraft began in 1962 as a quick-and-easy, low-cost and low-performance flying machine. While the wood construction and general layout resembled some of the secondary gliders that were popular in the late 1920s, the oddity of the design was in the powerplant department.

Calculations showed that an efficient glider could fly on 10 horsepower. A few glider pilots had added small two-stroke engines to existing sailplanes over the years, but they had trouble getting them into the air without assistance — and then were only able to stretch the glide a little. There was a big difference between calculated horsepower and horsepower that was delivered through a small-diameter propeller turning 4,000 to 6,000 rpm.

Replogle, a former bench mechanic at Boeing, installed a 10-horsepower West Bend chain-saw motor in the nose of the Gold Bug and two eight-horsepower models at each side to create the world's first homebuilt trimotor. That combination worked — sort of — as long as all three engines kept running at full power, which was seldom.

One day one of the side engines broke the shaft and the detached propeller chewed up the bench seat on which Replogle was sitting. To avoid a repeat performance, he turned the side engines around so that the props were further ahead of his vulnerable position.

A new landing gear was installed after the plane ran out of gas and knocked the wheels off during an off-airport forced landing.

Following another crash during a loss of power on take-off, the fuselage was rebuilt. The cabin and engine installation were cleaned up and made more aerodynamic, and the trimotor continued to fly as Gold Bug II. It didn't last long as such, however. Another crack-up due to the temperamental two-cycle engines, plus the fact that someone stole two of them, convinced Replogle to redesign the ship with a single

engine. What made the Gold Bug III a real airplane was his own conversion of a Volkswagen automobile engine.

Replogle retired from Boeing in 1966 and moved to Arizona for health reasons, taking Gold Bug with him on a trailer. Later that year he accomplished what might be regarded as the homebuilt flight of the year by making a 3,000-mile round trip from Arizona to the EAA Convention in Rockford, Illinois.

Just to show that that was no fluke, he did it again in 1968. That year he added big flaps to the wing, which gave great slow-flight performance; he could practically hover in a strong breeze. I recall going around the Rockford fly-by pattern twice in a Fly Baby homebuilt while Replogle was shaking up the EAA and FAA officials by traversing the straightaway in super-slow flight.

Replogle's pioneering efforts pointed the way, as can be seen in all the ultra-light hang gliders that were soon flying around with two-stroke engines. The Gold Bug, meanwhile, has been honorably retired to a museum.

The photographs

1. The first homebuilt trimotor, Merle Replogle's Gold Bug, was powered with a 10-horsepower West Bend chain-saw motor in the nose and two eight-horsepower models at the sides. The engines weren't intended to operate with instruments, but the FAA insisted that Replogle install tachometers. There wasn't room in the panel, so he used a single three-way electrical unit with a selector switch.

2. That's Replogle seated in the first version of his homebuilt trimotor, the Gold Bug I. The first change was to turn the side engines around to become tractors. The shock-absorbing landing gear is a tapered aluminum channel.

3. Gold Bug II was the same airplane with a redesigned fuselage, new cantilever landing gear, and enclosed engines. Adequate and continuous power was still the major problem; the new trimotor configuration did not last long.

4. Gold Bug III's final configuration featured a single Volkswagen engine in the nose. The flaps were added after the first Arizona-to-Illinois flight in 1966. This photo was taken near Seattle during Replogle's roundabout return from Rockford, Illinois, through Arizona in 1968.

1

2

3

4

Obsolete but still in need

When new monoplanes didn't work out, the Curtiss SOC biplane lasted through WWII

1st February 1979

In the normal course of progress, obsolete equipment usually gets replaced and thus forgotten by nearly everyone except the historians. How satisfying, however, to find an established design that simply refuses to die. The replacement cannot do the job, so the old-timer carries on long past expectations.

Such an airplane is the Curtiss SOC line of naval scout-observation planes that carried the popular name of Seagull. Actually, this plane was the second Curtiss model to carry the name. The first was a 1919 commercial flying boat that had been developed from a wartime trainer.

The first 1933 Seagull was designed to a U.S. Navy requirement for a traditional two-seat biplane that could operate on wheels or floats and could be catapulted from battleships. Operation from the decks of aircraft carriers was not a requirement at the time.

The new Seagull was an interesting mix of old and new. The structure was traditional, with welded steel-tube fuselage and metal-frame wings, all fabric covered. It was loaded with new gadgetry, however, in the form of full-span flaps on the upper wing and retractable leading-edge slats to improve slow-flight characteristics for observation missions.

The powerplant was the well-proven (since 1926) 550-horsepower Pratt & Whitney air-cooled radial under a modern NACA cowling. An oddity of the time was the use of a single stainless-steel amphibious float to allow land or sea operations without the lay-up time needed to make the usual change from wheels to floats.

Since it was designed for the observation role, the prototype of the new Seagull was designated XO3C-1, for the third observation model designed by Curtiss for the Navy. Before testing was completed, however, the Navy changed the mission concept to combine observation with scouting, so the designation was changed to XSOC-1 for scout-observation.

After some refinements to the prototype, including canopies over the cockpits, orders were placed for 135 production SOC-1s, with deliveries beginning in November 1935. The amphibious feature was deleted, and the planes operated on a single main pontoon with tip floats or a new single-leg landing gear. Again, no carrier operations were anticipated.

Further orders followed for 40 wheels-only SOC-2s and 83 dual-purpose SOC-3s. To supplement Curtiss production, the U.S. Naval Aircraft Factory built an additional 64 SOC-3s under the Navy designation SON-1. By 1938 the

Seagull was the only model that was used on cruisers as a scout and on battleships as an observation plane. Three more SOC-4s were built to the requirements of the U.S. Coast Guard.

Even before SOC deliveries were completed, it was obvious that the design was obsolescent. The new monoplanes with all-metal construction were coming on fast and the old biplane types were on the way out. Consequently, the Navy held another design contest for a replacement with the requirement that the new design be a monoplane.

Curtiss won that competition with the XSO3C-1 that it also named Seagull. The prototype flew in October 1939, with deliveries to the fleet beginning in July 1942.

Since the United States was now in World War II, The SOC's duties were expanding until such time as the replacements would be available. Some were modified to SOC-1A, SON-1A, etc., by adding arrester hooks for deck landings on carriers. The letter A in the designation indicated that arrester gear had been added to a model that did not originally carry it. Also, the three SOC-4s were taken over by the Navy, modified to full SOC-3A standards, and redesignated as such.

When SO3C-1 deliveries got underway, the old SOC biplanes were pulled out of the fleet and sent to schools as trainers. That situation, however, didn't last. The monoplanes, due partly to the Navy's insistence on an unsuitable engine and partly to its overloading the design with a lot of equipment that it was not designed to carry, proved to be inadequate for the job.

Consequently, the new monoplanes were themselves pulled out of the fleet, and a big effort was made to round up the old biplanes and send them back to sea. Those splendid anachronisms stayed on the job right up to the end of hostilities.

No new design came along to replace them this time. The Navy quit using airplanes on cruisers and battleships as "The Eyes of the Fleet" and turned the job over to helicopters. The SOC then retired for good, satisfied with having outlived its designated successor and carrying on its obsolete 1933 capability well into the dawn of the jet era.

The photographs

1. The 1933 XSOC-3 prototype featured full-span flaps on the top wing, a retractable leading-edge slat, and a stainless-steel amphibious pontoon. The aircraft was redesignated XSOC-1 and was entered into production as the SOC-1.

2. The SOCs had folding wings to reduce storage space

on board ships. This SOC-1 from Scouting Squadron Six aboard the cruiser USS Minneapolis is on wheels during shore leave.

3. Some but not all SOCs were modified to permit carrier landings. Here an SOC-3A makes the 2,000th landing on the USS Long Island, on April 20, 1942.

4. An SOC-3 leaves the catapult of a battleship. Note the partially lowered flaps on the upper wing. Scouting squadrons operated from cruisers; observation squadrons operated from battleships. Both also operated from carriers.

Evolution of a mail plane

A Wasp in the hand helped Boeing, Hubbard land a ground-breaking government contract

2nd February 1979

The present U.S. airline network dates to April 1926, when the Post Office, which had monopolized the carriage of domestic air mail since 1918, began to turn its established routes over to private contractors. There were no recognized airlines in the country at the time; many had been formed since the end of World War I, but all had failed because they could not survive on passenger revenues alone.

So when some of today's major airlines began their operations in 1926, they were primarily mail carriers. Some even started by using the same rebuilt, single-engine, single-seat, war-surplus airplanes that the Post Office had been using. A few that flew later equipment carried an occasional passenger if the mail load was light and there was room on top of the sacks in the front cockpit.

In the summer of 1926 the Post Office invited bids to turn the San Francisco-to-Chicago route over to a private contractor on July 1, 1927. Edward Hubbard was then the operator of the Seattle-to-Victoria contract international air-mail route. He had great faith in the future of commercial air mail and was also a close associate of Bill Boeing, head of the airplane factory that bore his name. When Hubbard heard of the availability of the San Francisco-to-Chicago route, he did some figuring and soon convinced Boeing that a combination of the Hubbard know-how and the resources of the Boeing company could operate the route at a profit. To that end, Boeing and Hubbard jointly bid for the route.

That seemed like an audacious move at the time. Though Boeing was a well-established and respected manufacturer, its market was entirely military; it had no commercial models and certainly no suitable mail plane in production. Further, the Boeing-Hubbard bid was considered by others in the industry to be far too low to assure a profit. However, it turned out that the audacious pair had an ace up their sleeve that the competition didn't know about.

Although it didn't have a mail plane in production, Boeing did have some mail-plane design experience. Back in 1925 the Post Office had held a fly-off design competition for a new single-engine mail plane to replace the obsolete wartime de Havilland observation planes that were then the standard of the fleet. One requirement was that the new model had to use the same 400-horsepower war-surplus water-cooled Liberty engine that powered the de Havilland. Boeing and nearly a dozen others submitted new models for the winner-take-all competition, which was won by Douglas with its M-1 (for mail plane), a minor variation of the O-2 observation model that it was building for the U.S. Army.

Competitors for the San Francisco-to-Chicago route were expected to use the Douglas M or a very similar airplane powered by the Liberty since the big V-12 was still the only engine of its power that was available for nonmilitary use. The combination pretty well fixed the payload of the airplane and its operating costs and potential revenues. Hubbard, however, knew the limitations of the Liberty from long experience and spotted the means of beating its weight and financial handicaps right there in the Boeing factory.

Boeing had just developed a new fighter plane, the F2B, for the U.S. Navy (Page 242), and had won a contract for 32 production articles. The significant feature of the new model was its powerplant — the brand-new Pratt & Whitney Wasp, a 420-horsepower air-cooled radial, instead of the heavy water-cooled Curtiss and Packard V-12 models then in use on contemporary fighters.

Hubbard realized the tremendous advantage that this engine offered for commercial operations: less weight and a corresponding increase in payload for a given airframe, simplified maintenance, longer operating life, and a large reduction in operating costs. Those factors prompted his suggestion to Bill Boeing. Hubbard figured that by redesigning the unsuccessful 1925 Boeing Model 40 mail plane to use the new Wasp engine he could reduce the empty weight and the operating cost while increasing the payload to the point where two paying passengers could be carried regularly in addition to the required mail load.

Air-cooled radial engines had been on the market for several years, and their basic advantages were well-known to the airplane manufacturers. However, the most powerful models commercially available were only 200 horsepower, half of what a big mail plane needed. The new Wasp was obviously the perfect engine for a mail plane, but there was one catch: It was a military engine, developed under the auspices of the U.S. Navy, and had not been released for commercial use.

Bill Boeing's advantage in the route competition was his opportunity to acquire the supply of Navy-owned Wasp engines that were then in his factory but were not needed for installation in the new fighters for many months. As a result of considerable discussion between Boeing and the president of Pratt & Whitney, the Navy agreed to release the in-plant engines to Boeing on the engine manufacturer's assurance that replacement Wasps would be available for the new Navy planes when needed.

The Boeing-Hubbard bid was submitted on the basis of Hubbard's figures for a redesigned Model 40 powered by the Wasp. After they were awarded the route on a low bid that confounded the industry, the two established an operating company called Boeing Air Transport, Inc., and the factory got busy on development of the new Model 40A and construction of 24 articles for use on the route. The airplanes

1

2

3

4

were all delivered in time for the inauguration on July 1, per the contract.

The 40A was a big airplane that clearly showed its traditional mail-plane ancestry. The pilot still sat in an open cockpit behind the wings, but the two passengers, instead of riding in an open cockpit as before, sat side-by-side in a cozy cabin between the forward and aft compartments that held 1,000 pounds of mail and express. The availability of a new 525-horsepower Pratt & Whitney Hornet engine in 1928 resulted in most of the 1927 40A models being returned to the factory for engine changes and redesignation as Boeing Model 40Bs.

Increasing passenger demand resulted in removal of the rear mail compartment for two more passenger seats in the 10 1928 Model 40Cs that were otherwise identical to the 40A. The most popular model of the series, however, with 37 examples built, was the 40B-4. It combined the more powerful engine of the 40B with the increased passenger capacity of the 40C along with a number of significant state-of-the-art improvements. The older 40Bs were then redesignated 40B-2s to reflect their two-passenger capacity. Several 40B-4s were built in Boeing's Canadian plant as Model 40H-4s, and other Model 40 variants were delivered to non-airline customers before production ended in November 1931.

Boeing Air Transport, meanwhile, expanded through the acquisition of other airlines and eventually became the separate company known today as United Air Lines.

The photographs

1. The original Boeing Model 40 was built for the government's mail-plane competition of 1925. It had a laminated wood veneer fuselage but was handicapped by the required use of a war-surplus Liberty V-12 water-cooled engine.

2. The 1927 redesign of the Boeing 40 was the 40A, which featured a welded steel-tube fuselage and the new air-cooled Pratt & Whitney Wasp radial engine. Taking advantage of the weight it saved, it carried two revenue-paying passengers in a comfortable cabin. The pilot stayed outside.

3. A four-passenger Boeing 40C of the Pacific Air Transport Division of United Air Lines after it was brought up to 40B-4 standards with a 525-horsepower Hornet engine. Though the Model 40s had brakes, they still used tail skids in the early 1930s.

4. Loading passengers on a Varney Air Lines Boeing 40C. The passengers were snug in the four-place cabin, but the pilot was still out in the open, as he had been in mail planes since 1918.

Zeppelin rigid airships

Sabotage, vandalism actually helped German company survive post-WWI climate

1st March 1979

Most acts of vandalism or sabotage are the result of protest, dissatisfaction or to deprive someone of something. Seldom does such an act see benefits.

One rare example, however, with benefits to the Zeppelin Company and to the U.S. Navy, was the destruction of seven German Navy Zeppelin airships by their crews a few months after World War I ended.

When it lost the war, Germany was forced to turn over much of its military and naval equipment to the Allies, including airplanes, airships, ,battleships and cannon. Things were going pretty much according to schedule by mid-1919. The remnants of the German High Seas Fleet had been sailed into the harbor at Scapa Flow, Scotland, but before the British could take the ships over, their German crews sank them.

When the naval airship crews back in Germany heard of that, they thought it was a great idea. Their ships were still intact, but their gas cells were deflated so that they could not fly immediately.

The rigid structures were, in fact, suspended by cables from the roofs of their hangars. Of 15 surviving Zeppelins, the crews cut the cables on seven and let them crash to their hangar floors.

The U.S. Navy was set to receive three of the Zeppelins as war reparations. It was very interested in rigid airships and was actually designing one of its own (Page 298) that was completed as the unfortunate Shenandoah (ZR-1). It was also buying another (ZR-2) that was part of England's own rigid airship-building program.

The German naval Zeps, which were high-altitude bombers, were not the type of ship that the Navy really wanted, but at the time any Zeppelins were better than no Zeppelins.

With their three war trophies destroyed, Navy brass got the Allied Control Commission to agree that they should be replaced. However, instead of three obsolescent models, the Navy would settle for one brand-new, up-to-date version from the Zeppelin works and paid for by the German government.

That didn't set too well with the Allied Control Commission. It had allowed Zeppelin to build two small commercial ships in 1919 but seized the first after only four months of service and the second before it could be used. Over the vehement protests of Zeppelin officials, who maintained that the ships were private and not government property, the first was given to France and the second to Italy as replacements for other sabotaged Zeps they were to have received.

One Allied excuse was that the pair had been built from wartime materials (which was true) and were therefore legitimate war booty. Further, the commission had every intention of putting the Zeppelin works entirely out of business.

When the Navy got Allied approval for one new airship, the Zeppelin works got a reprieve to build what was then supposed to be the last Zeppelin. It carried Works No. LZ-126 as the 126th Zeppelin, but it was only the 117th built because of end-of-the-war cancellations and some postwar design studies for commercial ships that did not get built because of the Allied Control Commission's restrictions on size. The LZ-126 carried the U.S. Navy designation ZR-3 and was named the Los Angeles.

Another complication then arose. The value that the Allied Control Commission placed on the three sabotaged ships, which it had directed the German government to pay to the Zeppelin Company for replacement, was considerably less than the engineering and production costs of a new one-only ship. The Navy wanted it enough, however, that it agreed to pay the $100,000-plus difference in price.

After it was delivered across the Atlantic in a spectacular 1924 flight, the political climate moderated a bit and the Zeppelin works, broke and with no customers in sight, was allowed to survive. Improving relations between the former Allies and Germany resulted in the Locarno Treaty of 1925, which, among other concessions to postwar restrictions on Germany, lifted the weight, power and size limitations on German aircraft production. That put Zeppelin back in business, enabling it to raise funds directly from the public for a new ship, the LZ-127 Graf Zeppelin, which was completed in 1928.

Although no one bought it, its widely publicized success permitted the financing of enlarged building facilities and the construction of two greatly improved ships, the LZ-129 that was eventually named Hindenburg upon completion in 1936, and the LZ-130 Graf Zeppelin II, which was finished in 1938.

The Hindenburg's story is well known, but neither it, the Los Angeles nor the two Graf Zeppelins would have existed if those seven wartime Zeps had not crashed on the hangar floors in 1919.

1

2

3

4

The photographs

1. The German Zeppelin L-48, typical of the 15 World War I ships that were to be turned over to the Allies under the terms of the Armistice. The black paint helped hide it from searchlights at night; the white top minimized gas expansion from solar heating.

2. Naval Zeppelins L-63 and L-42 were among the seven that the crews destroyed in their hangars to prevent their delivery to the Allies. These and three others were at the Nordholz Airship Station.

3. The U.S. Navy was due to receive three of the sabotaged Zeppelins. This is another view of the L-63 (LZ-110; the Navy L-numbers did not match the Zeppelin Company's sequential airframe numbers).

4. LZ-126, named the Los Angeles, was built by the Zeppelin Company as a replacement for the three wartime ships the Navy lost to sabotage. At the time of its completion in 1924, it was the world's largest and most modern airship. It was decommissioned in 1932 but was used for ground testing until it was scrapped in 1939.

From boom to bust

They became bona fide fuselages when they began to carry people

2nd March 1979

In past columns (pages 296 and 306) we have seen the tail booms of the old pre-World War I pusher designs evolve into thin fuselage-like structures that eventually grew to the point where they could contain engines and landing gear but no personnel. Now we see the final steps: putting bodies in the booms to qualify them as bona fide fuselages, plus a few cases of putting two fuselages of an established design together to create an entirely new model. Examples are so numerous that they will be presented in two installments. Part 1 here covers most of World War I and up to 1930.

The photographs

1. This French Voisin of 1915 represents a double oddity. Originally, the firm had developed a single-engine pusher with tandem wheels built into the bottom of the pod and used wingtip skids to keep the wings level on the ground. Figuring that two wrongs might make a right, Voisin put two of the singles together to make a twin-engine, four-wheel pusher. There was no production model.

2. The one-only Fokker K-1 of 1915 was publicized as a "Battleplane" but never strayed far from the factory. Two fuselages of a current singe-engine Fokker model, complete with individual tail surfaces, were combined to make a push-pull twin-engine model with the pilot in the pod between the engines. The former fuselages still qualified as such, rather than as mere fat booms, because a gunner was supposed to ride in the nose of each. The first flight convinced Fokker that the design was a lemon.

3. It's more accurate to call this German Siemens R-1 of 1915 a "split fuselage" design rather than a twin. The crew and engines were all in the single part of the fuselage up forward, with the propellers driven by gears and long extension shafts. The reason for the "over and under" aft fuselage was to give gunners in the main portion a clear field of fire directly to the rear, an indefensible blind spot on most multi-engine bombers of the time. This basic design saw limited production and use in World War I.

4. The British Beardmore seaplane of 1916 is probably the first twin-fuselage airplane actually designed as such instead of being an adaptation. It had no central pod. The crew, powerplants and controls were all in the fuselages. An interesting question: Since those old rotary engines didn't have starters, how did the props get swung when the plane was afloat?

5. The French La Bourdette-Halbron triplane of 1917 was the first attempt at a twin-hull flying boat. The pilot and an observer rode in a central pod, but there were cockpits in the bow of each hull for gunners. A basic disadvantage of such flying boats is the terrific additional stress put on the interconnecting structure by rough water.

6. It's doubtful that the U.S. Thomas-Morse firm was aware of the Fokker K-1 when it designed the MB-4 mail plane in 1919, but the concept is identical, even down to the use of separate tail surfaces. The only significant difference was putting the mail compartment instead of the pilot between the engines and putting the pilots and controls in the fuselages. The U.S. Post Office actually tried that on its routes, but soon dropped it.

7. The trimotor French Bordelaise of 1930 is hard to define. The area between the two "fuselages" is filled in from the central pilot's cockpit to a point well aft of the wing in the style of the famous Burnelli "lifting fuselage" designs. Note the windows. Whether the tail surfaces are supported by bona fide fuselages or large booms is open to question. They seem to qualify as fuselages because the forward portions are occupied, but are they truly independent structures at this point?

8. Little is known of this twin-hull Russian Krilov ASK design beyond this photo. The hulls were obviously intended to carry passengers, but the pilot sat in a central pod. The photo is not clear enough to reveal whether this is an amphibian resting on its wheels or a pure flying boat on beaching gear.

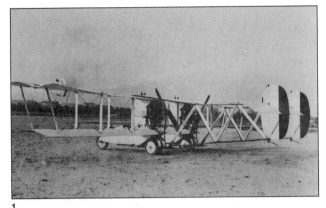

1

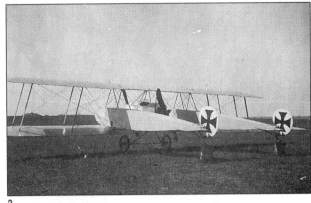

2

3

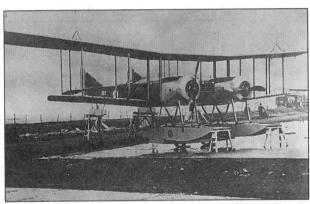

4

5

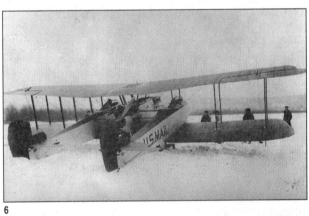

6

7

8

Selling single-seaters

Slow sales have been an ongoing problem since 1919

3rd March 1979

Since many pilots fly primarily for the fun of it, and since little single-seat airplanes give snappier performance than two-seaters for a given powerplant, you would think there would be a significant market for a good, low-cost, production single-seater. Some serious designers and manufactures have thought so too over the years. Yet while many prototypes have been built, there has been a notable lack of customers. Why?

The story is a long one. Efforts to sell production single-seaters go all the way back to 1919, but the basic problems remain.

While single-seaters are somewhat smaller than two-seaters that use the same engine, there is no significant price break due to any reduced quantity of material. Most of the standard instruments, wheels, etc., are the same whether the plane has one seat or two. The structure is not appreciably simpler, so there is little if any savings in man hours of constructions or in tooling costs.

Then there is the matter of utility. The single-seater appeals mainly to the sport pilot who wants a livelier airplane for a given power. A faster plane is not usually his objective. The single-seater is useful only to the established pilot for sport and transportation. With no cost break, there is no point in schools using them as cheap trainers for their students to build time. Also, the fact that they have only one seat creates resistance from people who have the all-important veto power in personal flying – spouses who want to fly along.

To retain the utility of two seats and still give the sport pilot a livelier airplane, industry beefed up some stock models like the Cessna 150 and the Beech Musketeer to give them the structural capability for normal aerobatics. With one exception, that pretty well took care of the sport pilot's need for a commercial single-seater and actually helped the aerobatic movement. With good two-seaters available for commercial training, the serious aerobats could get checked out properly and then move on to the hot homebuilts and custom-built exhibition models.

One exception is the Pitts S-1, a pre-WWII design that appeared as a custom model on the exhibition scene after the war. A world aerobatic champion, it has been one of the most popular homebuilts over the years. It is type-certified and available from the factory. Production is limited, and it has a long way to go before it catches the only other single-seaters that have seen significant production: the 45-horsepower Buhl Bull Pup of 1931 and the 65-horsepower Mooney Mite of 1948-52.

The photos here show five of the post-WWII single-seaters built by established manufacturers that did not get beyond the prototype stage.

The photographs

1. The Luscombe Model 10 is a case of a manufacturer developing a single-seat fuselage and using cut-down wing and tail assemblies from its established two-seat model. Luscombe wings were used on other single-seaters when amateur builders adapted them to their homebuilt designs.

2. The Lockheed Little Dipper was designed by John Thorpe when Lockheed considered entering the personal-plane market after World War II. It was also offered to the Army as short-range transportation for individual soldiers. Neither market materialized, so the design was dropped.

3. The Midget Mustang was designed by Piper's chief engineer, Dave Long, as a more practical type than the Skycycle. Only two were built, and they gained reputations

as racers when they were entered in the 1948 and subsequent Midget Races. The design has been popular for years in the homebuilt market.

4. The Piper Skycycle used a surplus WWII fighter drop tank as the main part of the fuselage. Wings, tail and landing gear were designed to fit. Piper quietly dropped the aircraft in favor of the more utilitarian Cub two-seater.

5. The Champion Pro was introduced in 1968 as a 180-horsepower single-seat version of the contemporary Citabria, itself a beefed-up Aeronca Champ. The fuselage superstructure was cut down to give the design the added sporting appeal of an open cockpit, but it didn't sell.

The earliest mail planes

The de Havilland 4 replaced the Curtiss Jenny and gave way to the Douglas M-2

2nd April 1979

Air mail began in the United States on May 15, 1918, when the Army opened a route from New York City to Washington, DC.

After proving the operation workable, the Army turned the job over to the Post Office a few months later. This government monopoly of the service, which stifled the development of airlines in the country, continued into 1926 and did not end completely until September 1927, when the last government route was turned over to a private contractor.

The Army started by using Curtiss JN-4H Jenny airplanes with a mail pit replacing the front cockpit. The Post Office tried a great variety of models. Some were conversions of established World War I military types and some were new. A modification of the de Havilland 4 was finally the plane of choice. It was a British design that originated in 1916 as a versatile light bomber and observation type. It was so outstanding in its day that it was selected for mass production in the United States in 1917, with the new American Liberty engine replacing the original Rolls-Royce. It was obsolete by the time the U.S. version, officially called the "Liberty Plane," but nicknamed "Flaming Coffin," got to the front in late 1918. After extensive modification, the DH-4 was a mainstay of U.S. Army aviation until the mid-1920s, and a few remained in service until 1932. The DH offered several advantages for the Post Office. First, it could carry the required load at the required speed. Further, it was available in quantity, and the price was right. All the Post Office had to do was ask the

Army to transfer X number of DHs and there they were. Finally, there was an unlimited supply of replacement engines at a time when major overhaul periods were less than 100 hours.

Finally, not much modification was required. The front cockpit became a 400-pound mail pit, the fuselage was skinned with clear-varnished birch plywood instead of fabric, and the wheels were enlarged and moved forward slightly to alleviate a chronic tendency of the military DH-4 to nose over during soft-field landings. When night flying began, an electrical system was added for the flying and landing lights. Exhaust stacks were extended aft of the cockpit to keep glare out of the pilot's eyes – until it was discovered that red-hot extensions were a major fire hazard in the event of an accident.

The relatively trusty DH did a good job for several years, but the requirements eventually got beyond it. The Post Office had various aircraft firms work up modifications to improve the aircraft's payload and performance, but they were not worth the effort and the cost.

Finally in 1925 the Post Office held a fly-off design contest for a new mail plane. The principal design requirement was that it be powered with the wartime Liberty engine, of which a big stock was still on hand. Douglas won with the M-1, a minor adaptation of its current O-2 Army observation model, and got a 50-plane order for the M-2.

Although these were on the routes when the Post Office started to turn business over to private contractors, plenty

1

2

3

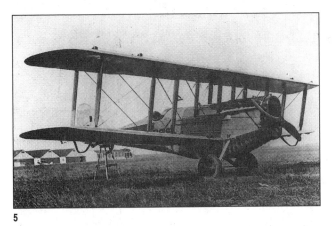

4

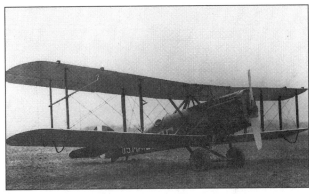

5

6

of old DHs were still in service. Some of the contractors bought the old crates when taking over the route and kept them in operation until 1928, when the new commercial models finally became available.

The photographs

1. The standard configuration of the de Havilland 4 mail plane in the early 1920s, with landing lights and long exhaust stacks for night operations. Standard coloring was silver-doped wings and tail, and clear-varnished plywood fuselage.

2. The most extreme DH-4 modification was this twin-engine version, which replaced the single 400-horsepower Liberty with a pair of 200-horsepower Hall-Scotts. At least 20 were built. They proved entirely unsuitable as mail planes,

however, so the Post Office turned them over to the Army.

3. Entirely different wings were tried by the well-known designer Guiseppe Bellanca. Note the novel addition of airfoils to the struts in an attempt to add lift. Again, this was a one-only design.

4. A quick and easy way to increase payload on the DH was to increase the wingspan. The Wittman-Lewis firm built a wider center section for a few, while keeping the original outer wing panels.

5. A new airfoil section was tried on this one-only version to increase lift, and a deeper belly was added to increase mail-carrying capacity.

6. One popular DH-4 modification was to use wings from the new Loening amphibian. The Army, Navy and Post Office used Loening wings on their DH-4s.

Twin fuselages

From the Savoia-Marchetti S-55 to Harold Wagner's Double Cub

2nd April 1979

Our short series on the evolution of the twin-tail boom airplanes into twin-fuselage aircraft has passed from the pod-and-boom stage, with the occupants in the pod (Page 296), to true twin-fuselage types (Page 322), with the occupants in either or both of the true fuselages. The last installment covered some of the more interesting designs from 1915 into the 1920s. In this final installment we look at some from the 1920s to the late 1950s.

The photographs

1. The best known and most numerous of the true twin-fuselage (or hull) designs was the Italian Savoia-Marchetti S-55 that appeared in 1926 and achieved major production. Though used on a number of notable exploration and long-distance flights, the major event in the S-55's career came when Marshal Balbo led 24 of them on a flight from Italy to the Chicago's World's Fair in 1933.

2. Little is known of most Russian designs between the two world wars. This Antonov ANT-22 flying boat owes much to the Marchetti S-55 but has full-length hulls and six engines instead of two.

3. A little evolution was involved in the World War II Italian Siai-Marchetti SM-92. The earlier SM-91 was a pure pod-and-boom type, with the crew in the pod. The SM-92 eliminated the pod, moved the fuselages closer together and put the crew under a canopy on the left fuselage only.

4. Necessity was the mother of invention in the case of the wartime German Heinkel He.111Z Zwilling, or Twin. Contemporary transports were not able to tow the giant Messerschmitt 321 troop gliders, so two He.111H bombers were spliced together at the end of their center sections, and a fifth engine was added at the joint. No cross-connection was made at the tail. More than a dozen of these splice jobs were made before the Luftwaffe gave up on the big gliders, hung six engines on them, and converted them to Me.323 airplanes.

5. The North American P-82 Twin Mustang partly followed the He.111Z idea in putting two fuselages of an established design on a single airplane. The fuselages and vertical tail were nearly identical to the famous P-51, and the outer wing panels were the same. The pod attached to the center section housed night-fighter radar. Note that the propellers rotate in opposite directions, as on the Lockheed P-38.

6. More mating of existing fuselages took place when this Twin Ercoupe was put together in 1948 for air-show work. Like the He.111Z, the two were joined at the ends of their center sections, but in this case the tails were joined too. It worked so well that brief consideration was given to adapting it to production.

7. Harold Wagner's Double Cub followed the Twin Ercoupe idea but put the fuselages a little closer together and did not use two complete horizontal tail assemblies. With the fuselages so close together, the props did not have adequate clearance, so Wagner put a short hub extension on the left one so that it overlapped the right.

The Hall XFH-1

Single-engine shipboard fighter used watertight fuselage for floatation

1st May 1979

One of the more unorthodox airplanes that was developed for the ultra-conservative aerial arm of the U.S. Navy was the Hall XFH-1 single-engine shipboard fighter.

Back in 1927 the introduction of the 450-horsepower Pratt & Whitney Wasp, an air-cooled radial engine, had pretty well revolutionized the fighter business for the Army and the Navy, and encouraged the Navy to adopt an "air-cooled engines only" policy for its carrier-based planes.

The XFH-1 (X for experimental, F for fighter and H for Hall) was one of several new fighter prototypes that the Navy contracted for in 1927. The contract with Charles Ward Hall, a pioneer in aluminum aircraft construction, was dated November 1927.

The Navy specification to which it was designed was pretty tight with regard to some of the details. First, the Wasp engine was the required powerplant. Next, the fuselage was to be metal monocoque construction and also be watertight in order to keep the plane afloat in case of an inadvertent ditching at sea.

Previously, clear back to World War I, the Navy had used various installations of the floatation bags in the wings or fuselage, inflating them after the ditching to keep the plane afloat. The watertight fuselage concept did not work too well, so the Navy stayed with the floatation bags for a few more years before switching to personnel rafts for crew survival.

In conjunction with the floating fuselage concept, it was also specified that the landing gear could be jettisoned for a smooth ditching. Back in World War I and for a few years thereafter, small hydrovanes had been fitted ahead of

the wheels of land planes that were expected to ditch in the water to keep them from nosing over. It turns out that this gimmick would have been more useful on the XFH-1 than the jettison feature.

The Navy also seemed to have a thing going for swept-back upper wings on its new biplanes of the time, as shown on such well-known designs as the Boeing F3B-1, the Vought O2U-1 Corsair, the Curtiss F7C-1 Sea Hawk, and the later Curtiss F8C Helldiver series and the Experimental Eberhard XFG-1.

The Hall also used the swept-back upper wing, but the physical relationship of the lower to the upper was such that the lower had to be swept forward for aerodynamic reasons, an oddity shared with the Eberhard design.

Because of headaches involved in developing all the special features, the XFH-1 was not delivered to the Navy until June 1929. Official tests were delayed by squabbling between the Navy and Hall over contract compliance. When flying did get underway, there was a partial structural failure of the upper wing, so a new one had to be built. As the tests progressed, the Navy showed great disappointment in the design, which showed a top speed of only 152 mph compared to 157 for the two-year-old F3B-1 and 168 for the 1928 Boeing F4B-1, both of which used the same Wasp engine.

The end came ignominiously on Feb. 18, 1930, when the XFH-1 had an engine failure over water. The pilot either did not have time to jettison the gear or could not get the thing to work, so that feature remained untested. The XFH-1 hit the water like any other land plane, nosing up and inflicting damage to the lower forward fuselage structure.

1

2

Despite a few leaks that might not have developed had the ditching been done without wheels, the XFH-1 finally proved the workability of its major design feature by staying afloat without the use of floatation bags.

The photographs

1. A side view of the all-metal Hall XFH-1 Navy fighter shows off the unusual wing arrangement, with the sweep-back on the upper panels and sweep-forward on the lower.

Note the streamlined fairings behind the cylinders of the air-cooled Wasp engine. It was an early attempt to cut down the drag of radial engines before the introduction of the NACA cowling and the Townend anti-drag ring of later years.

2. This three-quarters front view shows the XFH-1's landing gear, which could be jettisoned. The simplified wing structure eliminated the conventional center section and associated rigging by attaching the upper wing panels directly to cabane struts over the center line of the fuselage.

The Horton Wingless

Odd Bamboo Bomber derivative flew, but just barely

2nd May 1979

The Horton Wingless seems to qualify as an airplane despite its odd shape. It was built in Southern California in the early 1950s and was tested at Orange County Airport near Santa Ana in late 1952. The photos I obtained carry an early 1953 date. A designation of X-26-52 on one of them could be interpreted to mean that the thing was built in 1952.

Lynn Johnson, a Boeing engineer who was investigating lifting-body aircraft in the early 1970s, borrowed the photos and circulated them in the hopes of turning up some information on the origins of the design and its effectiveness, if any.

It seems to have been assembled from the major components of a World War II surplus Cessna UC-78 or AT-17 twin that was popularly known as the Bamboo Bomber. The Wingless reportedly substituted a pair of 450-horsepower Pratt & Whitney Wasp Jr. engines for the original 245-horsepower Jacobs. The propellers were on long extension shafts to put them well ahead of the square "lifting body." The body appears to have been built over the center section and engine nacelles of the Cessna. The original Cessna landing gear that retracted into the nacelles was retained but the rear fuselage was cut off. The standard vertical tail was replaced with a new one further forward, and separate elevators were fitted just behind and below the trailing edge of the body.

The Cessna wings from the ailerons outboard seem to have been retained, but the panels do not line up with the original center section and nacelles. Some cutting was done here, or a wing from another Bamboo bomber was used, because the original Cessna wing was built in one piece from tip to tip, with the generous dihedral angle built in. The dihedral appears to be about right for a stock Cessna wing, but the absence of a tight fit between the sides of the body and the wing makes one wonder if the projecting wing sections were supposed to move, either telescoping in and out or pivoting.

Johnson obtained background information and an eyewitness account of flight from a man in Santa Ana, California, in 1972. Just going on memory, the witness recalled that the plane was built by a William Horton in Huntington Beach, California, and was the subject of a vigorous stock promotion. The Wingless flew, but barely. Horton took off in it at Santa Ana in November 1952. Since he couldn't turn it, he landed it straight ahead beyond the runway.

Four more hops were made on Sept. 10, 1953, with liftoff in about 1,000 feet to an altitude of 30 feet, followed by a straight-ahead landing on the same runway. The witness said he knows of no subsequent flights. Apparently a lot of litigation ensued; the plane was stripped of useful hardware and just rotted away in the Santa Ana Airport bone yard.

The photographs

1. This side view shows how far the Horton Wingless' propellers were extended ahead of the engines. The message on the side reads, "This Experimental 'Horton Wingless' was built to prove that this configuration would fly. See our folder for production models."

2. This view of the Horton Wingless shows the wide lifting body with deep end plates, projecting Cessna Bamboo Bomber wingtips and the landing gear below the original Cessna nacelles.

3. Here's an interesting comparison of the boxy Wingless and a standard Cessna Bamboo Bomber (left). Note the projecting Cessna wing and Horton's unusual elevators.

1

2

3

Turning bombers into passenger planes

Curtiss Condor, Consolidated B-24 were altered on the drawing board

1st June 1979

Aviation history going back to 1919 shows that efforts have been made to convert military planes to civilian use. One of the best examples is the effort to capitalize on the range and load-carrying capability of bombers by making passenger planes of them. There are different ways to go here. We'll examine several in a sort of mini-series.

The easiest way, of course, is to take an airframe already built as a bomber, pull out the military equipment, add seats and windows, and presto, instant transport. That scenario was done frequently in Europe after World War I, before multi-engine planes were designed and built strictly as transports. The practice was followed again briefly, again in Europe, after World War II, when there was an acute shortage of bona fide transports for immediate commercial needs.

A slightly different approach was to alter an existing bomber design on the drawing board, making minor structural changes and then building an altered model that was better suited for carrying passengers. Two examples are illustrated here.

The first is the Curtiss Condor. The U.S. Army ordered a single XB-2 bomber prototype from Curtiss in 1926. It was Curtiss' own refinement of a 1920 Martin design that Curtiss had built under license. The XB-2 was a good airplane, and the Army ordered a dozen production models, a relatively big order for 1927-28.

With civil aviation booming at the time, Curtiss got Army permission to produce a civilian version of the B-2. Changes were minimal; the fuselage was widened slightly in the cabin area, which could now hold 15 passengers. The nose gunner and bombardier stations were eliminated, and the pilots were moved forward. The former open cockpit was converted to an enclosed cabin. Wings, tail, engines and landing gear were identical to the bomber. The machine-gun nests in the rear of the engine nacelles were simply faired over.

The civilian Condor was a good transport by the standards of the day, but it was the victim of bad timing. Only six were built before the Great Depression, which practically wiped out large civil airplane production.

A very similar adaptation took place in 1942, when the Army needed more long-range transports than the industry was able to provide at the time. Some bombers, notably the four-engine Consolidated B-24 Liberator, had been pressed into service as such but were pretty inadequate from the passenger's point of view. So, a little work at the drawing board developed a new model, and the C-87 in the C-for-cargo-transport series emerged. The C-87 used the roomy interior of the bomber for a proper 25-passenger cabin, with real seats, doors, windows, lavatory and the other essentials of a transport. The fact that the C-87 was not economical was not important at the time; there was a war on, and the C-87s were for the military, not the airlines. Two hundred seventy-six C-87s were delivered, compared to approximately 18,000 B-24s.

After the war the builder, now Consolidated-Vultee (ConVair) tried to market a Liberator Liner airline development of the B-24/C-87. Unable to compete with bona fide transports like the Douglas DC-4 (Army C-54) and the Lockheed Constellation (Army C-69) that were then being surplussed by the military and being built new in the factories, it never got beyond the prototype stage.

The photographs

1. The Curtiss B-2 Condor Army bomber carried machine-gun nests in the rear of the engine nacelles. This one is equipped with an early automatic pilot. The crew is demonstrating its effectiveness by having the pilot stand up in his seat while the copilot lies flat on top of the fuselage behind the cockpit.

2. The civilian version of the Condor was identical to the B-2 airframe except for the modified nose and widened fuselage. The letters TAT stood for Transcontinental Air Transport, a predecessor of TWA, or Trans World Airlines.

3. The Consolidated B-24 Liberator of World War II fame. This is a B-24D, before the model received powered nose and tail-gun turrets. Crew and passenger entry was

1

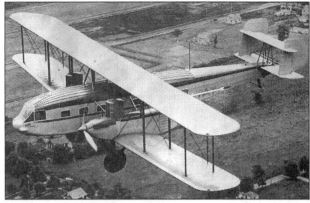

2

3

4

through the opened bomb-bay doors, which rolled up the sides of the fuselage in the manner of a roll-top desk.

4. C-87s could be distinguished from B24s by their smooth, elongated noses and their airline-type cabin windows. This is a rare bird. It's not a true C-87 or even a true B-24 airframe. It's an early Liberator model built for England before the corresponding Army B-24 design was finalized.

The Army drafted a number of them from the British orders, and a few got the C-87 conversion without ever acquiring standard U.S. Army designations. Both bomber and transport versions were operated under the designation LB-30 and flew under their original British serial numbers. Some became private transports after the war, but no C-87s or LB-30s were ever certified for airline use.

Censored swastikas

Ancient symbol is not a Nazi original

2nd June 1979

A newspaper item a few days ago indicated that a concerned group had put pressure on one of the country's biggest toy makers and a major producer of model airplane kits to quit using the Nazi swastika on World War II military toys and models.

The feeling of certain groups, and of entire peoples, toward that design is understandable. However, it does not deserve the condemnation that is now being heaped upon it. It was not originated by Adolph Hitler and his Nazis, and its use on aircraft was not a monopoly of the Luftwaffe from 1933-45.

For starters, the device is several thousands of years old, going back as far as art can be found. Besides being simply decorative, it has been highly symbolic, representing at various times the sun, infinity, continuing re-creation and, most recently, German national socialism. It appears in the works of the ancient Greeks, Chinese, Scandinavians, Incas, American Indians and Bhuddists.

Both Finland and Latvia used the swastika on a white circle as their military aircraft marking since the end of World War I. The Finnish marking had the swastika "flat," that is, with the two opposite arms parallel to the center line of the airplane and pointing clockwise, or to the right at the top. The Latvians had the marking standing on a corner, all arms at 45 degrees to the center line and pointing counterclockwise, or to the left.

Hitler's swastika, or "hakenkreuze" ("hooked cross" in German) was cornered like the Latvian and right-handed like the Finnish. It was also centered on a white circle. His major difference was the use of a red background for the circle as used on banners, arm bands and eventually airplanes.

After he came to power in Germany in 1933, Hitler decreed that the swastika should become part of the German national aircraft markings. Consequently, a wide red band was painted chordwise on the left side of all civil aircraft (there weren't supposed to be any German military planes then, but there were). The circle was centered between the leading edge of the fin and the trailing edge of the rudder. For nearly two years the markings on the right side of the tail was a chordwise set of three equal-width black, white and red strips in the pattern of the German flag. They were dropped in 1935 for the swastika on both sides, and the Luftwaffe also carried it on the tail as a supplement to the crosses on wings and fuselage. For camouflaged military types after 1938, the red band and white circle were deleted in favor of a narrow white border to reduce conspicuity.

The swastika had seen plenty of use as a personal aircraft marking by various World War I pilots, and it showed up in the Indian headdress of the famous Lafayette Escadrille in 1916. In the 1930s the U.S. 55th Pursuit Squadron used it as the main detail in its squadron insignia.

Hitler's atrocities seem to have wiped out all historical appreciation of the ancient swastika. Its display in postwar Germany is so forbidden that some publications, when using photos of airplanes carrying the Nazi marking, touch the offending symbol out of the photo before publishing it.

Even in the United States, manufacturers of model kits omit the swastika from World War II models, even though they are meticulously accurate in other marking details. In such cases, builders have to make them up themselves or buy separate marking sheets made up by firms that specialize in that area.

The photographs

1. In addition to standard military markings, this four-wheeled Voisin pusher of 1915 carried "flat" swastikas as the personal decoration of its crew.

2. Swastikas actually knew no nationality. This German WWI pilot backed his personal swastika with a big white square so it would be visible against the dark paint of his Albatros D-V fighter.

3. When used on this U.S. Army Boeing P-12B, the insignia of the 55th Pursuit Squadron, it was intended as an American Indian symbol of good luck.

4. One of the first countries to use the swastika as a national marking on aircraft was Finland. This plane, a U.S. Curtiss Hawk 75, was sold to France at the start of World War II. It was captured by the Germans and sold to Finland for use against the Soviets. After the war, the Finns replaced their swastika markings with white-blue-white circles.

5. Hitler's hakenkreuze, or swastika, was originally applied to German civil airplanes in 1933. Beginning in 1935 they were also applied to military airplanes inside a white circle and against a red band. Civilian airplanes retained the circle and band through the end of the war, but the military used only a narrow white border after 1938. The airplane is a Dornier Do-17M prototype.

6. This censored photo of a 1930s-era German Junkers Ju-52/3M airliner comes from a historical press release. The swastika was rather crudely painted over on the tail, making some viewers more conscious of it than if it had been left alone.

1

2

3

4

5

6

Phoney combat photos

Incorrect application of Allied markings exposed German propaganda

1st July 1979

As an avid collector of airplane photos, I have acquired prints from a vast variety of sources, some directly and some in very roundabout manner. The accompanying illustrations are an example of the latter. They are German news-service photos, copied out of strips of movie film and released in December 1940, soon after the fall of France. They are supposed to show a German Dornier Do.17 light bomber under attack by a British Supermarine Spitfire and a U.S.-built but British-operated Curtiss Mohawk during a low-level raid over England.

The photos were acquired as a pair, and yours truly was dissatisfied with them from the start. Other than the oddity of two different fighters making identical passes on the same airplane, and being photographed in the act at the same relative moment, something just didn't seem quite right. I couldn't put my finger on it at the time, so the prints were filed and left for a while. They reappeared from time to time, got a quick glance, and then went back into hiding.

All of a sudden the key to the puzzle turned up while I was doing some research into World War II German fighter markings. In the 1939-40 period, when these photos were supposedly taken, the specification under which the wing crosses of Luftwaffe fighters were applied called for the markings to be halfway between the fuselage and the wingtip, which was considerably further inboard than other powers placed their markings, and relatively small compared to the chord of the wing at that point.

Now an earlier suspicion was confirmed. The fighters were not defending England against Nazi invaders; the planes were flown by German pilots for propaganda purposes.

The first giveaway was the "German" location of the insignia. The Germans had captured plenty of British and French planes during the Allied reverses of 1939-40, and painted them in their own markings for test and evaluation. Naturally, when they did that, they applied the markings per their own specifications, hence the inboard location of the wing crosses. When it was decided to put British markings on the captured ships for the propaganda photos, the circles were put on in the German position instead of in the further-outboard French and British locations.

(Don't think for a minute that the Germans were the only ones to pull this kind of minor goof. When U.S. Army North American AT-6s were painted up to represent Japanese Zeroes in World War II movies, the Japanese markings were applied according to U.S. specifications, which also resulted in improper sizes and locations. This is still going on, as seen in the "Baa Baa Black Sheep" TV series of the 1970s and other aerial warfare epics in movies and TV.)

Another giveaway was the ex-French Mohawk. Quite a few escaped from France and got to England, where they were pressed into the RAF. However, they got the British sand-and-spinach camouflage (seen on the Spitfire) before going into service. Some of the Mohawks operated by the French were in the natural metal finish, as received from Curtiss, and some were painted light gray in France. Others had a much darker camouflage in the British style. The one in the combat scene is light colored, either natural metal or gray, even though it has the British insignia. This is a further point of suspicion, made more so by the fact that the British did not consider the Mohawk suitable for combat. They either used them as trainers or gave them away to colonial air forces and did not use them as fighters.

Years later I got confirmation that the photos were indeed fakes. While the use of improperly located Allied markings would seem to refute the famous German reputation for meticulous attention to detail, it's very easy to see what happened. No one had accurately recorded the proper size and location of the original Allied markings when the planes were repainted for the Luftwaffe. Then, when they were repainted as Allied types, no one had the specifications. No doubt someone knowledgeable in the subject pointed out the error, but things were too far along to change, as though anyone in authority really cared. Again, there is plenty of parallel in the Hollywood operation. The studios hire high-priced and sometimes really knowledgeable talent to advise them in such matters, and then proceed to ignore easy-to-verify accuracy and go hog-wild with something that someone like the producer's third cousin dreamed up.

It has happened, continues to happen and, I guess, will keep on happening. C'est la guerre cinamatique!

The photographs

1. This photo supposedly shows a German Do.17 bomber being attacked over England by a Supermarine Spitfire of the Royal Air Force. Real combat shots, showing two opposing planes this close together, are so rare as to be virtually nonexistent. The photo proved to be a setup made by the Germans, who used a captured Spitfire.

2. This companion photo shows a U.S.-built Curtiss 75 operating with British markings as a Mohawk. It's supposedly attacking the same Do.17. The initial clue that these propaganda photos included captured Allied fighters is the wing insignia: They were applied according to German specifications rather than Allied. Long after their initial release, the photos were proven to be fakes. The opposing airplanes were genuine, but the combat scenes were fabricated.

1

2

The Boeing 367-80

Prototype to the 707 and KC-135, it ushered in the airline jet age

2nd July 1979

July 15, 1954, is one of the most significant dates in aviation history. That day saw the first flight of the Boeing 367-80 (Dash-80) prototype of the 707 transport and the Air Force KC-135 tanker-transport. Both designs are in wide use today, and the last of more than 950 707s will not roll out of the Boeing factory until 1981.

Boeing achieved fame for its transport aircraft with the Model 40 of 1925-31, the big Model 80 trimotor of 1928-30, and the revolutionary Model 247 transport of 1933-35. Those aircraft were followed by the luxurious Clipper Flying Boats and the pressurized Model 307 Stratoliner, both of which saw their production end when World War II came along.

The company got back into transports after the war with the Model 377 Stratocruiser, a derivative of the military C-97, which itself was derived from the B-29. The 377, with its costly double-decker configuration, did not get a big share of the postwar airline market. It did become preeminent in jet bombers, however, with the revolutionary B-37 Stratojet and the giant B-52 Stratofortress. When it became evident that jet power was the way to go, the technology was adopted to the transport field.

The 367-80 was not the first jet transport, but it was far ahead of the British de Havilland Comet that opened the jet transport age in 1949.

Boeing developed the Jet Stratoliner strictly on its own as a colossal gamble, with the board of directors appropriating $16 million in company funds in May 1952. The prototype, designated as a far-removed derivative of the Air Force C-97 transport (Boeing 367), was designed to meet civil and military needs. The Air Force, in fact, was the first customer, ordering KC-135A tanker-transports only two months after the prototype flew.

The airlines were in sort of a dilemma at the time. If the 707 was as good as it was supposed to be, it would make existing piston-powered and Comet jet fleets obsolete. However, the airlines had invested heavily in late piston transports, and it took a little time to arrange the massive financing required for the new equipment before the old was significantly depreciated.

A novel feature of the Dash-80 compared to other transport types was that it was never intended to become a certifi-cated transport in revenue service. It was a flying guinea pig, pure and simple, and the non-certification allowed a lot of lee-way in making modifications. In its 18-year flying career, it became what is undoubtedly the world's most modified airplane. The accompanying photos show a few of the more notable configurations.

The much-patched Dash-80 was refurbished by Boeing in 1972 and flown to Washington, DC, for presentation to the National Air and Space Museum during Expo '72. Since there was no place in Washington to adequately display the aircraft, it was flown to Tucson, Arizona, for dry storage. It still sits there today.

2000 update: The Dash-80 is in a Boeing hangar under-going a slow refurbishment to its original condition. It's scheduled for eventual display in the National Air and Space Museum in Washington, DC.

The photographs

1. Rollout of the Boeing 367-80, prototype of the 707 and later jet transports, took place May 14, 1954. Topside color was yellow, the dark areas were brown, and the remain-der was natural metal.

2. The first customer for the new Boeing jet was the Air Force, which ordered an eventual 820 as tankers and straight transports. Here the Dash-80 tests an improved version of the Boeing-developed "flying boom" system on a Boeing B-52.

3. How's this for mixing engines? The outboard (No. 1 and No. 4) engines at this time are Pratt & Whitney JT-3s, commercial equivalents of the 10,000-pound-thrust J-57s that were used on B-52s. The left inboard (No. 2) is a 25,000-pound-thrust Pratt & Whitney J-57 and the right inboard (No. 3) is a later 17,000-pound-thrust J-57. The nose has been modified to test the AN/AMQ-15 weather-reconnaissance ra-dar for the Air Force.

4. With wing modifications and a 14,000-pound-thrust Pratt & Whitney JT-8 engine attached to the side of the fuse-lage, the Dash-80 became the five-engine prototype of the Boeing 727 Trijet. It was not convenient to raise the horizontal tail of the Dash-80 to the T-position that it would occupy on the 727, so the exhaust of the side-mounted jet was deflected over the tail.

1

2

3

4

5

6

5. Wing and tail modifications were completed on the Dash-80. Here the leading-edge slats and triple-slatted trailing-edge flaps of the 727 are being tested. Changes to the Model 720's wing planform were also worked out on the Dash-80.

6. The Dash-80 was flown for a while with special 90 degree flaps that had bleed air for the new JT-8D turbofans blown over them to create high lift. The plane could fly as slowly as 80 knots, the lower limit of its conventional flight controls.

The channel race

Louis Bleriot was the first to fly from France to England

1st August 1979

July 25 is another memorable date in aviation and world history. In 1909 Louis Bleriot of France flew a 25-horsepower monoplane of his own design across the English Channel from Calais, France, to Dover, England.

As a flight hop it wasn't much. Just a little over 21 miles and 36 minutes. Airplanes had flown greater distances before that, and a few had exceeded an hour's duration, so the flight set no records. The significance was in the locations of the takeoff and landing points, which gave the flight political and strategic significance.

For centuries the channel had isolated England from the rest of Europe, blocking invaders but also affecting the relationship of England with countries on the continent. With Bleriot's flight, the effectiveness of the channel as a physical and political barrier ended. The results are still being felt.

Actually, that first channel flight was a race. The Daily Mail, a British newspaper, was vigorously promoting aviation by putting up cash prizes for point-to-point flights. In 1908 it offered 500 pounds ($2,500 dollars at the time) for the first flight from England to France, or vice versa. With no takers that year, the prize was doubled in 1909.

The first contender to actually start was a wealthy 26-year-old Frenchman named Hubert Latham. He started from Sangatte, near Calais, in a 50-horsepower Antoinette monoplane. He had an impressive record, having made flights of 25 and 50 miles a few weeks earlier in the same ship. Fate, however, was her usual fickle self, and engine failure caused Latham to ditch in the channel, only seven miles out.

Another French competitor now appeared, the 37-year-old Bleriot. By the time he was ready to go, Latham had obtained another Antoinette and was also waiting for a break in the weather. Everything was right on the morning of the 25th. Bleriot was awakened at 2:30 a.m. and got his plane ready. Latham had also left instructions to be awakened at 3 a.m., but for some reason his crew let him sleep until after Bleriot had started.

Takeoff was at 4:41 British time after a short test hop. The French navy had generously provided a destroyer as a navigation aid and possible rescue ship. Bleriot caught up with the ship in seven minutes. He was so low, 250 feet, that he was out of sight of land in both directions. With no compass, he took his heading from the ship, which was supposed to be pointed in the right direction.

After 10 minutes of such "blind" flying, he spotted Dover Castle on its high cliff, although by now his heading was off by a few miles. He corrected that, fought increasing winds, and flew through a gap in the cliffs to land in a steeply sloping meadow behind the castle.

Latham was furious that he had been allowed to oversleep, but telegraphed his congratulations to Bleriot when he heard of his safe arrival. Bleriot replied with an offer to split the prize money with Latham if he could make it over the same day. By that time, however, the wind had come up and made another flight over the same route impossible.

Latham did try to be No. 2, however, on July 27. He was almost there when his engine quit again. He ditched in the channel once more, less than a mile from Dover.

The photographs

1. The Bleriot Model XI monoplane that made the first successful crossing of the English Channel on July 25, 1909. The engine was a 25-horsepower, three-cylinder Fan Anzani. Note that the elevators were mounted on the ends of the fixed

1

2

horizontal stabilizer. There were no ailerons; lateral control was by wing-warping.

    2. Latham's first Antoinette monoplane, which he used on his initial cross-channel attempt. The controls were oper-ated by two wheels, one at each side of the cockpit. Note that the ailerons were completely aft of the trailing edge of the wings. Latham's next Antoinette didn't have ailerons; it too used wing-warping for lateral control.

The Marines in Nicaragua

To help maintain order, they used rebuilt de Havilland 4 biplanes

2nd August 1979

Recent political doings in the Republic of Nicaragua bring to mind some aeronautical history from that turbulent country.

Because of the unsettled political situation in 1912, the Nicaraguan president asked the United States to send in the Marines to help maintain order. They stayed until 1925, but had to return again in 1926. That time they brought some effective though ancient air power with them. The airplanes were World War I de Havilland 4 biplanes that had been modernized to some extent after the war and were then known as DH-4Bs. Still later rebuilds of DH-4s turned out by Boeing in 1924 used welded steel-tube fuselage frames instead of the original wood and were then known as O2B-1s.

The airplanes made history by being used as dive bombers in the vicinity of Ocotal on July 16, 1927. Dive bombing had been known since World War I, but was largely an individual matter. Some legends credit its origin to Marine pilot Lieutenant H.M. Sanderson. Later Marines say they got the idea from the Army, and the Army says it got the idea from the British. Whatever the origin of the technique, the Marine operation at Ocotal is recognized as the first organized use of dive bombing.

Almost coincidentally with the Ocotal bombing, the Marines got some replacements for their venerable DHs and O2Bs: brand new Vought O2U-1 Corsair biplanes that picked up operations right where the oldies left off. One, however, made history of a different sort.

The Marines at Quilali, a remote village, were surrounded by insurgents and could not fight their way out. The only way to get the wounded out was to fly them. So a 400-yard airstrip was cleared and, on Jan. 6-8, 1928, Lieutenant Christian Schilt made 10 round trips in his Corsair through heavy ground fire to bring in supplies and evacuate the wounded.

As delivered, the Corsair had narrow-tire wheels that were equipped with brakes, a relatively new feature on the aeronautical scene. For the soft Nicaraguan fields, however, the Marines put bigger DH-4 wheels on the new ships. Unfortunately, the old wheels did not have brakes. The field at Quilali was so short that Schilt had to use "human arresting gear" in which the Marines and natives grabbed the wings of his plane near the end of the runway to stop its landing roll.

Schilt was awarded the Medal of Honor for his heroic achievement.

The Marines remained in Nicaragua until 1933 and continued to make aviation history. In 1926 the Army and Navy ordered military transport versions of the new commercial Fokker Trimotor airliner.

The Marines got three of the Navy versions late in 1927 for use in Nicaragua. Originally, they were designated TA-1 (T for transport, A for Atlantic, the original name of the American Fokker Company) but became RA-1 after someone realized that the T duplicated the T-for-torpedo-plane designation.

The range of trimotors had them making history from the beginning. They were delivered to Nicaragua by 1,200-mile nonstop flights across the Caribbean from Florida. Once in Nicaragua, they quickly proved the value of large cargo airplanes to military operations in the wilderness areas. They carried personnel and bulk cargo, and in some cases where things like replacement wing panels for a damaged airplane could not be carried inside the cabin, they were tied to the outside.

Dive bombing, air evacuation, overseas delivery flights

1

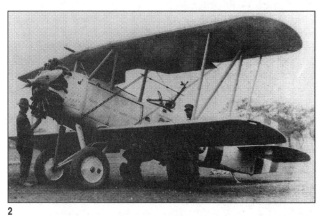

2

3

and military air cargo operations – all pioneered by the U.S. Marines in Nicaragua between 1927 and 1929.

The photographs

1. Marine Corps Boeing O2B-1s, de Havilland 4 observation planes during World War I, were rebuilt in 1924 with steel-tube fuselages. They were part of the first organized dive-bombing operations in Nicaragua in July 1927.

2. Marine pilot Christian Schilt won the Medal of Honor for his volunteer air-evacuation missions in January 1928 in his new Vought O2U-1 Corsair. Note the large DH-4/O2B wheels without brakes for operations from the crude fields of Nicaragua.

3. The Fokker TA-1/RA-1 Trimotor was the first modern airplane (i.e., not WWI design concept) to be used in support of remote military operations in wilderness areas. The Marines pioneered their use in Nicaragua from late 1927 into 1933.

The Super DC-3

When the airlines and Air Force took a pass, it found a home in the Navy as the C-117D

3rd August 1979

The principal transport plane of World War II, both civil and military, was the DC-3. First flown in 1935, it served on both sides of the war. Japan had been building them under license before Pearl Harbor and continued to do so after. The Soviets were also building under license, and the Germans had captured quite a few during their 1939-40 conquests.

By war's end, Douglas was in production on the larger four-engine DC-4, but there was still a need for a twin to replace the DC-3. Martin and Convair came out with very similar postwar DC-3 "replacements" that were bigger, faster and more expensive. They never became true DC-3 replacements, however; they were in a new class halfway between the DC-3 and DC-4.

Douglas, seeing that a need still existed for a DC-3 type but heavily committed to the DC-6 and DC-7 follow-ons to the DC-4, was reluctant to invest the time and expense of developing a whole new design. Instead, it decided to revamp the existing DC-3 and produce what it called the Super DC-3.

To that end, the company bought a former U.S. Army C-47, the military cargo version of the DC-3, that had been converted to a civil transport after the war and was being used by Western Air Lines. Douglas pulled out the 1,200-horsepower Pratt & Whitney R-1830 Twin Wasp engines and replaced them with 1,450-horsepower Pratt & Whitney R-2000-7s as used on the DC-4. The fuselage was stretched by adding a 39-inch section ahead of the wing and a 40-inch section at the rear of the cabin for a total increase of 79 inches. An entirely new tail assembly was built, and the outer wing panels were shorted by 2-1/2 feet each and swept back 4 degrees. The lower portions of the engine nacelles were modified to completely enclose the wheels when retracted. Gross weight increased from 29,000 pounds to 31,000, and top speed went from 227 mph to 270.

Douglas offered the new Super DC-3, which first flew on June 23, 1949, to the airlines on a trade-in basis – turn in an old DC-3 and, for about the price of a new one in the late 1930s, get a Super in return. The airlines didn't go for that, and very few Super DC-3s were sold, so Douglas decided to try the military market.

The company took another former C-47 and gave it the same treatment, except the cargo doors and heavy flooring were retained. Instead of the R-2000 engines, the 1,475-horsepower Wright R-1820-80 Cyclone was used. The Air Force bought the prototype, which it originally designated the YC-129, and gave it a new serial number in one of the few cases of buying an airplane that it had previously owned. The use of a new model number for an airplane that was so basically a C-47 could not be justified, so it was quickly redesignated a YC-47. The Air Force soon decided that the Super didn't fit its current needs and turned it over to the Navy.

Things went better there. Under the naval designation of R4D-8X, the prototype got a favorable response and the Navy ordered 100 production versions to be converted from R4Ds (the Navy equivalent of the Army Air Force C-47) that it had on hand. The R4Ds retained their original Navy serial numbers after conversion. Deliveries began early in 1952.

In 1962 the Air Force and Navy aircraft designations were combined, so the R4D-8s became C-117Ds. Why C-117D instead of a high-letter suffix on the C-47 designation? No one seems to know. The C-117 was another Air Force DC-3, but it was strictly a passenger version without the C-47's cargo features. Other Navy R4Ds up to -7 got revised C-47 designations; R4D-5s became C-47Hs, -6s became C-47Js and -7s became C-47Ks.

The Supers did a great job for the Navy, serving in the Antarctic, landing at the South Pole, and in other special tasks. Also, it was the only twin-engine type that the Navy permitted to fly from the mainland United States to Hawaii. The last examples of this tough old workhorse have only recently been retired, more than 30 years after the last one was built and nearly 25 years after their conversion from standard to Super.

The photographs

1. The first military Super DC-3 was the YC-47F for the U.S. Air Force. It was originally designated the YC-129. Note the larger tail surfaces and the deepened nacelles that completely enclosed the new dual wheels.

2. To permit very short takeoffs, Douglas added 16 solid-fuel JATO (jet-assisted takeoff) bottles to the YC-129/YC-47F.

3. The Navy's R4D-8/C-117D Super DC-3s did not use the dual wheels of the YC-129/YC-47F. The lengthened cabin allowed for two more windows one each side, for a total of eight on the left and nine on the right.

1

2

3

Cosmic Wind racers

Tony LeVier and 'Fish' Salmon built them with a production-line approach in mind

1st September 1979

Before World War II, the National Air Races featured pylon racing for a number of limited-engine-displacement classes as well as the unlimiteds. When racing resumed in 1946, there were only two categories: The unlimiteds, which were surplus wartime fighters, and a class for surplus North American AT-6NJ Texan trainers with 1,340-cubic-inch engines.

The 1947 event saw something new: the Goodyear Class for midget racers powered with engines of less than 190 cubic inches. The class was named for the Goodyear Aircraft Division of the Goodyear Tire and Rubber Co., which sponsored the event for three years. Today they are officially known as Formula 1 racers.

Only a dozen Goodyear racers competed at Cleveland in 1947. Of those, seven were prewar designs rebuilt to qualify under the new rules. Other than Art Chester's unique V-tail "Swee' Pea," the most interesting newcomers were the two Cosmic Winds, designed and built by Lockheed test pilots Tony LeVier and Herman "Fish" Salmon, with engineering assistance from Glenn Fulkerson.

Where other racers were one of a kind, the little Cosmics took a production-line approach to building racers and eventually completed four. They were all-metal, low-wing monoplanes powered with 85-horsepower Continental C-85 engines. Their wingspan was 18 feet 11 inches, length 17 feet even, wing area 69 square feet, and gross weight 850 pounds. Following modifications, they flew at over 200 mph, with the engine turning around 3,600 rpm, far above the 2,575 rpm red line of the certificated engines.

Only two Cosmics were finished for the 1947 race. LeVier's got Race No. 3 and was registered NX67888. It was finished in natural metal and carried the name "Little Toni." Salmon's had Race No. 10, was registered as NX67889, and was yellow with black trim. It had no name in 1947, but carried the emblem of a flying fish. It was later officially named "Minnow."

Despite their professional design and construction, the Cosmics didn't finish in the top money in the 1947 Goodyear. Salmon placed third and LeVier came in fourth. Their competitors were also very well designed.

For 1948, both 1947 ships were cleaned up and a third was completed in the revised configuration. Salmon's ship got a new overall bronze color, new registration number (N20C) and a new race number (4). The third Cosmic, named "Ballerina," got registration N22C, Race No. 5, and a metallic-green paint job.

The rework paid off. Salmon won the Goodyear, with Bill Robinson in "Little Toni" placing fifth and Bob Downey in "Ballerina" seventh.

Unfortunately they didn't leave well enough alone and completely reworked "Minnow" into a new airplane for 1949. A new steel-tube fuselage was added aft of the cockpit, new tail surfaces were fitted, and a wooden wing without dihedral was placed in the high mid-wing position. Despite being almost a new airplane, the identity, registration, race number and color remained the same.

"Ballerina" placed fourth in the 1949 Goodyear, outclassing "Minnow," which placed fifth.

That year a fourth Cosmic Wind was completed in the revised configuration of "Minnow," but it was not very successful. "Minnow" soon reverted to its 1948 form but the 1949 model, with registration N36C and Race No. 6, stayed in the new configuration.

The photographs

1. The second Cosmic Wind racer as it appeared at the National Air Races in Cleveland. Note the high aft turtledeck that streamlines the cockpit canopy and the neat fairing of the low wing into the fuselage. The oil companies supplied free gas and oil to racers who carried their decals, as shown here.

2. For 1948, the same racer got a new paint job plus new registration and racing numbers, and the name "Minnow." Structural cleanup included a cutdown rear turtledeck, bubble canopy, landing-gear-strut fairings, and long slim

1

2

3

wheelpants. The improvements paid off with a first-place finish in the Goodyear Trophy Race.

3. "Minnow" was greatly modified for 1949 but the changes did not pay off. It placed fifth in the Goodyear Race and was beaten by the standard-configuration third Cosmic Wind, "Ballerina." "Minnow" soon reverted to its 1948 form, but the fourth LeVier and Associates racer was completed in "Minnow's" 1949 form.

'Old Glory' never made it

Fokker F-VII's New York-to-Rome flight ended off coast of Newfoundland

2nd September 1979

After Lindbergh proved it could be done, a rash of transatlantic flight attempts broke out. The first two to follow him, the Chamberlain and Byrd flights, were already established contestants in the initial race for the $25,000 Ortieg prize. Lindy beat them by merely taking off and going while others were conducting test flights and bickering over crews. Those that followed declared other goals than Paris and gave different reasons for their flights now that the Ortieg prize money was no longer up for grabs.

As a promotion stunt for his newspaper, New York Daily Mirror Publisher William Randolph Hearst sponsored a flight from New York to Rome. The pilot, an air-mail flier named Lloyd Bertaud, was thoroughly experienced. Earlier in the year, he'd been hired as navigator for Charles Levine's Bellanca "Columbia," but he withdrew from that operation and Clarence Chamberlain was finally selected as the pilot. The copilot and navigator was another air-mail pilot, James D. Hill. The third member of the party was pure super-cargo: Philip Payne, editor of the Daily Mirror.

The airplane was a Dutch-built Fokker F-VII powered by a British Bristol Jupiter radial engine, and flown under U.S. ownership and registration. At Hearst's request, it was named "Old Glory." Coincidentally, Lindbergh wanted to make his crossing in a Fokker. Before he ordered his Ryan, Lindbergh was turned down because Fokker didn't like his record – four emergency parachute jumps in less than two years. Lindbergh had also tried to buy the "Columbia" late in 1926, but ended up having an airplane designed and built while the "Columbia's" owners were fooling around and wasting time.

To help the heavily loaded "Old Glory" get started, it was placed on the top of a takeoff ramp that gave it a run-ning start. The starting point was something new for 1927 transatlantic fliers. All the others had taken off from Roosevelt Field near New York City. Bertaud and crew decided on a Sept. 6 departure from Old Orchard Beach, Maine, which saved some mileage and also provided a longer runway. The fliers carried a wreath that was to be dropped in the middle of the Atlantic to honor the French fliers Nungesser and Coli, who had disappeared on a flight from Paris to New York a few days before Lindbergh's successful flight.

"Old Glory" got underway, in one of the few cases where good photographs of the departure were taken by an accompanying airplane. That was the last anyone saw of plane and crew together. Two SOS signals were heard around 4 a.m. the next morning. Then nothing. Five days later, the floating wreckage of "Old Glory" was found some 600 miles off of Newfoundland. As a result, the plane had the rather dubious distinction of being the first of several missing transatlantic planes to be found. No trace was ever found of the three crew members.

The photographs

1. The sloping ramp gave "Old Glory" a gravity-assisted start on its takeoff roll. The publicity-conscious manufacturer saw that the aircraft was well sprinkled with Fokker trademarks. Under the wing were paintings of the U.S. flag, and an eagle and "Old Glory" adorned the fuselage.

2. "Old Glory" on a test run. Note how the tail skid digs into the ground at low speed and acts as a brake. Some transatlantic pilots overcame the drag by putting their tail skids on a wheeled dolly for the takeoff run.

3. "Old Glory" off the cost of Maine on Sept. 6, 1927. The navigator used the hatch at the trailing edge of the wing for sighting.

1

2

3

Mob scene

Mass takeoffs used to be relatively routine

1st October 1979

Most pilots who have been trained since World War II are used to having an entire runway to themselves while taking off and landing. On a controlled field, the tower takes care of pilots and directs them into traffic. There are no surprises like finding a plane settling down just off the wingtip of another that's starting a takeoff roll. Even at uncontrolled fields, established procedures have the pilot looking for traffic before rolling onto the runway for takeoff and checking the area from the air before entering the pattern for landing.

The very thought of getting involved today in mass takeoffs like those shown in the accompanying photos would probably be an exercise in pure terror, but such things used to be relatively routine.

Back in the old days, airports didn't have runways. Big, open fields (hence the names like Mills Field, Wright Field, etc.) invited pilots to take off and land in the most suitable direction. With no runways, there was no long taxi trip to the head of the active, or a mile-long detour back to the hangar. Planes were started up in front of their hangars and usually took off from the spot where the propeller was swung. Landings were usually set up so that the plane rolled to a stop quite close to the hangar. In the days of no wheel brakes, taxiing crosswind or downwind was quite a chore, and it was often necessary for line boys to run out and grab a wingtip to gently turn the plane and "walk" it back to the line. The shorter the trip, the better.

For individual operations, pilots had few problems with other traffic; usually only one plane took off or landed at a time. As military operations got underway with World War I, however, it was necessary for several to take off together in a "scramble." Although it wasn't an actual formation takeoff, the pilots at least had formation flying experience and knew how to watch out for nearby planes on the same heading.

On occasion, some really big operations were conducted that must have been high-adrenaline affairs. Photo No. 1 shows nearly 50 Consolidated trainers taking off for a pass in review at the Army's primary training base at Brooks

Field in San Antonio in early 1927. What's really frightening is that the pilots are mostly primary students with little formation experience, the planes have no brakes and no radio, and tail skids instead of steerable tailwheels. The dust and turbulence certainly added to visibility and control problems. How would you like to tackle an operation like that with fewer than 30 hours in your logbook?

The second operation (Photo No. 2) was not quite as risky. Again, it involved a larger-than-ordinary mass takeoff from an open field, Kelly Field in San Antonio. The occasion was the shooting of the movie, "I Wanted Wings," in 1940.

That's Paul Mantz's Lockheed Orion camera plane in the foreground, and the Army ships are North American AT-6 trainers. This time, instead of turning into a swarm, the planes took off in elements of three, flown by pilots who were well-versed in formation flying. Thanks to brakes, steerable tail wheels and radios, control was much tighter.

Some fun, huh?

The photographs

1. Nearly 50 Consolidated trainers, some hidden in the background by dust, take off for a "pass in review" at Brooks Field in San Antonio in early 1927. Note how quickly some of the lightweight Consolidated PT-1s have gotten into the air. The Army had just changed tail markings and color schemes, but not all of its planes had yet been repainted. The result is an interesting mixture, as seen here.

2. The plane in the foreground ready to film AT-6 training ships at Kelly Field in San Antonio is flown by veteran Hollywood stunt pilot Paul Mantz. The sleek and shiny aircraft are ready to perform for Paramount's "I Wanted Wings," a saga of Army Air Corps training and tactics. More than $25 million worth of training planes, pursuits and bombers served as a backdrop for action that featured Ray Milland, William Holden, Wayne Morris, Brian Donlevy, Constance Moore and Veronica Lake. A company of 130 people spent a month at Randolph and Kelly fields to get realistic backgrounds and actual conditions under which pilots trained.

1

2

The pregnant Guppy

When its airliner career ended, The Boeing 377 was turned into a super-cargo plane

2nd October 1979

From 1949-59, the world's premier airliner was the Boeing Model 377 Stratocruiser, a double-decker design that evolved from the wartime B-29 bomber through the Army Air Force's C-97 cargo plane. It carried anywhere from 55 to 117 passengers, and for oceanic runs like New York to Paris in 12 hours, it was fitted with Pullman-like berths.

In 1959 the three major airlines that were still flying the Stratocruisers forced the bulbous aircraft into early retirement. Jet transports were making their mark, and the flying public was eagerly accepting them. But the Stratocruisers were not ready to call it a career. Some were outfitted with high-density seating for tourist operations, and others ended up as freighters after C-97-style cargo doors were installed on their upper decks.

A few more made aviation history by undergoing one of the most radical modifications ever performed on a conventional airplane. Aero Spacelines and the On-Mark Engineering Co., both of Van Nuys, California, combined to convert Boeing Stratocruisers into specialized cargo planes. The newly configured aircraft transported large but low-density articles like airplane and spacecraft major assemblies from West Coast factories to Eastern assembly areas.

The work started by lengthening the fuselage nearly 17 feet. Sections of other Stratocruiser fuselages were spliced in. Next, the upper cabin of the inverted figure-eight fuselage was cut away and a much larger structure, also of circular form, was built in place to create a cabin 20 feet wide and nearly as high. Because of its ungainly appearance, someone called the conversion "The Pregnant Guppy," and the name stuck. In fact, when a supplemental type certificate was issued, the FAA officially recorded the airplane as Model 377PG.

Creating a 20-foot-wide cabin was one thing; getting big cargo into it was something else. Doors that size couldn't be cut into the wall without weakening the structure. On the first Guppy, the problem was solved by unbolting the rear portion of the fuselage at an existing structural break. That section was then rolled backward on a special demountable

dolly that could be transported in the plane. Getting the cargo aboard through the open end by crane, forklift or ramp was then an easy matter. Later Guppies used a quicker swing-nose system.

The final model of the Guppy series, bigger and more powerful than the others, was called the Super Guppy. Instead of the original 3,500-horsepower Pratt & Whitney R-4360 piston engines, it was powered with 5,700-horsepower Pratt & Whitney YT-34 turboprops. The YT-34s were from two surplus YC-97Js that the Air Force had Boeing convert form standard KC-97Gs to service test the new engines in a proven cargo airplane. The Super Guppy had an even wider cabin than the others, and the wingspan was increased since a wider center section had to be built to get the larger diameter inboard propellers to clear the fatter fuselage.

It is a bit ironic that the Super Guppy, basically a Boeing airplane despite the modifications, was used in France to transport components of the competing European Airbus from the various builders to the final assembly plant.

The photographs

1. The first Boeing Stratocruiser, which flew in 1947, evolved from the B-29 through the improved B-29D (which was redesignated B-50), and then through the following YC-97As and -Bs. Note the unique double-lobed, double-decked fuselage.

2. The first pregnant Guppy featured a lengthened fuselage and a greatly enlarged upper deck. Due to the increased width, the diameter of the inboard propellers had to be decreased slightly to maintain clearance.

3. The final Super Guppy featured an even larger upper deck, turboprop instead of piston engines, more wingspan and a taller tail. It was used by Airbus Industrie in France to airlift components of the European Airbus jetliner to the assembly plant.

4. The swing-open nose of a Super Guppy. This French-registered model contains a fuselage section of a French Airbus. Note the supports for the fuselage and rear part of swing-nose/

1

2

3

4

Long-nose radial engines

While V-12s were dominant among WWII fighters, the round engines did well in P-47s

1st November 1979

Big engines have always been the principal feature of high-performance fighter planes. After the end of World War I, when the light, air-cooled rotary engine passed the peak of its development, the water-cooled V-type engine became the primary powerplant of choice in fighter aircraft. After the introduction of the 435-horsepower Curtiss D-12 in 1923, the V-12 rose to the top of the engine pyramid and remained there until the advent of the jet era.

The air-cooled radial, however, itself a follow-on to the rotary, began catching up to the V-12 in power, and by the late 1920s it was becoming a significant factor in military aircraft design. In fact, the two engine types became quite competitive, with the 600-horsepower Curtiss Conqueror in the 1929 Curtiss P-6 series, and the lighter 450- to 550-horsepower Pratt & Whitney Wasp radial in the contemporary Boeing P-12.

By 1933, the Conqueror had reached the peak of its development. With no suitable replacement in the works, the new radials in the 600- to 1,000-horsepower range monopolized the Army fighter-plane business until the 1,000-horsepower Allison V-12 came along in 1938.

While the engines produced equal power, the radial was lighter, didn't have a vulnerable cooling system, and had fewer parts. The layout of what came to be called the "big round engine," however, had an inherent aerodynamic handicap: its large diameter. The much narrower V-12 permitted better streamlining of the airplane, which in turn produced more speed per horsepower. It wasn't a big problem in the days of 200-mph or slower aircraft, but it became a serious handicap when speeds began passing 300 mph.

With the V-12s again taking the lead, advocates of radial-engine fighters took some extreme steps to save their breed. They got Pratt & Whitney to build special variants of its standard 1,000-horsepower Twin Wasp, an 18-cylinder twin-row model that was powering the Seversky P-35 and the Curtiss P-36, the Army's standard fighters of the late 1930s. The engine featured a greatly lengthened propeller shaft and gearbox that put the propeller far ahead of the cylinders. The combination allowed the airplane to have a long, pointed nose with the streamlining advantages of the V-12s. It was enough to convince a group of airplane designers to work with it.

When Curtiss took the fourth P-36A off the production line and put one of the new long-nose Twin Wasps in it, the Army redesignated the airplane the XP-42. A smaller firm, Vultee, came out with a new fighter in 1939 that it called the Vanguard. It too used the long-nose radial as initial equipment.

While the longer radials improved streamlining and increased speed somewhat, they didn't live up to expectations and never posed a serious threat to the established V-12s, namely the Allison and the U.S.-built version of the British Rolls-Royce Merlin.

Another engine change in a P-36 was much more successful. An Allison was put in the P-36A, which then became the XP-40. That led to production of more than 14,000 P-40s from 1940 into 1944. Vultee, meanwhile, also dropped the long-nose radial and used the standard Twin Wasp in the relatively small number of Vanguards that it produced.

Though the V-12s were predominant among the Army's World War II fighters, the big radial did hold its own in the famous Republic P-47 Thunderbolt, also called the Jug because of its blunt front end.

Altogether, 15,579 P-47s were built, the most of any single U.S. fighter model and a thorough vindication of the role radial engines played in fighters. It is significant to note that only fighters used the V-12s in other Army designs. The bombers and transports all used radials until the jets made piston powerplants obsolete for high-performance aircraft.

It should also be pointed out that the U.S. Navy did not figure in the radial-versus-V controversy of the 1930s and 1940s. As far back as 1928 it had switched to air-cooled engines for all fleet aircraft for other than aerodynamic reasons.

The photographs

1. The Vultee Vanguard, intended as a low-cost escort fighter, started out with the long-nose version of the Twin Wasp but ended up with the standard configuration in the production models despite a decrease in speed from 358 mph to 340 at 15,000 feet.

2. The fourth PA-36A became the XP-42 when it was outfitted with a long-nose Twin Wasp. The big increase in speed to 315 mph at 15,000 feet was not entirely due to improved streamlining. The experimental aircraft was nearly a thousand pounds lighter than the standard fighter. The camouflage paint was applied for the 1940 War Games.

3. The Curtiss P-36A with the 1,050-horsepower Pratt & Whitney Twin Wasp radial engine was the principal U.S. Army fighter of 1939-41. It was not, however, as fast as contemporary designs that used liquid-cooled V-12 engines. Top speed was 300 mph at 10,000 feet.

4. With the standard Twin Wasp engine, the production Vultee Vanguard had a much shorter nose. An early sale to Sweden was blocked by the prevailing arms embargo. England took them later, and even assigned serial numbers. Those are British markings shown here. The Vanguard didn't measure up to British fighter standards, however, so the U.S. Army finally took them and designated them P-66s. Those that were not sent to China were used as trainers.

1

2

3

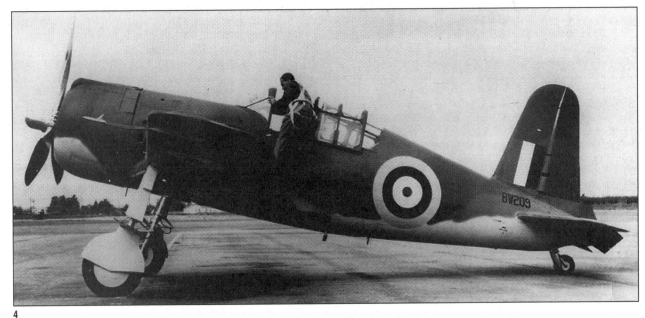

4

Stretched Zeppelins

In 1919, a 32-foot straight section was added to the 'Bodensee'

2nd November 1979

The term "stretched airliner," in common use today, is generally considered to be of recent origin. In airplane usage, the first to become a stretch version without actually being built as a follow-on model was the Douglas DC-3S, or Super DC-3, of 1949. An existing DC-3 airframe was lengthened by splicing in a section of fuselage and adding other modifications. The airlines didn't go for such an expensive update of a near antique, but the U.S. Navy had Douglas rework 100 of its existing R4Ds, as the Navy DC-3s were called, into "Supers" (Page 346).

After the jet transport era got underway, "stretch" became a big thing in airliner sales. There were "stretched" Boeing 707s and 727s, and Douglas DC-8s, but they were follow-ons to original models and were built that way from scratch. They were not existing articles returned to the factory for modification.

Actually, lengthening an airliner is not a post-WWII phenomenon. It was first done in 1919, but not to an airplane.

At the end of World War I, the Allied Control Commission moved into Germany and virtually shut down most of the aircraft industry. The aircraft that were allowed to be built had very severe limitations on size, power and performance. Most important, there was no tolerance for military potential.

The Zeppelin firm was one of the few major wartime producers that was allowed to continue. As early as April 1919, it completed the design of a passenger airship that the commission approved. Although some really giant Zeppelins had been built during the war, with gas volume as great as 2.5 million cubic feet and lengths of nearly 750 feet, the new commercial ship was limited to less than 1 million cubic feet and ended up with 706,200, about the same as a 1913 passenger model. Length was 396 feet.

The new ship carried the factory designation LZ-120, for the 120th by Luftschiffbau Zeppelin. Completed in August 1919 and named Bodensee for the large lake adjacent to the factory in Friedrichshafen, it was the world's first airship for scheduled point-to-point passenger service. The prewar passenger Zeppelins had been used only for local sightseeing tours from fixed bases, not intercity transportation.

The Bodensee was put on the 370-mile Friedrichshafen-to-Berlin run, which it usually made in less than five hours (trains took 16). The schedule called for a trip north one day, with a return the next. If enough time was left after arrival in Berlin, a local sightseeing flight was conducted. Altogether, the Bodensee made 40 round trips over a 98-day period and carried 2,380 paying passengers with only a few cancellations due to weather. It was a remarkable performance for the era. On-line flying time totaled 533 hours at an average speed of 62 mph.

While the Bodensee was a very efficient airship compared to its predecessors, it was a little marginal on lift, and hence payload. Zeppelin took care of that by splicing in a 32-foot straight section at the ship's widest point, thus increasing volume by 88,000 cubic feet. It wasn't a new trick. It had been done on a few wartime military Zeppelins with notable success.

Meanwhile, a second commercial ship, the LZ-121 Nordstern, had been designed to the new length and was nearing completion. Unfortunately for the Zeppelin organization, neither the stretched Bodensee nor the new Nordstern went into service for their original owners. The Allied Control Commission seized both of them in December 1919 and turned them over to the Allies. Italy got the Bodensee and France got the Nordstern. The explanation was that ships were legitimate war booty because they had been built with wartime materials and used wartime military engines.

Despite its short career, the Bodensee has the double distinction of being the first dirigible used for scheduled airline service (of three used for that purpose) and the world's first "stretched" airliner.

The photographs

1. The postwar Zeppelin LZ-120 Bodensee was the first airship to be used on scheduled airline service. It made 40 round trips between Friedrichshafen and Berlin in 98 days from August to December 1919. At its original 396 feet, shown here, it was a midget compared to the largest wartime military Zeppelins.

2. The Bodensee's small volume was a handicap, so the ship was cut in two amidships and a 32-foot straight section was spliced in to increase the length to 426 feet and the volume to 795,000 cubic feet. Despite the change in hull fineness ratio, it was still the most aerodynamically efficient Zeppelin built to that time.

3. The Bodensee now had the same length and configuration as her new sister ship, the LZ-121 Nordstern, shown here. Neither of the "long" ships got into passenger service. The Allied Control Commission seized them both as war booty. The Nordstern, which went to France, was scrapped in September 1926. The Bodensee, given to Italy, lasted until July 1928.

1

2

3

Slingshot air-mail service, Part 1

The Germans speeded up deliveries by launching airplanes from passenger ships

1st December 1979

One of the world's more unusual air-mail operations was conducted from 1929 to 1936 through the cooperation of a major steamship company and an airline.

Commercial air-mail flights across the North Atlantic were a long way in the future when the North German Lloyd shipping company (Norddeutscher Lloyd, or NDL for short) came upon an idea to speed up the delivery of transatlantic mail. In 1929, the mail was getting across in six days, as fast as it could go on NDL's two new ships, the Bremen and Europa.

While airplanes didn't have the range to go the full distance, they could be carried most of the way on the ship and then launched within range of shore to fly the remaining distance. Toward that end, NDL teamed up with the German national airline, Deutsche Lufthansa, or DLH.

1

The airline operated and maintained two Heinkel single-engine mail planes, and NDL had the two ships equipped with Heinkel-designed compressed-air catapults.

The devices, which could accelerate the three-ton planes to 110 mph in a distance of 65 feet, were quite a surprise to the world of aviation, coming as they did from a nation that had no military aircraft that would ordinarily use catapults.

The U.S., British, French and Italian navies, as well as Japan, had been catapulting naval seaplanes regularly from battleships and cruisers since shortly after World War I, but Germany was still denied such equipment by the treaty of Versailles. The NDL-DLH operation was the only catapult operation conducted before or since from a civilian passenger ship.

Service started July 22, 1929, with one two-seat Heinkel He.12 seaplane on the Bremen and a later but quite similar He.58 on the Europa. Each could carry up to 750 pounds of mail. Only one of each model was built, each specifically for the ship-plane operation. For the first delivery, the He.12 left the Bremen while it was 250 miles from New York. It reached the city in 2-1/2 hours.

Later, the westbound procedure was standardized, with the seaplanes being catapulted about 750 miles from New York. With cruise speeds averaging 120 mph compared to around 30 for the ships, nearly a full day was saved. The westbound seaplanes landed in New York Harbor. After the ships arrived, they were hoisted aboard for the return trip.

Eastbound, the airplanes saved even more time on direct mail to Germany since they docked at Cherbourg, France, before heading for their home port of Bremerhaven. At first, the seaplanes flew 500 miles directly to Bremerhaven from the ships just before they docked at Cherbourg, but later they were launched from further out in the Atlantic.

The slingshot air-mail service, in which the airplanes were auxiliaries to transatlantic ships, continued through 1935. There were 24 flights in 1930, 31 in 1931, 36 in 1932, 34 in 1933, 36 in 1934, and 34 in 1935.

Next we'll look at a reversal of roles, with ships becoming auxiliaries to a transatlantic airline operation.

The photographs

1. A Heinkel He.12 seaplane is catapulted from the sun deck of the North German Lloyd steamer Bremen. The two-seater, with tandem cockpits, was christened "New York" after its first arrival in the Big Apple. It was later repainted and carried the name "Bremen" on its side.

2. The Heinkel He.58 was quite similar to the He.12 and used the same 500-horsepower Pratt & Whitney Hornet engine. The major difference was seating. The two crew members sat side-by-side instead of tandem. The He.58 was originally named "Atlantik." When it was repainted and the NACA cowling was added to the engine, it carried the name "Europa." In this photo, it carries the name "Bremen" but is aboard the Europa.

3. Faster airplanes with more capacity were needed by 1932, so the Heinkel seaplanes were replaced by a pair of Junkers Ju-46s. Again, the name on the airplane matches that of the ship.

2

3

Slingshot air-mail service, Part II

Lufthansa used Dornier Wals and Do-18s for its South Atlantic operations

2nd December 1979

Last issue we saw how airplanes were used as shipboard auxiliaries to speed delivery of mail across the North Atlantic. Since cargo-carrying airplanes were not capable of going long distances on their own in the early in 1930s, catapults were used to launch them at mid-ocean.

The South Atlantic presented a different situation, however. The straight-across distance from Bathurst, on the west coast of Africa, and Natal, Brazil, on the east of South America, was considerably shorter but still too far for a plane to make nonstop. There were no halfway points.

As airplane range increased in the early 1930s, Lufthansa settled on a ship-and-plane combination like the one used on the northern route. The aircraft that Lufthansa chose were large twin-engine flying boats that were used elsewhere for passenger operations. In the South Atlantic, Lufthansa used them exclusively for mail.

The company chartered a couple of freighters and had Heinkel develop more powerful catapults that were capable of launching the big Dornier Wal (Whale) flying boats. On one ship, the Westfalen, the fixed catapult was positioned between the cabin and the bow. On Schwabenland, the catapult was installed aft, with the Wal taking off over the stern.

Both ships had a unique system for taking on the airplanes. They steamed forward while trailing a large reinforced canvas ramp. The planes taxied onto the canvas, and were secured and then hoisted aboard by a crane that was permanently mounted on the stern. Since the catapult on the Westfalen was forward, the planes were moved forward on a track along the starboard side of the ship.

The South Atlantic operation started on June 6, 1933, with Westfalen maneuvering 900 miles off the African coast. An eight-ton Dornier Wal took off from the water near Bathurst, Africa, landed next to the ship, and was hoisted aboard. After refueling, it was catapulted into the air and continued its flight to Natal, Brazil.

The eastward flight was different. This time the Westfalen carried a plane to mid-ocean. Another plane then took off from Natal, landed alongside, and the mail was transferred to the plane on the catapult. Total Brazil-to-Africa time was 14 hours 5 minutes. The system continued with regularly scheduled flights from Berlin to Rio, a distance of 8,700 miles, starting in February 1934.

Since the mid-ocean landings weren't very desirable, another change was soon made. Both ship and plane left Bathurst or Natal together. After the ship had steamed seaward for three hours, the plane was catapulted and made the rest of the distance on its own. That operation was slower but much safer.

Late in 1934, 10-ton Wals with greater range were able to cover the distance nonstop, so they were catapulted from the ships while anchored in the harbor. Catapulting continued because the big boost was needed. The big flying boats could not take off from water under their own power and retain enough fuel to go the full distance. Also, a quick catapult launch was easier on the airplanes than long takeoff runs through rough water at maximum weight.

Late in 1936, much faster Dornier Do-18 flying boats were put on the run, and two more ships were fitted with catapults so that the Westfalen and Schwabenland could move north to start survey flights for a similar operation on the North Atlantic. They were flown between New York City and Horta, in the Azores, using Do-18s. The aircraft were supplemented by four-engine Blohm & Voss Ha-139 twin-float seaplanes. The survey flights continued for two years, but no commercial flights were made. The imminence of World War II shut down both operations in 1939.

The photographs

1. The steamer Westfalen, chartered by the Deutsche Lufthansa airline and carrying the airline's flag and markings, pioneered the practice of catapulting large multi-engine seaplanes to increase their range. The airplane was a standard eight-ton Dornier Wal.

2. The Dornier Wal flying boat taxies onto a flexible ramp that's towed by the Westfalen while underway. Note

1

3

2

4

the open three-seat front cockpit and the Dornier-developed sponsons that were used for stability on water instead of the more traditional wingtip floats that were used on most other flying boats.

3. The Schwabenland differed from the Westfalen by catapulting its planes from the stern. Here a four-engine

Blohm & Voss Ha-139 is hoisted aboard.

4. Big seaplane catapult operations were not limited to Dornier Wal and Do-18 flying boats. Here the Blohm & Voss Ha-139 is launched over the stern of the Schwabenland. The catapult has been offset to port, and the crane has been lowered to starboard to provide adequate clearance.

Index

Because this book is not arranged by traditional chapters or subjects, the only way that a specific aircraft or activity can be found is through this index.

In addition to listing all of the subject aircraft alphabetically by manufacturer, the index also includes special-interest headings, which sometimes result in the same aircraft being indexed twice: once under its manufacturer's heading and again under the special-interest heading (markings, racers, flying boats, special operations, etc.).

Under manufacturer's headings, as BELL, the entry "P-39 Airacobra development" includes all the significant variants in the development of the P-39 series, but the index does not identify them separately, as XP-39, P-39C, P-39Q, etc. An entry for a specific P-39, as P-39D, also appears under BELL, but the page number shown is for another column in which that particular P-39D appears for a reason other than model development.

In cases where the products of a major manufacturer like Boeing are widely known in one area by their military designations (B-17, P-26, etc.), and in another by their Boeing model numbers (40, 314, etc.), the two identities are indexed under separate BOEING headings (one for military and one for Boeing designations) rather than mixing the two under a single BOEING heading.

PETER M. BOWERS: *His single-seat Fly Baby won the EAA Design Contest in 1962.*

About the author

Peter M. Bowers began his aviation career by building model airplanes soon after Lindbergh crossed the Atlantic in 1927. Much of his high-school lunch money was spent on World War I airplane photos from the U.S. Army Signal Corps and commercial dealers. After building all of the famous Cleveland three-quarter-inch scale WWI models, he designed and built his own from three-view drawings and photographs in the model magazines.

Bowers began to write for publications in the mid-1930s when magazine editors asked for submissions based on his outstanding models. His byline has appeared many times over the years in numerous aviation periodicals and books.

From 1940 to 1942 he studied aeronautical engineering at the prestigious Boeing School of Aeronautics. During that time he began to amass one of the largest and most comprehensive private collections of airplane photos and reference data in the United States. Authors and publishers worldwide draw extensively from his files.

After five years in the U.S. Army Air Forces as a maintenance and technical intelligence officer, he joined the Boeing Airplane Company as an engineer, retiring in 1983 after 36 years. In the meantime, his model building expanded into the design and construction of man-carrying homebuilt airplanes. His single-seat Fly Baby won a national design contest in 1962, and he has been selling plans ever since. More than 500 have been built to date.

Bowers earned his pilot's license on Feb. 29, 1948, and he followed with numerous ratings, including designated flight examiner. He has logged more than 8,000 hours of pilot-in-command time, mostly in relatively low-power (150 horsepower down to 36) and no-power aircraft. Twelve hundred of those hours are in gliders.

Over the years, his many books and magazine articles have led to worldwide recognition as an aviation historian, model builder and airplane designer. A stroke in 1985 ended his flying, but at age 82 he remains active as a writer.

He is looking forward to writing his 804th *Flyer* column in December 2003, which will commemorate the 100th anniversary of the Wright brothers' first manned, powered flight.